The Divided School

Routledge Education Books

Advisory editor: John Eggleston
Professor of Education
University of Keele

The Divided School

Peter Woods

Routledge & Kegan Paul
London, Boston and Henley

First published in 1979
by Routledge & Kegan Paul Ltd
39 Store Street, London WC1E 7DD,
Broadway House, Newtown Road,
Henley-on-Thames, Oxon RG9 1EN and
9 Park Street, Boston, Mass. 02108, USA
Set by Hope Services, Abingdon,
and printed in Great Britain by
Lowe and Brydone Ltd
Thetford, Norfolk

British Library Cataloguing in Publication Data

Woods, Peter, b. 1934

The divided school.
1. Teacher-student realationships — Case studies
2. Parent-teacher relationships — Case studies
3. Teachers — England — Case studies
4. Students — England — Case studies
5. Parent and child — England — Case studies
I. Title
371.1'04   LB1033   78-40971

ISBN 0 7100 0124 X

For Kath

Contents

Acknowledgments

Many people have commented on parts of this book in various forms and at various stages, and among these I would especially like to thank David Hargreaves, Frank Musgrove, Roger Dale, Donald Mackinnon, Bob Stebbins, Ivor Goodson, Cidella and Alun Morten. I owe a special debt of gratitude to Don Swift and Martyn Hammersley, who have read the whole text through various drafts and made many helpful suggestions, though this does not mean they will agree with all I have written. John Eggleston and David Godwin rendered valuable and much appreciated aid in converting the discrete elements of the original manuscript into an entity. My most sincere thanks are due to the teachers, pupils and parents of Lowfield School. Their willing co-operation made the study possible; their generous hospitality made it a pleasure. I owe much, in particular to Mike, Ian, Bruce, Clive, Mark, Beverley, Elaine, Teresa, and especially Jimmie. Expert secretarial assistance was given by Marion Richards, Gill Norman and Pat O'Farrell, and much moral support by my wife and family.

For permission to reproduce material previously published, my thanks to the editors of the *British Journal of Sociology*, June 1976 (parts of chapter 2) and of *Educational Review* 28 (2), February 1976 (parts of chapter 4); and to the Open University for parts of units 7-8 and 11 of E202 (parts of chapter 3 and Appendix 2). John Wakeford of the University of Lancaster kindly allowed me to reproduce the figure from *The Cloistered Elite* which appears here as Fig. 3.1.

Readers are recommended to consult the Note on Sources which precedes the Notes at the end of this book.

Introduction

The research on which this work is based arose from an interest in certain educational questions, and a commitment to a particular kind of sociological approach. The educational questions concern interpersonal relationships and intrapersonal processes and came to have a mutual focus in the concept of division. This is topical at least, for the school featuring in this study, like others of the day, is ostensibly on an egalitarian quest to repair divisions. They appear on two levels. One is between groups, such as teachers, pupils and parents. Purportedly on a joint, co-operative enterprise, few seem to be clear about the terms of the contract on which the 'co-operation' is based. Each group, however, is relatively clear about its own purposes, which, ironically perhaps, are often in conflict with those of the other groups. I was interested to explore, therefore, those connections which evidence these concerns and conflicts: for teachers and pupils primarily classroom activity; and for teachers and parents, two of the main linking media, the subject choice process and school reports. These were to reveal further equally deep-seated divisions within the groups but none the less an appearance, and at times quite a convincing one, of unity and common purpose. The form, generation and maintenance of this 'appearance' was therefore another concern.

There is another kind of division, arising from the compartmentalization of school life, the roles within it and its separation from the outside world and from other institutions. Thus pupils might appear to be completely different people in and out of school. Some of these differences might be evidenced in the 'private' areas of school. Again this contrasts with the psychological unity some of the teachers sought to impose on their charges. Teachers themselves appeared to wear different 'hats', depending on the situation, now acting as 'educationists', now as 'strategists', now as 'professionals', now as 'private persons'. It is as if school consists of a number of invisible doors, and people change as they go through them from one context to another. I was interested therefore to chart these movements and changes, and in the properties of the different contexts.

These divisions, often involving strongly contrasting situations and differentiation from each other along opposing lines, give rise to much confusion and bewilderment, as perspectives across the groups do not always lock into the same framework. They also help to account for the extremes of behaviour and responses that seem so typical of our schools, between hope and despair, great excitement and crashing boredom, laughter and sorrow, the joy of fellowship and the pain of humiliation. These expressions of division, being such a large element in school life and prime foci of concern, constitute an important part of this book. Laughter especially seemed an outstanding ingredient of the school day, contrasting strongly with the grim pictures conjured up by many sociological accounts. I describe its nature and incidence, both among pupils and among teachers, and analyse its social referents. But degradation is also prominent, pupils getting 'shown up' and 'picked on', and teachers subjected to mass onslaught on their status. These phenomena are also examined.

The sociological approach which informs the work derives from symbolic interactionism. This concentrates on how the social world is constructed by people, how they are continually striving to make sense of the world, and assigning meanings and interpretations to events, and on the symbols used to represent them. It puts the emphasis on pupils' and teachers' own subjective constructions of events, rather than on the sociologist's assumptions of them, and elevates the process of meaning-assignation and situation-defining to prime importance. Hence the emphasis on 'perspectives', the frameworks through which we make sense of the world, and on different 'contexts' which influence the formation and operation of these perspectives. Pupils' views of school differ according to cultural background, which might depend on class differences. But they also differ in relation to institutional and curriculum factors, and according to different teachers. Thus perspectives have both 'causal' and 'reasoned' aspects, depending on whence they derive and to what they are directed.

These perceptual frameworks are then linked to action. The action is thus impregnated with the meaning assigned to it by the participants, and is revealed as a mixture of strategies, adaptations and accommodations. Wherever they go in the school, pupils and teachers are continually adjusting, reckoning, evaluating, bargaining, acting and changing. The school has many stages, and there are various roles and scripts, some with traditional, routine qualities which carry a sense of having been worked through the years, others, more sporadically, convey inspirational freshness. I am interested, therefore, in the 'rules' that govern these processes, not so much the official rules of the institution, but the informal, implicit rules that apply in practice and that are arrived at through complex negotiations. Where opportunity arises I explore the boundaries of tolerance and factors that help promote conflict or inhibit its successful resolution. Through all of this interchange, which sometimes takes on the tone of warfare, sometimes idyllic companionship, the individual nurtures and jealously protects his identity. This is what he is in the business for. Factors that promise to enhance identity bring greatest reward, factors that threaten it bring greatest concern. This is true of both pupils and teachers. Identity therefore is the ultimate concept in this book, and the division of identity that parallels Laing's division of self is the ultimate division.[1] These introductory notes are developed and linked to similar work in chapter 1.

The method employed in seeking access to meanings, interpretations, perspectives and strategical orientations was 'participant observation'. A more detailed account of my own practice is given in Appendix 1. Here I will simply note that this entailed me 'living' in the school for a period of about a year, sharing in its activities as far as possible, observing events as they happened and seeking information from people in a variety of ways, chiefly by informal talk, in a variety of contexts. The major themes emerged in the course of the study. I did not go into the school with the aim of studying 'division' or 'strategies'. They occurred to me and gained increasing importance during the developing research. It might be argued that this is one intuitive judgment in one case study. I would reply that the methods that link that judgment with inmates' meanings are quite rigorous and now belong to an accepted tradition. That it is one case study cannot be denied. It has certain typical features, as I shall show, and I draw on my own experience as well as that of others, in other schools. But these are inadequate compensation for other case studies of schools, which we sorely need.

In the circumstances it might seem premature to seek the possibilities of generalizing from a single study. Sharp and Green, however, have argued that 'the social scientist has to begin to develop a perspective which enables him to develop the connection between macro-sociological and historical processes on the one hand and individual biographies on the other',[2] and I would agree with them. There is, therefore, a further aspect to this study, necessarily more speculative than the representation of life at the school, which looks at possible linkages with wider society. These are most clearly evident, I suggest, when school and society address each other, as in the process of subject choice and in the case of school reports. The influence of social class is suggested in both, but also another potent form of division between professional and layman, between the 'expert' and the ordinary man and between public and private arenas, which has equally, if not more,

powerful repercussions for action. These external factors are inves-
tigated, in purely exploratory fashion, in relation to the innermost
happenings in the school to which I had access — the 'showing up'
of pupils, and teachers' efforts to survive (as opposed to trying to
teach). The material is 'suggestive' in certain ways, but I make no claim
to definitive statements about the relationship between school and
society, let alone the developments of a perspective that would allow
us to do so. A small, but realistic, contribution toward the latter would
be appropriate, I feel, its further development depending on further
detailed studies. The material on the school, on the other hand, does
permit somewhat stronger analysis of the impact on action of institutional factors, and this will be a persistent theme.

The school

Before presenting the analysis I shall give a brief thumbnail sketch
of the school in which the research was conducted. My aim is to convey
an impression of what kind of school it was, and what were its essential
processes, through the eyes and in the language of a quasi-member of
staff. This is the manifest picture of the school, the semi-official image,
and it is the essential starting point before we move to deeper sociological analysis.

I call the school 'Lowfield Secondary School', which, of course, is
a pseudonym, as are the names of teachers and pupils which appear in
the text later. The fact that it was a secondary modern might appear
to date the school, but as I shall show, its status was irrelevant to my
concerns, its basic structures and processes being common amongst
secondary schools generally. Built in 1956, with 560 boys and girls
on roll and 30 teachers, the school serves a rural area in the Midlands
which includes some urbanized villages on the boundaries of a larger
manufacturing town and several small village communities. It is well
accommodated, with adequate classrooms, laboratories, domestic
science rooms, needlecraft and commerce rooms, lecture theatre,
hall, library, an impressive technical block, gymnasium, swimming-
pool and generous playing-fields. The pupils came mainly from working-
class homes, parents working mainly in light industry, farmwork or
service occupations in the nearby large town; though quite a large
minority of parents were in clerical or professional work, or relatively
senior positions in industry.

At times there is an atmosphere of balmy bliss at Lowfield. And
certainly one of the predominant impressions the school makes is one
of a certain 'ease'. Shortly after my arrival, the headmaster told me,
'They're all good children in this school. I've been headmaster here
since 1956 and I've never had any trouble, any real trouble that is.

They're not violent.' Another teacher, speaking of a group with the reputation of the 'worst' pupils in the school, said, 'They're not stroppy — they just won't be motivated.' And another, with eight previous years' experience teaching in the nearby town where pupils were 'getting progessively rougher', found those at Lowfield 'very affable'. The generalized aims of the teachers which aided this affability were to make 'happy marriages', and the children 'decent citizens' as one teacher said, or 'good Christian gentlefolk' as the headmaster put it. At other times the ease is tinged with despair as the teachers seek to inspire and motivate what they see as a predominantly apathetic clientele.

> 'We get them from nine to four with one and a half hours off for lunch. How can we hope to change them from what they already are? They come here *expecting* to go to the factory. I wonder if what we're doing is consolidating the class structure, teaching them good middle-class ways of living, and others their place. "4L — you're 4L, 4A — you're 4A". I know there's got to be factory hands and dustbinmen, but they don't seem to realise there's possibilities beyond that, they're fated from the word go.'

The 'factory' referred to here is located in the village, makes car components and employs over two thousand people. Inevitably most of these went to Lowfield at one time or another and in some ways its relationship with the school and the village is similar to those self-contained communities around the factory built on paternalistic lines during the nineteenth century. Its owner, for example, had a long and reputedly very influential association with the school, including a lengthy period as chairman of the governors. It is still the major employer of Lowfield school-leavers and among several families appears to be accepted, as equally as school, as an inevitable sphere of life. The headmaster spoke of 'the dead-end prospects of these kids. Many of their parents saw the top of the ladder being the tool-room in the local factory.' Thus it was seen by the teachers primarily, not as a beneficial agency providing employment and prospects to the people of the village, but as a breeder of apathy among pupils and parents as far as schoolwork is concerned. 'You needn't ask what most of the staff think of ROSLA. The kids' attitude is, "We're going to the factory anyway, what the hell's use is a couple of CSEs to us?"' Even, at the time of writing, with unemployment beginning to bite in the area, a deep-seated apathy lives on, suggesting more pervasive and elusive referents than 'the factory'. This lack of motivation, whilst primarily associated with factors promoting 'ease', was thus also responsible at times for the opposite atmosphere, a sense of urgency. For the teachers, from time to time, expressed concern in various ways to inspire to possibly better things, to create awareness of new opportunities,

5

and to stimulate and develop possibly unsuspected talents. Apart from which, low motivation can produce other problems, worrying to the teacher's conscience. While it might be part of a syndrome of factors promoting easy relationships, it is reckoned to be an unhealthy habit of mind associated with other undesirable traits and attitudes. So that, although enjoying and appreciating the benefits in the form of good relationships, the teachers seek to alter the base on which they rest. On such occasions there is a sense of the irresistible force, in the form of teachers' best intentions and indomitable will-power, meeting the immovable object, in the form of the pupils' intransigence. But running beside this, contemporaneously, is a sense of fraternity. 'It's impossible not to like them', one teacher told me, after a particular unsuccessful lesson. 'One of the things I shall miss most is the teachers'', said one particularly rebellious pupil. 'They're not such a bad lot really.'

However, this pertained only during 'time off' moments. The school is part of a national system and its rating is firmly governed by certification. This determined the orientation and organization of the school. The school entered candidates for both 'O' level and CSE. examinations. Officially pupils were placed in three mixed-ability groups in the 1st and 2nd years with setting in English and mathematics. In practice there was a kind of disguised streaming, which was made manifest in the 3rd year on the basis of pupils' ability in English. These graded forms, 3A, 3B and 3C, then studied a more examination-orientated curriculum than in the previous two years (for example, chemistry, physics and biology as separate disciplines instead of 'science'; history, geography and RI instead of 'Integrated studies' and examination syllabuses were actually begun by some), together with some vocational elements such as technical drawing and commerce. During the third year a system of 'subject choice' operated and pupils were allocated among four fourth-year forms – two examination forms (4A and 4B), one commerce form (4C) and one non-examination form (4L). The examination forms were able to choose between various groups of fairly traditional subjects which enabled 'individual' timetables (see Table). The commerce form, composed entirely of girls, had a mainly secretarial diet of typing and bookkeeping; the non-examination form had 'block' activities, with large doses of social studies, environmental studies, practical activities and games. In addition the school ran a 'Community service' programme in which senior pupils visited local hospitals, centres for the physically and mentally handicapped, community centres, playgroups and old people's homes. The school had no 6th form. Pupils wishing to continue studies transferred either to the grammar school or technical college in the nearby town.

The school was run on traditional lines with no frills or pretensions to progressivism or any other unusual or ambitious projects. The basic unit was the form and the form teacher. Each year had a year tutor, responsible for the pastoral care of the year. A traditional House system, mainly but not entirely geared to games, was the basis of much of the school's social activities. And all of the teachers, without exception, taught traditional subject matter by traditional methods.

Examination courses

'O' level	CSE
English language	English
English literature	mathematics
mathematics	chemistry
chemistry	physics
physics	biology
history	general science
French	history
woodwork	geography
metalwork	French
engineering drawing	commercial arithmetic
art	shorthand
domestic science	typewriting
needlecraft	office practice
	woodwork
	metalwork
	engineering drawing
	art
	domestic science
	needlecraft
	music

In the 4th and 5th years, courses are provided for both the examination and non-examination pupils. Examination courses are offered in the above subjects. English, mathematics and four or more subjects of the pupil's choice form the examination course. As the examination and non-examination courses form an integrated programme in the 4th and 5th years, less able pupils are not required to offer all six subjects to examination standard.

'We're all caught up in the rush for certification — staff, pupils and parents — now more than ever', one teacher told me. 'I resent it rather. Once upon a time, and I've been here sixteen years, we took things more easily, kids just transferred to the grammar or the tech, no fuss.' This may reflect a general trend in the increasing emphasis on results. But it was exacerbated in the case of Lowfield by an impending change in status. Under the proposals for the reorganization of secondary education in the area, it was scheduled to accept a six-form fully comprehensive entry in the near future. It was anticipated that

7

ultimately accommodation would be required for some 1,000 pupils in the 11–18 age range. Pupils who would previously have gone to the grammar in town and whose prospects in life were definitely not 'dead-end', as long as they could achieve the necessary qualifications, would go to Lowfield. This made for an interesting situation at the school. On the one hand there was a feeling of 'the end of the road' about the school in its present state aided by the incumbent head-master's impending retirement, due before the change. Its roots were solidly in the tripartite past, its teachers doing an honest and thorough job as best they could with recalcitrant material, with no frills, a minimum of experimentation, and firmly based on tradition, with its assemblies, House system, prefectorial system, school uniform and rules, Protestant ethic-type morals and largely congenial personal relation-ships. On the other hand, there was an air of hope and expectation, tinged at times with frustration. The hope was for a new era, more resources, greater fulfilment, better career prospects with the advent of the grammar-type children. The sense of frustration came with reflecting on the realities, what they saw as the lack of a forward-looking policy on the part of the head, the feet of clay stuck in the past, uncertainty about their own positions, a general anxiety about the unknown and above all the increased pressure these teachers felt under to produce 'results', to legitimate the school in the eyes of parents of prospective grammar-type children. In the past it had been accepted that they had had a tough job, dealing as they were with 'failures'; in the future they would properly be expected to achieve much with a fully comprehensive intake; but in the meantime, as one teacher put it, 'We're expected to get blood out of stones and make silk purses out of sows' ears.' For the transitional period, then, the teachers felt called on, indeed pressed on, by the headmaster, to make superhuman efforts to make the school appear a respectable repository for 'bright' children. The sort of effort which largely led to 'artificial' results and which one reserved for prize days or other occasions of public presentation, tolerable because of its rarity, was now demanded continually in one's day-to-day teaching.

These contrasts of ease and urgency, hope and despair, excitement and frustration provided me with points of focus during my research in the school. I was concerned initially with the very broad question, 'What do people do in school and what do they do to each other?' With such an open approach, no specific criteria were laid down for choice of school, other than accessibility and typicality. As it happened Lowfield was very accessible and ultra-typical in a sense. Pressure was put on the teachers to prosecute their professional task with extra zeal; both that task, and the strategies which supported or cushioned it, were, I believe, highlighted in consequence. In turn, the pressures on the pupils being greater, their resources in coping were stretched to great limits and appeared in sharper relief. Thus, though the school could be said to be going through a transitional phase, it was one in which, I believe, typical processes and interrelationships were revealed, often in particularly vivid form.

Chapter 1

Theoretical approach

It is standard practice to locate one's research within the general field, and to identify one's approach in relation to others. This is the aim of this chapter, expanding on some of the points in the Introduction. In addition I give an overview of the contents of the rest of the book.

Previous work on the school

Sociological interest in school processes has increased in recent years. In the 1950s attention was directed almost exclusively to input-output factors, namely the relationship between variables associated with social class and education achievement.[1] What came in between – the manner of achievement and non-achievement and what else went on in schools besides – was not examined at that stage. School processes were largely taken for granted, teachers regarded as co-research workers and school aims commonly understood and accepted.

During the 1960s a number of people in different areas and from different traditions began to focus on classroom activities. The reformist zeal of the 1950s, after all, seemed insufficiently productive in practical outcomes, both here and in the USA, and this failure, together with the pressure of other socio-political events which had implications for the education system, brought a change in focus.[2] One had to account, for example, for the failure of the reformist drive. Deschoolers and free-schoolers were among the first to make an impact, and in subjecting the educative process itself to critical scrutiny indulged in what formerly might have been regarded as heresy.[3] However, they pointed to vast new areas for study in the area of what has been termed 'the hidden curriculum'. This kind of work received a legitimizing academic imprint towards the end of the 1960s with the work in America of

Smith and Geoffrey, and Jackson, which derived from certain anthropological traditions,[4] and in Britain of Hargreaves and Lacey which was certainly reformist, but different from previous studies.[5] The difference, especially with Jackson and Hargreaves, lay in providing a vivid sense of touching the realities of the situation, which escaped more formal studies of the school.[6]

The broad areas these new studies came to focus on were, for example, distortions of the manifest curriculum, teacher and pupil strategies, the 'unalterable framework of the system', or they were concerned to create an evocation of life in an institutional setting. At the same time as these perspectives were being imported into Britain from the States, interest grew in a long-standing American tradition, that of classroom interaction analysis.[7] Systematic observation however, in which the researcher acts as analyst, preconstructs his categories and uses quantitative measures, meant that researchers had to ignore much of the action, as well as actors' meanings and intentions, and the general cultural milieu of the situation. However, sociologists entering the field in Britain in the early 1970s began to mix in more ethnographic techniques such as non-participant observation and retaining schedules for demographic and other quantifiable data.[8]

At the same time, interest in the school and the classroom grew from another quarter, the sociology of knowledge, inspired by the publication of *Knowledge and Control* in 1971 and the Open University Course, 'School and Society'.[9] To the 'new' sociologists, the sociology of education was inseparable from the sociology of knowledge. For an outline, students are often referred to an article by Gorbutt:[10]

> . . . Within the perspective it proposes, society is conceived of in broad terms as being socially constructed, sustained and changed through the ongoing interaction of man. The relationship between man and society is a dialectical one and is essentially dynamic . . . Man constantly makes his world in that he is continually faced with the problem of constructing his social reality, of making sense of the world. The meaning of men and things within his environment must be actively interpreted and negotiated . . .

The only way of operationalizing this approach was by moving into schools and classrooms and using close or 'participant' observation. Thus, for example, Keddie studied the processes by which pupils were categorized in a comprehensive school, by 'considering two aspects of classroom knowledge; what knowledge teachers have of pupils, and what counts as knowledge to be made available and evaluated in the classroom'.[11] Beck studied the techniques of transfer into a secondary school and accompanied a group of children around the school all day, observing, making field notes, tape-recording and interviewing.[12] Vulliamy examined the consequences of a lack of fit between teachers' and pupils' criteria of relevance with regard to school music.[13] The shift of focus is well illustrated by an American study by Estelle Fuchs, where she reports how one teacher initially attributed children's failures to her own inadequacy, but was persuaded by colleagues that the real cause lay in the pupils' home background.[14] The important element, Fuchs claims, is teacher belief, rather than the background itself. Nash's study comes to a similar conclusion.[15]

It was not long, however, before such studies were meeting the criticism that[16]

> such a narrow focus for empirical research . . . tends to assign, if by implication only, an implausible degree of autonomy to teachers. The reorientation of sociological studies of education has seemed to stress that definitions of legitimate knowledge are not absolute, and that the activities of classroom teachers are not irrelevant to the ways that these definitions are sustained. In doing so, it has some-times even seemed to place teachers at the *centre* of the process whereby conceptions of school knowledge (and, by implication, aspects of the social structure) are legitimated and changed.

Such work had another possible implication, following on from this supposed attribution of autonomy to teachers. In the 1950s they were implicitly accorded the status of co-research workers; reformist atten-tion focused firmly on indices of social class, and had its logical prac-tical fulfilment in the compensatory programmes following the Plow-den Report.[17] When attention turned to the school during the 1960s, and teacher activities in particular, some described it as a 'teacher-bashing', or 'blame the teacher' phase. Since the 'new sociology' was concerned with how man actively made his world and constructed his meaning, the teacher became a popular subject for study. In the enthusiastic rush to redress the balance upset by previous omissions, all manner of 'sins', 'errors', 'inconsistencies' and 'contradictions' were revealed in teacher behaviour. Though this often may not have been the intent, the implications for some of this kind of work, focus-ing on teacher action, for so long ignored by sociologists, were that teachers were responsible since these were matters of consciousness and presumably could be changed by an act of will.[18] Inevitably, perhaps with the enthusiastic indulgence in these new theoretical perspectives and new areas of investigation, the rectifying of the old imbalance carried the dangers of a new distortion, as indicated in the Whitty quotation above. For teachers are not free agents, and it is not entirely a matter of consciousness. This is a major criticism that might be levelled at *Deviance in Classrooms*, by Hargreaves, Hester and Mellor.[19] In conducting their study at the level of teacher conscious-ness, for example on how they typify pupils (revealed by depth inter-view), they do not take into account factors external to the school which constrain teacher behaviour, which might affect how they actually typify pupils in the situation. It might be claimed that their analysis is valid regardless, and that it is made available both for further refinement or adaptation and for explanations on a wider level. That would be another task.

Another recent work on the school, however, in reaction to such 'idealist' work, claims that it is impossible to understand school processes without reference to external factors, and indeed that 'the sociology of the school' or 'of the classroom' is impossible.[20] For Sharp and Green the quest is not just to describe teacher action and portray inconsistencies and dichotomies, but to investigate what problems for the teacher these are viable solutions to. This takes these authors out of the classroom and into the wider structure of social relationships.

Their central thesis is that the rise of progressivism in our schools is a function of its greater effectiveness for social control. They claim to illustrate how, despite the ideology of child-centred progressivism, social stratification is reproduced in the classroom, and children's identities are socially structured. These are explained in terms of 'common features in the material and social environment of the teachers which cannot merely be intended away in consciousness, and which structure the activities of each and produce similar patterns in the social structuring of pupil identities'.[21] They emphasize the constraints of the situation within which teacher action is generated, and their analysis of the implications of this and its relationship with teacher ideology and operational consciousness is a considerable advance. However, there are problems with their account. For in removing the focus so forcefully once more to structure, much autonomy and many decision-making powers are denied the actor, who is portrayed as the unwitting victim of external forces. School processes are interpreted in terms of social structure and this marks, perhaps, a changing emphasis.

But the interpretation of those processes and the way in which they are conceived remain firmly with the authors. The point of departure from the field of research, from interviews and observation, is too stark and too sudden. The phenomenological approach Sharp and Green criticize so strongly can, in turn, level the criticism at them that they neglect situational realities and local contexts. The 'meaning' attributed to an action or utterance can vary according to actor's or speaker's definition of the situation. If we do not know the latter, we cannot assume the former. In Sharp and Green's case there is every indication that there was a gulf of difference in interpretation between teachers and researchers. They state that 'we employ a concept of false consciousness and implicitly highlight in critical fashion the falsity, where it is substantively incorrect, and naivety, where it is superficial, of the actor's consciousness',[22] without, however, examining the teachers' frames of reference when producing the supposed 'falsity' and 'naivety'.

This is without doubt a serious and difficult problem epitomized in these two books, all too briefly discussed here.[23] On the one hand, Hargreaves and his colleagues *are* very much concerned with exact and faithful representation of the situation and inmates' definitions, but in their preoccupation with that, ignore other factors bearing on that situation which might help us contextualize them. On the other, Sharp and Green, acknowledging the valuable but limited aid such theoretical and methodological approaches can afford, and capitalizing on it to some extent, centre their analysis of what goes on in school in social structure, but at the same cost at the interactionist level. I make no claims to having resolved this problem, but simply make the point that my approach in this respect is predominantly interactionist, though I am concerned to explore some of the connections with the wider social structure where they seemed particularly relevant.[24]

A similar problem — of mismatch between inmates' definitions and researchers' understandings of them — has been evident with work done on pupils and their reactions to school. With the new approaches which stressed the individual's constructions it might have been expected that attention should turn to pupils also, with emphasis on their own point of view. Apart from Hargreaves's and Lacey's pioneering work, however, there have been few such studies, and the reports of them have been largely confined to the academic journals. These show a variety of approaches to 'the pupil's own point of view', some of them still encased within official frameworks. The range extends from inferences derived from preconstructed categories[25] through 'naturally-elicited' constructs based on the personality theory of George Kelly[26] and symbolic interactionist studies relying on observation techniques but strong researcher analysis,[27] to phenomenological and ethnomethodological studies which seek to preserve the 'integrity' of the situation still further.[28]

Methodologically there are vast differences among these offerings, but some common ground might be discovered. We learn that Hargreaves's and Lacey's polarization of pupils' subcultures within the school into 'academic' and 'delinquescent' is too rigid,[29] and that there is not necessarily an anti-school group.[30] Pupils are overwhelmingly utilitarian unless they are not doing examinations, when they might have expressive interests.[31] Teachers do not always act as they say they do or will.[32] Pupils like good order, warm friendly relations, teachers who 'explain' and are interesting, and dislike weak, unfair, unfriendly, boring teachers.[33] Pupils have their own rules, which teachers would do well to know about.[34] However, there are problems in relating these studies together. It is well known that pre-constructing categories delimits the area of investigation and channels responses.

The channel such studies sail up may be a minor tributary in the pupils' scheme of things. While not entirely invalidated, they can mislead out of context. Smithers, for example (following Morton-Williams), infers too much about the meaning pupils attach to his 'expressive' items, having assumed already, of course, that school 'objectives' generally are of importance to them. School-leavers may well value 'social' or 'expressive' goals more than 'stayers', but they may not be the school's social goals. Quine goes some way toward acknowledging this. He found nearly all his sample seeing school as a means to an end, thus frustrating the hopes of the champions of ROSLA who had emphasized the social benefits of the extra year. However, he does say that some appeared not to understand the question asking them about how school might aid their leisure, maturity and citizenship; while that on vocational ends was relatively clear cut. Quine also found most of his pupils saying they liked school, and 'this acceptance of the school regime was stronger in the bottom sets or streams.' We are given no indication of *why* they liked school, and if this differed at all among the pupils.

Much of this shortfall comes from a static conception of school and teaching. A more dynamic analysis would take into account all three elements — pupils' own interpretive processes, the manifold structure of the school and its own activities, and the pupils' dynamic relationship to it.[35]

Furthermore, pupil views, as school processes in general, need relating to wider, societal forces. The investigation of pupil views in their own terms, not ours, will reveal patterned differences, and in seeking to understand the basis of these, we shall be led further afield. Certainly a concern of early British sociology of education was to examine different cultural properties and different frames of reference bred by different social class positions. But the researchers, not the bearers of the culture, provided the definitions, and cultural differences were either conceived of as 'cultural deprivation',[36] or interpreted widely as such, as with Bernstein's elaborated and restricted codes.[37] We should, of course, make no such assumptions, beginning with pupil views, properly ascertained, and working outwards from there. As yet we have hardly started in this field.[38]

Symbolic interaction

The general conceptual framework of my approach to school processes is within the symbolic interactionist tradition of Mead, Blumer, Goffman and Becker.[39] This has three basic postulates.

(1) Human beings act towards things on the basis of the *meanings* that the things have for them. Man inhabits two different worlds:

the 'natural' world wherein he is an organism of drives and instincts and where the external world exists independently of him; and the social world, where the existence of symbols, such as language, enables him to give meanings to objects. This attribution of meanings, this interpreting, is what makes him distinctively human, and social. Interactionists therefore focus on the world of subjective meanings and the symbols by which they are produced and represented.

This means not making any prior assumptions about what is going on in an institution, and taking seriously, indeed giving priority to, inmates' own accounts. Thus, if pupils appear preoccupied for much of the time with 'being bored', 'mucking about', 'having a laugh', 'bunking off' or 'being shown up', the interactionist is keen to explore the properties and dimensions of these processes.

(2) This attribution of meaning to objects through symbols is a continuous *process*. Action is not simply a consequence of psychological attributes such as 'drives', 'attitudes' or 'personalities', or determined by external social facts such as social structures or roles, but results from a continuous process of meaning attribution which is always emerging in a state of flux and subject to change. The individual constructs, modifies, pieces together, weighs up the pros and cons and bargains. Hence, at Lowfield, I was interested not only in the kinds of pupil adaptation to school, but how individuals move among them; how teachers 'negotiate' with pupils, but then how teachers themselves react differently in different situations, and how these activities are differently interpreted by others — pupils and parents. The emphasis on process gets behind the psychological facade of such items as subject choice. Here the reckoning, pushing, prodding, considering, deliberating, discussing; as well as the worrying, grieving, fighting, rejoicing which are all components of the process, are starkly revealed. The different patterns of response are equally evident, and these can then be related to wider, structural forces.

(3) This process takes place in a *social* context. Each individual aligns his action to that of others. He does this by 'taking the role of the other', by making indications to his 'self' about the 'other's' likely response. He constructs how others wish or might act in a certain circumstance, and how he himself might act. He might try to 'manage' the impressions others have of him, put on a 'performance', try to influence the other's 'definition of the situation'.[40] Such projections are most clearly evident in the teacher's section on subject choice (chapter 2), in their 'presentation of front' to parents in reports (chapter 8), to pupils in the classroom (chapters 7 and 6) and to themselves (chapter 9); while pupils reveal the various personae, realities and definitions that they deploy, principally in chapters 3, 5 and 8.[41]

Constant negotiations are required to preserve an equilibrium, and as they proceed, people become more committed to their 'presentations' as they are progressively adjusted and refined. When events contradict presentations, breakdown of social interaction occurs, leading to embarassment, anger, discomfort, shame and so on. There was plenty of this at Lowfield. Hence my interest, again, in 'showing up'; in what I term 'heavy conflict' in chapter 5, and in 'laughter inhibitors' in chapter 9.

These constitute the main principles behind the examination of school processes. My analysis, however, is not confined to subjective meanings, for I have been concerned to relate the patterns thus revealed to more traditional conceptions of social structure, and to place them within a wider social and temporal framework.[42] It should be said, however, that this part of the study is necessarily more tentative and speculative for two reasons. First, while it may be true that there is a sense in which we can find the whole of mankind encapsulated in a moment, we cannot pretend that one case study will provide the answer to the question of how society operates. We need more detailed studies to build up the general picture. Secondly, the general framework which seemed appropriate to my analysis of Lowfield is perhaps one that has excited more strong feelings than cool detached reasoning, perhaps because of its very content. Both need more thorough investigation, and this study is offered as a pointer in both respects.

The relation to structure

My analysis owes something to Weber, something to Marx and something to certain strands of functionalist theory. Lest this seem an unduly eclectic group of theoretical sources, it should be noted that this is not at all at variance with the interactionist's typical view of society. This is as a fairly loosely structured entity, showing certain discernible patterns, but with many large gaps between the prominent features of those patterns, and a number of contradictions at any given time. This contrasts with hard deterministic viewpoints which regard the economy as overwhelmingly paramount and the real source of all action.[43]

The book is primarily about processes, about what goes on in school. To understand those processes they can, to some degree and for certain purposes, be analysed in their own terms as a product of the institution in which they occur. But for a wider understanding we need to go outside the school. My analysis indicated two kinds of linkages which seem particularly appropriate to the material thrown up by my research, one encapsulated by the other. The first is the school's place in the prevailing social structure. Early in my research I identified two broad groups of 'perspectives', or ways of seeing the world, among the pupils, which seemed associated with cultural properties of social class background. Inasmuch as the school fostered this division, indeed, as I show in chapter 2, crystallized it, notably in the subject choice process by sweeping up some anomalies, it is serving the predominant interests in a stratified society. This would appear to be in line with a larger body of opinion which argues that the school's main function in capitalist societies is to preserve and legitimate inequality. There is a sense in which it can hardly avoid doing so, as I demonstrate in chapter 2. But this is far removed from the teachers' intentions, at least in the case of Lowfield, and at least in as crude a form as that. The questions then arise of how the school can maintain this function against the wishes of the teachers, and how teachers accommodate the anomaly.

To answer the first question I lean toward functionalist theory, which points to the interdependence of systems and institutions in a mutually supportive and ongoing process. However, systems do not have purposes, only people, and the analysis is linked to the self through the classic interactionist concept of commitment (chapter 7).

To answer the second question — how teachers accept the anomaly of promoting some outcomes while intending others — I shall refer to a different tradition originating with Weber and his work on bureaucracy, and for my purposes receiving the most vital inputs from Goffman with his analyses of the individual's attempt to cope with society, and Peter Berger, especially in his analysis (with Berger and Kellner) of the effect on consciousness of technocracy.[44] The keynote is rationality. Weber saw Western civilization as having developed from supernatural to rational bases of action. The world has become 'disenchanted', no longer living by faith, but by rules and regulations, laws and records and systematic processes to discover adequate means of achieving clearly specified ends. We are in the era of the 'right solution', the division of labour, and the 'expert' and 'functionary'. Bureaucracy — the form of social organization adopted by institutions in advanced industrial societies — epitomizes the effects. As Weber put it:[45]

> Bureaucratization offers above all the optimum possibility for carrying through the principle of specializing administrative functions according to purely objective considerations. Individual performances are allocated to functionaries who have specialized training and who by constant practice learn more and more. The 'objective' discharge of business primarily means a discharge of business according to *calculable rules* and 'without regard for persons' . . .
>
> When fully developed, bureaucracy also stands, in a specific sense, under the principle *sine ira ac studio*. Its specific nature, which is welcomed by capitalism, develops the more perfectly the more bureaucracy is 'dehumanized', the more completely it succeeds in eliminating from artificial business love, hatred and all purely personal, irrational and emotional elements which escape calculation.

Schools are to varying degrees bureaucratized. Indeed, Musgrove has persuasively argued that schools are structured to foster bureaucratic personalities, and that trouble arises when children do not fit the mould.[46] Arguably, in the move to comprehensive education and larger schools, this element will be increased, since size of institution is a known associated factor. Inevitably, therefore, there is a strain toward impersonality in the prosecution of its main task, preparation of the young for present society.

I shall touch on this theme throughout the study, returning to a fuller consideration in the final chapter. I should say that I do not adopt a view of 'rationality' or 'bureaucracy' as necessarily implacable enemies of the human race. In some respects they are enormous facilitators. However, at Lowfield at least, there was strong evidence that human control of these processes had been, or was being, lost.

Organization and summary of the book

Though I have given certain basic details about the school in the Introduction, this tells us little about how the school actually works behind the official facade. In chapter 2 I seek to uncover some actual and basic processes and frameworks, the intentions behind them and their fundamental relation to society as revealed in the subject-choice process. The basic structure of the school, the relationship to it of teachers, pupils and parents, and the connection between the internal processes of the school and the macro elements in society, are all crystallized in the subject-choice process. In the official programme it appears as the fulcrum of the pupil's school career. All before has been preparatory, all after is the real stuff of education on which life-chances depend — preparing for examinations and aligning for future jobs.

Parents are sensitive to this and go through a period of high concern. They sense that it is an important step in life and that there can be no turning back. For teachers too, for their peace of mind and future prospects, a lot hangs by the results. Not for nothing has this process become a considerable industry. At Lowfield, for example, it takes up the whole of the third term in the 3rd year, and involves lectures, counselling, parents' meetings, examinations and a high degree of personal commitment from most concerned. It all takes place in a cultivated atmosphere of 'choice'. The choice is to be the best informed possible, hence there is an enormous input of data from all quarters, aided by specialist advice, rehearsals of combinations and permutations of subjects, soul-searching and crystal-ball-gazing, yielding the result most suitable for the individual pupil in the light of all known circumstances. However, an examination of the process revealed other factors more influential than pupils' interest, the most potent of them lying

19

outside the school. In their approach to making the choice I found pupils used different frames of reference or 'group perspectives' in two broad groups which could be systematically related to social class background. Teacher strategies in guiding pupils into making the 'right' choices were examined, and shown to be contributing to a 'contest' system of education behind a meritocratic mask. Given the basic group perspectives of the pupils, located originally in different lifestyles according to different positions in the social structure, the teachers could be held, albeit against their will, to be driving the wedges more firmly between these divisions. The external factors so constrain the process that the notion of 'choice', so fashionable perhaps among progressive ideologies, is almost the inversion of what actually occurs. At least, it operates within very narrow limits, within other decisions or consequences that are determined by other forces.

Pupils thus have different perceptions of school, it has different meanings for them and different impact upon them. If the mainstream activity of the school has relevance for some only, and possibly only partial relevance for many of those, the question arises as to how they adjust. They do this in various ways. In chapter 3 I develop a typology of pupil modes of adaptation, indicating the major ways in which pupils adjusted to school at Lowfield. Typologies are useful in that because all our thinking is a form of categorizing or typifying, they can improve our vision and sharpen our focus by drawing together a mass of detail into an organized structure wherein the major types are indicated. They give us an idea of the range of such types and point up relationships and interconnections, in this case linking pupil response to official aims and techniques. Primarily, they offer a basis for comparison, but they must be aligned to the realities of the subject matter they refer to. In observing and talking to pupils I was ultimately impressed by the relevance of a typology devised by Wakeford.[47] This I adapted to Lowfield.

In chapters 4 and 5 I examine two aspects of pupils' school experience. The first follows the careers of the two separated groups identified in chapter 2, now in the 4th year, and looks at their views on the official programme and structure of the school. These are informative as indicators of factors conducive to conformity, one of the major modes of pupil adaptation, though, as we shall see, teachers do not feel that the provision of such factors is entirely within their power, being themselves assailed by similar forces. The two groups represented here were those at the extremes of the ability structure — the top examination form, 4A, and the bottom, 4L, which included a large number of non-examinees. The different frames of reference or 'group perspectives' identified in subject choice are seen to persist; but also evident is the many-sided nature of pupils' interests and reactions in relation to such matters as the content of school subjects, teacher

20

personalities, school structure and institutional factors. Though separate, these are, of course, related. For example, institutional factors can determine the teacher personality witnessed by the pupil in the classroom.

The second aspect, examined in chapter 5, is what I discovered to be the most prominent feature of the school-generated lifestyles of those going through phases of the broadly dissonant modes of adaptation, indeed what might be regarded as the colonizing activity par excellence − 'having a laugh' − the 'hidden curriculum' of pupilhood. This study is more broadly based than that in chapter 4, being derived from conversations with 5L in the first place, but ultimately with over 200 pupils in the 3rd, 4th and 5th years. Both studies illustrate the degree and nature of the influence of the institutional framework of the school as a factor in pupil, and indeed teacher adaptations.

Chapter 6 strikes a sharp contrast so typical of the ups and downs of school life − one moment, laughter and jollity and amicable relations all round, the next pain and suffering, degradation and humiliation. At Lowfield humiliation was acutely painful, a frequent occurrence, an overriding concern, its practice suggestive of certain associations with teacher styles of pedagogy.

'Concern with dignity and degradation runs through the interviews. These teachers realize that if they refuse to humiliate their pupils they will be considered ineffective.'[48] So comments Frank Musgrove on his talks with rank-and-file teachers. They are 'humiliated by the power of children and by the power of headteachers, and feel degraded and brutalized by exercising power themselves. The real enemy is "the system".'[49]

Humiliation is the other side of the coin to laughter, and it is the other chief feature of many pupils' school lives. Quite often the balmy world of pupil adaptations is disrupted by excesses on the pupils' part or non-participation on the teachers'. If, in their laughter in search of respect and dignity, meaning and identity, pupils foul official or tacit norms, the most customary antidote employed by teachers at Lowfield is a tactic deliberately aimed at undermining dignity and producing embarrassment, shame and degradation. In the pupils' terms it is 'showing them up', and this was by far the most painful experience, the most feared and detested, the biggest outrage against the human person in their school lives.

In chapters 7, 8 and 9 I analyse what appeared at Lowfield to be the major components of the teacher's activity − 'survival', 'professionalism' and 'being human'. In many of our state secondary schools, and Lowfield was no exception, teachers are mainly busy with basic techniques of survival. To take an example it is essential for the teacher to have control in order to teach. But often the problem of control is so enormous as to be insoluble, and it becomes an end in itself − the only end. I was alerted to the pervasiveness of this problem, and the many latent ways teachers try to resolve it, during my stay at Lowfield. Indeed, though individual teachers differ enormously in this respect, I was left with the feeling that 'survival' was undoubtedly the teachers' predominant activity as a group, at least in the sense of demands on their time and energies. I examine this 'survival' aspect in chapter 7.

Teachers are never more professional than when writing school reports. Reports are one way in which teachers appear as neutral professional mediators, rather like doctors pronouncing on the state of health of their clients and diagnosing what needs to be done, if anything, to improve it. But, taken against its initial reference — school aims and organization — the basic commodity is seen to be somewhat more variable than 'good health'. What the report indicates, in short, is how far the pupil measures up to a teacher's present intention, and that cannot always be taken for granted. Chapter 8 is aimed at uncovering some of those intentions. If, however, we look for brilliance and invention, and sheer *joie de vivre*, it does not take place in the classroom at all, nor in any areas connected with the prosecution of the teacher's job. There is a striking amount of it in school, but evident mostly in the staffroom, and other 'private areas'. Its chief manifestation is laughter.

A major theme of this book is that the institutional structure of the school does impose constraints and conditions on relationships, which effectively removes them from the 'personal' sphere. The mass nature of schooling, the heavily standardized and systematic requirements, the formal traditions of teaching, which emphasize role distance, firm discipline, and routinization, the culture gap between most teachers and most children, and increasing tendencies amongst many of the latter against the purpose of the school; not to mention all the trappings of rooms, timetables, bells and rituals — all these items produce strain for both pupils and teachers. The pupils accommodate to it by 'having a laugh'. The teachers do likewise. At Lowfield, 'real' selves were mostly not to be found, for either pupils or teachers, in the formal structure and programme of the school, but in private areas and moments. Laughter was a bridge between the two, a magical device by which potentially damaging, unwelcome, or alienating circumstances or people were transformed to tolerance, and transported to the plane of 'truer' self.[50]

This is not, of course, to say that all lessons and teacher-pupil contacts are humourless. Pupils 'have their laughs' and teachers 'fraternize', or use humour as an instrument of policy.[51] Teachers also take time off from their formal roles in 'asides', as it were, to joke with pupils. But for the most part they are heavily constrained by circumstances. This is why, contrarily enough, it can sometimes be more 'pleasant' to teach a non-examination than an examination form.

The latter requires total professional commitment. With the former, with only very vaguely defined aims, one can take 'time off' and be more 'human'. Since there is nothing in the school for them, they are thrown back upon their personal human resources. Those teachers accepting, or at least sensing, this can indeed enter into a 'special' relationship with such forms when all the usual criteria surrounding the teacher-pupil role are released; though conversely those who contrive with too strict an interpretation of aims and roles are likely to have uncommon difficulty − they are not playing the same game. For the most part, however, Lowfield teachers depart from the social world that contains their preferred identities when they leave the staffroom, bound for classrooms, and re-enter it when they return. Laughter is the passport back. It is the mechanism that restores them as persons, that puts a perspective on what has happened 'out there' to make it more manageable, that emphasizes individuality after the experience of depersonalized structures and faceless crowds, that recovers face, confidence, status; in short one's identity as a person. This is why the staffroom is sacred; why in many schools pupils are debarred and headteachers knock before entering. It is the teacher's private area where he can reconstitute those elements of 'himself' without the tension-ridden interference of higher authority or conflictual opposition of pupils.

In fact, of course, much of the catharsis that takes place through laughter concerns those items. And not only do headteachers and their deputies and pupils impinge greatly on teachers and cause tension in their own rights, but the fact that they induce contrary tendencies and expectations sets up the biggest conflict of all for teachers, which they must resolve in some way, if they are to survive. Laughter has this supremely important function of not resolving conflict, but dissipating it, transforming it to a zone of reality where it doesn't matter any more. Through laughter, the teachers can resist the headteacher and cope with the pupils and thus do their job. Of all the contrasts, inconsistencies and divisions I experienced at Lowfield, I encountered none greater or sharper than this, between joyous laughter and soul-less despair. I examine staffroom humour and teachers as persons in chapter 9.

In the final chapter I reconsider the main themes of the study and their interconnections. I attempt to demonstrate the relevance in relation to an empirical study of a typical secondary school in the English state system, and the fruitfulness, both for sociological theory and for present educational concern, of a focus on the classic interactionist concepts of perspectives, contexts, strategies, rules and identities. I summarize the various ways in which institutional factors, as opposed to external factors, have emerged throughout the study as influences on school processes. I then review the external factors suggested by

certain aspects of the research. I conclude with some of the implications for educational practice, as I see them.

Chapter 2

Patterns of choice[*]

Pupil and teacher strategies and adaptations take place within an institutional framework which is related to the general educational system which, in turn, is related to society. A perplexing question, which will recur throughout this book, is how much those activities owe to purely institutional factors, and how much to external factors.

The difficulty lies not only in the point of linkage between micro and macro, but also in the diverse and often contradictory elements of school life. Thus, in our attempts to resolve the one, we may not do justice to the other. We either get a neat theoretical account which embraces part of school activity only, or an accurate and further description of school life, which is comparatively atheoretical. We rarely get both together.

Certain possible connections, which linked interactionist concepts like meaning-construction, perspectives and mediation to structural matters like the social class system and the school's role in society, occurred to me during the summer term of 1975 when I witnessed various aspects of Lowfield's subject-choice system. This system also illustrated certain important properties of the school's overall organization, indeed, it could be represented as one process operating at the heart of the school, with implications for all its components, lending itself most readily to analysis. In this chapter, therefore, I depict the framework within which the action of subsequent chapters occurs, suggesting certain linkages between process and structure, using subject choice as a case study. Ultimately, however, the detailed study of action and process in these later chapters leads to the conclusion that this framework is not entirely sufficient to account for all the prominent areas of activity observed in the school, a deficiency I attempt to remedy in later chapters.

The mode of exposition here will be to examine, in turn, pupils', parents' and teachers' parts in the process of subject choice, ultimately looking at the implications for the school's relationship to society. First, however, I set out the model and the major concepts that I came to use in making sense of the materials. As far as method is concerned, briefly, my own engagement at the school enabled me to monitor the process through the summer term, and to follow it up the next year. I talked to all the pupils in the 3rd year, at least once, in interviews ranging from half to two hours, and discussed freely with teachers from day to day. I sent a questionnaire to all parents of 3rd-year pupils (see Appendix 2), and visited as many as I could before the end of term (25 per cent). This involvement over a long period enabled me to cross-check results, follow up promising leads and to explore in some depth the reactions of those concerned.[1]

A sociological model of subject choice

The first important concept arising from my discussions with pupils, was that of *group perspectives*. As used by Becker[2] these refer to:

> modes of thought and action developed by a group which faces the same problematic situation. They are the customary ways members of the group think about such situations and act in them . . . which appear to group members as the natural and legitimate ones to use in such situations.

They arise when people face 'choice points', where previous thought and experience does not guide their actions, though if a particular kind of situation recurs frequently, the perspective will probably become an established part of a person's way of dealing with the world. They develop and gain strength as a result of group interaction and they are situationally specific. I shall show how, among the pupils, two broad 'group perspectives' seem indicated.

The second key concept, focusing more on pupils' parents is *social class*. The relationship between social class and educational experience is well known, as is the culture clash between working-class children and teachers.[3] My materials suggest that parental definitions of the situation differ along class lines, and thus the parental influences brought to bear on children in making their choices are both quantitatively and qualitatively different in accordance with these broad groupings.

There is a strong connection between social class and the development of group perspectives. Underpinning these are different frames of reference and self-conceptions,[4] which are products of the position a family occupies within the overall class structure. Bernstein,[5] for example, has pointed up the differences in socialization between lower-working-class and the professional and managerial middle-class families. Among the former, the child is brought up to see the world in terms of the immediate present, and he is taught to acknowledge without question the bases of his relationships with others.[6]

> The range of alternatives which inhere in the roles is relatively limited, consequently the communication system reduces the degree of individual selection from alternatives. These children are less likely to learn to cope with problems of role ambiguity and ambivalence. They are more likely to avoid or foreclose upon activities or problems which carry this potential.

The middle-class child on the other hand has a wide range of discretion, and an 'open' communication system. The child learns to *make* his role, rather than this being formally assigned to him. Judgments and decision-making are a function of the quality of the person rather than the status of the member.

How these frames of reference are stabilized and reinforced by the child's experience of others within the school (thus facilitating the development of group perspectives) is discussed by Ashton.[7] For the 'careerless' (mainly products of position-orientated families)

> their [initial] allocation to positions in the lower streams effectively denies them the opportunity to develop their cognitive and manipulative skills beyond a minimum level . . . On moving through the third and fourth forms these young people face a situation that reinforces their concern with the here and now. Pupils in higher streams face the problem of mastering academic subjects as a means of obtaining future academic qualifications, but for these young people there are no such future rewards . . . The problems they face . . . are those of obtaining some sort of reward or satisfaction in the here and now — problems that are frequently solved in the classroom through 'rulebreaking', and 'messing about'.

My study supports this general analysis.

However, school decisions such as subject choice are triangular affairs, involving children, parents and teachers. I found teachers important as *choice mediators* operating within a framework of *institutional channelling*. These concepts owe a great deal to the work of Cicourel and Kitsuse.[8] As against explanations of academic attitudes and achievements mainly or directly in terms of class-related differentials and peer group culture,[9] Cicourel and Kitsuse in their study of the American 'Lakeshore High School' presented an alternative view which saw the differentiation of students as a consequence of the administrative organization and decisions of personnel in the school. The counsellor's role in students' ultimate admission to college was shown to be crucial. Assignment to college and non-college course was dependent upon the interpretations of a student's ability and aptitude by admissions personnel; and since parents knew little about college entrance requirements, his opportunities were to a great extent decided by counsellor's perceptions of him. These perceptions of the student were made purely in terms of the characteristics of the student, that is to say that any variations in performance, for instance, would not even be thought to be attributable to, say, teaching methods. Furthermore, a counsellor would not base his judgments on test scores alone. There are other important factors, such as social class, which operate in subtle ways. For example, administrators 'spend more time with the processing of middle- and upper-class students for college entrance, for it is the students from these social classes who have the best means at hand to validate the effectiveness of the high school's programme of developing the talent'. The highly bureaucratic organization of the school helped create the problem, for (a) the classification of students 'routinely initiates organization actions that may progressively define and limit the development of such careers', and (b) in their concern for professional status, counsellors produced a greater range and frequency of student problems. This reminds one of Becker's 'moral entrepreneur',[10] who originates and leads crusades against particular problems and extends his outrage to other problems as he becomes knowledgeable about them. Dickson[11] emphasizes that organizational structures give rise to moral entrepreneurs, whose function is to instil the organization's ideology and legitimation in the eyes of the public. All this serves to support Cicourel and Kitsuse's conclusion that 'the advances and setbacks in the process of mobility in such a system are governed less by the folk norms of the larger society than by the doctrines and practices of a professionalized bureaucracy.'

There are many analogies between the Cicourel and Kitsuse study and my own. The school has a similar bifurcation of routes; and institutional processes and teacher counselling (though frequently indirect and subsidiary to their teaching role) play a large part in the distribution of pupils between them. However, there is another important concept which bears on teachers as 'choice mediators' which does not figure in the Cicourel and Kitsuse account. They explain their counsellors' actions in terms of motivation in celebration of the self within the framework of professionalization, and in the self-fulfilling outcomes of bureaucratic structures. This may do as an explanation for the actions of American high school counsellors, but there were other factors bearing on teachers in my account, which I term *critical area influences*. To a great extent they direct and constrain teacher actions and thus serve to modify the Cicourel and Kitsuse conclusion above, at least in relation to this particular school.

How I relate these concepts together in a general model is illustrated in Figure 2.1. Differences in social class origins produce different educational experiences. These are reflected in school structure, which is serving societal rather than individual aims, and hence feeds back into social structure. From all of these, singly and collectively, values, attitudes and actions form. Group perspectives develop in reaction to 'pedagogical orientation', which includes aims, methods and organization of teaching, themselves determined by teacher philosophies and ideologies and sustained or intensified by critical area influences (these are frequently mediated by the headteacher). The particular pedagogical orientation dominant in a school then bears on life in the school (culture) and the school's organization (structure). Most educational decisions in school, including subject choice, are made within this framework.

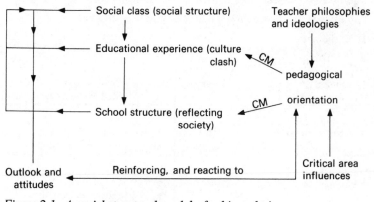

Figure 2.1 A social structural model of subject choice
CM = choice mediation

The school's system of subject choice

During the summer term of the 3rd year all pupils are required to complete a form expressing their choice of subjects to study in the 4th and 5th year (see Table 2.1). The rationale behind the scheme is governed by four crucial criteria. (1) Prevailing custom which allows choice encouraged by current ideologies such as progressivism and pupil-directed learning. (2) Prevailing state of knowledge and current patterns of educational career, largely dictated by the extended examination system, the requirements of further education and employers and the disposition of pupils. Thus there are the traditional subjects, and traditional groupings available (e.g. sciences, arts, commerce, non-examination subjects); and English, maths and games are considered so important as to be compulsory. (3) Type of child. All the pupils at this school had been unsuccessful at the 11+ examination and for the greater majority it was considered that more than six examination subjects might well prove counter-productive, and in any case were quite sufficient for all purposes. Hence the four 'choice' groups, in addition to the compulsory maths and English. (4) Resources (size of school, number of teachers, space and equipment).

TABLE 2.1 Fourth Year Options: September 1974

Before entering the 4th Form you are given an opportunity to select the subjects which you would like to study for the next two years. English and Mathematics are compulsory, but, within certain limits, you may choose the remaining four subjects of your course.

Choose ONE subject from EACH of the following groups.

Put a tick in the box below the subject you have chosen.

1 Mathematics
2 English

3	Commerce	Chemistry	Geography	Art	Environmental Studies (non-examination)		
4	Commerce	Physics	English Literature	General Science	General Science (non-examination)		
5	Commerce	Biology	History	Tech. Drawing	Social Studies (non-examination)		
6	Woodwork	Metal-work	Needle-craft	House-craft	Music	French	Art & Craft (non-exam.)

Further information

(a)   Your programme will include 4 periods of Games and PE.
(b)   Pupils not entered for examinations in Woodwork, Metalwork, Needlecraft, Housecraft, French or Music will be able to participate in the School's Community Service programme. A limited number will be able to spend further time in the practical areas of their choice.

The pupils: the development of group perspectives

Within this framework the pupils chose. Each pupil was asked to state, in an informal interview situation,[12] his or her reasons for each of the original choices. Table 2.2 summarizes the results. The three forms were streamed by ability. In the first two years pupils had been un-streamed, but setted for English and mathematics.

TABLE 2.2 Pupils' reasons for choices

Forms		Nos	Liking for sub-ject	Dislike of others	Job	Good ability	Poor ability at others	Liking for teachers	Dislike of teachers	Others
3A	Boys	15	29	5	15	19	1	1	2	8
	Girls	21	29	26	44	12	5	5	11	2
	Total	36	58	31	59	31	6	6	13	10
3B	Boys	14	18	9	12	23	6	1	3	10
	Girls	20	31	17	13	8	5	3	1	5
	Total	34	49	26	25	31	11	4	4	15
3C	Boys	15	13	6	10	3	13	0	1	2
	Girls	15	9	22	8	0	3	0	1	2
	Total	30	22	28	18	3	16	0	2	4
All boys		44	60	20	37	45	20	2	6	20
All girls		56	69	65	65	20	13	8	13	9
	Total	100	129	75	102	65	33	10	19	29

There appear to be two main factors, an affective one (liking, or disliking), and a utilitarian one (career and ability), and they seem to hold in roughly equal proportions overall. However, there are some interesting differences within, illustrative of two basic group perspectives. The positive reasons (liking, good ability) are much stronger in 3A and 3B than in 3C, where good ability is hardly a factor at all. 'Liking for subject' includes, of course, a strong teacher element. The like/dislike teacher categories are for responses indicating direct personal reasons — 'I can't stand the teacher', 'She picks on me all the time, I'd never get through the course', 'He's the only teacher I seem to get on with', 'She hates me so she won't teach me nothing. If she don't like yer, she won't learn yer.' This was a factor in only 7 per cent of cases, with nearly three times as many girls being involved as boys. The like/dislike of subject response focuses on the subject as mediated by the teacher. But this response begs a further question — why do they 'like' certain subjects? The interviews showed these reasons to fall into two types which point up the contrast between 3A and 3C more vividly. Thus the former tended to like subjects for official, supportive, traditional educational reasons, the latter for unofficial, anti-school, counter-cultural social reasons. Thus the first type might like a subject because the teacher makes it interesting, is well organized, can keep order, and gives them to feel that they are learning something; the second type for almost directly opposite reasons, such as having few demands made on them, having great freedom, and even 'having a muck-about'. As this is an important illustration of these vastly different attitudes towards school, I give some examples of each type.

Type 1 Liking/disliking subjects and/or teachers for 'supportive' reasons

Sandra: I like history and I like Mrs Nelson and she makes history really interesting, and I don't think I could do it if she didn't, an' she does — very interesting.

PW: So if any other teacher took you for history you'd have second thoughts?

Sandra: Yes!

Leslie: Mrs Nelson we all get on very well with her, don't we, I mean I don't think I'd take it, if Mr Hanly was doing it . . . Mrs Nelson, she really does get down to it, she makes the lesson clear. If you don't understand she'll go over it again.

Julie: An' she really can keep control of the class can't she? Without having to raise her voice — an' she's ever so quiet — an' everyone's quiet, 'in't they?

PW: What do you reckon the secret is then of winning everybody's respect?

Leslie: Maybe, it's personality coming out of Mrs Nelson. She just has to stand there and the room fills with her personality.

PW: What happens if somebody messes about — you've got some pretty rough characters in your form?

Leslie: You've said it, but they *don't*, not with her, because of her personality and her way of doing things, even the rogues are interested.

Sandra: When she's done she gives us homework and everybody does it, don't they?

One can also dislike subjects for 'supportive' reasons (i.e. using official criteria). I asked one girl why she chose needlecraft on line 6 (see Table 2.1).

Susan: Well, I can't take woodwork or metalwork. French — I don't get on with French very well and I can't do it, and I can't take art/craft (*because she's doing that on line 1*). I was considering taking music, but I thought it's only the basics I need and I thought I'm not too keen on Mr Greig's way of doing things so I think two years of that would drive me round the bend. And housecraft — I forgot my kit at that time, so it wasn't worth my doing that, so needlecraft was the only one left.

PW: Don't you need materials for that?
Susan: Yes, but not so often. Cookery you need stuff every week and it costs, and mums get fed up with it.

Type 2 Liking/disliking subjects and/or teachers for counter-official reasons

I would include in this those who chose subjects for transient 'right' reasons. Thus a recent event, rather than studied and closely considered opinion, might be fastened upon in an otherwise lost situation. Why had one boy chosen biology at first?

'I dunno. Well, we done some'at about the body, I thought that were good . . . you know, animals an' that.'

Many ruled some subjects out because they were too hard work.

Yvonne: I hate geography.
PW: Why?
Yvonne: Do hard work. These map things. He give you maps and you have to write names on.

In this regard, 'writing' was by far the most onerous activity. Several pupils had been cooled out of subjects by the sheer fatigue of the writing they were required to do. They would be equally impressed though in the opposite direction with subjects where the demands were few.

'Because you have an easy time and I like it.'

'I like it because 'e's great. You never do no work, we 'ave a great time. Good laugh that is.'

'I like it because I'm with all me mates and we 'ave a right old laugh. Not like some subjects where we do nothing but work. Gives yer a 'eadache all day that does.'

To return to Table 2.2, 3A also seem more swayed by thoughts of career, but this is a somewhat misleading result since this is due mainly to the girls opting for the commerce course. There are some interesting differences between boys' and girls' responses. Boys appear to take ability and lack of it more into account than girls, while girls are more influenced than boys by likes and dislikes. One might speculate that this is a consequence of sexual socialization, boys as ultimate careerists and breadwinners not allowing themselves to be swayed by likes and dislikes to the same extent as the girls.

Another striking result, again indicative of group perspectives, was the difference in number of responses among forms. The average number of responses per pupil decreases with stream, with a big drop in 3C. I take this, as with their reasons for likes and dislikes, to be a reflection of their basic attitudes to school. For 3C, it is largely characterized by estrangement from its main objectives. As one of the teachers said to me, 'You won't find many of their parents [i.e. of 3C pupils] here tonight [at the headmaster's talk], they know it's not for them.' Such pupils, alienated from the school's processes, go through the organizational motions that are required of them, inventing their own rationale for existence. It is hardly surprising then that when faced with making a decision of their own relating to the school's processes many were sunk. It was an unreal situation for them.

Example 1

Dave: I filled that form in in about 20 seconds (*laughs*).
PW: Did you ask anybody's advice about what to do?
Dave: I didn't 'ave time. See, I filled my paper in, I took it 'ome, see what me dad think, an' I forgot all about it, an' then, oh, [deputy head] came in and gi' me another form an' I filled it in quick so I wouldn't lose it, because I've got a bad memory, I always forget things an' I just filled it in quick.
PW: Did you talk about it amongst yourselves?
Dave and Philip: No.
Kevin: We just said what we were doing.

Example 2

PW: What subjects did you choose?
Paul: The non-exam ones.
PW: Why did you choose those?
Paul: Because I ain't no good at anything, so I chose those.

Examples 3 and 4

Malcolm, though with three of his friends, seemed to know very little about the process, what was required of him, as well as how he met it. Though he had chosen four subjects, he was unable to say why he had chosen them. Sheila did the same as her sister because 'She was no good at anything' (in fact her sister filled in the form for her), and she was unable to remember the subjects she had chosen, even when shown the list.

Example 5

> *Gary*: I only done two out of these, I didn't fill the other two places in.
> *PW*: Why is that?
> *Gary*: All the others I'm not any good at.

Example 6

> *PW*: What subjects have you chosen, Susan?
> *Susan*: I dunno. I forget. (*I show her the form.*) I think it was [four subjects].
> *PW*: Why did you choose those?
> *Susan*: I dunno.
> *PW*: Did you ask anybody's advice?
> *Susan*: Yeah, I asked Mr Lewis's. First of all, I put all sciences down because I want to be a nurse . . . and he said they're no good . . .
> *PW*: Why did he say that?
> *Susan*: I dunno.

Example 7

> *Claire*: I'm doing the non-exam course.
> *PW*: Why?
> *Claire*: Because I don't like any of the other courses.
> *PW*: Why do general science non-exam rather general science exam?
> *Claire*: Because that's an exam course, in't it?
> *PW*: How do you know you won't like it?
> *Claire*: I don't like science anyway.
> *PW*: Why put down for it then?
> *Claire*: Well I 'ad to pick something, di'nt I?

These suggest the nature of the non-event it was for many pupils. In Example 1, Dave turns the procedure into material for his own use, as he does for many other events relating to school. He makes a laugh of it. Examples 2, 3 and 4 illustrate the problems set up by pupils' lack of success by the school's single criterion of ability. If you are not any good at anything there are no grounds for making a choice and you gravitate towards the non-examination subjects. Nobody selects those subjects for positive reasons. Examples 3, 4 and 6 perhaps give some idea of the massive vagueness or unawareness that some of these pupils displayed. Several of them were hardly conscious of anything having happened at all. Example 7 shows the unerring logic of a pupil with a sound grasp of the situation.

For these pupils, then, there is not much 'choice'. Inasmuch as they 'choose' at all, it is a diffident, social, counter-cultural choice. In making their choices, they employ the kind of dichotomous model

Table 2.3 Kinds of subjects

1 Hard work	Easy
2 Examination	Non-examination
3 Nasty, horrible	Fun
4 Boring	Interesting
5 Without friends	With friends
6 Control	Freedom

set out in Table 2.3. There is a sense of immediate gratification, and jocular acceptance of ultimate destiny. Years of interactions, tests and examinations have taught them their place. By the time of the 3rd year these processes have completed the sifting and groups have worked out their *modus vivendi*. They may choose only within their pre-ordained route, and for some in 3C, as we have seen, that means no choice at all.

For another group of pupils, mostly found in 3A, subject choice, like all other school decisions, is a real and positive affair, and is defined in school terms. For them society is a contest system and they are in the contest with a chance. Comparative success in assessment and selection mechanisms reinforced by social factors (like within-group pressure and parental encouragement, discussed shortly) will have cued them in to this. This means they do see the future in progressively structured terms, and they do believe their choices have relevance to their future careers. Thus they are much more likely to think in terms of career, ability, examination success and other factors that promote it. Here is an example of the sort of reasoning involved:

Stephen: I chose chemistry instead of geography because someone advised me it would be better for the RAF than geography. I thought geography would be better, but the bloke next door thought chemistry. He knows a bloke in the Air Force, pretty important, and he was talking to Mum and Dad one night and he said chemistry was more important. I would much rather do chemistry myself than geography because you can't do geography 'O' level, but you can chemistry.
PW: Why physics?
Stephen: Well, the only other one I thought of was English literature and I'm not really interested in that, so I chose physics.
PW: The others are out, are they?
Stephen: Yeah — general science — I'm already doing chemistry. I'm not interested in biology, so I might as well do physics and

specialize in something else rather than do general science.

PW: Tell me about technical drawing.

Stephen: Well, I wanted to do both that and history, I just couldn't make my mind up.

PW: What was hard about it?

Stephen: Well if I join the RAF, I want to be a draughtsman, so tech. drawing is obviously the one to do. But I'm interested in history and I enjoy it. I put history down first then thought again and changed it later.

PW: Did you talk to anybody about it?

Stephen: No. I told Mum and Dad I was thinking of changing it, and they said, 'we won't say "yes" or "no" either way.'

PW: And why woodwork in group 6?

Stephen: Well I'm not good at metalwork, I don't do needlework or housecraft, I'm no good at music, shan't mention French. I quite enjoy woodwork, but I'm not much good at it.

Contrast this with the replies given on pp. 34—5. The close commitment to school values, the logical and ebullient application to the task in hand, the instrumental reasoning tinctured with the educational reciprocation all point to this pupil's close approximation to the 'ideal', and emphasizes the distance the others are away from it. His major criteria in choosing are shown in Table 2.4.

Table 2.4

Job-related	Non-related
Good ability	Poor ability
Good learning situation	Poor learning situation
Interest	No interest

The existence of two polar sub-cultures in the school is well documented. Hargreaves[13] showed in his study of 'Lumley Secondary Modern' that the higher the stream a pupil was in the more likely he was to conform with pro-academic culture and behaviour, while lower streams were disposed toward contrary norms. Lacey[14] also claimed that pupils' internalization of self-identities was in accordance with their place in the school's structure. While King[15] found evidence to suggest a direct link between the values highly approved by the teachers and values of 'undeniably middle-class connotations' on work, interest, activities and opinions of children. My study again illustrates the connection with school structure, but further shows the existence and illustrates the different perspectives of these two broad groups of pupils confronted with the specific problem of subject choice. They employ different interpretative models, distinguished by instrumentalism on the one hand, and social and counter-institutional factors on the other. These underwrite the more general and potentially misleading affective factor of 'liking' or 'disliking', which applies to some degree to both groups. The values and attitudes which provide the bases of these group perspectives derive in large part, I suggest, from position in the social class structure.[16] Differences among parental perspectives along class lines are examined in the next section.

Parents: some differences emerging from social class

Conversations were held with six pairs of parents on subject choice, and on the basis of these a questionnaire was devised and sent to all parents of all 3rd-year children in the middle of the summer term when pupils were resolving their choices (see Appendix 2). Replies were received from 73 per cent of homes and 56 per cent of parents, as in Table 2.5a.

Table 2.5a Parents' questionnaire response rate

	3A		3B		3C		Total
	Boys	Girls	Boys	Girls	Boys	Girls	
Fathers (alone)	5	1	1	3	3	0	13
Mothers (alone)	1	8	3	5	3	6	26
Both parents	4	6	8	9	7	5	39
Pupils represented	10	15	12	17	13	11	78
Nos in form	14	20	17	21	20	15	107

There were over twice as many mothers replying alone for daughters than there were fathers replying alone for sons. This mildly suggests the possibility of girls having more influence directed at them in the form of their mothers than boys.

One-quarter of homes of all 3rd-year children were visited by me before the end of the summer term at the invitation of parents. Visits were made as questionnaires were returned. Table 2.5b gives the details.

Parental advice

The responses were analysed by form. Unfortunately, insufficient precise detail of father's occupation was available for it to be of use.

However, the connection between social class and stream is so well known for us to assume reasonably that it holds in this case, an assumption well supported by the interviews (see pp. 32–7).

Table 2.5b Parents interviewed

	3A		3B		3C		All		Total
	Boys	Girls	Boys	Girls	Boys	Girls	Boys	Girls	
Fathers (alone)	0	1	1	2	0	0	1	3	4
Mothers (alone)	0	3	1	2	2	1	3	6	9
Both	3	3	4	3	1	0	8	6	14
Totals	3	7	6	7	3	1	12	15	27

The questionnaire replies supported the social structure model in some respects, in that 3C parents in making certain different responses from 3A showed that they do hold different, less-supportive attitudes towards school, and their replies give some indication of what this might mean in terms of influence. Table 2.5c summarizes the replies on projected 'advice to children'.

Table 2.5c Parents' projected advice to children

	Very important			Quite important			Of some importance			Not very important			Not at all important		
	3A	3B	3C	3A	3B	3C	3A	3B	3C	3A	3B	3C	3A	3B	3C
Ability	23	21	22	8	24	8	2	3	0	0	0	1	0	0	0
Interest	19	28	27	12	16	7	2	1	0	0	0	0	0	0	0
Best teachers	8	9	15	8	7	8	12	20	8	3	9	0	2	1	1
Own choice	15	19	27	11	20	3	7	5	3	0	1	0	0	0	0
Good job	20	25	26	7	13	4	6	7	3	0	1	0	0	0	0
Teacher advice	12	13	9	18	17	10	2	13	8	1	1	2	0	0	3

Fewer thought 'teacher advice' as important as some of the others, but 3C parents thought it even less so than others. 3C parents would be more inclined than others to say 'do those subjects you want to', and they also put more emphasis on doing subjects with the best teachers, and (compared with 3A) 'interest'. These results are consistent with a model implying a differential fit between outlook of parents of different class, and aims and ethos of school. The 'own choice' and 'teacher advice' differences in particular suggest less involvement and perhaps suspicion of teachers among 3C parents. More of these proportionately also put more emphasis on 'interest'. Interviews showed that 3A parents were inclined to be more involved, and to use more complex reasoning. Thus they would be less likely to settle first for 'interest', 'best teachers', or 'own choice' and would more closely accord with the school's policy of 'guided choice', reasoning their way through a complex set of factors; while the replies of parents in the lower form accord with the 'drop-out' syndrome shown by many of their children. This squares with replies to question 1 which asked if their children consulted them about what subjects to choose. Table 2.5d shows there are signs of less consultation in 3C than in 3A. Attendance at the two parents' meetings

TABLE 2.5d Parental consultation: parents' views

	3A	3B	3C	Totals
Yes	26	33	21	80
No	7	13	15	35
Totals	33	46	36	115

held to discuss subject choice also reflects this relationship (see Table 2.5e). It is also supported by pupils' own responses on parental advice

Table 2.5e Parents' attendance at either school meeting

	3A	3B	3C
Yes	29	31	12
No	4	15	23

(see Table 2.5f). They were asked in interview, whether they had discussed the matter with anyone. With regard to parents there appeared to be two types of discussion, brief and detailed. A higher proportion of 3A pupils claimed to have had detailed discussions with parents than other pupils, while those in 3C had the smallest proportion of any kind of discussion.

Stronger attachment to unofficial functions of the school by 3C parents is also suggested by the replies on school aims. A much larger proportion of 3C parents attached great importance to 'keeping children occupied till they go out to work', than did other parents.

On influences bearing on their views of their child's suitability for certain groups of subjects (see Table 2.5g) fewer 3C parents reckon they are influenced by school reports, examination results or teachers' recommendations (i.e. a 'school' factor). With others, most of them claim to be strongly influenced by a 'personal' factor (own knowledge of the child, knowledge of the rest of the family). This again squares with the social, uncommitted outlook of their children and a distancing from official policy and processes.

Table 2.5f Parental consultation: pupils' view

	Brief	Detailed	None
3A boys	5	6	3
girls	8	12	0
Total	13	18	3
3B boys	11	4	2
girls	12	6	3
Total	23	10	5
3C boys	5	4	11
girls	6	4	5
Total	11	8	16
Grand total	47	36	24

Such a position does not necessarily involve criticism of school processes. Being alienated from them, criticism does not arise, is not an issue. This may explain the large majority of favourable answers received to those questions about how they viewed the school's programme (questions 5, 6 and 7). Of all respondents, 84 per cent thought the school offered a reasonable choice of subjects, though only 68 per cent thought the school gave enough information and advice, and 70 per cent thought the school did as much as it reasonably could to see pupils get the subjects which they choose.

Table 2.5g Perceived influences on parents

	Very influential 3A 3B 3C			Quite influential 3A 3B 3C			A little 3A 3B 3C			Not very influential 3A 3B 3C		
Reports	10	12	3	17	22	19	4	8	9	2	0	5
Examinations	11	12	2	15	22	15	4	6	13	3	0	2
Own knowledge	25	23	23	7	14	11	0	3	1	1	1	0
Family knowledge	10	9	18	8	11	9	3	7	3	9	13	5
Teachers	11	13	5	19	22	13	2	5	7	1	1	8
Child's view	12	17	7	16	20	23	4	4	2	1	2	3
Other children	0	2	4	2	12	9	6	10	10	17	17	10

Parental influence

None of this, of course, gets anywhere near telling us how parents actually do influence their children. I used the interviews to try to get a little closer to this, comparing pupils' and parents' accounts. Pitt considered that 'the influence of the parents appears to be neutral'.[17] Reid, however, while finding a large number of pupils who make their choices unaided, found that 44 per cent of mothers and 41 per cent of fathers had discussed the choice of options with their children in some depth; and that a higher proportion of pupils of non-manual parents select parental influence as the most important, as compared with manual.[18] My results square with Reid's; and both support the social structure model. From my interviews with pupils and parents, I identified five types of parental influence: (1) Compulsion; (2) Strong guidance; (3) Mutual resolution; (4) Reassurance; (5) Little or nil. Table 2.6 shows how these were spread among the twenty-seven homes that I visited. Though numbers are small, the trend towards stronger counselling to the middle-class child is clearly visible, confirming 3rd-year pupils' own accounts, as given in Table 2.5f. Further, as I illustrate in Table 2.6 where working-class parents give strong guidance, it tends to be less well informed about school processes and subjects and their linkage with future careers. Some examples might illuminate the quality of these various types of guidance.

Table 2.6 Distribution of types of parental influence

Type of influence	Middle class			Total	Working class			Total
	3A	3B	3C		3A	3B	3C	
Compulsion	0	2	0	2	0	0	0	0
Strong guidance	1	3	0	4	1	0	1	2
Mutual resolution	2	1	0	3	1	4	1	6
Reassurance	3	0	0	3	0	1	2	3
Little/nil	0	0	0	0	0	1	2	3
Total	6	6	0	12	2	6	6	14

1 Compulsion

This seems to have been used in cases where parents greatly feared their child was in danger of selecting the 'wrong' route with all its disadvantageous consequences. I only found middle-class parents using it, and it is another instance of how the middle-class child who, for whatever reason, might have adopted the social, counter-cultural model, can be cushioned against a possible fall into the drop-out zone (if this cushion is lacking, teachers might provide an alternative one, see p. 51).

'My boy was in the L form — an absolute waste of time — feeding the hens and pruning the bushes in their final year. He got very bored. I wouldn't like to see that happen to her.'

'There is a fringe element left out in the cold, and we have feared Andrea might be in there but for the grace of God.'

Here are two examples of pupils being rescued from this fate, one in the pupil's words, the other in the parent's.

Linda: I didn't want to do commerce.
PW: Why have you chosen it then?
Linda: Because my mother said so.
PW: Why did she say that?
Linda: Because she wants me to work in an office.
PW: And what do you want to do?
Linda: Be a hairdresser.
PW: If it were left to you what to do, what would you have chosen?
Linda: I haven't thought about it.
PW: Will you be allowed to do commerce, do you think?
Linda: I hope I'm knocked out.
PW: What form will you go in?
Linda: I'd go in 4L straight away.

Linda is employing the diffident, social model of subject choice, and her mother is kicking against it. Here is a directive father explaining how he went about it:

'I suggested commerce at first — you can get a nice little office job, meet good people and so on — otherwise you might be stuck behind a bench. But when I saw that commerce was all they did — and talking to other people a general course leading to a broader education seemed more suitable. Oh, there's a lot of conniving gone into it. I've been up to the school and seen the teachers. Teaching is equally socially acceptable, but it might be something else in two years' time, so a broad base is necessary. Sandra was stuck in Group 3 — all horrible she said — so we eliminated the worst, then I came to geography. He's a good teacher, and by looking at her book, it's nice and orderly, and he's got through some stuff — and by talking to him on the night, I decided that was the best one to do.'

Again, the choice was a non-event to this girl. She told me she would have preferred to carry on in the same way, rather than be faced with these choices. Her father, a managing director, made up for her lack of resolution.

2 Strong guidance

This is similar to the above, except that it contains an element of persuasion.

> 'He told us which ones he wanted to take and then we got at him. We went to Open Night, saw his teachers and then we saw him again and changed his mind on one. He was talking about the Royal Navy. We said woodwork's no good for that. Mrs Foster said he could do French if he put his mind to it, so we persuaded him to do it. We tried to talk to him along the lines of "Are those subjects likely to lead to a good job?" The problem is he doesn't know what he wants to do, and it's difficult to know what to choose as a consequence.' (Police officer)

Sometimes the influence is subtly concealed, at least in the parent's eyes. This extract suggests the continual involvement typical of the middle-class parent:

> 'It goes back over a period of time. There's been a careful channelling of opportunities as they've presented themselves. From experience of life, I'm biased towards a child going into secretarial work, because if you're not academic, the only alternative is factory work. It goes back two or three years really. I would say, "If you don't get good results you'll land up in a factory on the line, and you've seen them factory girls in their hair nets." Sara actually made her own choice — I think I influenced her unknowingly. She told me she wanted to be a secretary, and that's what I've wanted her to do! None of the subjects on the bottom line would be helpful to her in the sort of occupation I wanted for her, so I chose housecraft for her, for general use, later. (Factory manager)

3 Mutual resolution

This, with reassurance, was the most common form among those I interviewed. Working-class families were well represented here. However, though they might show as much concern as middle-class families, their guidance tended to be less well informed. Middle-class parents told me in detail how they monitored their children's thinking on the matter, making sure that they themselves were well informed, by, for example, frequent consultations with teachers; then employing this knowledge, and that of the child, and of the world in general to feed gently into the decision-making process when requested. By contrast, working-class parents seemed as puzzled as their children. To many of these, school is an alien though desirable agency where professionals practise their considerable expertise behind well-defined boundaries. They have little idea either of their own child's achievements and capabilities or of the career prospects and how they are associated with educational routes. Another 'disadvantage' for working-class parents was that they tended to be less instrumentally orientated than middle-class parents, though every parent I met thought primarily of the child's future career.

The following examples illustrate these differences:

'Over the past year we've known subject choice was coming up. She wanted guidance in those subjects she was reasonably good at. We went to the school and had a long talk with Mrs Nelson in early May. Ann said she wanted a commerce course, but we thought we were leading her. And also of course the limiting nature of the commerce course. She would be opting out of a lot of other things, and with her grasshopper mind, we thought it too much to ram down her throat and she'd become bored and uninterested. She's very good with children so I said, "What about 'child nurse'", and I said, "It's not the end of the world if you want to change", and she said, "Yes, that's what I want to do." We then had to decide which subjects were most suitable for that.' (Managing director)

And here is Ann's account:

'I talked to Mum about it a lot and we've been through it. It would often crop up over dinner and we'd talk about it . . . She often said to me I had to have a lot of advice in everything . . . I wanted something to help me with my child nurse . . . and housecraft, that was essential really − cooking − And general science − you have to have something to do with science. And I like history, and I like Mrs Nelson. Mum likes geography, and I like it anyway, and that was the only one in that group I wanted to do.'

One captures the sense that school, and what goes on there, is part of the way of life of this family. They recognized the implications of the decision and laid down the foundations accordingly.

Compare this account:

'He asked me what would be the best if he was going in for diving. I said, "Well, you'll have to meet people, English is always good." He sat a long time in front of the list. I didn't want to tell him what to put, but he said, "What do you think?" ' (Farm labourer's wife)

This shows another pupil, equally lost as to what to choose, ultimately receiving strong guidance, though it is not nearly so well informed.

4 Reassurance

Here, typically, the pupil would make the choice, then show parents, often asking if it seemed reasonable to them.

'She chose, then asked our advice. She knows what she wants to do, she was seeking reassurance mainly. I leave the choice up to her really, she's quite sensible. I'll support her judgment. If she sets her mind to something she can do it.'

'Kathryn did ask our advice, but she also had her own set ideas on the subject she wanted to do, as she has firmly made her own mind to go into the medical profession of some kind depending on exam results. (School secretary, wife of works manager)

Many parents approached in this manner gave general advice such as 'do those you're best at' or 'do those you want to'. There was again a suggestion of class difference in type of reassurance offered, middle-class parents supporting their children through confidence in them to make the best choices, working-class parents supporting their children as they would in any enterprise as part of the socio-emotional bond between them.

5 Very little or nil, or disregarded or not consulted

Many of those who simply advise 'do what you want to' might more properly belong in this category. But at least they were asked and gave some advice. Several pupils claimed they never showed the form to their parents.

'Mum wanted me to do commerce, because you can get a good job, and that. But I didn't want to do it because it's too boring. I didn't ask my Dad at all. I don't think Mum knows the subjects I've chosen.'

'I showed the form to Mum and she said, "It's up to you, I don't know your ability at school." '

As Table 2.6 shows, I only found working-class parents giving very little or no advice.

It seems fairly clear, in this school at least, that regarding parents' influence over their children's choice of subjects, the higher the social class, the more considerable, both quantitatively and qualitatively, it is likely to be.

Parental types

Parents influence the choice in other ways – through teachers for example. All the parents I saw were, not surprisingly, anxious for their child to 'do the right thing'. But as already said, parents do not have equal resources to bring to bear on the situation, and again, these differences tend to follow class divisions. There are, as far as school and its knowledge, pedagogy and selection processes are concerned, a number of *uninformed* parents. They have little idea either of their own child's achievements and capabilities or of the career prospects and how they are associated with educational routes. They tend to be working class.

'The teachers should tell them what to do, or at least go further than the parents. We didn't know what to say – we "ummed" and "ahd" – then went to the school and the teacher says, "Why don't you do tech. drawing? He's ever so good at that." So we came back, but of course if you say *do* this, he'll rebel. You just don't know their ability, so I said, "Do them you think you're good at and some of those you think you're not so good at because as you get older your views change and you see things differently." ' (Electrician)

Several parents were clearly in desperate need of help, accepting responsibility for advising their child and anxious to do so, but reluctant and unconfident in an area with so many unknown variables. Ultimately it seems advice of a general nature would be given, as above, or the child would be left to make his/her own choice. Some 'uninformed' parents on the other hand were less anxious, the situation impinging on them in less of a traumatic way. Similar general advice would be given, but there would be very little knowledge of particular subjects and how to distinguish between them in relating to the future. Some would be reduced simply to saying, 'It's up to you.' Other parents differed in their confidence though not all had equal knowledge of the school. Some were very *supportive* of the school, its staff and its functions and hence by implication sure that the best would be done for their child.

'They've got every facility there. A child only needs a bit of initiative, the school certainly gives them every opportunity.'

'It works on the principle of first come, first served; you know your first options are honoured as long as your exam results are O.K. Without a doubt you've got to give them with brains first choice really.' (Metal polisher)

'You can't complain about the school now, it's a lovely place. If they don't make the best of it — it's up to them. They're there five years, it's for their own good, I mean. You know times are not going to get easier, they'll get harder.' (Petrol pump attendant)

There were a number of *critical* and *coercive* parents. These tend to come from the middle classes. They have a low opinion of the school and are distinguished by the extent to which they will put themselves out to achieve their ends. This may take the form of aggressive postures at meetings, and frequent visits and phone calls to the school. I have no evidence of their effect, but one social trick that worked was brought to my notice:

'Alan pranged an exam, he only got 12 per cent and was very depressed, quite sure the teacher wouldn't let him take it because that teacher always goes on the exam, and not term work. So I advised him to go to the teacher and apologize, and promise to try hard in the future'. (Estate agent's wife)

We cannot know for sure, of course, what effect this boy's methods, as coached by his mother, had on teachers, but at least some of his contemporaries were in no doubt.

John: Alan Snowling has been accepted for chemistry —, and he only got 20 per cent. Gary got 40 per cent and he can't do it.
David: Neil got 27 per cent and he can't do it.
Mike: Yeah, well Alan Snowling only got 12 per cent for — and he was accepted; and Mr Garrett had second thoughts about Neil with 27 per cent.
PW: Why do you think Alan Snowling was accepted?
John: Well he went up to him and *pleaded*, said he was sorry and all that and how he could do it if he worked hard, so, [the teacher] said, 'If you work hard, I'll help you.'
PW: Why don't you do that?
John: I'm unlucky in things like that.

This is not a stray idiosyncratic example. It suggests again the social advantages enjoyed by some children.

Parental characteristics

I was impressed during the interviews with certain characteristics of parents which have repercussions for their views on subject choice, as indeed on all school processes.

1 Particularism

All parents, naturally, showed to some degree or other, particularistic concern for their own child as opposed to the totality of the pupil body. Many acknowledged this, of course, and their fears centred on whether the teacher's concern for the latter would work to their own child's disadvantage. One parent ruefully reported the headmaster as stating, ' "It's for the benefit of the pupils at large", full stop, and we were told, "ours not to reason why", we're lucky to get what we get.' There is bound to be tension between these particularistic and general concerns. Indeed it is one of the chief sources of role conflict in head-teachers.[19] Particularism is rarely unprejudiced. It leads some into criticism of the subject-choice arrangements on two main grounds: (a) that it is too severe a restriction on the number of subjects one can take, and (b) pupils are debarred from choosing more than one subject in a group. Here is one parent following through the implications both for her own particular child, and for the school:

> 'If a child has decided the subjects she needs for her job on leaving school, she may find she is unable to take all subjects required if they come in the same group. Therefore she may have to take one or two subjects she has no interest in whatsoever, and have no bear-ing on her career in mind. This tends to lead to the child being thoroughly bored, wasting time, and feeling discouraged. Then they start messing about.' (Housewife)

The administrative reasons underlying the structure are, of course, unacceptable answers to this particularism. It seems to be fanned by teacher criticism of a parent's child on parents' evenings. Different interpretive structures are being brought to bear, teachers being much more likely to use an ideal-typical framework. I shall expand on this in chapter 8.

2 Instrumentality

Every parent I met thought primarily of the child's future career, though working-class parents were less instrumentally oriented. As far as the school programme is concerned, all the 'trimmings' such as Com-munity Service (unless of course it served the purpose of career in some way) come under attack. It is connected with status consciousness.

3 Status consciousness

Many parents, particularly middle-class 'critical' and 'coercive' ones, were very sensitive to the difference between the two main routes.

> 'The headmaster said his usual piece about it not being very shameful to be non-examination, but this is all whitewash. Everybody knows it's a waste of time in the non-examination group.' (Insurance broker)

The school might dress the activities of this group in widely accepted educational theory, but in parents' eyes the product is ill-defined, there are no visible rewards and it is extra-mainstream. One parent described their curriculum as consisting of 'hobby jobs' (social crafts, car maintenance, gardening, painting) and 'lazy subjects' (art, pottery).

4 Traditional pedagogy

Parents invariably strongly supported traditional forms of pedagogy, of which they had had most experience themselves, of course. Thus support was common for things like firm control, neatness, 'good' behaviour, respect for authority, a clearly identifiable and tangible body of work, forceful teaching and good results. As a body, the parents seemed much more entrenched in this paradigm than the teachers. Comments focused on the general running of the school, discipline, and teacher-pupil relations.

> 'We teach our children good manners and that, and then it's all undone outside. You should hear some of the language, and then they come home and tell us what they did to teachers — we did *this*, and we did *that* — honestly!' (Housewife)

> 'They ought to *make* them work. Old Brown at my old school was a miserable old bastard and we hated his guts, but as we got older we appreciated what he did for us. Kids get away with murder today. We'd get a good hiding till we did it.'

I pointed out to this father that teachers would probably say they would give more attention to those who were interested.

> 'If my lad didn't show interest [he replied], I'd beat hell out of him!' (Building site agent)

> 'They need more discipline because I hear if they don't want to do anything they don't do it. They should be *made* to do it because if they did only what they wanted and not what was needed they wouldn't get anywhere. The school's all right for those who are clever, but they don't do enough for those who need an extra shove. Linda needed pushing — me and her had great battles. It's been a struggle, but she's grateful now. Oh! It's so exhausting, constantly

nagging, and adolescence is such a rotten time, ever so moody, falling in love every five minutes.' (School clerk)

These characteristics add a further dimension to the study of parental influence. The utilitarian aims of the school which underwrite processes like subject choice clearly have strong support among the parent body. But there is a dialectic relationship between school and parents. Many, in fact, believe that the wishes of parents have a deterministic effect on school aims and policies. More will be said about this later.

In this section I have shown that there are different kinds and amounts of parental advice and influence operating on the different groups of pupils identified previously. These suggest a connection with social class.[20] Middle-class parents are more likely to be more involved with school processes, show more complex reasoning in accordance with school criteria in advising their children, be more persuaded by 'school' factors; working class parents display less 'involvement', are less instrumentally oriented, possibly entertain suspicions of school and teachers, have less consultation with teachers and their own children, are more likely to be persuaded by 'personal' factors. Middle-class parents tend to give strong guidance, be well informed, critical and coercive, instrumentally oriented and status conscious. Working-class parents tend to give less guidance, and to be uninformed. Indications have been given of the subtle ways in which class can work towards differential opportunity, for example, through 'knowledge of the world' and 'how to handle men'. It also operates, of course, through the teachers.

The teachers: choice mediators

Teachers do acknowledge that there is not a completely free choice, but there is a belief that the advice and guidance offered is given in the best interests of the pupil. This is a view I wish to contest in this section. As with Cicourel and Kitsuse's Lakeshore High School, this school's structure is determined by what happens at the end of the pupil's career in this case the taking (or not) of examinations. Pupils are streamed and/or setted in the early years to facilitate optimum overall academic performance as defined by skills and knowledge deemed useful in the 5th-year examinations. As at Lakeshore, early decisions can be crucial. Of one 5L group I was able to trace back, twenty-seven out of thirty-one had come through the school in the bottom stream. This institutional channelling creates its own effects,[21] and in association with the group perspectives that form within the channels and the development of teachers' typifications,[22] brings about a crystallization of opportunities at a very early stage.

This is vividly illustrated by one aspect of the subject choice process, the rechannelling of misdirected choices. Teachers view pupils' subject choice in a way akin to Figure 2.2 which shows four basic types of

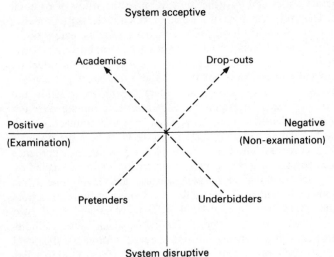

Figure 2.2 Teachers' perceptions of subject choice

choice from the teachers' point of view. The 'system acceptive' type pupil is one who interprets correctly the school and its processes and his relationship to it, and hence the implications of the subject choice, be it for examination or non-examination subjects. The 'system disruptive' pupils, however, have misinterpreted the cues, and made unrealistic choices, selecting examination subjects when they should have chosen non-examination (by ability), or vice versa. The problem for teachers then becomes one of moving pupils along the lines indicated.

But who are these 'pretenders' and 'underbidders'? Table 2.7 shows the changes that were made from pupils' first choices to final allocation. 'Positive' changes are those from non-examination to examination subjects; 'negative' vice versa; and 'neutral' are changes within the same standard. Of the whole, 44 per cent and proportionately twice as many boys as girls had at least one subject changed from his or her original choice, and 60 per cent of these changes were 'negative' ones. Nearly half of these came from 3C, even though many in that form had already made negative choices and therefore did not come into the reckoning. Most of the rest came from 3B, which is here showing its 'in-between' status, having some 'good' pupils, some 'bad'. 3A had two or three 'bad' boys who blotted 3A's copybook. Of the boys, 62 per cent were involved in changes, compared with 30 per cent of the girls. Clearly the vast majority of those requiring rechannelling came from the lower part

Table 2.7a Choice changes

Form	Nos	No. in form	Changes	Positive	Negative	Neutral
3A boys	5	15	10	2	5	3
girls	3	21	3	1	0	2
Total	8	36	13	3	5	5
3B boys	15	17	24	2	12	10
girls	10	20	16	2	7	7
Total	25	37	40	4	19	17
3C boys	9	15	15	0	13	2
girls	4	15	10	0	9	1
Total	13	30	25	0	22	3
All boys	29	47	49	4	30	15
All girls	17	56	29	3	16	10
Total	46	103	78	7	46	25

Table 2.7b Perceived reasons for choice changes

Form	Set full	Ability	Behaviour	Job	Don't know	Others
3A boys	1	5	1	1	0	0
girls	0	0	0	0	0	1
Total	1	5	1	1	0	1
3B boys	4	5	2	4	2	0
girls	2	4	0	1	3	1
Total	6	9	2	5	5	1
3C boys	0	5	0	0	4	1
girls	2	6	1	0	0	0
Total	2	11	1	0	4	1
All boys	5	15	3	5	6	1
All girls	4	10	1	1	3	2
Total	9	25	4	6	9	3

of the streaming structure. There is also the suggestion of a sex difference.

Table 2.2 suggested that boys set more store by ability in choosing
their subjects; Tables 2.7a and 2.7b show girls to be perhaps the greater
realists, for far fewer of them were required to change, even though
there are more of them in the year; and the most quoted perceived
reason for having to change a subject was 'not good enough'.

Thus, for many of those in 3C and 3B, this subject options scheme
foreclosed options in that they were debarred from taking those few
subjects which they felt positive towards, and which hitherto they had
found rewarding. The 'integrated' nature of the scheme was proved

in practice to be a gloss, and when these pupils reassembled at the beginning of their 4th year, the 'non-examination' pupils found themselves together in as neat a package as before. The institutional channelling momentarily challenged was thus restored.

There is another problem, again shown by Figure 2.2, namely the line between academics and non-academics. There can be no appeal to an absolute standard in drawing this line just as with the line separating success and failure in the 11+. It is determined by the teachers, each for his own subject, and as with the 11+, it might fall at different points, for much the same reason — resources. Consider Figure 2.3,

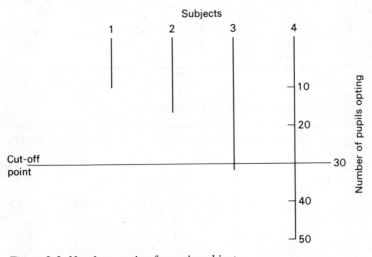

Figure 2.3 Numbers opting for main subjects

illustrating the number of applicants for four mainline subjects (optimum number thirty) and the 'resources' cut-off point in relation to each. With subjects 1 and 2, there is no problem from the resources point of view; but with subject 3, 6 per cent need to be excluded, and with subject 4, 41 per cent.

This points up the uneven nature of the redistribution problem. But teachers will already have exerted influence to try to achieve these results less brutally beforehand. Their teaching and assessment, culminating in the all-important examinations at the end of the 3rd year, gives most pupils a sound idea of their 'ability' at school subjects.

This is the most powerful factor underlying all others in the acceptance of pupils to subjects — i.e. teachers' definitions of success and failure.[23] We have already seen in the section on the pupils how many of them (and their parents) had internalized these definitions, accepted the consequences, and chosen 'realistically'.

'We're not the brainy ones, they are.'

'How do you know?'

'Well, they are.'

Though occasionally there is a spark of protest:

> *Amanda*: They think because we're in a lower form they think, we're dibby and we can't do it on our own. But then they never give us a chance to try do they? That's why we have gone off homework and don't like it, 'cos everybody thinks we're dibby and they don't give us a chance, you know, that's why we don't want to take exams and don't like teachers.
> *PW*: Do you ever get called 'dibby' or anything like that?'
> *Amanda*: Well, they put in a nice way. They say, 'You're not as intelligent as all the others, and you ought to do so-and-so.'
> *Linda*: Or they'll give you that strong impression, you know, talk to you like babies. One teacher goes over and over it so we understand, and he goes 'Do-you-understand?' (*mimicking a babyish measured voice*).

Interestingly, those who interpret teachers' behaviour towards them in this way are usually those who overreach themselves in subject choice and have to be corrected. To guard against this, a teacher might use special pre-option techniques. The teacher of subject 4 for example, possibly anticipating a big redistribution problem, gave a talk which had the effect of cooling out several 'pretenders'.

> *PW*: Why didn't you choose subject 4 in that group?
> *June*: We'd get too much homework.
> *Mavis*: Yeah! She don't 'alf put it on ... 'you'll 'ave to work all the time!' — an' homework! You think, 'Oh, I can't do that — oh!' Talking about it made me feel ill.

As with Cicourel and Kitsuse's counsellors, teachers' judgments are not based simply on past achievement. In estimating the likelihood of future examination success, other factors are also important. I asked the teacher of subject 4 what were her principles of exclusion. In making up the optimum number she employed three: (1) the 'best ones'; (2) those who seemed to have the 'right' attitude; and (3), from 3C, the three who seemed a 'cut above the rest'. It was no good having problem people like John Church.

> 'He's too lazy, he lays around, and if he gets his pen out, he lolls around saying "Oh Miss!" I can't take the risk, it spreads like a cancer. Who starts it, initiates it, I don't know. It's cruel, I know, but what else can I do? I haven't time to motivate, inspire, correct for behaviour and so on, so you must cut out all the miscreants and

thickies. You just haven't got time. They do drag you down. Now Sharon Brown, nice girl, parents didn't want her in that form, I think once she gets out and in with this other lot, they'll pull these three [*from 3C*] up.'

This teacher is articulating the system's rules, and by tidying up the 'misplacements' illustrates how the wedge is even more firmly driven between two types of pupil. These two types, and who falls into them, are clearly identified, as is their within-group influences. So also are the criteria for success, which include, apart from past performance, 'attitude' and a 'cut above the rest'. The social undertones and divisiveness become explicit towards the end. Family background can be decisive. It can rescue, or condemn at the eleventh hour.

Apparent also is the classic dilemma of the upper secondary school teacher — concern for the individual while operating within the constraints of a structure which allows very little room for manoeuvre.

Figure 2.4 illustrates this structure. The three blocks relate to three groups of children characterized by expectation of performance in the 16+ examination. The shaded areas are where adjacent groups overlap.

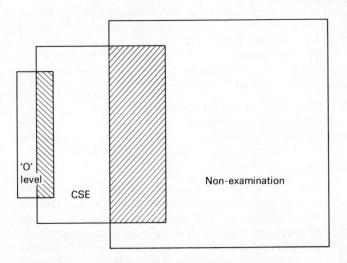

Figure 2.4 Examination overlaps

For teachers, they can be high tension generators, for there is pressure on the teacher to achieve a high proportion of examination passes. Usually this might be interpreted, as Cicourel and Kitsuse with their counsellors, and Becker with his moral entrepreneurs, purely through the concept of professionalization. Here, however, a critical external agency increases the pressure, indeed, for some teachers, could be held responsible for it. In the ordinary course of events, a teacher might gain relief by ensuring that the shaded area in Figure 2.4 is as small as possible, ideally non-existent, which would mean 100 per cent examination passes; or, of course, he might not feel under any pressure, especially if his results are deemed reasonable. But at this particular point in the school's history, numbers are seen to be very important. For the school is about to become comprehensive, and to receive pupils formerly admitted to the high status town grammar and high schools. The strain towards better and better examination results is seen by the teachers[24] as a public relations exercise in honour of the parents of such children to convince them of the school's credibility as a respectable academic institution. One of the effects on teachers is to cause them to monitor the selecting of subjects with great care. It is unavoidable, even in traditionally less constrained subjects like creative design.

'A lot choose art, yes, and you know why, don't you? I'm not fooled. I say to them, "Why do you want to do art?" I say, "*I* know, but come on, you tell me," and they say, "Huh, I don't want to do old biology or whatever, all that homework and so on." It's an easy option, and they go for it on both lines. My results this year were pretty poor which rather proves my point. But what I do is this. I pick those with most artistic ability and I like it to be seen to be fair. I don't spring this on them either. I tell them all this at the beginning of the third year. I tell them they'll be judged on the quality of work that goes into their folders, and then, towards the end of the year, I get them to lay it all out, so they can all see, and, of course, some are very good and some are pathetic. There's no other way, not if they want to take the exam. If they just want a skive, they can do it somewhere else.'

Here is 'justice' being seen to be done, and opportunity given for pupils to make their cases. With its free and informal atmosphere, and its different, non-exacting work-task, the 'art' options are a natural attraction for the diffident counter-cultural chooser (see p. 35). But the art teacher is subject to the same forces as his colleagues, and the same criteria must apply.

What direct counselling of children by teachers came to my attention also seemed directed towards the preservation of institutional channels, while expounding the rhetoric which legitimated it. In his address to the 3rd-year pupils, for example, the headmaster showed a conservative, selection-orientated, instrumental and elitist approach. The 'choice' pupils made was represented as the most crucial decision they would make in their school career, indeed as one of the most important decisions of their lives. Hitherto they had been merely 'getting a taste' of subjects, but the next two years were 'for real'. They counted for something in the world at large. This essential link with the occupational structure was emphasized in his advice on their approach to choice. They would obviously think in terms of 'what they wanted to do' after school. He gave examples, then warned against choosing subjects because they liked the teacher or 'environmental studies because they were interested in what goes on round the canals'. They were urged to think first if they were 'good at it', and second, 'what use was it going to be to them'. The importance and meaning of examinations was explained, and they needed (besides working hard when they got in an exam form) to ask themselves whether they were good enough in the first place to take an exam subject, or if they ought to take a non-exam subject, in which of course there was 'nothing shameful' — people were needed for all sorts of occupations. Where there was competition for places, they could only resolve it by the fairest method — having a test to see who was 'the best'. Throughout his talks, the headmaster stressed the basic utilitarianism of the decision, and the school's traditional ways of resolving difficulties.

This is interesting for what it adds to our knowledge about the philosophy behind the scheme and about the kind of advice being directed at pupils. We might hypothesize, however, in view of pupils' different group perspectives on subject choice, that the signals would reach one group but not the other. This seemed certainly true of the latter, for of twenty 3C pupils interviewed during the three days including and following the address, only two could remember anything about it. I received comments like:

'I never listen.'

'It's too boring, he goes on for so long.'

'I was asleep.'

'She was showing me her photographs.'

'Advice' therefore could hardly be considered a factor, for this group at least. The same applies to the senior master's 'counselling'. Empowered with responsibility for running the scheme, he had more involvement in it overall than any other teacher. But his individual 'counselling' came at the end of the chain, and, as we have seen, was channel-restorative. He told me that the process worked like this: first, pupils filled in forms indicating their first preferences; second, subject teachers were informed, and asked if they would accept those selecting their subjects; some 'thirty or forty' were thus referred back and required to make second choices. These he was 'able to give a fair amount of his time to', and proceeded to 'negotiate with teachers on their behalf'. He was also on the lookout for 'choices for friendship' and 'correcting for career' which involved 'going through the whole list'. However, though 'guidance was available, a great deal of responsibility was placed on their shoulders'. No doubt some individuals benefited from this advice and intervention, but clearly it is operating within the very severe constraints of the institutional channelling current in the school; and any scheme requiring a large amount of self-responsibility surrenders decisions not to individuals, but to group perspectives.

Taking into account the various examples given in this section it appears that teacher mediation does not operate in the interests of the individual pupil, but is predicated rather on considerations of status, career and professionalization, rendered particularly acute by the critical external agency of parental pressure. Mediation then takes the form basically of alerting pupils to the ideal-types (and their own approximations to them) which serve the purpose of those ends through the agency of 'good examination results'.

Some of the staff at least were not blind to the hypocrisies in the system and wanted it scrapped and incorporated fully into their professional jurisdiction. They would question however, not the criteria of their mediation, but the mechanics and the products of it. They were the only ones who knew which children 'stood a reasonable chance', yet this system put them under pressure from pupils, parents and headmasters at both ends of the examination course. They 'bent over backwards' to accommodate everyone, then when it came to homework, the pupils 'didn't want to know'. In other words, when they relaxed the strict application of their criteria for selection, and enlarged the shaded zones in Figure 2.4, the pupils concerned failed to observe the norms required of the group. Another thought it 'ridiculous making these decisions before the examinations, and misleading parents in many cases about the actualities, encouraging them to think their kids are more capable than they really are'. Others blamed parents for not honouring implicit pledges to keep their children up to the mark.[25]

In summary, it appears that teachers do most of the 'choosing', albeit by rather tortuous routes, which leads some to protest and yearn for 'cleaner' decisions. Pre-choice tactics include communicating to pupils a 'proper' notion of their ability and of their 'rightful' place in the school structure; heading off pretenders, encouraging underbidders (though this last was not very evident − perhaps because unnecessary); removing the stigma of the drop-out choice; and establishing the legitimacy of the whole procedure by, for example, extolling the fairness of selection techniques. Post-choice tactics include persuasion based on the criteria of ability and aptitude, which appear to have social class overtones, and only in the last resort ruthless exclusion. The overall aim is to get the pupils to articulate the teachers' decisions. That teachers go to such lengths is a testament to the pervasiveness of the progressive, pupil-directed ideology. The reality, as revealed in this study, is an indication of the power of basic structural forces.

Conclusion

A comparison between within-system and extra-system functions provides another perspective. Within the system, schemes like this have four main functions. (1) There is some option within groups of subjects, if not of routes. However, we have seen that some groups of pupils have more option than others. (2) It does give some pupils and parents an opportunity to relate, to some extent, their school careers with prospective occupations. For those on the 'deviant' route, for whom school has a different meaning, it is an opportunity to select those subjects which best support that meaning, though there will be problems if a subject is also an examination one, as with art above. (3) It helps to consolidate the image of the school as a meritocratic and democratic institution. (4) It serves as a kind of hiatus in the school programme which can be used as yet another motivating device. As we saw earlier, pupils are urged to regard the past three years as a kind of limbering-up for the real business of the final two years. With self-selected subjects and teachers, new courses ahead, the prizes within sight and the past all behind, the activity attending the process of subject choice, with parents drawn into the act, is visited with an urgency and a seriousness which might hopefully wash off on to the studies which follow, to the credit of both pupils and school.

However, in a wider sense, the subject-choice scheme is serving the implicit school policy of selection inasmuch as (1) subjects are grouped in accordance with recognized patterns associated with occupation career. (2) Two broad channels allow for those who 'opt in' and those who 'opt' or are ruled 'out'. The non-examination provision can be viewed, therefore, as a form of social control.[26] (3) Pupils are encouraged to choose those subjects in which they have most ability and which are most related to their likely future occupational careers. (4) In rationalizing the picture that emerges from the last point, teachers apply those criteria which promise to lead to the best overall examination results. Priority is given to the elite. (5) 'Interest' and 'liking' are played down.

The four within-system functions therefore are serving a system of sponsorship mobility behind a 'contest' mask.[27] There is an illusion of a range of choice, of selection of personnel delayed to the last moment (immediately prior to the commencement of examination courses), of a common starting-line (everybody in with a chance), and of common fare (roughly the same subjects up to the end of the 3rd year). In fact the range of choice is variable among the pupils, non-existent for some; the pupils have been 'channelled', that is to say selected (at 11+, and no doubt earlier) and selected again (in the school's streaming arrangements, and possibly 'hidden' streaming before) long before they come to the 3rd year; different social origins lead to different educational experiences, the difference being reinforced by the prevailing pedagogical paradigm; and these differences have repercussions for what is taught to different groups. Despite meritocratic overtones, by the 3rd year most pupils have developed group perspectives; they know their places, having internalized teacher definitions of success and failure and their application to themselves with the usual labels ('thick', 'dibby', 'lazy', 'pest').

For them, subject choice has different meanings. Generally speaking, to the initiated, generally middle-class pupils it is his choice, and he makes it carefully with a view to job, ability and prospects. To the estranged, generally working-class pupil it is a line of least resistance, and even that at times presents problems. This scenario is complicated, but sharpened still further by the changing status of the school wherein the unseen and unspoken influence of potential 'sponsoring' parents is felt by teachers to exert great pressure on them, through the mediation of the headmaster, to produce better and better examination results. While this ultimately might mean more joining the élite ranks of the examination pupils, it does not, of course, alter the basic division and the principles on which it rests; in fact it increases it, since teachers will feel compelled to sharpen their selective and pedagogic techniques to guard against the increased risk of 'contamination'.

With these powerful forces structuring their policies and activities, teachers 'mediate', choosing the arena, making the rules and providing most of the equipment (including the pupil's own view of himself) for the game of subject choice. For them, the game is to guide pupils into the right channels to get the bell of examination results to ring. The criteria they use are past achievement and future potential. For all of these factors we know that there is a strong connection with social class, though it is not a simple one. The middle classes are at home in this arena, the working classes strangers. It is in this sense, most powerfully, that pupils' subject choice is socially structured. But we have seen also how, even within these severe limitations, social factors such as degree and type of parental advice, within-group influences, cultural impressions on teachers (a 'cut above the rest') or simply parents' *savoir-faire* of the middle-class milieu can exert an influence, and indeed at times retrieve apparently lost situations.[28]

One of the basic questions arising from this analysis of school structure and function as evidenced in the subject-choice process is, 'how is school possible?' Given teachers' humane commitment and dedication to altruistic ends, how can they accept, indeed prosecute with such vigour, their role in exacerbating these divisions? And how can pupils, on the receiving end, put up with it? I shall examine the teachers' position later. First, I look at the pupils. A great deal of heat and passion is generated in certain areas during the summer term of the 3rd year over subject choice. However, the crucial decisions having been mooted, discussed, argued about, grieved over; given rise to great hopes, consternation, bewilderment and anger; analysed, spurned or ignored, and eventually, ultimately and irrevocably made or accepted, pupils go through the 3rd-year gates on their next great journey in life.

In fact, the 'gates' are an illusion, the same divisions remain, now even more acute, and the same structures press. These divisions evidenced in the subject-choice process are also reflected in pupils' everyday reactions to school. The two broad, basic kinds of group perspective, for example, are associated with two broad groups of pupil modes of adaptation to school, which we might term 'conformity' and 'dissonance'. These, in turn, contain subdivisions which bring us nearer the 'pupil reality' of school. In the next chapter I seek to establish a means of achieving an overview of such types without losing this sense of 'reality'.

Chapter 3

Pupil adaptations

Pupil activity

In trying to make sense of pupil activity we search for common denominators that promise to yield some sort of pattern which embraces the greater majority of them, and that are sufficiently important to account for much of their activity. An obvious place to start is in their response to the official programme, since this is something that affects them all, which cannot be ignored, and forces clear and definite reactions of one sort or another. It might be argued that there is a great deal of variable 'space' hanging round the official programme for many pupils, especially in a secondary modern school, and that another basis of comparison might therefore be preferable. There is some truth in this and in chapter 5 I offer an approach which seeks to get to the heart of 'unofficial' pupil activity. The first task, however, is to situate that within a framework which embraces the entire range of pupil commitment.

To give an idea of the kind of activity this framework is directed towards I first give a number of examples from Lowfield. For convenience I have chosen extracts from interview material, but that they are typical of groups of pupils, rather than peculiar to the actual people mentioned, was strongly substantiated by other interviews and by observation over time. How can we begin to make sense of this variable and 'messy' activity? I go on to develop a schema which relates these examples, and much other pupil behaviour, to the aims of the school and the means of achieving them. Finally I analyse the examples in the terms of the schema.

Pupil adaptations

Example 1

> *Karen*: If Jane does something, she gets ignored. If she don't do any-
> thing she never gets told off, all the teachers favour her.
> *Susan*: She's so *good* in lessons, behaviour and work. She does *more*
> than they give them, she does *extra* work. If we have a film, she'll
> watch it, whereas others might talk a bit. If we have a book to read,
> she'll do it in a couple of days, and pointedly go and ask teacher for
> another one.
> *Lisa*: She goes up the library every lunchtime. She used to creep
> round.
> *Karen*: If we do anything wrong, we get shouted at. If Jane does it,
> it's 'Oh Jane, do stop, please, dear.'
> *Susan*: She copies in maths to get ahead, and gets ratty if she falls
> behind. She's not so good in maths, so she has to copy to keep up.
> She says, 'Come on, let's have a look.'
> *Lisa*: She *always* does homework, so never gets into trouble.
> *Susan*: She had a cousin from France who came over, she was
> flouting [*sic.*] her about.
> *Karen*: One teacher said, 'This is a girl who's going to get on in life.'
> It makes you sick.
> *Lisa*: Reading a passage in French, she'd volunteer. Beefy would say,
> 'I think you've done enough, Jane.' She'd say, 'I want to do it, I
> want to.'
> *Karen*: Mr Timpson told her, 'Oh, Jane! You should have been in the
> top stream, you know!' as if she didn't know.
> *Lisa*: Paddy asked her, 'Will you look after the library for me?'
> 'Oh yes, sir,' she said, 'certainly, sir, thank you very much, sir.'

Example 2

> *Geoff*: It's not really hard work, you get used to it. Maths — you had
> to do that. Phil never does any homework. Me and Martin copy each
> other, you see we have different strengths and weaknesses. I do the
> maths and he does the history. If I could do it pretty easy, I'd do it,
> or compare the answers with somebody else . . . we get things right
> mostly, we're skilled operators.
> *Martin*: It's been a good laugh, mostly. I do a bit of work for
> teachers I enjoy, like Mr Harvey. He tells us a joke. We get on all
> right with him and will do some work for him. He's friendly, talks
> to you, he's more free, let's you do other things, you can ask
> questions any time. Not like Martell, you can't interrupt him. He's
> too busy writing on the blackboard and droning on.
> *Geoff*: Miss Leacock, she's all right, but we don't do any work. She's

got no control over us. Phillers will go mad and belt someone, if you muck about while he's talking he'll go spare.

Martin: Whiteoak makes us work. He split me and Phil up. Phil never made a single piece of work. He brought his brother's in for the CSE moderator. See, his brother had passed the year before.

Geoff: We enjoyed going to history, didn't do much in chemistry — dreary, boring it was. He'd set work for us, give us a few chemicals and let us get on with it. Gives you three questions, we asked him to go through them and he'd give us the answers — we'd write 'em down quick.

Martin: Do you remember Mick Langley? He bust everything on the desk as a rule, he just liked causing trouble — lobbing test tubes out of the window, changing labels on bottles, watering down acids.

Example 3

Don: Metalwork's been a good laugh, but it's been a drag as well at times. We used to take the mickey out of the teacher behind his back, things like that.

Paul: What about that time we put stuff in his coffee, metal shavings and God knows what!

Don: And he still drank it!

Paul: And then chemistry's pretty good as well, because there's a kid in there — all the rest of us used to sit on the back row and teacher never used to take any notice of us. He just used to talk to the front row, and like ignore us lot at the back — and this kid he used to smoke at the back, and the teacher would take no notice — got on your nerves really 'cos they kind of ignored it — don't like want to tell you off or nothing stupid!

Don: There used to be these drawers and there used to be loads of paper stuffed in there, and they used to set fire to them and you used to see the smoke coming out the keyhole — and he used to take no notice of that. We used to set fire to the paper, shut the drawers and the smoke would come out of the keyhole.

Alan: In the 4th year you done all the work, in the 5th, you was just going over it, reading it, and filling your folders up what you 'adn't done. You 'ad to do that else you couldn't take the English exam. There were about four of us that never did them until we had to. I'd done about five essays when most had done nearly all of 'em.

Paul: Yeah, then we just copied other people's out.

PW: How did you get away with that?

Alan: It's the oldest game in the world, just changing the words.

Paul: We used to change every alternate word, just copied it so's they were practically the same. I managed to do five at one time in about an hour.

Don: Yeah, I used to borrow this girl's folder, Pat Mitchell, she's left, she was good she was, yeah, her essays were massive length. I just used to copy paragraphs out. I did about five in an hour, that soon took the number up.

PW: Wasn't the teacher suspicious about these essays being all the same?

Alan: They weren't exactly the same. We used to have story-books, they'd all be about the same thing — it was about a book, you just had to write about it, what you thought about it, what happened, or certain chapters. So that girl's would be the same, so would everybody else's, so they couldn't tell whether they'd been copied or not.

Example 4

Pat: I think I've been worse behaved the last two years than I 'ave before. It's ever since that time when they said we couldn't take exams — now we're all misbehaved 'cos we couldn't take exams . . . we're all just takin' no interest in lessons.

PW: Did you have a choice?

Pat: Yeah, you had a choice, but when you chose they said you couldn't do it. You know in maths and English an' that, what as some of us like, an' they just went in 'cos they got higher in something else you know . . . I've got a chip on me shoulder since then . . . 'Cos in my form I was higher than some of them — and it gets on your nerves when they get on. You know, you think, 'Bugger the school, I ain't goin' to do anything for the school now!' If I was taking exams I suppose I'd be a completely different person. I'd be taking more interest in the lessons but I'm not. I'm not taking no exam, so I'm not interested, and that's it!

Elaine: We're not taught, we're forgotten about. We are, aren't we? We're just layabouts, really. When there's any trouble in the school it's always our form.

Julie: We're left on the side as you might say — left to do the dirty work.

PW: Is there no point staying on if you're not doing exams?

Julie: No, you could be out working. If we was learning something interesting, like the boys bricklaying, and girls typing and things like that, then it might be a bit better, but we don't do nothing like that. We're treated like 1st-years, ain't we? 'Cos in English we're doing these things an' I remember doing them in the 1st year.

Elaine: I'm repeating work. It's making me sick, because I can remember doing it before an' it was quite exciting then, but now we're painting and washing up and everything else.

Example 5

Mick: We're quite good at football, because the first game we ever played we won it 6–2.
Len: It's a rough game rugby, I don't like it, I done my arm in.
PW: Do most of the boys think like you?
Gary: 3A and 3B yeah, but you've got all the poofs in 3A and they'd rather do *work*. You get them little idiots playing rugger wi' yer . . .
Len: Yeah, little small kids . . .
Mick: You've got a big kid called John Harvey, he's like a fairy.
PW: Do you get a choice in games?
Mick: We done what we're told. It's just a big bore, school is.
Len: We do whatever we can to get a day off school.

Example 6

Julie: I like history and I like Mrs Brown, and she makes history sound really interesting, and I don't think I could do it if she didn't, an' she does, very interesting.
PW: Would you still like history if some other teacher took you for it?
Julie: No, Mrs Nelson we all get on very well with her, don't we? I mean, I don't think I'd take it if Mr Harvey was doing it.
Others: No! No!
Pam: We had him 1st and 2nd years.
PW: And why wouldn't you have him?
Pam: Well, he makes a laugh and joke of it. We've had him for RI this year and we haven't even had a book. He tells us jokes and when not, we just read out of a book, just reading, about a fifth of our time.
Dianne: Mrs Nelson she really does get down to it, she makes the lesson clear.
Julie: If you don't understand she'll go over it again — won't shout at us if we don't understand.
Dianne: And she can really keep control of the class, can't she, without having to raise her voice, and she's ever so quiet, and everyone's quiet, aren't they? But with Mr Dunsdale and everything, oh, that's terrible!
PW: What do you think the secret is then, of winning everybody's respect?
Julie: Maybe it's personality coming out of Mrs Nelson. She just has to stand there and the room fills with her personality.
PW: What happens if somebody messes about, you've got some pretty tough characters in your form?

Dianne: You said it! But they don't, not with Mrs Nelson, because her personality and her way of doing things — even the rogues are interested.

Example 7

Carol: I hate school.
Michelle: So do I, hate it, Gina and Deirdre do too.
PW: Why's that?
Carol: Miss Sparkes tells me to get me hair cut, Marne is always moaning at me 'cos I don't like games very often. Reckon she talks about me behind my back. I've got that feeling. Martell — dunno really, just can't stand 'im, way 'e talks to yer, Gina and Deirdre, just 'cos we muck about. He says, 'Shut up you lot!' — mostly to Gina. He calls us 'chappies'.
Michelle: When you get your work wrong he shouts at you and makes you do it again till you get it right. He doesn't help us — Mr Jones used to. Mr Clayton shouts at us.
PW: How long have you hated school?
Carol: Since we've been here. Junior School used to be fun, good fun.
Michelle: Yeah, at Bishton it was fun. You could muck about and teachers didn't tell you off. What we could do with here is a little more freedom for a muck-about. We could do with a smoking room for example.

Example 8

PW: Do you agree with having to come to school?
Ray: No.
Paul: Well, it's to learn 'in't it, it's only for your own good, 'in't it?
Kevin: I don't. It's not a benefit if you've nothing to do all day, you're stuck there and you're not learning anything.
Lawrence: But if we weren't at school, we'd be getting a job wouldn't we, so it don't really matter — you could work on a farm, say, when you're old enough.
PW: What would you rather be doing, Ray?
Ray: Working, get some more money, I think.
Lawrence: It would be all right if we got paid at school.
Kevin: They should let you play darts.
Lawrence: Yeah, an' a canteen I reckon we should 'ave, nice ice-cold drinks, where teachers 'in't allowed, 'cos they've got their little private corners.

A typology of pupil adaptations

Clearly pupils adapt to schools in various ways. One mode of analysis is that employed by Wakeford, who elaborated a model originally devised by Merton, and informed by Goffman's work on total institutions.[1] Merton's original formulation was based on the perceived relationship between the institution's socio-cultural structure and the individual's experience and behaviour. Concerning the former, he identified two critical elements: (i) the culturally defined goals 'held out as legitimate objective for all or for diversely located members of the society', and (ii) institutionally prescribed means of reaching these goals. He envisaged individuals either accepting or rejecting goals and/or means, the shades and combinations of which produced five modes of adaptation, such as 'conformity' (acceptance of both goals and means) and 'retreatism' (rejection of both goals and means). This typology gave rise to much interest, and others developed it. An individual might not simply 'accept' or 'reject', he might be 'indifferent' or 'ambivalent'; or if he 'rejects', he might reject with nothing else in mind, or with some 'replacement' in mind.[2] Wakeford used Harary's reformulation and produced this scheme (Figure 3.1) of major adaptations with regard to the public boarding schools he studied.

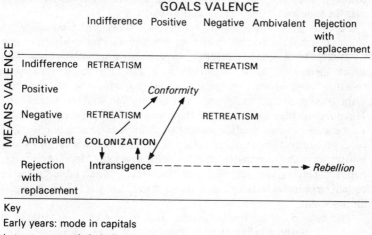

Key

Early years: mode in capitals

Later years: mode in italics

Major movements in careers of boys shown by arrows

Modes characteristic of
    early years in school: Colonization (+ retreat)
        middle years: Intransigence (+ colonization and retreat)
           later years: Colonization (+ conformity, rebellion and retreat)

Figure 3.1 Revised typology of modes of individual adaptation, showing principal modes of adaptation by boys to the public boarding school

Now these, of course, are sociologists' categories. The sociologist has devised them in accordance with his observations. It is also a fairly rigid typology, pupils assuming either one mode of adaptation or another, and 'goals' and 'means' being rather tautly defined. That might, of course, reflect the public schools of the research. In adapting the typology to the state education system, I would argue that we need to make allowances for: (a) great variety among and within schools, (b) consideration of the constructs of pupils. With regard to 'goals' it might be possible to perceive broad, general, institutional goals, such as 'to teach', 'to educate', 'to train', 'to get past examinations', 'to humanize', 'socialize' and 'civilize' etc. The vaguer ones might be only dimly perceived by pupils, but most, in my experience, have a good grasp of the instrumental ones ('training', 'examinations'), and are well able to articulate them. However, as well as these broad, institutional goals, aspired towards in varying degrees by teachers, teachers might have their own aims. To be sure, if they conflict with the school's, they will be in difficulty. Usually they can be subsumed under the official ones. Consider, for example, a rebellious non-examination form in a secondary school — one teacher might aim to 'hammer some sense into them' to achieve some objective standard; another to humour them with a view to teaching them something 'about life'; another simply to pass the time away as agreeably as possible.

Further, within his own framework, a teacher might vary. For example, one environmental studies teacher told me that he aimed to give a certain class 'a general education, to teach them something about life, about themselves, their surroundings, where they came from, their ancestors, and where they were likely to go, with a view to making them good husbands and wives, and fathers and mothers and so on.' The point is, that apart from anything else, the varying content of such a programme carried implications for pupil response. Some pupils might be consistently turned on or off by the school as a whole, or by one subject, say environmental studies, on the whole. More likely most pupils display varying responses to school, teachers and subjects, and to certain aspects of teachers and topics within subjects. The examples illustrate this.

The same point applies to 'means'. It is more profitable to think of them in a personal rather than an institutional sense. Teachers vary in their methods, which they are at quite some liberty to do in the autonomy of their classrooms, and pupils vary in their responses. To give an obvious example, a pupil might reject formal methods, and accept informal ones. In short, there needs to be more recognition in the model of variations in individual pupils' responses in accordance with the above discussion of goals and means.

In seeking to understand the culture of a group, it is important to get at the constructs of members of the group, or we might be in danger of imposing our own categories. However, the sociologist's constructs are not entirely worthless. On the contrary, they can be very useful – as long as they are in line with actors' constructs. They can be useful in providing an overall view, by showing how members' categories relate together, by suggesting how they relate to wider considerations, such as institutional or external factors, by refining them (but not changing them) in line with considerations the member has no knowledge of, but which it is the sociologist's business to have knowledge of, and so on. As long as they remain faithful to member constructs, they are valid. Thus the basis of the revised typology is located in the life-world of the majority of the pupils.

I shall examine each mode of adaptation in turn, but in the light of secondary schools in the state educational system, and informed primarily by my research at Lowfield.

Conformity

This results from a positive attitude to both goals and means. Wakeford found (as Goffman suggested) a minority of boys adopting this mode, and they were mainly senior inmates. He relates them to prisoner-of-war camp 'suckers' and prison 'square johns'. They often aim for posts of responsibility and prestige within the school and present themselves as having 'enthusiasm for the school and for its reputation [which] equalled or even exceeded that of the staff'. Boys adopting this mode early in their school career risk unpopularity with their fellows and accusations of 'sucking up'. However, though there are interesting similarities, schools do differ from prisons and prisoner-of-war camps. One of the major differences lies in the specification of goals. The latter are explicitly correctional, constraining, anti-inmate, pro-'the rest of society' institutions. Schools claim to be educational, liberating, pro-inmate. Also they are almost a 'natural' part of life – everyone experiences them. Through certification they link with the job structure.

The point is that to 'conform' does not necessarily imply 'sucking up', 'creeping' or becoming pets. This indicates a weakness in the typology which has only one space for 'conforming' adaptations, and a possibility of twenty-four for 'non-conformity'. The mode that Wakeford is talking of here, when applied to the wider system, is a kind of hyper-conformity, akin to 'ingratiation'. So for possibly benevolent institutions, like schools for example, as opposed to coercive institutions, like prisoner-of-war camps, the typology needs widening to include more shades of conformity. We might do this by breaking down the 'positive' response in the Wakeford typology (see Figure 3.1). A strongly positive response to goals and means, we might term 'indulgence'. Indulgence towards goals and means yields the *ingratiation*

71

mode of adaptation. Ingratiators aim to maximize their benefits by earning the favour of those with power, and are usually undisturbed by unpopularity among their peers. Often they are individuals operating alone. To use the pupils' terms, you can become a 'pet' by 'creeping', for example 'by always being in there dinnertime and breaktime, offering to do jobs; *volunteering* to do things'. Why do some teachers have pets?

> *June*: I dunno. He just has pets. And if they do something they don't get told off: if we do something, we get blinking killed!
> *PW*: Why don't they get told off?
> *June*: They do jobs for them. They go round always doing little jobs.

A more moderate positive response to goals and means we might term 'identification'. The pupil relates to, feels some affinity for and identification with, the goals and means. This yields a mode of adaptation we might call 'compliance'. There might be several forms of this. In the schools I have studied, for example, there have been two large 'compliant' groups at either end of the school. In the lower forms, particularly the 1st forms of secondary schools, there seems to be a lot of acceptance of goals on trust, though they might be vaguely perceived. Many pupils beginning a new school have an air of hope and expectancy. Inasmuch as the goals are vaguely perceived but strongly identified with, we might term this *optimistic compliance*. In the upper school pupils on examination routes are coming within sight of their examinations and many seem to have a very clear perception of what they are doing and why. At Lowfield they were very instrumentally oriented. In one form I interviewed, for example, subjects were associated either with jobs they wanted, or more generally were ones that would lead to a certain class of job. Indeed in only one instance out of twenty-nine interviewed did a pupil express a satisfaction for a subject because she liked it (this was for music), and even then she rated it below chemistry and biology, which 'could be handy for a job in a hospital'. Further discussion of pupil instrumentalism follows in chapter 4. We might term this *instrumental compliance*. Here are some examples:

> 'I want qualifications when I leave, the more chance of getting a job, a good job with good money. It's no good going into the 4L form, they've got to stay on as long as us, it's no good just mucking around for two years.'

> 'I think physics is the most important subject. When I look through the paper, the adverts for jobs mainly include 'O' level in physics. This is the reason I got out of English literature. I changed over to physics. That's a pretty good combination with chemistry and

biology, you can get a pretty good job with physics. I'm not really bothered about geography because I can't see how it's going to help you later on.'

Another kind of conformity, omitted by Wakeford, but in Merton's original typology, is that of *ritualism*. In Harary's revised version this involves a positive relationship to (or, as we would say, identification with) means, and an indifference to goals. Whereas the 'optimistic compliant' has a strong identification with the school's goals, the ritualist is not interested, or does not consider them very important, or has no knowledge or conception of them, and no inclination to find out. But he accepts that he has to come to school and he accepts the official norms of behaviour within the school.

PW: What sort of pupil would you say you were?
Derek: Pretty average really. I do me work. I behave meself.
PW: What do you hope to get out of it?
Derek: Dunno, really. I just do what I'm told.
PW: What do you come to school for?
Derek: Well, you have to, don't you? Ain't got much choice.
PW: Why do you have to?
Derek: That's the law, in't it?

Another kind of 'conformity' arises from an ambivalence towards both goals and means, which I would term 'opportunism'. Characteristically it develops in the 2nd year of secondary school, as a reaction sets in against the optimism of the 1st. It involves less consistent application to work and frequent but momentary leanings towards other modes. It is a 'trying out' phase before settling into another style, but while the experimenting goes on, 'conformity' of one sort or another represents the basic mode. The behaviour of a pupil during an opportunistic phase can seem unaccountable with wild fluctuations in school performance, attitude and allegiance to peers. In short, there are various types of conformity within schools. I have identified ingratiation, optimistic and instrumental compliance, ritualism and opportunism and there may well be others. It would be better perhaps to do without the term 'conformity' altogether, except as an umbrella term for a group of styles.

Retreatism

This is characterized by an indifference to or rejection (without replacement) of both goals and means. In the state secondary schools of my experience it is more common in middle and later, rather than in earlier years, and the 'retreatism' tends to intensify the longer it goes on.

The retreatist is *'in* the society but not *of* it'.[3] Because he has no 'replacement', his life at school is very empty and boring. For him, it is a 'waste of time', and the time hangs heavily. Many pupils caught by the raising of the school-leaving age regard it as deprivation of a year from their working lives. For them the immediate problem is how to pass the time, and they do this by 'doing nothing', 'mucking about', 'having a laugh'. They might also practise 'being away'; a kind of mental removal from the scene, like daydreaming during lessons, and indulge much more than others in 'removal activities' which are 'voluntary unserious pursuits which are sufficiently engrossing and exciting to lift the participant out of himself, making him oblivious for the time being to his actual situation'.[4] Such activities in schools would include unofficial games, playing cards, group smoking, listening to the radio, contra-school conversations (i.e. 'talking' as an undercover activity) and reading 'illicit' literature.

Colonization

This mode combines indifference to goals with ambivalence about means. The colonizer[5]

> accepts that the school is to provide his basic social environment during term-time for five years and attempts to establish a relatively contented existence within it by maximising what he perceives as the available gratifications, whether they are officially permitted or proscribed.

This is possibly the most prevalent mode of adaptation in our schools, and is particularly evident in middle and later years. Typically the colonizer employs both official and unofficial means to achieve either official or unofficial ends. He accepts the official programme in part, and is concerned about 'keeping his nose clean', 'getting on', 'making the grade', in short, getting what he can out of the system. He might be genuinely interested in aspects of the education offered him, and perform services and fill offices in the system. It makes for an easier life. But the colonizer has a different kind of investment from the 'ingratiator', for he might use at times illegal means, or 'short cuts' at least, such as copying someone else's homework, cribbing in tests and examinations, or lying to avoid punishment. It is also much more of a group activity than ingratiation; association aiding the achievement of its ends. You can take turns to do the homework, or make the unpopular or risky move by which the group stands to gain, such as complaining about work or criticizing features of the teacher's style or lesson or organization of the school which might have unfortunate consequences for the colonizer's pleasure.

The colonizer also 'works the system', that is to say he learns to use legal means beyond the point intended by the organization. Close observance of rules can frequently avoid some more unpleasant activity; volunteering for one job might avoid a more onerous one (note the difference here from the ingratiator's motives for volunteering); playing off one teacher against another is common, or parents against teachers, such as in the endless stream of notes some bring to 'excuse them from games'.

Goffman distinguishes between 'primary' and 'secondary' adjustments. The former 'fit in' with the roles and expectations the organization has for them. The latter provide ways of standing apart from the role prescribed by the institution and 'making out' or 'getting by'. Wakeford describes 'rigged' rugger matches, where the teams agreed on strategies beforehand to give a semblance of keenness and effort. There are many classroom dispositions of activities which are not what they seem. On occasions a whole class may appear attentive, but not be so.[6] In the English state system with its high degree of selection — much of it now disguised, but as keen and widespread as ever — there is much colonization among those who are selected 'out', such as those in non-examination streams. Interestingly the staff, in attempting to solve their problem with 'difficult' pupils, usually offer an 'official' secondary adjustment formula by defining new goals; stressing social objectives and talking in terms of 'education for life' and 'education for citizenship' as opposed to the examination streams' instrumental or academic objectives and devising new means — such as more 'project' work, integrated teaching, link courses, films, visiting speakers, trips and so forth — which are all characterized by some quality of institutional escape. Many accept these official secondary adjustments. In a sense the concept may seem a contradiction, but it is not. Rather it is a good illustration of how 'inverted' people can become in total institutions. Where there is no release from the institution and hence no solution to its problems, stresses and tensions outside, it must solve them itself. When it can no longer do this through its own official processes — as our schools are increasingly finding — then it has recourse to inmate solutions, but in official disguise. In other words, the school *aids* colonization.

It also does this in more obvious ways. Not all teachers are strict interpreters or enforcers of the rules and regulations. They too are bound by constraints and bothered by tension, and need to adapt. One way of doing this is to ignore, or even facilitate, inmate colonization by turning a deaf ear or a blind eye to many a breach of the law, such as smoking groups, and not invading 'free places' (areas where pupils are *de facto* but not *de jure* free from surveillance, such as the toilets, 'behind the cycle sheds', 'on the far side of the playing field', 'under the stairs'). Many a teacher understands and indulges colonizers'

75

working of the system. Both in terms of his own well-being *and* the functioning of the institution, it is a much more acceptable mode of adaptation than intransigence or rebellion, which I discuss below, and for the pupils concerned, those are frequently the only alternatives.

Intransigence

The pupil adopting this mode is indifferent to the school's ends and rejects its means. He may not care about the future and is characterized mainly by persistent and powerful detestation of rules, rituals and regulations and much of his 'front' and presentation of self is based on that simple fact. He replaces the school's means with his own antipathy to them. He is 'agin the government', 'bolshie'. He is bored by the school's normal procedure and outraged by attempts to interest or discipline him. He is very awkward to handle. His rejection of the school's methods involves lesson disruption, hidden and open, verbal, non-verbal and sometimes physical assaults on staff, open and disguised truancy, destruction of school property, pronounced misbehaviour in public while in school uniform or on school business. His opposition is frequently symbolized by his appearance, taking on the style of dress, hair and demeanour of whichever youth sub-cultural group he identifies with — teds, skin 'eads, greasers and so on.

A good example of intransigence is given by Hargreaves:[7]

> Clint summarized the A clique's attitude to school when he said:
>
> > I think school's a waste of time. If I don't like a lesson, I don't do it.

The behavioural counterpart of this attitude was fully confirmed by my own observation of this clique in lessons. During one Mathematics lesson, all the 4C boys were working from various sections of the text-book. Clint as usual was sitting next to Chris, surrounded by other A clique members. Throughout the lesson Clint never opened his book or used his pen. The time was spent in gossiping, day-dreaming, combing his hair and threatening smaller boys in the form. During Library periods, he wasted the majority of his time in an apparent search for a book, playing hide-and-seek with the teacher behind the partitions. For Clint, any form of academic work was irksome; it would be avoided scrupulously and flagrantly. Yet Clint was, by the eleven plus results, one of the more intelligent boys in the school. His ingenuity for avoiding getting into trouble with the teachers was remarkable. More often he would goad other boys into pranks which inevitably led to a rebuke or punishment from the teacher. When a situation seemed unlikely to provoke retaliation from the teacher, Clint lost no opportunity to break the rules. This approach produced a norm which forbade any kind of academic achievement to his followers.

Many of the school's resources are channelled into dealing with the intransigents. They are the most immediate threat to the institution and must be neutralized for it to survive. If there are many of them in a single class, as often happens, they can be accommodated in the poorest, worst-equipped rooms where they can do least costly damage, and given a mixture of the most dominative (those likely to instil respect by fear) and the most fraternal (those likely to instil respect by sympathy) teachers. However, as Wakeford notes, this is commonly a transitory phase, shading into some form of colonization or rebellion.

Rebellion

This involves rejection of both goals and means, involving the substitution of other goals and means. It is more common in later than in earlier years at school. This is not surprising since, in the nature of things, one might expect alternative modes of adaptation to be tried first; and the institution presses harder on junior than senior inmates.

The alternative goals might be connected with future work. Thus girls hoping to be hairdressers might spend their day 'doing' each other's hair; or those bound for the factory shop floor will begin acting out aspects of shop-floor culture. Particularly among girls the displacing goals might be associated with future marriage and family life, evidenced in the enormous and continuous attention to personal appearance, endless conversations about the opposite sex, past activities and future programme. Interestingly such girls are frequently captivated by parts of the official curriculum that deal with these matters, such as courses in child care, and for those periods adopt a 'conformist' attitude. Girls also are much more drawn towards the 'pop' scene, and for many it provides an instant and complete world. At school they will play their transistors, sing the songs, dance, discuss the private lives of the stars and read the 'pop' literature.

Because they have 'replacement' of 'goals' they are less of a threat to the institution than intransigents — as long as their alternative can be accommodated. Schools that conduct massive conformity drives might succeed, but do run the risk of turning both rebels and colonizers into intransigents.

A revised typology

Figure 3.2 shows my revised typology of modes of adaptation. Figure 3.3 illustrates the incidence of dominant modes of adaptation in

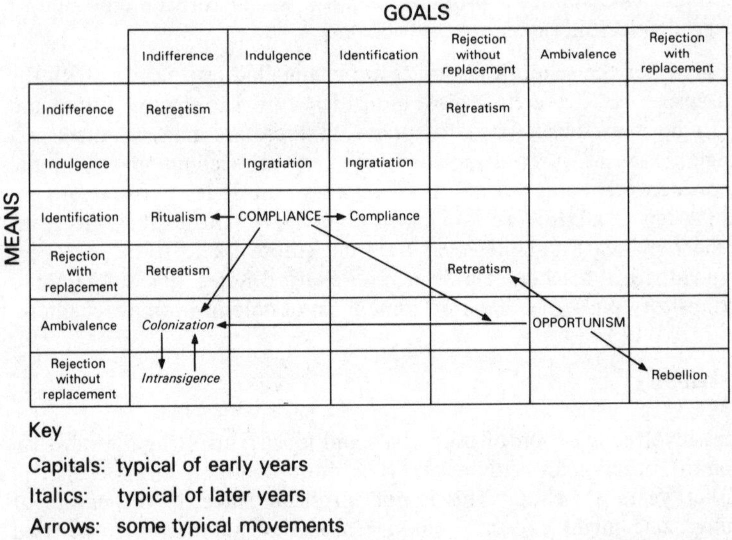

GOALS

MEANS	Indifference	Indulgence	Identification	Rejection without replacement	Ambivalence	Rejection with replacement
Indifference	Retreatism			Retreatism		
Indulgence		Ingratiation	Ingratiation			
Identification	Ritualism ◄— COMPLIANCE —► Compliance					
Rejection with replacement	Retreatism				Retreatism	
Ambivalence	Colonization ◄				OPPORTUNISM	
Rejection without replacement	Intransigence					Rebellion

Key

Capitals: typical of early years
Italics: typical of later years
Arrows: some typical movements

Figure 3.2 Revised typology of modes of adaptation in the state secondary system

Lowfield. Broadly speaking, one route leads to adaptations that might be classed as 'conformity', the other to 'dissonance' involving opposition in some form to the official programme. However, it is not a rigid bi-polar model, since some in the 'reject' stream can achieve a kind of conformity through secondary adjustments, while some in the 'examination' stream can equally become 'dissonant'.

No school is quite as neatly structured in reality as this. There are all kinds of overlaps, blendings and contradictions. Figures 3.2 and 3.3 pull out of the morass the *predominant* modes. Similarly, an individual career and composition can be very complicated. A pupil might adopt one mode through his school life, though it is more likely he will move through a series. He might adopt one for a long time or less, usually oscillate back and forth between several. He might employ one mode for one section of the school, one subject or one teacher, and another for another. He might have a dominant mode, or a mixture of them. Though I have talked of the 'ritualist' and the 'retreatist' I have talked of them as abstracted people. It is really the *modes* that we have been discussing. There are bits of all of them in most people.

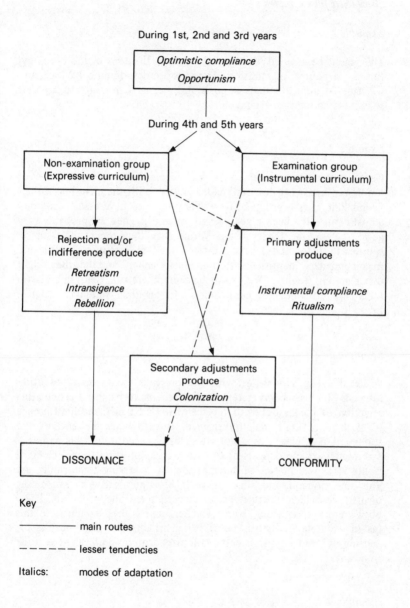

During 1st, 2nd and 3rd years

Optimistic compliance
Opportunism

During 4th and 5th years

Non-examination group
(Expressive curriculum)

Examination group
(Instrumental curriculum)

Rejection and/or
indifference produce

Retreatism
Intransigence
Rebellion

Primary adjustments
produce

Instrumental compliance
Ritualism

Secondary adjustments
produce

Colonization

DISSONANCE

CONFORMITY

Key

——————— main routes

– – – – – lesser tendencies

Italics: modes of adaptation

Figure 3.3 Incidence of dominant modes of adaptation

Comments on examples

Example 1

This might be entitled 'Portrait of a Creep'. In terms of the typology, this is, of course, ingratiation. The girls are describing behaviour, and we have to infer attitudes to goals and means. This is not to say that such information is unattainable.

Example 2

Geoff and Martin appear to be 'colonizers'. They give examples of 'unofficial' means to 'official' ends. Clearly, with the inclusion of their friend Phil, it is a group activity. They seem to have made secondary adjustments ('It's been a good laugh, mostly'). They are probably very good at 'working the system'. Notice that they report different responses to different teachers — a reminder that 'institutional ends and means' must be identified with individual teachers, and that they might differ among teachers. With some teachers, therefore, Geoff and Martin might be 'instrumental conformists'. In his final statement, Martin refers to a possible 'intransigent'.

Example 3

While this has similarities with the previous example, it has other interests. In his second statement, Paul seems to begin by articulating rejection of means but with replacement ('a laugh'), and indifference to goals — a kind of intransigence. But towards the end of the statement it is clear this is not altogether in accord with his wishes — a reminder of the dangers of too stark an application to real cases. It is not a simple matter of categorizing, or of saying some pupils are 'this' one moment, and 'that' the next. Most pupils have a complex set of attitudes which are triggered off by certain extraneous factors. These boys' remarks on their various teachers and colleagues illustrate this (as in example 2). Otherwise it is remarkable for more devices for 'getting by', more typical of the colonizer with his ambivalent attitude to means.

Example 4

Retreatism all round, teachers included apparently, involving rejection without replacement of either goals or means. But what are the goals?

The pupils here seem to think there aren't any for them. Some of the teachers said they were trying to 'provide them with a basis for living', others that they were 'just trying to keep them happy'. Either way, they are rejected. This example reminds us that schools can have a variety of goals for a variety of pupils, and some might be rejected and not others. Also the source of these pupils' rejection is the rejection of them by the school.

Example 5

These boys are a compound of colonization and intransigence. They are indifferent to goals, reject the major aim of the school ('work') but find solace in games, and thus have a certain ambivalence about means. Interesting also for group identification and differentiation from 'conformist' groups.

Example 6

Again this example shows that some pupils are compliant with some teachers, and others with other teachers. Here the girls express strong identification with the 'means' of Mrs Nelson and rejection of those of Mr Harvey, which the boys in example 2 were quite keen about. The means are quite clearly specified (Mr Harvey 'makes a laugh and a joke of it . . ., won't shout . . ., keeps control'). But for the girls, the most potent factor is the quality of Mrs Nelson's personality.

Example 7

These are retreatists, involving rejection without replacement of goals or means. Similar to example 4, except that there is a difference in inclination. Whereas the girls in example 4 claimed they had been rejected by the school and indicated a tendency to compliance had it been otherwise, these are still within the mainstream of the school and are rejecting the goals and means that the others would have identified with. The kind of scene these girls want is what the others in example 4 have, with its 'freedom' and its 'mucking about' potentiality. Of course, were they to achieve it there is no guarantee that they would become 'compliant'. They might equally as well articulate the same kind of retreatism as the girls in example 4.

Example 8

This is interesting for the variety of perspectives. There are shades of
the ritualist about Paul; Ray is certainly retreatist in his responses.
Kevin appears to accept goals and reject means. He seems to acknowledge that 'learning' is an acceptable goal, but, like those in example 4,
questions whether the school actually *has* any means directed to that
end as far as he is concerned. This reminds us again of the problematic
nature of institutional goals and means. We must bear in mind three
questions: (1) Does the school have goals and means with respect to
all its pupils, and if so, how do they differ among them? (b) Are they
clearly specifiable, or are they vague and diffuse? (c) Are there any
latent aims and means behind the more manifest ones? Lawrence makes
no mention of official aims, but simply specifies the nature of the
colonization that would appeal to him. There must be many like Kevin,
who accept the general goals of education, but feel the means are not
advancing them.

The origin of pupil adaptations

The immediate source of origin of pupil adaptations is pupil cultures.
These, in turn, owe something both to school and external factors.
The broad division into 'conformist' and 'dissonant' modes corresponds
to those general divisions with two subcultures identified by Hargreaves
and Lacey.[8] At Lumley, Hargreaves's school:[9]

> Those with positive orientations towards the values of the school
> will tend over the four years to converge on the higher streams; and
> those with negative orientations will tend to converge on the low
> streams. On every occasion that a boy is 'promoted' or 'demoted'
> on the basis of school examinations, the greater becomes the concen-
> tration of the two opposing subcultures. As boys with similar values
> and attitudes are drawn together by this selective process, the more
> we would expect these values to persist and the greater will become
> the domination of subcultural values, leading to an increase in pres-
> sure towards conformity to the peer group.

Thus school organization contributes towards 'differentiation', and
thereafter development within each group reinforces the ties,
strengthens its boundaries and leads to a polarization of values. Lacey
describes the process thus:[10]

> A fairly homogeneous body of pupils is sorted and ranked . . . that
> is, they are 'differentiated'. This initial process is therefore one
> which accentuates differences. The good are rewarded and the bad
> are punished. The good are frequently encouraged and the bad are

frequently discouraged. Differentiation is therefore unstable, and it leads to a situation where the opposite ends of the differentiated group are faced with different problems: the problems of success and the problems of failure. It is the resolution of these problems that gives rise to polarization.

Among the pro-school culture there is continuous reinforcement, but the anti-schoolers solve their problem by rejecting 'the pupil role and replacing it with an autonomous and independent peer culture'.[11] As Hargreaves points out this means a higher priority on *collective* behaviour and regard since the rewards of status can only come from the group, whereas in the pro-school culture rewards come from *individual* effort in competition with others. The content of the pro-school culture is strongly influenced by school values; emphasizing academic achievement, and more general middle-class values; emphasizing correct dress, attitude and conduct. The anti-school culture is a reaction against that, and is influenced by locally-derived working-class values. This association with external factors in the form of class cultures is supported, as is the general broad division, by the group perspectives identified at Lowfield. It should be said, however, that all these studies were purely exploratory in that respect and no exhaustive and generalizing claims can be made for their findings. The connection is a complex one, as most who have worked in the field acknowledge. Future research might explore these indications further.

With regard to the school, two broad sets of questions are raised by the analysis in this chapter. In the first place, what school factors are associated with movements into and between different modes of adaptation, *within* the broad groupings of 'conformity' and 'dissonance', and how are these factors mediated by pupils' interpretative frameworks? What actually do pupils do, and what constructions do they put on it? Second, while this typology has been developed in relation to 'goals and means', it has been seen that these vary. In other words, the 'goals and means' are mediated by other factors. They do not 'come at' the pupil as a result of his experience of school as an entity. We need therefore to examine these other factors, and see if pupil reaction is consistent among them, or if there are certain elements of school life that are more prominent in this respect than others. This is the subject of the next chapter. Some lines of approach towards answering the first question will be presented in chapters 5 and 6.

Chapter 4

Pupils' views[*]

Responses to notional institutional 'goals and means' provide a useful starting point, and yield an overview of pupil reactions to school. We can take in this broad spectrum of adaptations 'at a glance', and say that in general this is how groups of pupils *typically* react in the main. However, it is not sufficient to tell us how an individual pupil reacts, or the criteria by which he judges his reactions. As pointed out, the schools' 'goals and means' can be variable. Moreover, they are multi-faceted institutions, and reactions to different aspects of activity or organization can also be variable. According to my conversations with pupils, they distinguished between three such sub-divisions – curriculum, institution and teachers – and for practical purposes, 'goals' and 'means' should be seen in relation to these. Thus individual pupils can differ in respect of each of these, and among them, accepting some subjects or some teachers and rejecting others, or possibly being so swamped by institutional factors that no teacher or subject can compensate. Also, of course, the typology tells us nothing about the criteria of acceptance or rejection, which again might differ among pupils. The initial conceptualization provides a basis for comparison here. In this chapter I examine the reactions of two sets of representatives of these two groups in the shape of the top 'examination' form, 4A, and the 'non-examination' 4L. This particular study shows common curricular acceptance, though for different reasons, suggesting instrumental conformity on the part of one, and a form of colonization on the part of the other. Equally, both groups show common opposition to certain 'institutional' factors. In their appraisal of teacher qualities which they are likely to accept or reject, both groups are inclined to accept 'teacher-person' qualities and reject 'teacher-bureaucratic' qualities. Interestingly, this is even more significant with the more bureaucratically oppressed examination form. Aspects of teachers that are disliked are often in the area where the teachers are impinged on by the institution, or where they are acting in strict interpretation of their 'teacher' role. This supports the main thesis of this book, that it is the bureaucratic apparatus of the school, rather than its educative function, that divides and oppresses, and that this bears on all pupils regardless of their social background.

Indeed, inasmuch as greater bureaucratization is brought to bear on pupils in the examination form, who are of generally higher social class background in the school's mainstream programme of instrumental certification, they might be the greater sufferers in this respect. Their general instrumental conformity therefore has to be qualified in this respect.

It might be thought, given a basic conflict situation, that pupils might frequently manufacture grievances or make more of them than is actually the case. In this instance at least, however, the teachers of these forms agreed with their pupils, particularly over 'institutional' matters. It is perceived, therefore, as a common enemy which all too frequently intrudes into the teacher-pupil relationship. Teacher views are given at the end of the chapter, together with examples of their different aims for these two forms. Those for 4A are marked by a distinct instrumentality, those for 4L a more indistinct generality. One wonders whether this is tacit recognition of 'colonization', or even encouragement of it in fear of 'rebellion' or 'intransigence'. Thus what might appear as equal 'conformity' on the part of both these forms to 'curriculum' is in fact 'colonization' on the part of 4L, and a readjustment in school aims in line with that, to achieve a kind of spurious conformity. It makes for a more peaceful life.

I begin by recalling the basic model linking these forms of adaptation to group perspectives (Figure 4.1). I then discuss the reactions of these two groups of pupils to aspects of curriculum, institution and teachers, with teachers' own comments following.

The central concept is 'group perspectives'. I described in chapter 1 how, faced with the problem of subject choice, pupils employed different interpretive models, choosing subjects on the one hand for instrumental reasons (job-related, ability, etc.) and on the other for social or expressive reasons. These, however, were *their* social reasons (easy work, fun with friends, etc.) rather than educators' (leisure, citizenship, maturity, etc.). These group perspectives are shown as emerging from the social class structure. The two broad groups referred to above went their separate ways — either to a largely examination-oriented or to a non-examination-oriented curriculum. Teachers are shown as influencing this routing in the usual ways. The examination groups, mostly instrumentally oriented already, are processed through a heavily instrumental programme geared to examinations. They have made 'primary adjustments', which 'fit in' with the roles and expectations the organization has for them.[1] It is not surprising that they have large

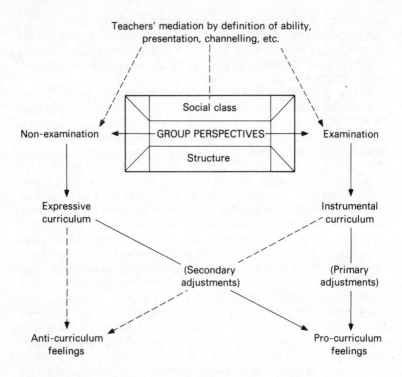

Figure 4.1 Group perspectives, teachers and the curriculum

pro-curriculum feelings. The non-examination group moved into an expressive curriculum, one deliberately geared to 'education for citizenship' (social studies, environmental studies, community, etc.). In some ways its social orientation coincided with their *own* social values: that is to say the work was easy, non-demanding, sometimes fun and interesting, they had more freedom and they were with friends.

It therefore aided them in making 'secondary adjustments', i.e. ways of standing apart from the role prescribed by the institution and 'making out' or 'getting by'.[2] Hence 'school' becomes more palatable, and this route can also lead to pro-curriculum feeling. This route could equally well lead to anti-curriculum feeling: pupils might fail to make secondary adjustments, or those they make might be insufficient.

Curriculum

I made an intensive study at Lowfield of two forms, one non-examination (4L) and one examination (4A). Both were curriculum supportive in accordance with the above model. 4L completed a questionnaire, indicating their liking for subjects (discounting the teacher as far as possible) on a five-point scale.

TABLE 4.1 4L pupils' liking of subjects

	Like a lot	Like a little	Neither like nor dislike	Dislike a little	Dislike a lot
Totals	81	75	29	12	17

This seems to indicate a generally favourable acceptance of the formal curriculum. As might be expected, the same was true of 4A, with even fewer dislikes. However, investigations into the reasons for their largely favourable disposition revealed vast differences. As might be anticipated from their attitude to subject choice, 4A's main reason was utilitarian; i.e. subjects were associated either with jobs they wanted, or more generally they would lead to a certain class of job. Indeed, as noted earlier, in only one instance out of twenty-nine interviewed did a pupil express a satisfaction for a subject because she liked it (this was for music), and even then she rated it below chemistry and biology which 'could be handy for a job in a hospital'. This is instrumental compliance and the examples quoted on p. 72 give the flavour of responses on this topic. Here are some others:

'I'm not really bothered about geography because I can't see how it's going to help you later on.'

'Only one I'm satisfied with is metalwork, because you can do things when you get out that you couldn't do without it; that's the only thing.'

'The most important subjects are chemistry, maths, English and history, because I need them for my future career. I need a science subject and an arts subject as well as English and maths.'

It is hardly surprising, therefore, if vocational orientation is the main criterion, that the girls on the 'commerce' course (in 4C) seemed the most contented of all from the point of view of subjects. This course has much greater linkage to actual jobs in terms of nature of work than more traditional courses.

The approach of 4L to school knowledge, though they profess a similar degree of contentment, appears to be very different. In that form only one pupil (out of thirty-one) seemed to be vocationally motivated in his appraisal of school subjects. The others judged by intrinsic interest or sheer physical pleasure. Thus 'games' is popular.

Other subjects might have their good points for 'unofficial' reasons, e.g. in the opportunities they provide for a 'laugh':

> 'Well, metalwork is quite interesting. Sometimes you have to chip down the walls. Last week me and Ken took two barrels across to empty them, and on the way back we were smashing into each other with 'em, sort of mucking about as we came back.'

Social and environmental studies are popular because they contain matter that is useful to know:

> 'Well, you want to know about the place where you're going to live and work all your life, don't you?'

> 'You learn a lot in social studies . . . not to take drugs . . . blinking mad . . . you kill yourself.'

This would appear to reflect the different curriculum paradigms contained in the model above, and in that applied to subject choice, as described in chapter 2.

For 4L the paradigm might be summed up in the term 'education for life' or 'education for citizenship' as opposed to 4A's 'education for achievement' or 'education for jobs'. With regard to jobs, 4L seem either to know definitely what job they are going into, and none of them requires any academic qualifications (e.g. farming, carpentry); or they do not know what job they are going into, and don't particularly care at this stage. Whereas 4A are 'aspiring' in their attitude to jobs and their relationship with school subjects, 4L are simply 'freewheeling'. It is hardly surprising that most wish to leave at the earliest opportunity.

Institution

High curriculum acceptance, for whatever reasons, must be seen against a background of institutional constraint. Hostility to the institutional aspects of school was common to both 4L and 4A.

There was much evidence of depersonalizing, bureaucratic and instrumental pressures:

> 'Recently my life's been all routine; I get up in the morning, have breakfast, get on the bus, you know. I don't know how I'm going to stop it when I leave school, you know.'

School was likened to 'the army', 'prison' (the most used term), 'Colditz' and 'Stalag Camp 13'. Its influence is pervasive:

> 'It's homework mainly. I don't think you ought to do it. When you get home you want to forget school. You want to go out and do

something instead of being stuck in working. It's like having continuous school, almost.'

This type of complaint is intermingled with those of the growing young adult:

'They've got too many rules. You're not allowed to go here, there, do this, do that . . . like every year it's worse. The area gets smaller and smaller.'

'I think the rules are too strict. Well, you know people smoke? In the summer they're caught smoking and the next day you're not allowed on the field in hot summer. You have to hang around here, and then they wonder why the windows get broke. And that gets me, that! They can't stop them smoking, because they smoke all the while. They'll always find another place.'

Favourable comments about the school can also be seen from the point of view of institutionalization. These took two main forms:

(i) Institutional provision for relief from the usual constraints (a whole afternoon of games, activities, Community Service); and institutional elasticity in interpretation of rules and constraints.

'I know people who go to other schools and they do envy us that we have so much outdoor activities, Community Service and so on, a half day of games, and choices in what we do.'

'You get a lot of games and things like that. I don't mind most of the subjects but you get a bit fed up.'

'We have quite a lot of freedom, really, compared with other schools.'

(ii) Institutional elasticity in interpretation of rules and constraints.

'I like coming to school because you meet all your friends and you can have a right good old time.'

'Uniform rules get on your nerves. They should allow you to wear what you want within reason. (*What happens if you don't come in uniform?*) All depends what teacher I see. Some don't mind, but others — well! (*You're not in uniform now, can you come dressed like this and get away with it?*) Yes, most of the time.'

Comments can thus be seen to hang upon the degree of institutionalization. This is not to suggest that all by any means unequivocally condemned the formal structure of the school. Some thought the rules quite fair by and large; others thought so except for particular grievances (among which school uniform figured prominently — but mainly the fashion rather than the principle). But the chief complaint here seemed to be about the exercise of power, and how this was manifested in the making and interpretation of rules:

> 'They're always telling us to go off and just sit down and talk and play a game of cards or something like that, and when we do, we always get thrown out, and I don't think . . . It's a bit daft, isn't it? But what can you do? They turn the rules around to make things suit themselves, so when we follow one rule they change to another.'

> 'It all depends what mood he's in.'

> 'Sometimes a rule is just set and not explained. One teacher will talk it over with us and explain why the rules are made in certain cases. Other teachers try and change the rules as well and make up their own rules.'

> 'They always think they know what you like best and that. What's best for you, like we're not allowed to go in the cloakroom at break. We're told to go to our classroom, because it's unhygienic for us, but everyone prefers to go there because our friends aren't necessarily in our form. All your friends go to the cloakroom; that's where my friends go, and if they're not in your class then you don't see them.'

Teachers

So far in these two forms we have a pro-curriculum feeling (for different reasons) and an anti-institutional one (for the same reasons). The third aspect of school — the teachers — contains elements of both.

The question is: which aspects of teacher behaviour having repercussions for pupils' affective feeling are considered to be most important and are these uniform among different groups of pupils? Discussing with these pupils the qualities they liked and disliked in teachers, I simply asked them to describe such teachers as fully as they could. To give a rough idea of the kind and distribution of responses, I categorized them into four types and counted as one mention each separate and distinct facet they attributed to each and every teacher who came into the reckoning. This gave the results summarized in Table 4.2.

The differences shown in Table 4.2 are perhaps not startling. We might expect 4A to be more articulate than 4L, and 4L as a form to encounter more problems of control. Otherwise, matters of technique and disposition are clearly of high general importance. It would be wrong to regard this as a scale of priorities. So often one category merges with another. Teacher disposition, for example, has clear links with 'control' and 'fairness' and may strongly influence the teaching

TABLE 4.2 Pupils' perceptions of teachers

	Number of mentions	
	4L (*N* = 31)	4A (*N* = 29)
Teacher technique	36	53
Teacher disposition	31	59
Teacher control	21	9
Teacher fairness	11	17

'techniques' adopted. This becomes clearer when we look at the components of each category:

1 Teaching techniques

Liked	*Disliked*
(a) Helpful, explains.	Unhelpful, ignores.
(b) Provides variety.	Boring, monotonous.
(c) Allows more freedom.	Little freedom.

Examples

(a) 'Helpful, explains' accounted for twenty-one out of thirty-six mentions from 4L in this category.
A teacher who is liked:

> 'Will explain if you don't understand it.'

> 'Come round and help you if you get stuck.'

> 'If you go wrong, says, "Go and have a go and then come back again." '

> 'Explains how to do things clearly, and if you're not too sure will go over it personally with you.'

> 'Spends more time with you.'

> 'Won't have a go at you for asking a question.'

A teacher who is disliked:

> 'Doesn't explain things properly.'

> 'Explains it only once.'

'Can't make anything clear to you.'

'Doesn't spend so much time with you.'

'Pays no attention to you, and don't help if you're lagging behind.'

'Thinks he knows but doesn't know his subject.'

(b) Variety. A teacher who is liked:

'Gives you interesting jobs.'

'Lets you do more jobs.'

'Gives you a choice of jobs.'

Frowned upon are:

'When you all have to do the same job.'

'Monotonous, boring stuff.'

'The same thing day after day.'

(c) Freedom (i.e. more democratic, not anarchic). A teacher who is liked:

'Allows you to talk.'

'Lets you get on without bothering you.'

'Lets you do what you want.'

'Leaves you to do things.'

'Lets you walk round the room.'

'Lets you finish work.'

A teacher who is disliked:

'Doesn't let you talk.'

'Every so often keeps telling you what to do.'

'Talks too much, stops you and lectures you.'

'Stands watching but doesn't help.'

'Never lets you finish.'

2 Teacher disposition

Disposition is preferred to 'personality' or 'personal qualities'. The latter two terms imply something fixed and immutable. The former is the outward manifestation of the inner self as 'state of mind', and may change from day to day.

The main sub-categories were:

(a) Cheerful, humorous, comical, etc.

(b) Friendly, kind, understanding, etc.

Examples:

(a) Cheerful, etc. A teacher who is liked:

'Makes you laugh and you can work faster.'

'Makes the lesson cheerful, makes it fun to do, even if you have got out of the wrong side of bed.'

'Nice, you know, you can have a laugh with him.'

'Gives us a load of jokes.'

A teacher who is disliked:

'Says, "Down to work", no pleasure, no nothing.'

'Is always moaning.'

'Loses his temper, shouts a lot, and bangs you about.'

'Gets on to you.'

(b) Friendly, etc. A teacher who is liked is:

'Willing to listen to you. You can talk to her . . . if there's anything wrong she's understanding, she'll help you out.'

'Calm, talks to you.'

'More like one of you.'

'One you can always talk to.'

A teacher who is disliked:

'Doesn't like us. Gets mad easily. Picks on us for little things.'

'Hits you.'

'You just can't speak to them as a person as well as a teacher.'

'Just tells you to get on with your work and that's that.'

3 Teacher control

This is closely related to the last category, and was often expressed in personal terms. 'Shouting', 'hitting', 'yelling', were universally condemned, though most appreciated 'firmness' of control. Teachers who are 'too soft' or who 'threaten and never do anything' are just as much criticized as those who 'bully you', 'fly off the handle', or 'show you up'. There is a difference between 'always telling you off' and being 'strict, but nice', and between being 'bossy' and 'not too strict, but telling you off when you do anything wrong'.

4 Teacher fairness

Again, this is closely connected with the two previous categories, but there were enough responses alleging discrimination to warrant a separate category. The two items most generally opposed were 'having pets' and 'picking on people'.

Examples of teachers who are disliked:

'Show you up in front of the class.'

(Such a strong category in the senior school as a whole that I examine it separately in chapter 6.)

'Pick on people instead of being able to stand a joke.'

'Teach only the boys and forget about the girls.'

'Take it out on the whole lot of you if one does something wrong.'

'Get on about your writing a lot.'

The above examples are taken from my discussions with 4L. They seemed to attach equal weight to technique and disposition. Table 4.3

TABLE 4.3 Perceptions of teachers: 4L and 4A compared

Major category	Sub-category	4L	4A
Teaching technique	Helpful, explains	21	25
	Variety	5	13
	Freedom	8	4
		34	42
		4L	4A
Teacher disposition	Cheerful, humorous	17	17
	Friendly, kind, etc.	14	35
	Others	0	7
		31	59

shows how 4A compares. The one outstanding difference this comparison reveals is the greater emphasis 4A puts on being 'friendly, kind,
understanding, etc.', both in comparison with their own other mentions, and with those of 4L. They seemed particularly impressed with
the teacher's ability to empathize with them (or not):

'If you sort of say something to him . . . some teachers would look
at you in disgust . . . like in connection with being young, he accepts
it from the pupil's point of view, he accepts that he was young once
and that he used the same language as we use and that sort of thing.'

'You don't have to be afraid to talk out or anything in his lessons.'

'If anything doesn't go their way it's the pupils' fault and they get
the blame for it.'

'You're taught one thing at home to speak your mind, and you get
to school and do it, and that's it — teachers are away!'

'A teacher should be fair to everybody, treat you almost as an equal,
not there to command you, but there to teach you.'

'Good teachers treat you like people, they come down to your level
— you know, don't talk down to you or treat you as something different — outside as well as in. Other teachers are just concerned
about their subject — they'll teach it almost because they have to.'

'If you had a personal problem you could go to him. He's just like
your dad, really, you could say anything to him. He was understanding, and he was a good teacher, he was just one of those we could
get on with.'

'The best approach to make an impression on me is for someone to
sit down and talk to you. A bad approach is someone who comes up
to you, grabs you by the collar and starts dragging you along, that
doesn't do anything really . . . When teachers do that, pupils dislike
them more and it makes for worse trouble.'

'More like a friend than a teacher.'

Comparing these with the 4L examples they are much more verbally
extensive, though qualitatively similar. This apart, it is fair to say that
they are making much more of it than 4L. Some possible explanations
are: (1) Perhaps they are more sensitive, aware and more mature than
4L. (2) Their experiences of different combinations of teachers might
have led them to different conclusions. (3) There may be more
emphasis on academic achievement with 4A, and consequently (a) less
time for fostering good personal relationships on the one hand, and
perhaps less perceived need for it (of the nine teachers concerned with
both forms who answered a questionnaire on this report, four agreed

there was less time, five did not), and (b) more occasion for personal conflict between teacher and pupil over standard of work (on this point, three teachers agreed, seven opposed).

Some of this shows through in the following contribution from a boy who said he liked the work but didn't like the place any more.

'I used to like it. There was an atmosphere of friendliness about the place – you could talk to most teachers, but now it's getting larger it's not . . . and the teachers, I don't know some of the teachers, and . . . there are some I've never even spoken to . . . well perhaps there were one or two you didn't know when you first came in the 1st year, but that was all. Now, I don't even know, not even spoken to five or six of them. The friendliness of the place is gone . . . and it's really gone, and it's really changed since the 1st or 2nd year. So I think I don't really like the school now . . . it's more like a school than it really was when I was in the 1st year, and that's why I don't really like it.'

I asked him what he meant by 'more like a school now'.

'Well, if you go into a house, there you feel some sort of security that you're in your own house, and when you came to this school, we didn't . . . it seemed different from the house, but you sort of . . . you was at home here, you could . . . you know, you knew what you could do and what you couldn't do, but now everything seems to be a sort of a . . . going away from pupils and teachers . . . and we don't seem to know them any more now than they know us better . . . and that in the 1st year we knew each other quite well and we knew what we liked and what we didn't like.'

Here we get a suggestion of how institutional change and forms affects relationships, in this case for the worse. Was this generally felt or acknowledged, for instance among the teachers?

Teacher mediation

Reactions from the staff were sought to this study of these two forms, and they were all given a copy of the results and a questionnaire. Two reactions were particularly strong and illustrate aspects of teacher mediation in the development and progress of the two groups as referred to in Figure 4.1. First, as we might expect from the subject-choice syndrome, all those who taught 4A agreed emphatically that there was more pressure on them there than with 4L type groups to 'achieve results'.

'There certainly is – on "O" levels. Mrs Gamble said, "this is the most academically run school for the least academic children I've ever been in" — and that just about sums it up. It's always getting mentioned; always with you. You're expected to get blood out of stones. The children here are less stupid than the working-class kids at my last school in town. Teaching my mixed-ability "O"-level, CSE groups, I tried talking, researching, filming — all that kind of thing and making their own notes, but they were not well done, so I reverted to dictating — and it's *terrible*! But they like it and prefer it, because it's less work. So there's pressure there. Some of the kids are very exam-success prone — John Starkman says, "Why can't we do 'O' level geography?" Parents also like it — that's what they want, and they're important.' (Mrs Nelson)

'The standards and presentation cause great concern in both. For the 4A type there is the yardstick of the exam, but they expect to be spoon-fed — an automatic route to exams without urgency or personal sacrifice, and so they settle for existence rather than pride in their work. The "L" child sees no point in standards, and the teacher has no sanctions to operate against academic indifference for the "L" child. With the lack of thought, and lack of cash in setting up ROSLA courses, it is hardly surprising the "L" child wants to be taken out of a captive situation. Equally so, the "L" child is captive to the teacher.' (Mr Timpson)

These differences are reflected again in the different aims teachers profess to have for the two groups. Some examples:

Example 1

Aims for 4A: To help them reach a good standard of work and become more confident in their work.
Aims for 4L: Basically we try and establish a good relationship with them and give them encouragement in their work. (Mrs Coles, Housecraft)

Example 2

Aims for 4A: To give them as good an examination qualification as possible commensurate with their ability, and to develop a love of learning, particularly a desire to discover by experimentation, so that on leaving school they have a deep desire to continue with a developing educational process.
Aims for 4L: To encourage an interest in and appreciation of science and scientific method so that the pupils have a desire to 'find out'. To give them an understanding of the world in which they live and

an appreciation of the major problems facing the world. (Mr Garrett, Science)

Example 3

Aims for 4A: To provide a sound springboard for examination success, but not merely to stuff them full of ammunition, rather to make them aware of the range of the subject by providing introductions; I like to trigger off interests (often within the exam syllabus) and then let them pursue.

Aims for 4L: Often to correct the missing links in *basic* knowledge, so that in the working situation there is not an 'embarassed' series of gaps in their general educational equipment. This is not 'textbook' knowledge, but geared to practical situations, and expressed in mundane terms. (Mr Timpson)

Example 4

Aims for 4A: Aiming at a successful exam result, but at the same time hoping to prepare them for the successful running of a home and looking after themselves (and a family).

Aims for 4L: As for 4A, but minus the examination result. A slightly broader approach because of the lack of restrictions. (Mr Stewart)

Example 5

Aims for 4A: To give a broad understanding of the way in which historical factors influence our lives and behaviour, to respect the past without sentimentalism, to attempt to inculcate the beginnings of wisdom − incidentally to let them obtain a piece of paper.

Aims for 4L: The same as 4L (less the incidental), but from a different approach (Mr Harvey)

Thus the differences between the two groups; the heavy instrumentalism of 4A, supported by parents and fostered by the school hierarchy, and the comparative purposelessness of 4L in school terms, throwing them back on their own cultural resources, together with differential aims and pressures teachers felt themselves in teaching the two groups, thus furthering the division, was supported by the staff.

The second point of interest was their support and sympathy for the boy who claimed 'the friendliness of the school had gone'. For many, it was the major factor, for it pinpointed their major concern −

school ethos, the atmosphere in which they work. For some it was part of a general *malaise* attributable to the declining powers and misguided schemes of those directing school policy. But for most, it was a consequence of increasing numbers, together with growing instrumentalism.

'Increased numbers. Less time to know pupils. Up to this year [500+] I knew by name and sight every pupil in the school. I still aim to do so, but it is becoming very difficult.' (Miss Sparkes)

'I agree with the boy that the loss of "friendliness" is due partly to the increasing size of the school. I am certain that 200 is an ideal number for a secondary school. This increase in size has brought an increase in unnecessary hierarchy — year tutors, duty rosters, etc. — all of which has had the unfortunate effect of removing responsibility from where it should belong: with the form teacher. In a small school, a form teacher has an opportunity to know and understand his form, and the pupils feel that they are the particular responsibility of one member of staff who has a personal interest in them and their welfare. I feel that many members of staff do not possess the same degree of sympathy with the problems of a 4th- or 5th-year pupil that they possess with the problems of a 1st- or 2nd-year pupil.' (Mr Garrett)

'Increasing conservatism in staff. External examination pressure. Need to prove worthy of new [comprehensive] status.' (Mr Groves)

'Because of (a) increased size of school, therefore less knowledge of individual pupils and (b) as a result, groups get taught rather than individuals, and (c) younger pupils have more enthusiasm and want to please more, and therefore a teaching situation is more friendly naturally.' (Mr Fuller)

'Obviously the growth of the school is a factor. Also the children are far more aware of the academic rat-race, and so become more self-orientated. The trend is more towards " taking" than "giving" to the school; they are more calculating than previously. Also, the breakdown into strict exam courses (often one teacher per subject for two years) means that it is rare to see the bulk of pupils regularly.' (Mr Timpson)

'Partly because of increasing numbers of newcomers not used to normal life; partly because children of this type become "pseudo-sophisticated" in their middle teens owing to social pressures; I would qualify these remarks by saying that there is greater empathy between myself and 4L pupils and between myself and the more able 4A pupils than with the mass of "in-betweens".' (Mr Harvey)

'(1) The increase of numbers. (2) A reaction (perhaps overreaction) against the familiar approach of young teachers. (3) A reaction

against the hurtful way some of our colleagues have been treated.'
(Mr Martell)

Clearly, teachers are equally at the mercy of many institutional
features, and feel helpless to change them. The effects are mediated
through them to the pupils, often quite consciously. Thus, even in reply
to a question based on the pupils' generalized complaint about teachers'
unreasonable use of power, eight accepted the point, while only six
opposed.

'But this is due largely to the very difficult position in which the
teacher himself has been placed.' (Mr Garrett)

These teacher comments lend support, sympathy and validity to the
pupil views expressed in this chapter, as well as indicating certain
features of teacher mediation. The question of institutional impact on
teachers will be taken up in later chapters.

Summary

Items such as 'liking school' and 'social values' are seen to be predicated
on other and different considerations when viewed through the frameworks of group perspectives. School is a multi-faceted institution and
pupil response can be uneven. At Lowfield, among one particular year,
there was a high curriculum acceptance rate, but for different reasons
between two groups; for the non-examination group, the 'social values'
they attributed to their curriculum were not at all the same as
educators' 'social' values. There was common feeling against institutional factors, even favourable comments about school in general
hingeing on relief from institutional constraint. Comments about
teachers could also be interpreted as depending on their degree of institutionalization; dislike arising from ultra-rule consciousness, uneven
and irrational use of power, formal and depersonalized relationships,
superior attitudes, as well as certain aspects of pedagogy and personality. Certain differences in reactions to the latter two aspects correspond
to differences in educational routes, and may be a product of them.
Teachers' own views supported these results, and gave indications of
how their mediation of institutional and other factors operates in the
4th and 5th years.

We have seen so far how pupils, influenced by group perspectives
which have their origin in social class backgrounds, are consolidated in
initial divisions by teacher policy and school organization; how, in the
face of these divisions, they adapt to school in various typical ways,
and how these adaptations might vary according to certain aspects of
the school. We have not yet seen how these adaptations work out in

pupil lifestyles. Colonization was the major mode of adaptation at Lowfield, and its chief manifestation was 'having a laugh'. I examine this prominent feature of pupil lifestyles in the next chapter.

Chapter 5

Having a laugh[*]

Q: What do you think about when you come through those gates in the morning?

A: Well I think . . . 'ere we go again, another day for mucking about.

'It's all right when you're at school, really, like when you can just talk to people, have a laugh.'

'It's the only place we have fun, isn't it?'

'We aren't silly at home, not very often anyway. You act silly at school for a laugh.'

The prominence in pupils' minds of 'institutional' elasticity and freedom, and the development of their own social values are indications that their school life-worlds are far wider than an investigation based on official norms and criteria can reveal. Often this world seems composed of an aimless, pointless, disorganized chaos of activity, a childish 'mucking about' or causing trouble through sheer devilment, or 'not paying attention', or simply loafing about 'doing nothing'. However, it is not as aimless and disorganized as it appears. Its central feature is laughter. That is the means by which pupils – and teachers as we shall see in chapter 9 – displace the grimness, the sourness and hostility that impinges upon them, and make their school lives more palatable, even enjoyable. In this sense schooldays can well be 'the happiest days of one's life'. However, for the most part it is not a naturally intended consequence of the official programme and policy, or youthful exuberance merely filling the spaces in between. Rather, it is a colonizing activity, a pleasant way of surviving, a means of infusing life, zest, interest and excitement into sometimes hostile and alien surroundings; and an activity which emphasizes togetherness, *camaraderie*, fortifies the group and provides identities within it.

I was alerted to it mainly by conversations with 5L, the senior 'non-examination' form in the school, many of whose pupils had run through the full gamut of adaptations ultimately to settle for a form of colonizing, with laughter as its chief expression, to form almost a little world of their own. As such, they can develop their own forms of laughter, but much is generated at the interface between their world and the official programme of the school.

Kate: I remember Mr Gantry calling Tracy 'my pet goat'.

Tracy: Always in trouble, me and Kate.

Kate: Lazy, horrible lot, pests, he used to call us. Lazy.

Tracy: You ain't 'eard 'is new saying, have you? 'E says to Joanne Mackie, 'Don't sit there looking pretty, will you', so Joanne says, 'One thing, I look a sight better than you.' (*Loud shrieks of laughter and suckings in of breath from girls.*)

Kate: We used to play 'im up in the 3rd year just so's he'd give us a lecture and we wouldn't have to do no work.

Tracy: ''Orrible, miserable lot', he used to say. 'Lazy'.

Kate: Yeah, we used to laugh at 'im.

Tracy: What about when 'e made us go outside and made us march back in properly.

Kate: What about when me and you fell out and I threw your book across the classroom and 'e sent me down to Miss Judge.

Dianne: What about when Mr Bridge stood just outside the door.

Tracy: Dianne fell off a chair first and as she went to get up, she got 'old of me skirt, she was 'aving a muck about, and there was I in me petticoat, me skirt came down round my ankles and Mr Bridge came in (*great screams of laughter from girls*). He'd been standing outside the door.

Kate: 'E told her she'd get suspended.

Tracy: He 'ad me mum up the school, telling her what a horrible child I was.

Kate: 'Nobody will marry you,' said Miss Judge.

Tracy: Oh yeah, Miss Judge sits there, 'n, nobody will want to marry *you*, Jones,' she said. I said, 'Well you ain't married, anyway.' (*Shrieks of laughter from girls.*)

Types of school laughter

Laughter can be an instrument of policy, its aim to forge better relationships and to create an atmosphere judged to be conducive to the achievement of the aims of the school. Laughter can also be a reaction against authority and routine, a socially divisive and disturbing element made in the interests of the preservation of one group and the

103

destruction of the other.[1] Both of these are chiefly teacher-initiated. We can find both, of course, in the same school. In chapter 3 I noted the importance pupils of all abilities attached to teachers being able to share a joke and have a laugh with them. During such incidents, teacher and pupil were seen to transcend the institution and become more 'human'. This seems apparent in such remarks about teachers as, 'he's more natural' and 'he's more like your friend than a teacher'. Conversely a prominent feature of disliked teachers was their lack of fun and propensity to laughter (e.g. 'he's always moaning'). I am not concerned here with the first type of teacher-initiated laughter, since my focus is on the pupils. Among them, I discerned two broad types of laughter which I term 'natural' and 'institutionalized' laughter.

Natural laughter

Laughing seems a natural function. The young especially like to laugh, so we can assume there will be a certain amount of seeking to push through the institutionalized constraints to the surface, whatever the character of the institution. However, there was plenty of evidence that much school laughter had its own peculiar characteristics. The pupils themselves distinguished readily between 'natural' and 'institutionalized' laughter.

> *Sandy*: It's different when we're outside, isn't it? When you're mixing with other people that are older than what you are, can't act stupid then.
> *PW*: You act with a ladylike deportment, do you?
> *Tracy* Eh?
> *Gill*: Well, we have a laugh when we go out.
> *Sandy*: I mean we don't muck about like we do in school.
> *Gill*: No, we don't stand there throwing bottles and plimsolls about.
> *Sandy*: We have a good laugh when we go out, anyway.
> *PW*: What, and still be sort of 'ladylike'?
> *Sandy*: Yeah, and still have a good laugh. When we are out of school uniform it's a lot different.
> *Gill*: I don't know, when you go out you sort of act your age, and I don't know.
> *Sandy*: We aren't silly at home, not very often anyway. You act silly at school for a laugh.
> *Gill*: Yeah, not all the time, but we muck about.

Many of the examples that appear in my notes I would interpret as natural laughter. Much of the laughing and joking with teachers (as opposed to against teachers) and between groups of friends I would place in this category. The content of this type of laughter is often extra-institutional. Girls, for example, make capital out of their evening social engagements. I would also include, as natural, certain high-spirited activities which occur and never come to the attention of staff. During my stay at the school, two that came to my attention were 'mass rapes' and 'FPs'. Mass rapes were calculated systematized 'assaults' on certain girls by one group of boys. 'FPs' were 'funny positions', which simply involved boys falling on top of each other, the aim seeming to be to do this in as bizarre a situation or in as massive a pile as possible. No doubt the fact that such activities are contrary to official norms adds extra piquancy to the enjoyment, but I feel that this type of laughter owes more to the natural exuberance of youth than to any institutional factor beyond the part it plays in bringing them together. Many of these activities might be conceptualized as 'side involvements', in that they are peripheral to the main official activity of the school and do not impinge on it.[2] The same is true of some other laughs dependent on the pupils' own interaction, such as those which involve socialization into a subculture.

Institutionalized laughter I: mucking about

Institutionalized laughter takes two main forms. (1) 'Mucking about', a kind of seemingly aimless behaviour, often labelled by teachers as 'silly' or 'childish' and (2) subversive laughter, aimed, deliberately or not, at undermining the authority structure of the school or the status of a particular teacher. Both forms of laughter seem to vary among pupils in proportion to their commitment to school.

Examination pupils generally were less bored and made less mention of having a laugh than non-examination pupils. This was confirmed by my observations. Examination pupils were more circumspectly behaved and officially orientated. Non-examination pupils seemed to exercise their minds mainly in devising their own forms of amusement, thus transforming the reality of the school. Laughter is an excellent vehicle for this. Goffman has observed that joking is a way in which the individual makes a plea for disqualifying some of the expressive features of the situation as source of definition of himself; and to participate with a group of one's similars in this kind of activity can lend strength to the show of role distance and to one's willingness to express it.[3] This, incidentally, illustrates the caution we must exercise in interpreting positive answers to asking children if they like school. Many of them might say yes, but only having transformed the reality of it.

In their conversations with me 5L talked to me about their life at school. Analysing these recorded discussions there was a remarkable contrast between on the one hand a set of factors which could be subsumed under 'boredom' and on the other those relating to fun and laughter. The former made for dour, grim recounting while we talked within the official definition of the school. Many regretted not having been allowed to take examinations. Some had lost out by choices in the 3rd year. The 'work' they were doing and had been doing since the beginning of the 4th year was 'too boring', 'too simple'; they were simply repeating work; or did 'useless', 'meaningless' work or 'nothing'; lessons were not 'helping for the future'; they were 'ignored', 'forgotten about', 'practised upon', 'made use of'; some teachers agreed with them, others 'didn't care', 'picked on them', 'took it out of them'.

The following examples are given to demonstrate how ingrained this boredom is within these pupils.

Example 1

PW: Do you get anything out of school subjects?
George: No, not very helpful I don't find them, just boring.
Len: Some of them interest yer.
Harry: Everybody likes an easy time, don't they? Like our English group now, it's mad ain't it? He tells you the answers before you ever do anything. Says, 'Oh well, I'll write it up on the blackboard first', and then I'll copy it out! Huh! Rubbish!
Len: It's like Mr Brown, you don't learn nothing on that, you just copy off the board.
Harry: Blackboards and blackboards of writing, it's just meaningless. You write it down. Can you tell me what we done last week?
George: Done nothing.
Len: I wasn't here last week.
PW: What use do you make of this writing, do you ever read it again, are you ever tested on it?
Len: No.
Harry: We haven't 'ad an exam in two years, it's pointless.

Example 2

Kim: I can do it, I just don't like it, it's too boring. The maps we are doing now are so simple, really.
Christine: I've not learnt anything these past two years. The English we're doing is exactly the same as my sister's doing in the 1st year, and the maths work, she's doing 'arder work than what I'm doing.
Kim: What I'm doing is fractions, but 'alf of this work is only 2nd-form stuff, I just sit around doing nothing either because it's too easy or because I'm not bothered about it.
Christine: See, we're not learning anything, we've done it all before.

I wish they'd give us some work, some proper work to do. It's so boring. We have two lessons with Mrs Nelson, that's interesting because she talks to us about life and things like that. Nobody plays about there because it's interesting. In chemistry the boys sit around and throw things about.

Example 3

Sally: I'm repeating work; it's making me sick because I can remember doing it before and it was quite exciting then, but now we're painting and washing up and everything else.
Susan: . . . Ever so easy . . . (*all talking at once in agreement*).
PW: Isn't there anything you enjoy doing?
Joanne: Art, and that's about all — for a laugh.

Example 4

John: There's nothing to do here. There's a long dinner hour, not that we mind that but us being 5th years, we can't have a room to ourselves where we can talk. If you go in the cloakroom you might be suspected of stealing if something goes wrong, but if we had us own room we could go in there and talk, but we're all outside bored stiff, there's no activity to do, it really does depress you. We ain't got nothing to do, you're just waiting for the next lesson and when it comes, you're bored stiff.

Example 5

PW: Looking back on school, what do you think you're going to remember about it most?
Paul: Boredom of all the lessons and that. Same thing day after day. I like primary school better, there were more things to do and I seemed to get on better there.

Example 6

Alan: When they had Speech Day everyone started ripping off these bits of foam under their chairs and started throwing them about. Suddenly I noticed a line of teachers at the door taking names, everyone in the hall, you know, spaced out, sort of Gestapo, spaced out, standing up for the interrogation . . . 'Did you throw?' . . .

'Were you in?' . . . Some people got the cane, but it was so *boring* it weren't true, Speech Days. If you're sat there for a whole afternoon with nothing to do, you do get bored, don't you?

Example 7

Simon: It's not a bad school really, you know. I don't mind it, you know, but . . . coming every day doing the same old thing one day after the other, same lessons, you know, gets a bit sickening. You can't wait until the end of the week or the end of the day, you know, when you get here.
PW: Do you find the work difficult?
Simon: No, it's not difficult, it's boring. You just sit there with a whole lot of work to do.
PW: What do you do, say in English?
Simon: Wednesday, teacher reads to you which you nearly fall off to sleep, I do anyway. You get so bored with it, you know.
PW: What else do you do?
Simon: It's hard to think. I remember once I got so bored I did fall off to sleep in English. Yeah, so bored with it.

Example 8

From field notes 5 March 1975; art — periods 1 and 2, 4th form

(Carol, Janice and Susan seem lost for anything to do.) 'Have you any jobs, sir?' The three of them shimmy idly over.
Teacher: How am I going to find jobs for you three for all of next term?' (*Teacher sets them arranging magazines in a file, the three exchange looks of resignation.*)

Teacher tells me they're not interested in art. They came to him for negative reasons. He sees some of them three times a week, twice for half days. There are four more terms to go yet.

A considerable amount of 'mucking about' was mentioned in association with expressions of boredom, itself often connected with routine, ritual and regulations. Thus Speech Days, assemblies and other forms of ritual which the vast majority of pupils I spoke to described as 'boring', 'useless', 'meaningless', 'a waste of time', taxed their ingenuity in remaining sane. I witnessed many assemblies. On the surface they seemed rigid, militaristic, well-drilled affairs. Pupils filed in by form, were inspected for uniform as they passed through the door, and lined up in serried ranks. Teachers ordered them, squaring off rough corners, tidying up lines, filling up spaces. They stood amongst them at strategic points while those not on 'duty' mounted the platform. There followed, usually, a talk, a hymn, prayers, then announcements. The beginning and end were monopolized by the band. For most of the pupils I spoke to in the senior school, it was twenty minutes of standing boredom. Here are some typical reactions:

> 'Assemblies are a waste of time. For religious people they're OK, it's a good morning's start, but there aren't many religious people in the school. You're all in there together, it's a great temptation to kick somebody's legs and make them fall down just for a laugh, just temptation to trouble.'

> 'No, we don't listen in assembly, we just muck about. Sing to drown everyone else and that.'

> 'Useless, rubbish.'

> 'The boys keep tickling yer . . . All mucking about . . . boys pulling your hair and that.'

> 'Waste of time, I reckon, 'cos while you're standing there you might as well have an extra ten minutes on your lessons. All you do is sing a song and say a prayer, and that's it, you're out again. You could do that any time, couldn't you, at home?'

Among the pupil assembly activities that I observed were the mutilating of hymn-books, whispering messages along the row, general scuffling, teasing the nearest teacher, communicating by coughs, making faces at the teachers on the stage. The hymns seemed to be quite an exciting affair. Among the competitions I witnessed were trying to be the last one to finish a verse, getting a word in in the middle of a pause (the most amusing one I heard was a cacophony of 'harks' in the pauses between the lines in 'Hark the Herald Angels Sing'), trying to drown the senior mistress, inventing new words for the hymn as you go along, mutilating your hymn-books some more.

Pupil rules: the backdrop to subversive laughter

Pupils not only make their own amusement during assemblies, they have their own sense of order determined by status amongst themselves. If this is disturbed by teachers, there is great annoyance.

> 'Look, as far as I can remember, ever since the 1st year the 5L used to stand at the back. Didn't they, Frankie? Back at the left-hand side; so you work your way up the school and you get there and you got to move and then we get moved. (*All talk heatedly at once.*)

109

Why should we suddenly get moved? All the other 5th-years have
been back there.'
PW: I don't follow.
'Well you ought to be able to find your own position, walk straight
up at the back but you have to be lined up, lined in half way down,
form by form . . . '

Similarly if their 'laughs' are seriously curtailed by an over-zealous
member of staff, they might bear him particular resentment since he is
forcing them back into boredom. It is a kind of second-order
annoyance. They have accepted the boredom and have invented certain
ways of coping with it — 'secondary adjustments' — the ways the individual stands apart from the role and the self, taken for granted for him
by the institutions and by which he 'makes out', 'gets by', 'plays the
system' and so on.[4] The maintenance of social order in the school
depends on staff not seeing, ignoring or accepting this. They are, in
fact, 'hidden norms'. Behind the apparently sterile officially ordered
facade, there is operating another system developed by the pupils
through time which transgresses the general rules of the institution
without appearing to do so. It is 'concealed deviance' from an official
point of view. But, from a pupil's point of view, time, tradition, lack of
detection and spiritual and physical necessity have legitimated such activity. Studies of deviance usually take an official line whether it is
regarded as a qualitative activity, one that is so labelled, or one
phenomenologically conceived, but pupils, commonly disregarded because they have less power, also have their notions of deviance.

Often this is confused with the official line which pupils are wont
to present to pseudo-official interviewers, which then they have mis-
takenly been perceived to have internalized. The activity of which I
speak here might be regarded as yet another part of the so-called hidden
curriculum, similar in essence to the unofficial strategies employed by
pupils to meet official criteria for, usually, certification. Here, however,
their intent is survival and sanity.

Pupils then have their own rules. The usual interpretation of rituals,
and that their chief function is to reinforce social order, is, of course,
uni-dimensional. It assumes a passive assembly who receive the ordering
and an active staff who impose it. I am saying that despite first appearances everybody is active but in different milieux. The pupils have their
own rules. H. L. Foster has noticed this in another educational setting,
namely that involving urban lower-class black children in the United
States.[5] He suggests that one of the reasons why the education of such
children is not working is that urban educators have been playing the
game of teaching and learning by the wrong rules:[6]

The formal organizational rules of the urban teachers and
administrators are not working. The rules actually running the schools

are the informal rules set by the students which evolve from lower-class urban black male street corner behavior and life style.

However, there was nothing in my study to suggest anything remotely like 'Street corner behavior'. This was a rural area and there were no signs of any integrated behaviour as in an inner city, though there are undoubtedly class differences between pupils and teachers, and this is connected with the development of group perspectives. The in-group, of course, does not need laughs as much as the out-group. For the latter, therefore, there are structural connotations but their behaviour, unlike Foster's 'street corner behavior', is much more institutionally produced. It is a response to circumstances and those circumstances shape and condition the response.

How do pupil rules work during lessons? In these micro units individuals have more influence and the situation has a more fluid penumbra. Thus pupil norms can vary from teacher to teacher and in accordance with their own composition.[7] I think it true to say, however, that there is a pupil-institutional core norm which all new teachers to a school have to discover and adjust to. Some of them never succeed and spend their time and energy in misguidedly trying to establish official rules. This infraction of pupil rules and norms can promote 'heavy' conflict displayed in anger.

> *Lorraine*: We 'ad a lady teacher and she picked on Angela and we all sort of went against 'er. We were shouting at her, moaning at her, telling her why was she 'itting Angela for nothing. You know she was 'itting Angela, and we just turned round, chucked our pencils all over the place, said, 'Right, we're not doing no more work', and we sat there, didn't we?
> *Yvonne*: Yeah. We all slammed our pencils down and just sat there.

Here is another group of girls' account of the same incident:

> *Lisa*: Some teachers say we're uncontrollable, like Miss Yates.
> *Others*: You can't talk to her . . . No you can't . . .
> *Tracy to Lisa*: When she 'it you, it weren't even you, were it?
> *Lisa*: No, she 'it me for nothing.
> *Beryl*: They all started shouting at 'er and she said, 'Sorry.'
> *Lisa*: She said, 'I'm ever so sorry.'
> *Tracy*: Someone said, 'You didn't 'ave to 'it 'er.' She went off her rocker, so she grabbed 'old of Lisa, slapped her face and 'You'll come down to the [*senior mistress*]', got to the door and there was a riot.

This teacher told me that she never understood these girls. As a new teacher she had tried to impose an inflexible static order on her classes, 'starting as she meant to carry on' in the folk wisdom of the trade. But

111

this could be dangerous practice. We must distinguish between school norms, teacher-class norms, and teacher-individual norms. As pupil and school come to terms with each other, so does each teacher and class and each teacher and individuals in each class. This is why starting teachers are in such a difficult position. They don't know the school norms and are often misled by seasoned teachers instructing them in their own class and individual norms. Their initial approach, therefore, could either be firm, and possibly misplaced, or tentative, in which case in repressive schools the sponge rubber behaviour of the pupils, traditionally suppressed, will naturally spring back at them, pupils taking what advantage of the negotiation they can.

Another illustration of the consequences of infraction of pupil rules came during a discussion about pupil antics I'd observed during certain lessons (such as walking over desks, swinging from beams, playing tape-recorders soft and loud, and playing 'find it' with the teacher, connecting bunsen burners to water-taps and directing fine jets to the ceiling, leaving the room and returning by various routes, etc.). Invariably, they did these things just 'for a laugh', but occasionally to annoy a teacher.

'. . . say if he's taken a pack of cards off someone, say, and we're just trying to get our own back to try and annoy him — we'd do everything we could think of to annoy him.'

Much of this reaction takes the form of subversive laughter, which I discuss below.

Aided colonization: the avoidance of subversive laughter

As noted in chapter 2, there was every indication that at Lowfield at least, pupil norms and rules were taken into account. What might have been a thoroughly anti-school group were given assistance in colonizing and in some ways encouraged by the staff, in the formation of a 'culture' which in ethos is pro-school. An interesting case in illustration of this is 'the smoking game'. There was a school rule against smoking, supposedly strict, but not explicitly against the possession of cigarettes. Many in the upper school were compulsive smokers. They must have their cigarettes, so they must smoke secretly. A club formed behind the swimming-pool, but that was highly dangerous because of the presence of oil, so the area was put out of bounds. This was strictly enforced. The club reconvened behind the potting-shed, another formed on the far side of the playing-fields, and these were disregarded. Clearly, it was more important to the staff that pupils should not blow themselves up than that they should not smoke. But they also realize that the smoking game is, in fact, one they cannot win, and that attempts at strict enforcement will only lead to unproductive trouble. 'There goes

Michael for a smoke', said one teacher to me during a lesson. 'What can you do?' – said with a humane grin rather than a tone of despair. I witnessed another teacher having an elaborate game with the boys in one class focused on the detection of cigarettes. 'Come on, Dogsbody, where are they, I know you've got some?' and searching a boy's clothing amidst jocular protests: finding some and confiscating them in mock triumph, only to return them with an indulgent grin at the end of the lesson. Pupils played the smoking game in my presence – teasing each other about the possession of cigarettes, threatening to light up in my presence, and so forth.

'Give us a fag, scruff.'

'I don't smoke.'

'What are these, then?' (*Fumbling in his pockets.*)

'Do you want a light?'

I took this to mean that I was entering into the same kind of tacit conspiracy with them as some teachers were, in recognition of their own norms and rules. Rule infraction is good substance for a laugh especially if those associated with official rule-making implicitly join in. In this sense pupils and teachers occasionally transcend the institution and find common cause in a common humanity.

In this respect teachers as law enforcers are acting in a similar way to Bittner's skid-row police.[8] They do not employ a strict interpretation of the rules, rather basing their discretion on 'a richly particularized knowledge of people and places'. They recognize that the law can be unjust. They often 'play by ear', using their own rules. We might regard this kind of teacher-pupil interaction as 'reciprocal indulgence' following Braroe's concept of reciprocal exploitation.[9] Children are refused the privilege of playing adult roles (teachers are allowed to smoke, wear jewellery, they have freedom of movement, speech, etc.), therefore children must define the self along defensible lines but in a way to permit validation of this self by teachers. Hence, for example, they smoke in secret. To some teachers, pupils are childish, irresponsible and stupid. The pupils, because they can bend the rules so easily and trick teachers, see themselves as taking the advantage. This suggests that bad feeling in a pupil might be caused more by teacher rejection of self as presented by the pupil rather than because of the specific instance. In other words, the many deep-felt complaints from certain pupils about being 'picked on' may not have anything to do with the actual justice of the matter but rest in the teacher's denial of the pupil's desired presentation of self. This is a delicate matter requiring keen teacher perception. Pupils offer an image of self consonant with a consensual definition of the situation supporting a social structure which includes the superordination of teachers over pupils. If this image of self is not recognized or accepted then the consensus may fail.

School is 'not so bad', therefore, for many pupils so long as they can 'have a laugh', primarily to relieve the boredom of the official programme. The lesson for teachers would appear to be that if they cannot make the programme more interesting to these pupils, they must take into account their need for creating their own interest to enable them to get through the day.

Teacher types: laughter initiators

This, however, does raise the question, considering classroom laughs, of wide differences among them depending on the teacher. The pupils in 5L did have a few likes — like 4A — mainly de-institutionalizing activities such as Community Service or social studies, 'When we go on trips and that', but mostly the official programme was dead for them. They seemed to see teachers in four categories:

(1) Those that keep you working.
(2) Those you can laugh and joke with.
(3) Those you can work and have a laugh with.
(4) Those that just don't bother.

Those in category 3 appear to be showing most awareness. In Bittner's terms they are using their knowledge of the pupils to mediate the school policy. Those in category 1 are seeking to impose it more literally. The difference is brought out in the following conversation.

> *Jane*: Sometimes you can hear him shouting in the other room. He won't laugh you see, they try to get him to laugh, they do these stupid things and they just want . . . If he'd laugh they'd be all right, he won't you see.
>
> *Anne*: Oh yeah, they'd do anything to try to make him laugh. He puts them in the report book and everything. They don't care.
>
> *Deirdre*: Every lesson somebody is going down for it.
>
> *Jane*: Yeah.
>
> *Deirdre*: He put one girl in twice in one day. They do it on purpose. If he was to be more friendly with them like Mr Lennox is, 'cos he'll have a laugh with you.
>
> *Jane*: You see, he won't smile and have a laugh with you like Mr Lennox will.
>
> *Deirdre*: 'Cos we can have a joke with him, can't we?
>
> *Jane*: Yeah, and we do work as well, but in there they play about and don't do any work.

Here the 'authoritarian' teacher intent solely on 'working' gets his come-uppance directly. A more 'successful' (in his own terms) authoritarian teacher usually succeeds in displacing it towards the category 2 type teacher. Let us examine this more closely. The teacher whom you can both work and laugh with is a respected person, who knows his job, can keep control, teaches them something sometimes, but above all retains his human qualities in the classroom. His perception of teacher role does not require of him any different behaviour pattern than that of human being role. He has no problems of role distance and correctly perceives the pupils' desired presentation of self through the constraining and dehumanizing institutionalized morass. The authoritarian teacher frequently adopts a different role from choice.

> *Kathleen*: What about when we 'ad Mr Bullet? He made us stand up straight when we walked in the classroom.
> *Deirdre*: Like being in the army, that was.
> *Kathleen*: He made us march out; if anyone spoke, he made us write about three essays out.
> *Sally*: There was a different side to him, though, 'cos me and Tracy used to go in his room at break times — he was ever so nice — didn't have to march in then, just sit on desks and chat to him, he was ever so nice.

This reminds us, as T. Burns noted, of the discreteness of status positions and the schizophrenic nature of our society.[10] I also perceived a marked change in some teachers between classroom and staffroom or between on-duty and off-duty. This suggests that many teachers' classroom attitudes are open to change. However, such is the nature of secondary school teaching today that control is valued above transmission. In other words, the authoritarian teacher enjoys high esteem because of his ability to perform the custodial function while others struggle in varying degrees. This is usually taken to be because of, either their own deficiencies, or the evil and difficult nature of the children. No doubt some teachers have more 'trouble' than others. It would be foolish to deny that they affected the situation and this would be particularly true of 'weak' or 'wet' teachers. But it is part of the thesis here presented that these difficulties, which largely take the form of the pupils 'having laughs', originate from the boredom they experience from the total institution. It needs humanizing, but the authoritarian works in the other direction in the service of the institution. There are no laughs in his lessons. If they are a bore (which they inevitably were for the pupils I studied), they would need to take and make more laughs elsewhere, wherever they could.

Institutionalized laughter II: subversive laughter

Thus, having a laugh can come to assume a political nature. Reaction against authority can be stirred by the authoritarian teacher, possibly in reaction to a laugh against boredom, and invariably fulfilled on the weak. When pupils get at the teacher directly, by, for example, putting pins on his chair, making strange noises, sitting on whoopee cushions, letting off stink-bombs, ventriloquizing nicknames and playing other sorts of games deliberately to annoy, they are seizing opportunities to get at the stereotypical teacher rather than that teacher personally. Certainly they will exploit what personality idiosyncrasies they can, but they are subsidiary to the major sociological factor. There are several forms of subversive laughter. One of the most common is 'subversive ironies'.[11] Among school-children one form of this is name-calling. Attaching nicknames to staff in depiction of character forms a status bridge which by displacing it in humour belittles it. Thus the headmaster and his deputy were known by some as 'Dick Dastardly' and 'Side-kick' and the senior mistress as 'Nellie' or 'Flossie'. Unfortunate facial characteristics or behavioural habits or postures were seized on with alacrity and teachers rapidly transformed from Mr or Miss So-and-So or 'Sir' to 'Deputy Dawg', 'Captain Pugwash', 'Cheetah', 'Fruitie', 'Beefy', etc. From this it is a short step to having them engage in all sorts of unlikely activity — usually illicit sexual activity. Numerous jingles, poems and anecdotes decorated the pupils' 'quarters'. Interestingly, sexual prowess and parts seemed to conform to the staff hierarchy. Much of this is closed humour, that is to say it is used only within, from one's own culture or to oneself for the purposes of making the enemy appear ludicrous and boosting one's own status and self-esteem. Many behind-the-hand sniggers occur in coactive teaching situations. There is a more open technique which has the effect of making the enemy appear ludicrous in his own eyes as well as everybody else's. This would include shouting out the teacher's nickname, firing missiles at him and arranging booby-traps.

Another form is 'confrontational laughter'. On one occasion, one girl, unaware of the senior mistress's presence, shouted for the television set to be turned up because 'I can't 'ear the bloody thing.' This immediate confrontation of cultures from which the senior mistress felt obliged to retreat produced much laughter, as did another occasion when a girl in anger told the senior mistress to 'get stuffed'. Both these incidents show the pupils' culture impacting against the teachers' culture to the detriment of the latter. It also illustrates the important role of vulgar language, which here helps the pupils to sustain their own definition of the situation and blocks a construction of the 'official' one. Such occasions provide superb and dynamic material for laughs in the countless retelling of the incidents which will take place. The relating of them to me was yet another one of these occasions for laughter.

The authoritarian teacher, jealous of his status and sensitive to

assaults on it, often tries to detect or anticipate subversive ironies. However, they are not easily detectable and he may pick on a form of
natural everyday laughter by mistake.

> *Wendy*: Remember when we were discussing . . .
> *All*: Oh, yeah! (*Much laughter.*)
> *Sharon*: That was in the 3rd year; he went off his rocker at us, didn't
> he?
> *Wendy*: What was it? I know, we were talking about Christmas
> pudding and my mum said me Nan's knickers caught fire (*great
> laughter*).
> *Sharon*: I remember, Wendy . . . it weren't very . . .
> *Wendy*: We were both sat on the front desk chatting away . . .
> *Sharon*: He went barmy, I told him he shouldn't be really listening
> (*general laughter*).

Here, a teacher has invaded a private area and earned a rebuke accompanied by laughter which could have done nothing for his self-esteem.

Subversive ironies in number could be regarded as 'gallows humour'
as mentioned above, a response to an atmosphere of tension and unease
wherein people seek an intellectual and emotional escape from disturbing realities.[12] Gallows humour can become a means of social control
in boosting the morale of the victim and at the same time undermining
that of the oppressors. As Obrdlik says:[13]

> He who has had no opportunity as a participant observer, to feel on
> his own skin as it were the beneficent influence of the gallows
> humor upon the mentality and emotions of people in invaded
> countries can hardly have an adequate idea of the importance of the
> social function exercized by this type of humor.

I would not wish to make many comparisons between schools and
countries downtrodden by the boot of the invader, but the social function of some of the humour, at least, is similar.[14]

> Gallows humor is a reliable index of the morale of the oppressed
> whereas the reaction to it on the part of the oppressors tells a long
> story about the actual strength of the dictators: if they can afford
> to ignore it, they are strong; if they react wildly with anger, striking
> their victims with severe reprisals and punishment, they are not sure
> of themselves, no matter how much they display their might on the
> surface.

There is another form of subversive laughter which I would call
'symbolic rebellion'. Some people make a career of open resistance, in
their terms 'playing teachers up'. As above with gallows humour,
success depends on response.

George: Jones, 'e isn't worth playing up because he don't do nothing.

Alan: He don't like me, he picks on me. The other day in activities we were all sitting around the table playing dominoes and he came over and clouted me. The others were doing the same.

George: Jones just goes a bit red, it's not worth the effort of playing 'im up unless you're going to get a response. Mr Cook goes livid.

PW: Do you plan what to do in advance.

Pete: We don't often plan. We sometimes go in late, that always gets their goat. Mr Diamond gets the chin, he knows all these big words, he called George 'a churl'. We just laugh at him.

Symbolic rebellion can also take the form of destruction of school property. Thus two glasshouses which it had taken one class of non-examination boys a full term to repair and make functional were destroyed by the same boys in the space of five minutes only a few weeks after completion of the task. Another example that occurred during my stay was the blazer-ripping incident. Of all the symbols of school authority and their own oppression none is more detested by the pupils, generally speaking, than school uniform. It is precisely because it is so closely associated with school norms and teacher authority that enforcement and conformity are pursued with vigour. After years of inspections and remonstrations about their clothing a tradition had developed among boys who were leaving that others would tear his blazer literally to shreds during the last week of term. My stay at the school encompassed the departure of one group of boys marked by blazer-rippings, which in spite of the fact that they were done so near the end of the school career of the pupils concerned, precipitated a teacher-pupil crisis. One boy's blazer was ripped to shreds early in the week of departure. He was seen on his way home by a member of staff and referred to the headmaster. A campaign was then launched for the detection of those responsible, which involved the whole form being retained for several periods of their free time, much vigorous interrogation and ultimately the caning of the offenders. It was a heated topic among both staff and pupils. The most quoted factor lying behind teachers' anger that I heard was connected with their *in loco parentis* role. They felt responsible for both person and property of the pupil. Thus one teacher thought the mother of the boy concerned deserved compensation for the destruction of the article. But the mother had sent a letter saying she had no objection and telling the teachers to forget the incident. However, by this time there was more at stake and the professional zeal with which the investigation was conducted is evidence of the extent to which teachers were sensitive to the symbolic assault on their authority. To the pupils, the teachers' case seemed unreasonable, unfair and altogether out of proportion to the event.

'What's one blazer, it wasn't all that good, anyway.'

'They'd been writing all over blazers, writing their names on them, it's a traditional activity at the end of yer school days.'

'They all get ripped on the last day, anyway. You can't do much about it. Last day they all come round and cut chunks out of your hair, tie up your hair, half cut up your blazer and then messing about all the way home, sticking scarves out of the window and things like that, but they can't do much about that because you've left.'

'On our bus when the last lot left there was maths books, all sorts of books, going out of the window and that gets their hair up because all the people round about complain. Bits of paper there were everywhere.'

Once leavers are clear of the school they can do what they like, but this blazer-ripping incident, occurring at the beginning of the week in which pupils left, impinged too much on school time and became, therefore, in the teachers' view not only a violation of school rules and norms and their authority but also an overstepping of the bounds of discretion most of them usually employed. Again, a situation redolent with laughter turned into heavy conflict, characterized by anger.

Conclusion

'Having a laugh' is not always enjoyable by any means. As a cure for painful experiences it is only partly efficacious. When it comes to leaving school, many, particularly the girls, may feel sad, even cry, forgetting the bad times, remembering the laughs, even summoning affection for those who have hurt them the most, possibly because the treatment led to particularly memorable laughter-making devices. Thus might authoritarian teachers be given more cause for self-congratulation. But, in the existential situation of the classroom, the laughter might have arisen from constraining situations in response to boredom or in reaction to oppressive authority. Many teachers understand this and this understanding will be reflected in their better personal relationships with the pupils. But the question of accounting for the boredom in its total and blanketing effect on some pupils is a much broader one involving structural and historical factors. There are also questions unanswered about the nature of the laughter and its incidence among the pupils. For example, to what extent is it a response or reaction to the dominant culture and/or how far is it an expression of their own culture? These are matters requiring further investigation. Neither must psychological aspects be forgotten, for example, laughter as tension release. This raises interesting questions about 'cards'. Among the pupils are particularly severe 'nut-cases'. Perceived manifestly as a great trial by teachers, they may, in fact, be extremely functional for a school in providing foci for tension release among whole groups of pupils. I shall take this up later in chapter 8, in relation to teacher humour.

Pupils have their own norms, rules and values and their school lives are well structured by them in ways not immediately apparent and not always based on official criteria. In their lives, laughter has a central place either as a natural product or as a life-saving response to the exigencies of the institution — boredom, ritual, routine, regulations, oppressive authority. Inasmuch as the latter predominate in a school, the laughter will not be consensual, contributing to control, but obstructive, subversive and rebellious, contributing to conflict. Thus might colonization shade into intransigence or rebellion.

Chapter 6

Showing them up*

In this chapter I shall examine in depth one of the most important criteria among the school factors promoting conflict. We have looked at the strain towards tolerance, making the best of it, and in the existential joy of companionship in the face of common afflictions, that is quite something in itself. At times, schools are, for one reason or another, very happy places. At other times, the misery they cause plumbs the depths of despondency. While teachers and pupils negotiate a *modus vivendi* which falls somewhere between teacher aims and pupil aspirations, the school ticks over, life is normal. Both teachers and pupils develop and operate on a 'school' plane of thought and life with its own rules, values and customs, reserving a 'personal' plane for off-duty moments and private areas. They do not do this consciously and it is often very much regretted by both sides, as when pupils complain of teachers not being persons — friendly, understanding, etc. (see chapter 4) — and teachers complain, for example, of 'not being able to get through to' such and such a pupil. But roles provide protection. If at times they are inhibiting, they are also, at others, insulatory. Thus a teacher can withstand some 'bad' forms by becoming the teacher for those moments, separating out his person for its own protection and leaving it behind in the staffroom, or even at home. The pupil does likewise. And by so doing they leave behind those attributes of the person that are most vulnerable, acute sensitivity, conscience, emotion. Much school life is an elaborate charade performed by apparitions. The price paid for 'playing safe' in any game is a kind of monotonous conformity, like hanging on to the ball for the purpose of playing out time for a draw in a match played away from home.

Thus while pupils feel that more of an investment of personal activity would enrich relationships, it also involves greater risk. This is well illustrated in instances of pupil humiliation. If 'having a laugh' was the main manifestation of pupils' colonizing activity, 'being shown up' was their most painful experience by a very long way. It involves being stripped of all one's defences, as pupil, as person, and held up nude under spotlights in exaggerated shame, and degraded by the most cutting taunts and insults. In this manoeuvre, teachers use what might be considered a rather unfair tactic in that, while retaining their own 'teacher' status for themselves with all its cushioned conscience, they invade the pupil's personal sphere with all its acute sensitivities, outside the common ground where they act out their parts with timeless predictability. And it hurts. It's a low blow; not only against the rules, but against the spirit of them. The only redress pupils have is to resort to clandestine cunning and invent even more ingenious ways of getting their own back, possibly through counter-ridicule, in subversive laughter.

As the biggest heavy-conflict producer among the pupils, and the one outstanding factor in teacher-pupil relationships fomenting dissonance in one form or another, I considered it merited detailed examination. Having been alerted to it by talks with the 5th-year pupils, I began a more systematic study of the phenomenon, talking to more pupils in the 3rd and 4th years, observing lessons, attending functions, ceremonies and so on. There seem to be three basic types of 'showing-up': those which result from pure accident; those which result from official policy as part of the official programme (not perpetrated as punishment, though that is how they are received); those deliberately performed for punishments.

The first type we can hardly cater for. Wherever people interact, some will cause embarrassment to others unintentionally, e.g. by seeing or hearing them in a disadvantaged situation, by interpreting them in a way different from that intended, by a slip of the tongue, and so forth.

Regarding the second category, many of these officially sponsored embarrassments are a by-product of institutional requirements. Among the best examples are those which stem from a pseudo-Olympic creed which extols the taking part in an event as opposed to the winning of it. It is perhaps most clearly manifested on the sports field and is closely associated with the House system, which itself is believed to be functional for the school. Slogans such as 'taking part', 'having a go', 'he does at least *try*', are used in the mystic folklore of inter-House competition as *a priori* justification for putting pressure on pupils to engage in activities in which the public manifestation of enormous differences in skill, ability and physique is positively degrading for the non-athletic.

At Lowfield each of the four Houses was required to enter teams for Sports Day. Each event demanded two competitors and one reserve from each House. The value placed on mere entry was emphasized by the award of a point (though the point was not awarded unless the event was begun). A morning was set aside to select these teams by trial, i.e. the House teachers undertook to find the best at each event by observation. I accompanied one male teacher concerned with the selection of the girls' team for one of the Houses. I was impressed by the difficulty he had in persuading them — particularly the senior girls — to take part in the events he wanted them to. Before he began he was approached by two members of his own form:

Shirley: Can we be excused games, please, to go and help Mr Groves?
Mr Town (frowning, hesitant): Whose Houses are you in? Go and see your Housemistress; I can't give you permission.
(They approached Mrs Stewart. Mrs Stewart was very busy organizing some other girls. She reasoned with Shirley, then finally dismissed the matter with Well . . . try a jump or something!' *Shirley looked aghast. I never saw her do it.)*

When he came to selecting his team, he began in a friendly, democratic way by asking for volunteers for events, with a slight touch of cajolery ('This is not the time to be modest, Susan, you are the best at the 100, aren't you?'). Before long, however, by the administrative necessity[1] of finding a team in the restricted space of time, he was forced into subterfuge (asking all of them, 'Who's the best at this?'), and later into authoritarianism. The following extract from my field notes is typical of these negotiations.

'Mr Town is trying to persuade Kim to do the high jump, Lee to do the 100 yard hurdles and long jump, and Sandra to do the shot. Kim and Lee bombard him with excuses, "I ain't any good at it", "I've hurt me ankle", "My mum said I ain't got to jump", "I can't do it".
Mr Town: It doesn't matter, we get a point. *(He turns to Sandra.)* You're a shot-putter aren't you, Sandy?
Sandra: No!
Mr Town: Yes you are! *(Writes her name in.)* Who are discus-throwers?
Girls: Tracy! Claire!
Mr Town: Right, you can both do it. *(Writes names in.)*
Claire: Javelin, she's *(Tracy)* good at.
Tracy: No I'm not, Claire does javelin.
Sandra (outside): It makes you sick, this.
Mr Town: So you're in high jump and discus, Barbara *(writes)*.
Barbara: No I'm not. Honestly, I haven't done high jump for three years.
Mr Town: I'll put you down for shot then.
Barbara: I can't do shot, I hurt my arm ski-ing.
Mr Town to Tracy: I'll put you down for shot as well *(goes)*.
Barbara: What I want to do is discus and long jump, and he won't let me do either of the bleeders.

There was much evasion, by silence, by denying any sort of ability at the event in question, or by deliberately under-performing the trial event. But the teacher was not to be taken in. After an apology of a long jump from one senior girl he simply said in weary, authoritarian tones: 'And again.' And after the next, slightly less of an apology: 'And again.' And after the next: 'You're in, Susan.'

In fact he was joking, but Susan turned, and very heatedly shouted, 'I'm not. Shut up!' and returned to her friends with a very high colour and many hostile glances at the teacher. When I asked her later what she felt so upset about she said, 'Well, they make you look such a fool in front of everybody . . . I wouldn't mind if I was some good at it.'

By tradition, apparently, all took part in the 100 yards senior girls' trial. But Tracy, a large girl, was reluctant.

Mr Town: Come on, Tracy.
Tracy: No! Show me up!
Mr Town (cajoling): Come on, come on!
Tracy: No, I show myself up. I always come last.
Mr Town (laughing): Come on, get up, everybody else is doing it.
(*Tracy got up, ran, and came last.*)

In interviews I talked with pupils about the sports while they were still topical. Some enjoyed them, of course, but many were not interested. 'It's all right for those who are good at them, but if you're not, you just look ridiculous.' I think it true to say that many did not want to take part simply because they did not want to, but I was satisfied that many perceived participation as a threat to their social identities.

I marvelled at the teacher's administrative and organizational expertise in parrying and countering the oppositional thrusts from the girls, and in getting his lists complete. 'We're experienced campaigners,' he said. In fact nearly all the encounters I witnessed had an air of ritual about them. Everybody seemed to know how everybody else would react. For example, the teacher would have been astonished if all had agreed first time; pupils likewise would have been astonished if the teacher had accepted their excuses. In this sense they seemed to be operating in clearly-defined roles, and with clear expectancies of others. This teacher incidentally was very popular among the pupils generally. It seems that if there is a strong element of ritual about the activity and, even more, if it is part of the sacred institutional order, the teacher can avoid personal hostility, as long as he keeps to the clearly defined teacher role. In turn, some pupils may be able to transcend the situation when it comes to running, jumping, throwing and so on, by performing as pupils rather than persons.[2] This, together with the lack of intent to punish, considerably softens the embarrassment felt in this type of 'showing up'.

We now come to the third category, deliberate punishment. This is the type of showing up that causes most distress, and I will therefore consider it in more detail. I want to look at the properties and functions of deliberate showings-up.

Properties

Showings-up require certain properties. They need a public arena. They are much more likely to occur in formal settings where there is probably considerable distance between the rules governing the formal procedure and the rules governing the everyday interaction – hence they frequently happen in meetings such as assemblies and co-active, formal teaching situations. They require an object who is sensitive to such treatment. Obviously he needs to be able to interpret the stimuli in the manner intended. (It is no use using wit or scorn that someone does not understand, or adopting a tactic that he will interpret in other ways, for example as a joke.) The victim must also be someone who has the ability to stand over against his 'self', take the role of the other and see himself as others see him. In Mead's terms, the 'me' is perceived as the object of humiliation, and the subject 'I' feels the humiliation.[3] The perpetrator acts deliberately, though quite often impulsively, with the intent of discrediting a person or persons in ways they themselves value.

Time and the progression of events are also relevant considerations.[4] The time can be very short or long and drawn-out, depending on the sub-type. For example, the 'cataclysmic explosion' relies partly on the rapidity of execution for its effect. Consideration of the 'progression of events' reminds us that showings-up have careers.[5] They begin, typically, with the perception, on the part of the perpetrator, of some sort of deviance. Often such deviance is embedded in interactions which to the pupils represent a reasonable reflection of their expectations (for example it is not unreasonable to them, though it may be against the rules, that people talk in assembly). The perpetrator then interrupts these expectations. The situation is fractured, and people must re-define it and their expectations of others anew. The exposed person experiences an assault on his 'identity' and feels confusion, since his previous identity was the basis of others' expectations of him. There are a number of possible outcomes. He may, for example, try to in-validate the manoeuvre by parrying the assault, trying to turn the tables and exposing the teacher; or by attempting to redefine it as unserious, by, for instance, smiling, laughing or by some such indication to his fellows with the object of gaining group support.[6] At the other extreme a showing-up can have such a poignant impact that the bases of one's whole presentation of self are permanently damaged.[7] The degree of discredit is dependent on its reception; i.e. if the victim shows no signs

125

of confusion, the discredit will be less.[8] Hence the attempts to cover signs of confusion, the compounding of confusion by the manifestation of it (by which he loses social poise) and the actual accumulation of credit to persons who can conduct themselves through such incidents with aplomb.

Further characteristics of showings-up might be revealed by comparison with this definition of embarrassment:[9]

> Embarrassment occurs whenever some central assumption in a transaction has been *unexpectedly* and unqualifiably discredited for at least one participant. The result is that he is incapacitated for continued role performance. Moreover embarrassment is infectious. It may spread out, incapacitating others not previously incapacitated. It is a destructive disease. In the wreckage left by embarrassment lie the broken foundations of social transactions.

While we may accept the first part of the definition as being equally true of showings-up, it has certain other and different properties, arising mainly from its institutional situationing. Showings-up are not always unexpected. In fact in some ways the expectations can have more severe repercussions in terms of punishment than the actual deed. Again, showings-up may or may not be infectious. Others present may in fact contribute to, rather than share in, the embarrassment, especially if the person is unpopular. Classrooms develop their own norms, and frequently those of society in general cannot be applied. Thus it is not uncommon for people in classrooms to shout at one another, hit one another or try to embarrass one another. Also, in some instances where perpetrated as an act of deliberate policy, showings-up may be intended to be constructive, inasmuch as they aim to restore social order.

Functions

Gross and Stone mention three functions of deliberate embarrassment: (1) as socialization, (2) as a negative sanction and (3) as a means of establishing and maintaining power. Showings-up might have these functions, but they could also have at least two others: (4) as a means of motivation and (5) revenge. I will consider each in turn.

(1) Socialization

Particularly apt here is Mead's definition of socialization: 'not an internalization of norms and values, but a cultivated capacity to take the roles of others effectively'.[10] What keener way could there be of encouraging the development of this capacity than by involving the individual in a process which depends on his perceptions of others and which focuses on himself? Thus teachers might be considered as having a legitimate role here. And since much learning requires emphasis and repetition, they might be excused what at times may appear to be unreasonable or exaggerated styles.

We might say pupils must learn how to behave in society. In the questionnaire sent to all parents of children in the 3rd year at the school concerning subject choice, this was rated as one of the two chief aims of the school. Attitude-training is an important part of the curriculum. A pupil must learn what to expect of others so that he can measure his own behaviour against that predicted of others. His peers are important here too (and they are also quite good at showing-up), but the teacher as a more fully socialized member of society has a deeper and wider knowledge of those expectations.

(2) Negative sanction

Many of the incidents causing the showings-up are seen as a threat to order: in relation either directly to goals, for example where an individual submits a particularly bad piece of work, especially when it is common knowledge; or, and this is more frequent, in relation to conduct deemed likely to jeopardize the normal running of the school, the most common instance of which is infraction of the learning situation. Thus, to stop an outbreak of talking in assembly, a teacher might make use of an outburst directed against one person, relying on the shock waves to silence the rest. Or in class, by developing a reputation for showing people up, a teacher might rely on its deterrent effect to secure general order. Otherwise and more frequently, showings-up might be directed at one individual to stop him doing something, the teacher relying on the implicit or explicit support of others present. The philosophy seems to be that just as people attempt to hide physical deformities so they will hide behavioural deformities if they can be made sufficiently conscious of them.

(3) Establishing and maintaining power

The teacher is continually having to face challenges to his authority, and assaults on his power and status through subversive laughter, as discussed in chapter 5, and particularly through symbolic rebellion. The 'trying out' of new teachers by pupils, seeing 'how far they can go', is well attested in the literature.[11] In the formalized power structure of most of our secondary schools, teachers are regarded as fair game for this kind of sport. Pupils may play up through sheer devilment, to 'look big', to embarrass the teacher, or to provoke certain responses such as blushing or loss of temper.

Throwing missiles around the room, directing reflected sunlight onto the teacher's face, ventriloquizing his nickname while his back is turned are commonly known items in the pupils' repertoire. Arriving late for lessons, walking out of the room, talking back to the teacher are all infractions of the rules governing the teacher-pupil relationship, and are explicit denials of his authority. If, in reply, the teacher miscues by, for example taking no action at all, or showing some signs of confusion, or by over-reacting, i.e. by losing his temper and thus self-control, he loses status in the eyes of the class as a whole, while some gains in prestige among the pupils might accrue for the perpetrators. If he continues to miscue over a period, he will lose all power as teacher, and all prestige ('respect') in the pupils' eyes as a person.

In a very real sense the teacher is on a hiding to nothing in the traditional co-active teaching situation that obtains in most of our secondary schools. For he is set up as an individual against the group. He is the focus of attention, and he it is who is making demands on the group that may not accord with their wishes. For many a pupil he is the agent of an alien, authoritarian world who is continually challenging the pupil's conception of self. Pupils therefore seek to neutralize the situation by showing the *teacher* up. There are a number of counter-moves a teacher can make, but none more appropriate perhaps than by turning the tables on the pupil or pupils concerned, making capital out of the situation and instead of losing status, *gaining* it at *their* expense. Teachers, like pupils, make representations to themselves. They need to maintain status in their own eyes. This may lie behind the rhetoric of toughness and pupil flagellation that prevails in many staffrooms, which lends such solid support to techniques such as 'showing-up'.

(4) Motivation

Teachers might attempt to 'shame' pupils into better work or an attitude more conducive to it. Most frequently this is done on an individual basis, and there is no public humiliation. But sometimes it is done in front of others, to inspire them also.[12] The belittling may be by reference to age — 'a child of five could have done this' — or perhaps insinuations will be made about one's personal standards or conduct such as to discredit one's cultural milieu — 'You're too busy knocking about with that boyfriend of yours!' Sometimes a direct assault is made on one's attributes or capacities — 'You're thick, lad, you're thick!' Or the same may be implied by 'long-suffering' oaths ('Oh my God!') and facial contortions, indicating in vivid style to all present that the student in question falls ludicrously short of requirements. Groups can be shown up in attempts to influence other groups. Even in the absence of the victims, word can get back to them and they can feel publicly outraged. For example, teachers often talk about year-groups as entities having characters of their own. Thus there are good and bad years for pupils just as there are for wines. Sometimes a particular vintage may get publicly lampooned, as if to say to another year, 'Look how ridiculous and stupid they are, don't you get like that!' A 5th-year girl told me: 'The 3rds were told we were a rotten year, always mucking about, wouldn't get many passes and that. I didn't think that was very nice.' This neatly illustrates the ethical clash involved.

A common ploy with pupils of supposedly high status is to emphasize their deficiencies in front of their 'inferiors'. Thus prefects, or senior pupils who are not conforming in the required manner, may get shown up in front of junior pupils. Again the thrust of the manoeuvre is double edged, for by displaying the conduct of the senior pupils as discreditable, the teachers are informing the juniors, who otherwise might seek to emulate them, either that it is unworthy in itself, or that it earns this sort of punishment. And they are informing the senior pupils that if they wish to earn and maintain status they must conform, otherwise teachers might make inroads into their positions in the informal structure of the school.[13]

(5) Revenge

A showing-up may have the functions (1)-(4) in varying degrees; but at the time the object may simply be to give as much hurt as possible. In his 'teacher-training' chapter on discipline, Hargreaves suggests that many experienced teachers have a limited repertoire of techniques, and these are nearly all *punishments*, because they see disorder as a threat to their control and mastery and therefore as a personal affront.[14] 'Almost instinctively, therefore, counter-attack seems the best form of defence.'[15] Hargreaves introduces Schutz's distinction between motives and intentions.[16] Taking into account only the latter, the teacher frequently acts out of a spirit of 'angry revenge'.[17] In estimating what will convey most hurt, some might resort to blows; others will choose a form of words designed to inflict psychological harm. In a cultural sense, the latter might seem more appropriate, that is, it might seem more of an 'intellectual' response. Some teachers become extremely skilled at delivering this kind of riposte even though under pressure in the heat of the moment.

Some examples of showings-up

Perhaps the most sophisticated, appropriate and least unpleasant way of showing somebody up is by the use of wit. But this is a scarce resource, and more commonly sarcasm is employed. This is strongly disliked:

'I could not stand that subject. The teacher kept being nasty and sarcastic. He called us louts and said we all had lice, that was the sort of thing, in front of all the class . . . because we had long hair, we were dirty . . . just because he had not got none.' (3rd-year boy)

'Sarcasm' was frequently mentioned. But it was difficult to get illustrative data sufficient for a satisfactory definition. It frequently seems to contain a sneering, deprecatory quality, it reflects on a pupil's person (as opposed to his role as pupil), and carries hurtful intent at least as perceived by the pupil.

The following extracts from a talk with four 5th-year boys illustrate some of these points, and also compare the 'mock' showing-up, which is pleasurable rather than hurtful, with the real thing:

PW: What are they like, these teachers that you don't like?
Andrew: Sarcastic.
Roy: One especially. Say you do something, then next day, say you don't do your homework or something, he will completely change round.
PW: Is that sarcasm?
Andrew: Well I don't mind sarcasm in a friendly way but when he means it I can't stick 'im.
PW: What do you mean?
Andrew: Well, another teacher, he's sarcastic but in a friendly way again, you know. We can all have a laugh with him, but can't with this other one.
Eric: He shows you up in front of the class.
Ian: You don't feel free with him, do you?
Andrew: He's not easy to get on with.

It is when an individual is singled out for 'shock' treatment that maximum feeling is aroused:

Christine: I don't like that subject because I can't stand the teacher. I've never really liked him since I got caught skiving, and he made that right fool of me, and I sat next to Kevin . . . Don't you remember? . . . When I was at the back of the class . . . Do you remember? . . . I've never been so bright red in all my life.
PW: What did he say?
Christine: Oh nothing. I'm not telling you.
PW: Come on, tell us what he said.

Christine: I was sitting next to Kevin, and he'd got this cartridge in his pen and he was going like that (*she indicates an obscene gesture*), and I just pushed him away, and the teacher was writing on the board and he must have eyes in the back of his head . . . and he says . . . he turns round with a fuming face and he says 'Will you two stop fiddling with each other!' I never went so bright red in all my life, and he pushed me over one side and him on the other . . . and everybody turned round, didn't they? . . . In front of all my friends! you know . . . he made such a . . . mockery . . . can't stand him! Everybody was scared stiff in that class, everyone just sits there, all quiet.

This vividly portrays the consumer's experience and a common teacher problem. So acutely had she felt the embarrassment that she found it very difficult to relate, but having started almost by accident, she responded to her three friends present, and addressed most of her remarks to them.[18] There was no doubting the intensity of the hostility felt towards the teacher in question, chiefly based on that one incident. According to Christine's account, she was the victim of both Kevin and teacher. With Kevin, however, it was privatized. The teacher made the matter public, implied illicit sexual activity (thus exploding one of the stanchions supporting Christine's presentation of self to her friends, viz. her moral propriety) very plausibly to others, perhaps because the pair were sitting at the back unseen, and everyone discontinued activity to turn around and gaze. This sudden transformation of position *vis-à-vis* others, from being at the back one moment to being at the front the next, is a necessary feature of the 'shock' show-up. That her closest friends were present made things worse, and that it was a 'mockery' of what had actually been happening compounded her sense of injustice.

The following extract from a discussion with four 3rd-year girls suggests that 'showing-up' is a commonly used technique in this school, and not a rare event; and how the embarrassment can be compounded by inter-sex rivalry.

PW: Are there any bad things about school?
Alison: Being put on report . . . getting into trouble.
PW: Do you get into trouble a lot?
Alison: Yeah, mostly from Mr Black, like today. I came in late.
PW: What's so bad about getting into trouble?
Alison: I go red.
PW: It embarrasses you, does it?
Alison: Yeah.
Kay: Yeah, all the teachers embarrass you! All the boys *look* . . . horrible it is . . . horrible.
PW: Give us an example.

Kay: One of my friends . . . a teacher belted her ever so hard and she started crying and all the boys started picking on her . . . calling her a baby.

PW: Do you think teachers show you up on purpose?

Kay: They probably think if they show us up we won't do it again because we're so embarrassed.

Implicit in all these showings-up is the 'display', even though the people concerned may not alter position. Some techniques used in schools make the display explicit, and economize perhaps on words and gestures. These follow the format of degradation rituals.[19] 'Standing out at the front' or 'on chairs', for example, is designed to preserve order amongst the mass by fear of embarrassment. This is a frequent occurrence in ritualized ceremonials, such as assemblies. In these formal and closely regulated public meetings nothing succeeds in restoring order better than the explosion directed at one individual and its accompanying shock-wave. Quite often, because of the depersonification of the occasion and the associated nature of the showing-up (which is likely to be a very sudden, sharp and loud command, full of sinister implications such as 'Wilson! Go and stand outside my room'), embarrassment is sharp, but brief. The individual is more likely to feel his emotions rising when reflecting on the *justice* of the matter. This accords with Lemert's suggestion that:[20]

> Degradation rituals . . . may dramatize the facts of deviance, but their 'success' is gauged less by their manner of enactment than by their prevailing consequence . . . The ancient ceremonial . . . may strike [the accused] with awe and fear, but if nothing much happens as a consequence, the memory fades or is retrospectively rationalized.

Degradation ceremonies are the symbol of order and authority. It is the multitude that counts, and the individual who is the scapegoat.

As a matter of policy, the headmaster in his address might seek to discredit an individual in the eyes of the multitude. One example that came my way concerned a 3rd-year boy, widely recognized as a deviant and leader of a group. The head had summoned him to talk about an offence, then the next day in assembly represented him as 'a boy who had gone to the head and "complained" about certain matters'.

Thus the leader of a deviant group was made to appear something of a 'creep', one of the most despicable types according to the group sub-culture. The boy concerned recounted this to me with great feeling. It is a good example of how to show up a deviant — it is no use abusing him in more customary ways!

Who does, and who doesn't, get shown up

Not all pupils are treated the same. There is a tendency among teachers
− very human and therefore difficult to detect and counteract − to
reward (in the fullest sense of the term; i.e. in continual day-to-day
interactions) those who conform most closely to the ideal pupil role as
they perceive it, and to punish those who deviate a long way from it.
This is quite well known. Lacey, for example, presents incidents to
illustrate that 'teacher behaviour, conditioned by the reputation of the
pupil, is one of the central factors producing differentiation'.[21] Hargreaves also discusses the categorization of pupils, a process which
'provides the plan for all future interaction between the two parties'.[22]

In relation to the phenomenon under discussion, there are two contrasting groups which predominate in pupils' perceptions of teacher-
pupil relations. There are first, 'pets' and 'creeps' (the 'ingratiators'
discussed in chapter 3), and second, those who get 'picked on'. In any
group, whether streamed or not, there are likely to be some of each.
The number of them, and who they are, might vary from teacher to
teacher, but usually there is a hard core of each. It is the latter who are
far more likely to get shown up, of course, as indeed to receive any
kind of punishment. In fact, in a sense, the two terms are synonymous.
To be 'picked on' is to be singled out, unjustly, for unfavourable
treatment, perhaps because of a teacher's dislike or perhaps simply
because he needs a scapegoat.

'Picked-ons' are usually 'known' deviants. Somehow or other, rightly
or wrongly, they have acquired reputations. Their behaviour is 'predictable'. Teachers have a great deal of police work to do, and in the work
of detection they have not always the time, nor would it necessarily
always be best policy, to conduct discreet enquiries. Moreover, they
need to maintain their own 'success' image. 'Good' teachers are those
who can keep order, and this involves knowing always everything that
is going on, and spotting the miscreants − or at least appearing to do so.
The rise or fall of many a deputy headmaster hangs on whether he can
carry off a successful 'police' image. Pressures of status, self-esteem and
good order demand that he find solutions. 'Picked-ons', in a sense,
offer themselves up for the slaughter.

Apart from the attribution of blame for deviant acts, teachers might
also interpret similar behaviour from 'pets' and 'picked-ons' in very
different ways. This is well attested in the literature.[23] The teacher's
problem in dispensing pure justice is compounded by unscrupulous
pupils, as the following extract from a talk with three 5th-year boys
shows:

Robert: In the classroom they'd tell us to get out and we'd ignore
them. Or they'd tell you to do a detention and we wouldn't go.

We swore at them — I got sent to the head for that — and we just said they were picking on us and we got fed up and swore at them. He just told us off.

PW: Were they picking on you?

Robert: No, we were just mucking about, they weren't really picking on us.

Results of showings-up

If effectively performed, showings-up might seem extraordinarily functional as far as immediate appearances are concerned. The sudden and complete transformation from general disorder to complete silence; the blushing and confusion of an individual who has threatened the teacher's authority; the ridicule of his peers; the self-satisfaction experienced; the deference shown by pupils who never challenge the teacher or misbehave in any way — all these would appear to testify to their effectiveness. But there have been hints throughout this chapter that this is more apparent than real.

Certainly what work we have on such matters breeds scepticism. Hargreaves, for instance, talks of a 'punishment illusion'.[24] A pupil might be stunned or humiliated into silence, but may smoulder in such resentment that he awaits the next opportunity for his revenge. Redl also distinguished between 'surface' and 'deeper' behaviour.[25] Are the pressures on teachers such as to direct their attention almost exclusively to the first to the detriment of the latter? Interestingly, Kounin in his experimental study found that the only correlation in his sample for both high and low motivated students concerning a desist that contained anger, was with some felt 'emotional discomfort', but not 'attention' or 'conformity'.[26]

My study also suggests that the more short-term the aims, the better the chance of success. For example, I witnessed many instances of the 'shock-wave' effect following an explosive showing-up designed to restore order at that particular moment. Individuals have ostensibly been changed from troublesome deviants to silent conformists. What is not so clear is how the pupils actually interpret these interactions, and whether the outcomes accord with the aims, or whether the long-term effects invalidate the short-term. Certainly those narrated to me were experienced with much bitterness.

There are two points I would like to make concerning these results. First, taking them at their face value, they are a good illustration of those perennial teacher problems of resolving instrumental and expressive, and particular and universal aims. The teacher might value expressive relationships and individuals, but above all, the school must be run, order maintained and his subject must be taught. In these interests, the individual might occasionally be sacrificed. What then are the effects for the individual? Showings-up can lead to a devaluation of the self. As Rose has suggested, employing Mead and Cooley's conception of the self:[27]

> A depreciated or 'mutilated' self is a major factor in the development of a neurosis . . . because an individual's ability to accept strongly held views of any kind and to act effectively to achieve those values is a function of his conception of himself — a conception that he is an adequate, worth-while, effective, and appreciated person.

I am not suggesting that most showings-up are so serious as to produce neuroses. They might do so, if kept up over any length of time, and especially if reinforced by the subject's peers. Most pupils seem able to draw strength from the group in their definition of self and of the situation, and instead of internalizing the humiliation, project it back onto the teacher in a feeling of intense dislike. It is for teachers to decide whether the restoration of order, the reinforcement of status, the quashing of the obnoxious individual and so on, is fair exchange.

The second point is this: if we accept a conflict model of teaching, such manifestations of tension and hostility may be a necessary feature of teacher-pupil interactions. They may be functional in that they provide relief mechanisms for the outlet of such tensions. Thus the showing-up may be one of a number of ways in which the teacher externalizes and defuses the conflict, just as the relating of it, together with all the other ways he tries to get at the teacher, does the same for the pupil.

There is conflict, certainly, in most teaching situations. There is an air of ritual about many interactions, as already noted, which suggests heavily structured situations. But it does not account for those teachers and classrooms where conflict does not occur; nor does it account for those conflicts which supersede the ritualized norm and which could not, by any stretch of the imagination, be considered as contributing to the stability of the institution. We need to look more closely at those teachers who habitually use the technique.

Who does the showing-up?

Not all teachers employ this technique. Perhaps there are schools that are entirely free of it. This is because, I suggest, 'showing-up', like corporal punishment, is associated with certain conditions, attitudes and ideologies which in turn support certain systems of rule. I will outline some of their main features here in relation to showing-up, preparatory to considering the teachers in more detail in chapter 7.

Several typologies of teaching have been presented recently.[28] The type which we are interested in, prominent in all of them, is what is often referred to as 'traditional' teaching. Hammersley calls it 'discipline-based' teaching and describes it thus:[29]

There is an authoritative teacher role legitimated in terms of and based on a curriculum. The teacher role is relatively narrowly defined and the orientation to pupils is characterized by universalism, a concern with product and a high degree of control of pupil action. The pupil is seen as an apprentice adult, his behaviour tends to be conceptualized in terms of an individualistic vocabulary of motives, and human nature is considered recalcitrant material. A definite curriculum is involved, knowledge is objective and universally valid, is hierarchically structured and is contained by distinct disciplines. Learning is seen as essentially an individual, competitive activity, as involving hearing about and reproducing some segment of the teacher's knowledge, and as requiring for its occurrence the teacher's mobilization of extrinsic rewards. The learning path pupils are to follow is conceived as external and pupils must be channelled along it, they would not follow it 'naturally', they would not 'learn' without direction. Preferred and predominant techniques are formal organization of the classroom, constant supervision and frequent intervention, the use of imperatives and positional appeals, class tests and grouping by age and ability.

The basic assumptions are:
(1) Knowledge is objective, bounded and 'out there'.[30]
(2) The child has a finite amount of intelligence or 'capacity'. Likewise he has other attributes which can be clearly labelled.
(3) Teaching therefore consists of fitting (1) into (2), and pedagogy is designed and school organized to facilitate this.
(4) The teacher is fully acquainted with (1), and has the expertise for (3).
(5) The child has a moral responsibility to seek to fulfil his capacity, and the teacher has a moral responsibility to provide the means for him to do it.
(6) However (if social Darwinism is added), the child is innately socially irresponsible, and therefore needs to be motivated to learn and to conform.
The emphasis on matters of control and discipline, the periodic expressions of conflict, the explicitness of the authority structure of the school follow from these premisses. So do certain systems of rule, such as paternalism.

The two key elements in *pater*'s position are (a) infallibly knowing what is good for those he governs, and (b) dispensing it in ways he chooses on the grounds of superior expertise. For the governed it follows logically from (a) that they are bound to benefit as long as they are loyal and obedient. Infractions of the latter invalidate the contract (in which the government, of course, has acted for both sides). Thus, in the case of infractions, the benevolence disappears and the deviants are punished in ways designed to remind them — and others — of the superiority of their mentors. Showing-up is a way of cutting down to size more in keeping with the spirit of this system of rule than detentions, reports, and even corporal punishment. If the victim accepts the humiliation, the contract will be restored and the benevolence return. Often a kindly remark or deed will follow a hurtful one, as long as the pupil is duly penitent.

Thus the showing-up technique is possibly the product of a system of beliefs which dictates how a teacher regards his pupils. This system has been around for a long time, but during the last thirty or forty years there have been profound changes in the teacher's raw material, and it is this which helps to make features of school such as showing-up such big issues for pupils today. A generation or two ago, pupils may have been more conditioned to accept the consequences. Since then we have gone through a period of 'child liberation' promoted by two concurrent factors. One is the quite enormous changes in child-rearing practices, focused on greater liberty, fewer rules, punishments and jobs;[31] the other is the consigning of a new status to teenagers by the business section of society in recognition of that greater liberty, and of a new economic independence.[32] All this provides a conception of self very much different from that of the pupil of thirty or forty years ago. It is one not inured to adult dominance and ridicule; on the contrary, it is hypersensitive to such assaults. The nascent conflict between teacher and pupil becomes then a clash of cultures to which there is no solution.[33] It has many manifestations. Pupils must not smoke; but mum hands the cigarettes round after tea. Pupils should conform to school regulations on dress and appearance which usually condemn all marks of individuality and require uniformity in accordance with the 'good pupil' image: the external pressures on the pupil stress individuality and for the teenager a sophistication quite out of character with the humble pupil role. Pupils are expected to be obedient, respectful and to accept the teacher's authority without question; elsewhere, they are encouraged to reason and to speak their minds. Thus pupils exposed to this pedagogical paradigm find powerful pressures being exerted on them to perform two quite distinct, and frequently contradictory, roles.

Some schools supporting this paradigm display some of the features of 'total institutions' quite prominently. Of particular interest to my theme is the 'mortification' of inmates:[34]

The recruit comes into the establishment with a conception of himself made possible by certain stable social arrangements in his home world. Upon entrance, he is immediately stripped of the support provided by these arrangements . . . he begins a series of abusements, degradations, humiliations, and profanations of self. His self is systematically if often unintentionally, mortified.

The insistence on austere uniforms, compulsory games, forced deference patterns, the opening up of hitherto private areas of the self (and their consignment to posterity in school records), forced social relationships, regimentation, the authority structure, the rules and punishments, especially if they include beatings and humiliations, could all be interpreted as mortification of the self. Further,[35]

> total institutions disrupt or defile precisely those actions that in civil society have the role of attesting the actor and those in his presence that he has some command over his world – that he is a person with 'adult' self-determination, autonomy and freedom of action.

The pressing problem of schools today is that so much education is lacking relevance. It remains outside the experience of the mass of the people, unrelated to their personal and human development. It applies to teachers as well as to pupils. Here is one form of it:[36]

> The content of lessons for the exam-orientated is seen as externally determined and inevitable. Any attempt by teachers at involving the pupils in decisions is seen either as weakness or as duplicity, since the teachers themselves are not thought to be free agents in the education process, the final arbiters of which are the 'O' level and CSE examiners. While this feeling is obviously weaker among pupils in the first two or three years of secondary school it is quite often passed on to them by parents who incline to be suspicious of too much 'freedom'. In this deeper sense pupils and parents who are committed to education are actually more alienated than those who openly reject it. Both groups perceive education as something 'outside' which can be borne for an ulterior reward and which may be rejected; but the rejectors at least have a genuine relation to such 'education': they despise it. Generally they consider that life is for living – at least when you're young. Education, as purveyed by schools and colleges, is an imposition, something that comes between you and living. Fulfilment is seen in terms of getting what you can when you can, of making the most of your bodily needs, for your mind is seldom your own. How can it be when you have no access to any decisions that matter? 'Things of the mind' are not seen as despicable, unless imposed in school: simply, they are irrelevant.

But not only pupils and parents are 'alienated' in this sense, for teachers are not the autonomous perpetrators of such 'education'. Teachers also, as I shall show in the next two chapters, are not engaged in a vocational activity of 'pure education' but, rather, a forced activity of 'survival' and 'professionalism'. 'Showing-up' is a kind of 'survival strategy' (discussed more fully in chapter 7). The conditions responsible result from the exigencies of the situation, and the means for the resolution of the problem are guided by one's pedagogical orientation.

Chapter 7

The hidden pedagogy of survival

It would be sensible to summarize the argument to date.

Divisions in school result, first, from its linkages with social structure. Society is divided, and to a certain extent teachers are forced into reproducing these divisions. Pupils aid their own stratification through group perspectives, and the supporting frameworks of these perspectives are driven further in by teacher policy and school organization. Divisions also result from institutionalization. Pupils 'adapt' to school in various ways, but many lead a 'double' life as 'pupil' and as 'person'. They themselves recognize instinctively the distinguishing features of the bureaucratic institution in the form of rules, routine, hierarchy and so on, and detect a similar division in teachers too, between what we might call teacher-bureaucrats, those whose teacher-styles are governed by the school's rational and bureaucratic processes, and teacher-persons, those whose images are governed by more humane considerations. There is an undercurrent of dissatisfaction about these divisions, but nonetheless a certain resignation, a feeling of 'that's the way it is'. That is the arena in which they have to work out their adaptations, and they do it. Occasionally the two arenas, pupil and personal, public and private, merge to mutual advantage as in 'warm' teacher-pupil relationships or collide, as in 'showing-up', and heavy conflict is produced.

These pupil divisions are mirrored among the teachers. They also instinctively distinguish between public and private, between professional and lay, and they also 'adapt' to school. As 'professionals' they are part of the technocratic apparatus of society. The rationalization of the world, and the growth of technological production and the social processes connected with it, have led to the development and consolidation of a structure of society and a consciousness which mirrors it, based on a belief in the omniscience of technical solutions, and a regime of experts trained and dedicated to providing them. Teachers are such experts. In the systematization of life that is such a prominent feature of the technocratic society, they control the passages from one arena to another. They alone know what it takes. Their area of untouchable competence is in the elaborate forms of certification and all that that implies in the processing of people through these gateways – CSEs, 'O' levels, apprenticeships, references. This is the teacher's area of competence. Just as doctors diagnose bodily health, vicars spiritual health or lawyers legal health, so teachers diagnose and minister to mental and personality health in the sense of fitness for job and for life. They are masters of mental and personality symptoms in a way that parents, or others unconnected in any direct sense with the certification process, cannot be.

However, they do not perform their professional duties in a vacuum. Their actual performance can be held to depend on other factors – resources, freedom, co-operation, conducive atmosphere and so on. Yet it is part of the ethos of professionalism never to admit to error. It is impervious to default, infallible and incontrovertible in its judgments, and those are 'facts', not dimensions. As the supportive factors grow less supportive, indeed begin to oppress, the reality of the teacher's job begins to change by degrees, until eventually, although he still gives the impression of teaching and is still attended by the professional aura, he is actually doing something else. It is a commonplace to say that we all do our jobs 'as best we can', and that in aiming for an ideal we inevitably fall short of it. That implies, however, a unidirection of aim. The goal is not in question; our efforts to reach it are merely conditioned by attendant factors. But in the case of teachers in the modern secondary school state system, of which Lowfield is a typical example, there *is* a change of goal on occasions among the staff, when the 'transmission of knowledge' or 'preparation for exams' gives way to more personal considerations of security and ease. The teacher cannot do his professional job without the right conditions. So he falters in this field, without, however, appearing to do so, thus creating the hidden pedagogy of survival. Lest this sound unduly condemnatory of teachers as lacking in dedication or worthiness in some way, let me say immediately that I am not passing judgment, merely seeking to construct a framework which will adequately explain my observations of and conversations with teachers at Lowfield and my own experience of teaching. In fact, as we shall see, my analysis of the constraints on teachers portrays them in the ever-tightening grip of a powerful pincer-movement, with 'professional demands' on one side, and 'recalcitrant material' in the form of reluctant or resentful pupils on the other, with shrinking aid or the ability to resist either. In the crush, the kernel of their real job, teaching, is lost, and only the cracked shell of their personal defences remains. Teachers labour to piece it together, and as is the nature of repaired shells, it can appear deceptively full.

This might be regarded, then, as one kind of mode of adaptation to circumstances that assail teachers. But there is another, equally as strong, and, as with pupils and their highly variable experience, it is the opposite of the trauma often accompanying the grim struggle for survival in the classroom. For teachers 'have their laughs' also. I refer not simply to casual chuckling, pleasantries, or the occasional joke or leg-pull. In the Lowfield staffroom, as in several others of my acquaintance, laughter was clearly something special, and it was quite separate from other activity. The customary sociological accounts of laughter were insufficient to explain this. It needed a broader backcloth. It might seem a long way from ribbing the headmaster to the technological society, but the connection is crucial. Laughter is the elixir by which teacher becomes person once more, and humanity and confidence is restored after the affliction to the person caused by the rationalizing, bureaucratic processes connected with the teaching task, and by the crushing and humiliating struggle for survival. This squares with the pupils' observations of teachers discussed in earlier chapters.

These three divisions, then, teachers as professionals, as survivors and as persons, represent one way of viewing the bulk of teacher activity in all its manifestations at school, and is suggestive, as was the pupil analysis, of certain links with society which I shall explore more fully in chapter 10. In the remainder of this chapter I shall examine the survival aspect of teacher activity. This involves a consideration of the conditions in which they work, and their association with their work, and these establish the reference points for the splintering of their school activity. I shall examine the manifest professional role in chapter 8, and teachers as persons in chapter 9.

An interactionist model of teaching

Institutions, once established, generate a certain momentum and interdependence. The establishment, development and gradual expansion of compulsory education and the drive since the last war for equality of educational opportunity created an ethos of beneficence about the education system, which has only been seriously disputed within the last decade. This disputation was the product of developments in society which were to bring into question the structures on which the education systems of industrialized societies rested – the changes accompanying advanced technology, the nature of work, upheavals of class and community cultures, the extension of the media, 'affluence', shifting definitions of morality, changes in child-rearing patterns and the growth of the social sciences. However, at the same time that the system was coming under attack, it was still, of course, receiving substantial support from within. Changes in structure, such as comprehensive education, and new developments in educational theory, notably child-centredness, were adaptations to the changing social scene, which carried an air of healthy reformism to those within, though it was rhetoric and reification to those without.

Now, one way to explain the resistance of the system to radical change is to see it as the agent of the capitalist state. It is then dependent on economic forces and structures in society, and only changes in those structures can bring about any real changes in the education system. Another way to explain it is to view it as the product of institutional momentum. We can secure a more interactional viewpoint which would allow the actors more autonomy and furthermore enable us to make distinctions among the actors, by introducing the notion of commitment. I refer to the term as used by Kanter:[1]

> Commitment is a consideration which arises at the intersection of organizational requisites and personal experience. On the one hand, social systems organize to meet systemic 'needs'; and on the other hand, people orient themselves positively and negatively, emotionally and intellectually, to situations. Since social orders are supported by people, one problem of collectivities is to meet organizational requisites in such a way that participants at the same time become positively involved with the system — loyal, loving, dedicated, and obedient. This requires solutions to organizational or systemic problems that are simultaneously mechanisms for ensuring commitment through their effects on individuals — their experience and orientations. Commitment, then, refers to the willingness of social actors to give their energy and loyalty to social systems, the attachment of personality systems to social relations which are seen as self-expressive.

This is particularly useful in my analysis, for, as Kanter has observed, it links maintenance of the self with maintenance of the system. We might regard institutional momentum as the collective sum of commitment of all the actors within the institution.

One of the major social system problems involving the commitment of actors is its continuance as an action system. This involves cognitive orientations bearing on profits and costs, and generally implies commitment to a social system role. 'The individual who makes a cognitive-continuance commitment finds that what is profitable to him is bound up with his position in the organisation, is contingent on his participating in the system.'[2] There is a profit in his remaining there and a deficit associated with leaving. Continuance is accompanied by 'sacrifice' and 'investment' processes. As a price of membership, members give up something, make sacrifices, which in turn *increases* commitment. So does investment, which promises future gain in the organization. The member takes out shares in the proceeds of the organization and thus has a stake in its future. He channels his expectations along the organization's path, and the more he does so, the more he increases the distance between this and other possibilities. They grow more remote as his commitment grows larger. In this way the process is self-validating, self-reinforcing and frequently irreversible. The member goes on further to lay down what Becker calls 'side-bets' as other, unanticipated, sources of reward appear, once the line of action has been chosen.[3]

Another process accompanying commitment is what I will term *accommodation*. This refers to the solving or riding of problems thrown up by the organization so as effectively to neutralize the threat to the actor's continuance in it. One of the most common techniques of accommodation is rationalization, which frequently follows decision-making. What previously might have been perceived as problems are explained away once a course of action has been chosen, and often reappear as benefits.

Continuance commitment among teachers is strong. It's their job — they are not trained for any other. Investment takes the form of career-bound choices — doing certain jobs, such as the timetable, accepting certain roles, taking courses. Also, the sorts of trials a teacher goes through in his first one or two years of teaching are a kind of initiation rite, a matter of pride to those who have successfully negotiated them. Sacrifice is considerable — alternative careers and the pleasures and profits associated with them. Once embarked on teaching, few turn back or alter course. Perhaps the large demands in commitment that teaching makes help to explain why so many opt out at training stage.[4]

Contributing towards institutional momentum is institutional development, reformist educational theory and much teaching tradition. A great deal of the latter already involves much 'accommodation' to perennial constraints and difficulties thrown up by such matters as the teacher-pupil ratio, the length of the teaching day, week and year, resources, such as book provision, buildings, compulsory education and examinations. While we cannot deny that generally conditions in schools have improved over the last hundred years, it is equally true that in some respects, in terms of demand on teachers' accommodation capacity, they have worsened in recent years. The leaving age has been raised, and though the 11+ has largely disappeared, 16+ examinations have become even more the yardstick by which secondary schools shall be judged, and, since CSE was begun, many more pupils have become involved. Further, it seems likely that in the foreseeable future the teacher-pupil ratio will increase and resources in general diminish.

Concerning reformist educational theory and institutional development, the teacher operates within a climate of dynamic change. The growth of departments, institutes and colleges of education, of the social sciences and their application to education, of in-service training, of general interest in and recognition of the importance of education have contributed to this. While theories about comprehensive education, mixed-ability teaching, the integrated day, Newsom courses, child-centred education, progressivism and so on also pressurize him to adapt further. Support of, and attachment to, these theories is itself, of course, a product of societal developments but all, or nearly all, are framed within the same institutional context and assume its continuance.

With regard to the trend of societal developments such as I spoke of earlier, the social consequences of technological growth are manifested for the teacher most prominently in the nature of his clientele. Musgrove has likened the school system to a 'network of bear pits'.[5] Webb found the teachers of Black School distinguished by fatigue, and hence motivated by the avoidance of circumstances that might add to it, and *fear* — fear that 'playground chaos' would spill over into the classroom.[6] That picture has become much more common today and the problems deeper and more diverse. Every week there is talk in the educational press of growing rates of violence and truancy in the schools. And there is much teacher disillusionment. One rank-and-file member told Musgrove, for example, 'because of the pressures teachers work under, because of the system, they find they have no real control over how they teach and how they carry out the job. And this is a very degrading experience.'[7]

I conclude, therefore, that the pressures on the teacher's accommodation capacities have increased, are increasing, and are likely to go on increasing. But, of course the pressures differ according to (a) type of school — there are enormous differences among secondary schools as well as between secondary and primary, and (b) teacher commitment — the less the commitment, the less the accommodation problem. If we envisage for a moment a teacher in the most besieged situation — strongly committed, but having to cope with a number of difficult classes — his problem might be construed as a crisis wherein the whole basis of his commitment may be called into question. The investments and sacrifices he has made, the side-bets he has laid down, are all at risk. He faces career bankruptcy. It is, in short, a *survival* problem. What is at risk is not only his physical, mental and nervous safety and well-being, but also his continuance in professional life, his future prospects, his professional identity, his way of life, his status, his self-esteem, all of which are the product of an accumulating investment process. Because of the concomitant sacrifices, for most people there is no second chance, no closing down and investing in another career. Teachers are stuck, and must do as best they can. They cannot leave their positions, they cannot change the social order, they therefore must adapt. They must accommodate these problems. Where the problems are numerous and intense, accommodation will prevail over teaching. In easier circumstances, the teacher can concentrate more on educational interests. However, it is not quite as clear cut as that. The problems are of such a nature, the teacher's commitment so complete, his position so circumscribed, that accommodation requires considerable ingenuity. It can, as I shall demonstrate, 'double' or masquerade as 'education'. I should make clear that I am talking of 'education' here as 'the transmission of knowledge', the model overwhelmingly subscribed to by all the teachers at Lowfield.

Survival strategies

Teachers accommodate by developing and using survival strategies. Normative means of control enshrined in the punishment structure are quite inadequate. They are after all devised for normative children. It is the kind of control one needs in order to teach. And survival, of course, involves more than simply control, though that is an important part of it. I define control in this instance as successfully dealing with incident which fractures the teacher's peace, or establishing one's power in a situation which pre-empts such an occurrence. We can illustrate this by the techniques Waller observed teachers using to secure control: (1) command; (2) punishment; (3) management or manipulation of personal and group relationships; (4) temper; (5) appeal.[8] These can be subsumed under more general strategies; for example, command, punishment and temper are all features of the general survival strategy which I term 'domination'; the others, of the general survival strategy of 'negotiation'. But these are only two out of eight survival strategies that I have observed in our secondary schools. The other six are socialization, fraternization, absence or removal, ritual and routine, occupational therapy, and morale-boosting. If control is conceived of as the handling of incident, survival includes that, but also involves the avoidance of incident, the masking or disguising of incident, the weathering of incident and the neutralizing of incident.

A feature of successful survival strategies is their permanence and ongoing refinement. They contain the seeds of their own continuance and growth, often outliving their usefulness, and festering, causing another problem for which another survival strategy must be devised. They do not take a problem out of the arena, as it were, leaving more room for teaching. Rather, they expand into teaching and around it, like some parasitic plant, and eventually in some cases the host might be completely killed off. However, like parasites, if they kill off the host, they are a failure and they must die too, for they stand starkly revealed for what they are. The best strategies are those that allow a modicum of education to seep through. Alternatively, they will appear *as* teaching, their survival value having a higher premium than their educational value. Theoretically, it is not difficult to point up the difference:[9]

> the intention of all teaching activities is that of bringing about learning . . . If therefore a teacher spends the whole afternoon in activities the concern of which is not that the pupils should learn . . . he cannot have been teaching at all. In these terms, it could be the case that quite a large number of professional teachers are in fact frauds most of their lives because their intentions are never clear . . . [they] may be lost in a welter of secondary intentions.

The term 'frauds', though technically correct, carries unfortunate moral connotations. My analysis shifts responsibility largely from the teacher to the situation in which he finds himself. The factors of which I have spoken have led to teachers suffering from 'a crippling sense of uncertainty about what they are for'.[10] This is how I would conceive of many of the paradoxes in the teachers' situation in Sharp and Green's study school. Only their commitment with its capacity for accommodation keeps them going. And the immediacy of the survival problem, as Jackson has noted, determines the action.[11] I want to emphasize this situationist point. Deutscher has stated the extreme case:[12]

> The social situation is a notion which is different in kind from the constructs culture, social structure and personality. These gross abstract forces not only provide little understanding of why people behave as they do in everyday life, but, unlike the social situation they are fictions constructed by the social scientist; none of them, in fact, exists . . . These concepts are all inventions, myths, fantasies, which often blind the analyst to the very real constraints imposed by the immediate situation in which the actor finds himself.

Becker also stresses the importance of the situation with regard to personal change in his notion of 'situational adjustment', whereby the individual turns himself into the kind of person the situation demands.[13]

> If we view situational adjustment as a major process of personal development, we must look to the character of the situation for the explanation of why people change as they do. We ask what there is in the situation that requires the person to act in a certain way or to hold certain beliefs. We do not ask what there is in him that requires the action or belief. All we need to know of the person is that for some reason or another he desires to continue his participation in the situation, or to do well in it.

Clearly I would not want to write off 'structure' as completely as Deutscher seems to do, since I am concerned to account for the situation in wider forces. But if we are to understand behaviour we must examine thoroughly the circumstances a person finds himself in, and his own perspectives on it.

One work which illustrates how teachers' perceptions of pupils contribute to this is that by Jenks.[14] The teachers in the primary school that he studied characterized most of their pupils as 'difficult'. Consequently they distinguished among them according to their 'controllability'. 'Thus the strategy of coping with the present situation involves a central notion of control, usually exercised as silence: this is what is sought often, and against this success in the classroom is measured.' Control became an important part of the curriculum. Instead of a curriculum of writing, spelling and maths, it became writing and control; spelling and control; maths and control. 'Child-centred' methods were considered inappropriate by the older teachers for *that* type of child. Similarly, Denscombe noticed in two London comprehensive schools that 'the aim of motivating the unmotivated appeared to owe as much to the practical attempt to avoid disruption in the classroom as to any pedagogic "ideology".'[15] On teachers' own accounts, 'pupil motivation in the practical context of teaching was of concern in a manner which transcended and was analytically distinct from "progressive" or "traditional" perspectives on education.'[16] Their competence as teachers was accordingly judged by their 'capacity to secure for themselves quiet orderliness in "their" classroom', the actual task structure of teaching involving 'the prevention of noise emanating from the classroom without recourse to help from other members of staff.'[17]

Sharp and Green also suggest that the 'notion of "child directed learning" is related to the categorization of the pupils via the control problems presented to the teacher in [an] open fluid context.' There are 'bright' pupils who are easily 'biddable' and dull ones, who are difficult to motivate. The teacher's solution to this problem of engaging all the pupils in work is 'busyness', where[18]

> children do something which they have chosen and are thus engaged in activity without requiring the constant attention which the teacher is unable to give them. To the teacher there is a logical relationship between the notion of busyness, her educational philosophy and her actions. However, there is also a contingent relation in that the situation is objectively given in the sense of the limitation of her time-space resources.

It is these contingencies that threaten to predominate in many schools. Westbury has observed:[19]

> The interaction between the demands on the classroom and the constraints within it cause it to be a social setting that has only limited potentiality for manipulation by teachers. The recitation is a teaching strategy that permits teachers to deal, in at least a minimally

satisfactory way, with the tensions that this interaction between demands and constraints creates; it has persisted through the fifty years that Hoetker and Ahlbrand have explored because the fundamental characteristics of the classroom that have made the recitation adaptive to the needs of teachers have persisted through these fifty years.

Westbury, however, concludes that 'the classroom does not alter the essential character of these teaching tasks, but it makes their execution more complex.' This provides us with a more humane view of traditional pedagogical processes such as formal teaching, question and answer and so on, whose inadequacies as educational vehicles are more usually simply exposed. It is what Westbury calls a *coping strategy*. However, survival entails more than coping, and I would contend that it does quite often alter the essential character of teaching tasks. Significantly, Westbury only takes into account rather mechanical or demographic constraints, such as rooms, desks, resources, *numbers* of pupils, within a general context of these other constraints. What we have to inject into this model is a more dynamic factor, namely the nature of the pupils, within the general context of these other constraints, which materially represents the pull of societal forces; together with an element of teacher creativity.[20]

I want now to give some illustrations of survival strategies that I noted during my year at Lowfield. I try to show in these illustrations how pervasive the survival aim is, as opposed to other aims that have been imputed, such as educating for 'social control' or 'educating for democracy' in some cases; lack of interest or anomie, for example, in others.

1 Socialization

'Teach them right'

Some regard conflict in schools as inevitable. Only the degree of it varies. Where there is little, it might be that fewer constraints are operating on the teachers, and/or they have perfected their survival techniques. Some, mainly private schools, enjoy the benefit of matching prior socialization. This is the ideal state for pedagogy, where both sides have common standards, values and beliefs. Most schools spend an enormous amount of time and effort in trying to inculcate them. While some of this might be in accordance with a general 'citizenship' aim, the volume and intensity of many programmes has to be understood in existential survival terms. As noted previously, many children take to schools a culture which is not conducive to good order in the institution. The culture might value, for example, initiative, single-mindedness, activity and individualism; the school, on the other hand, invariably favours receptivity, malleability, docility and conformity. Most schools have some blanketing techniques which achieve a veneer of these qualities and hence a working relationship. For example, many schools adopt 'mortifying techniques', as noted in chapter 6. They aim to strip pupils of certain parts of their 'selves'. Certain roles are proscribed, and the role of 'good pupil' highlighted. This will involve deference patterns (how to address members of staff, how to respond, etc.), loss of identity (as one of a group – a class, a House, a school, entities which submerge the individual), will-breaking contests, and rewards, of course, for 'proper' behaviour. Great emphasis is put on the management of the pupils' appearance. Clothing, hairstyles, cosmetics and jewellery are closely controlled, so that individual expression is limited. Most school uniforms in turn are drab and coarse, unless there is a well-presocialized intake. Pupils are given drill in how to move about the school, sit in desks, raise hands, speak to teachers, eat their dinners, treat their fellows; and the puritan ethic of hard work, sober living and good manners is continuously urged upon them. Some would interpret this as 'education for domestication', that is, concerned with the successful induction of the young into the industrial-political system.[21] It is perhaps better viewed as accommodation. This is hardly a survival strategy in itself. It is an anticipatory manoeuvre. It tries to fashion the pupil so that he will not cause other contingencies to arise. Thus other strategies depend upon its success or failure. Generally speaking, unless pupils are already well disposed toward the official culture, socialization programmes are just as likely to alienate as to win over, and most of them have a hollow ring to them. Most teachers, therefore, have to have recourse to other methods.

2 Domination

'Keep them down' (Headmaster's advice to new teacher)

Generally speaking, teachers are bigger, stronger and wiser than schoolchildren. If survival is basic, nothing is more basic than these facts and recourse is frequently had to them. Corporal punishment abounds in school. If formal use of the cane has been abolished in many schools, there is still a great deal of punching, knuckling, tweaking, clouting, slapping, slippering, hair-pulling, twisting, rulering and kicking. One teacher told Becker in his Chicago study:[22]

> Technically you're not supposed to lay a hand on a kid. Well, they don't, technically. But there are a lot of ways of handling a kid so that it doesn't show – and then it's the teacher's word against the kid's, so the kid hasn't got a chance. Like dear Mrs ——,

she gets mad at a kid, she takes him out in the hall, she gets him
stood up against the wall. Then she's got a way of chucking the
kid under the chin, only hard, so that it knocks his head back against
the wall. It doesn't leave a mark on him. But when he comes back in
that room he can hardly see straight, he's so knocked out. It's really
rough. There's a lot of little tricks like that you learn about.

I witnessed several such incidents. One teacher I asked about the
legality of this kind of treatment said: 'The secret is to hit them where
they don't bruise.'

Verbal aggression is even more widespread. Humiliation is common,
as recounted in chapter 6, as is the threat of physical aggression imbued
with a special tone of nastiness for extra effects:

'If I catch you chewing gum in my lesson again I'll ram it down your
throat; you'll have indigestion and you won't go for a week!'

The threat is often accompanied by 'transfixation' whereby the victim
is held in a vice-like grip and subjected to a wide and wild-eyed nose-
to-nose confrontation. Often, of course, anger is simulated − it is part
of the teacher's 'presentation of front'.[23]

With regard to commands, Waller noted some factors which might
weaken their efficacy. One should not explain a command, for that
immediately introduces doubt and weakens it. Nor should one express
a grievance, whine or moan, threaten or exhort. Waller, of course, is
talking about the establishing of authority, and in the 1930s when he
was writing that, traditional forms of teaching were much more universal and teacher-pupil relationships much more stable. There are still
many teachers who would agree with him, but given the nature of
the pupils today, it is extremely doubtful if the formalization and
mechanization of commands that he recommended as being most
efficacious in his time would still be so. This provides us with a good
example of a survival technique which has outlived its usefulness and
in fact turned into a problem itself, thus requiring some other
technique to accommodate it.

It is an accumulatory process, and there is something awfully inexorable about it. Webb speculates about a new idealistic teacher going to
Black School:[24]

Secretly he despises his colleagues. He will never be a drill-sergeant
as they are. In class he tries to be relaxed, treats the lads as equals.
This does not work, because they play him up. He is a chink in the
armour of the system which oppresses them. At first he looks upon
fighting for control as a game. So do the boys. Then he begins to
get tired. There is ridicule from colleagues. The head seems to be
saying 'good morning' rather coldly. A game's a game, the new
teacher thinks. But the 'blighters' don't seem to know when to

stop. And he has not enough energy left at the end of the day to do anything worthwhile. After spending the first week of the holidays in bed, he resolves to do as a kindly colleague advises — to 'really get on top of the blighters next term from the word go.' In a year or so, if he is not qualified to move, he is another drill-sergeant. Thus Black School perpetuates itself.

Physical superiority (and preparedness to use it in some way) and nastiness are useful attributes in maintaining order, for few pupils, like any other group of people, would push any interaction to the extremes where they are employed.

Sometimes this is an integral part of one's teaching. It is perhaps best illustrated in the gymnasium. It is no coincidence that many PE teachers progress to senior positions with special responsibility for discipline. For many of these, 'survival' and 'teaching' are synonymous. The survival techniques of games teachers are built into the structure of their teaching, and are based on relentless efficiency, continuous structured physical activity (which pre-empts any countering), strong strident voices (backed up by whistles, hooters, megaphones, etc.) used to prevent the activity from flagging, and a display of potential physical aggression (in shorts, singlets, track-suits, muscles, and the smell of sweat and embrocation, etc.). This is fused into the normative order, so that barked commands like 'Stand up straight!', 'Don't move!', 'Pull, boy, pull!' appear as part of the manifest curriculum. It is the accepted, legitimate technique for the aim in view.

A certain momentum is created:

'Well done! . . . This is where it begins to hurt! . . . Keep going! . . . This is where it counts! . . . Come on! . . . Another twenty seconds! . . . You can get three more in! . . . Pressure, now, pressure!'

The strict control of activities, the stentorian voice and the aggression are used to socialize:

'Somebody's changed places, who is it? Come down, whoever it was! (*Boy comes down from wall bars.*) Why did you change? I don't know why! (*Boy mumbles.*) Now why did you do it? (*Boy mumbles, inaudibly. Teacher, very loudly*) Don't be so dishonest, lad! Let's have some guts and courage here! If you don't like the people you're playing with because they're weak, do something about it to make them stronger! That's no way to show you're a superior sportsman, is it? You're here to learn to lose!'

Mortification techniques are freely at the disposal of the games staff. PE and games are often compulsory, there are the showers, and various stages of undress. Stripping people of their clothes strips them of part of their 'selves'.

'I made them all do PE in their pants the first week I was here, just to show them who's boss.' (Woman PE teacher)

Games and PE thus perform an important function in the life of the school. Not least, of course, they release a great deal of bottled-up drive and energy that otherwise might be released in more sedentary lessons. These techniques are employed variously by other teachers.

The same form of verbal aggression is employed during assemblies and other such rituals. Some moral message is usually offered, and enshrined in prayers and a hymn. These are often enunciated with frightening force, as if validated by holy authority. The function is both to alarm and to rally, but the aim is singlefold — conformity. Even if nobody joins in, the first function is hopefully achieved — the headmaster and music master, for example, by the sheer power of their voices and terror of countenance, establish themselves as forces to be reckoned with, backed by mystical power.

3 Negotiation

'You play ball with me, and I'll play ball with you'

The principle of this strategy is exchange. Commonly used are appeals, apologies, cajolery, flattery, promises, bribes, exchanges and threats:

'I'm sorry I'm talking a lot this morning but bear with me, please. I do want to get this finished.'

'We'll call it a day after this one, you've worked hard this morning, well done!'

'I thought in the second period we'd have a film, then I thought next week we'd do the nature trail in Aspley Forest, but first I want us to make up those notes.'

'You can go when you've finished, and not until.'

Often the commodity the teacher offers in exchange for good order and a representation of 'work' is escape from or relaxation of institutional constraint — films, records, visits, outings, breaks, an 'easy time'. In the pupils' reckoning, these are not 'work'. Nor are they always such in the teachers'. Thus on one occasion when a teacher found he had the wrong film, not even remotely to do with the subject in question, he felt he had to honour the bargain and offer the class the film regardless. Otherwise he might have had a survival problem. They accepted, for otherwise they might have had to do 'work'. 'Community Service' also comes under this rubric. Most pupils I spoke to 'had a good time' while doing it. Many did all that was required of them — gardening, shopping, making tea, etc. – but it was not that obnoxious commodity, 'work'.[25] Neither were 'projects', whether connected to CSE or not. One can hide somewhere, have a smoke, and fill in the worksheet later from somebody else's. The CSE, in fact, is the biggest aid to teacher survival introduced into schools since the war. It draws many more pupils into the mainstream culture of the school, and still allows pupils their secondary adjustments. Thus if you fall behind on your essays in English, you can always copy somebody else's, merely changing a few words; or you can submit your brother's or a friend's specimen in woodwork – and so on. The CSE has been a success because it has allowed for this – unlike many other innovations. These examples all support Bernstein's theory that[26]

> when [the pedagogical] frame is relaxed . . . to include everyday realities, it is often, and sometimes validly, not simply for the transmission of educational knowledge, but for purposes of social control of forms of deviancy. The weakening of this frame occurs usually with the less 'able' children whom we have given up educating.

All this adds to the teacher's resources. There are various types of admonitions teachers use. These include appeals to civilization and society in general, and the individual's fitting in to it. 'Right' conduct and attitude thus will provide access to the promised land. Waller mentions appeals to the parents' ideals, fair play, honesty, chivalry or self-esteem.[27] There are appeals against the fracturing of peer-group norms ('spoiling it for others', group punishments for individual offences), and appeals against the fracturing of a common bond between teacher and class. Of course, the particular strategies a teacher employs will depend on other factors – his conception of children, his view of teaching, his ideological make-up. Great contrasts can be found within one school. One teacher might be essentially dominative and to keep an edge on her techniques cultivate 'social distance' from her pupils; another might be predominantly negotiative, and aim for social nearness. Of particular interest here is the development of a sense of 'we-ness' between a teacher and a retrograde class of school 'failures'. These constitute the biggest potential menace to the school, and hence require a special security arrangement. This frequently involves assigning one teacher to the class full time, so that a notion of separateness develops between the backward class *and* their own teacher from the rest of the school. Strong identification is made within the unit, with feelings of loyalty, comradeship and regard, so that it acts as its own survival agent. Appeals, if made by their own teacher, rarely fail. Other teachers, however, are invariably driven to other techniques with these forms.

There is a more general negotiation strategy that teachers use based on compromises over rules, as discussed in chapter 5. Many teachers work out, through interaction, with each set of pupils, norms and standards common to the group as a whole. Everybody feels bound by such democratic procedure. Thus teachers might choose to ignore certain forms of behaviour as long as they are not perceived as institution-threatening or publicly flaunted. 'Smoking behind the cycle shed' is an obvious example. The same can apply to 'work'. Teachers often feel obliged to abandon their absolute standards and settle for what they can get from a class, or from an individual.

4 Fraternization

'If you can't beat them, join them'

'One of the ways to resolve extreme conflict between teachers and children is for the teachers to become less adult and in some sense enter into the world of children. This requires isolating oneself from adult interactions and assuming some of the language and style of children.'[28]

Some staff were[29]

not altogether sympathetic with the social aims of the school, but fulfilled an informal role which was functional for the school organisation in defusing conflict within the pupil identity of working class children which might otherwise have made it difficult for them to continue in the upper years at the school. As such, these staff acted . . . as a 'safety valve institution', channelling discontent and hostility, while keeping intact the relationship within which the antagonism arises.

The concern with interest and motivation as exhibited through practical problems in the schools owed as much to the aim of preventing disruption, as to the aim of promoting the inculcation of knowledge.[30]

A prominent survival strategy is to work for good relations with the pupils, thus mellowing the inherent conflict, increasing the pupils' sense of obligation, and reducing their desire to cause trouble. It might be thought that this is fairly central to 'progressivist' forms of teaching. But the teachers at Lowfield strongly opposed 'progressivism'. It is taking place therefore within more traditionalist styles.

Fraternization takes many forms. Young teachers, especially, by their appearance, style of dress, manner, speech and interests frequently identify strongly with the pupils. They are often very popular. Implicit alliances can form against the main structure of the school, but, as with teachers of 'backward classes', it can ultimately work in the school's interests, since much bad feeling is defused through this bond with members of staff. On the other hand, of course, pupils with their own survival problem might try to increase their benefits by play-ing off one teacher against another ('so and so lets us chew in *his* lesson'), so it can promote instability. Older teachers can assume parts of this role. For example, they can display signs of alienation from the official culture, especially where it seeks to dominate. Explicit or implicit disapproval before pupils of a rule or action, especially if perpetrated by the upper hierarchy, is common. In fact it has been suggested that a major function of the head and his deputies is to soak up a lot of the bad feeling in the school, leaving a pleasanter field for front-line teachers and pupils to work in. Some identify with the pupils against outside aspects of the establishment:

'I loathe the vicar, who goes up, takes his watch off — and you know you're going to get your twenty minutes' worth — and he says "I've got four points to make" — and he's only done two of them after fifteen minutes . . .'

(Interestingly, this teacher betrays himself before typical secondary modern pupils by identifying with the establishment at all!)

Many teachers share in cultural influences which cross generations. Thus some have recourse to an earthy humour which marks them not as 'a teacher, a man apart', but as 'a man of the people'. Dirty jokes are not excluded, and seem to be particularly appreciated by rebellious male elements in the school. Another shared cultural influence is tele-vision. Some lessons I observed abounded in references to popular tele-vision programmes, advertisements included. While this might have a pedagogical value, it also has important survival repercussions for the pupils' perceptions of the teacher's identity. Sport also can form a bridge. For example, gangs of adolescent boys follow a football cult. Their discourse consists of jocular abuse directed at others' chosen teams and vigorous championing of one's own at all costs. This aggress-ive banter is typical of their lifestyle and is indulged in as a form of play. On these terms it is open to teachers, and sometimes they take advantage of it.

Much survival teaching takes the form of entertainment. It is quite often reflected in styles of speech and associated with culture-identification. Thus one teacher I observed employed a local, chatty, pubby style of speech in his teaching, which he indulged to good effect from the control point of view. Another had a cosmopolitan, youthful, 'with-it' style which reinforced his identification with the pupils. Another related almost everything he said to television programmes, making liberal use of standard phrases, and copying situation and character comedy. Less 'identification' associated are forms of teacher wit and humour. A stage manner helps, and the fun is often directed good-naturedly and matily towards the inmates. The displacement of reality in humour neutralizes any potential conflict.

'Oh, my God, that smell. Is that that "Brut" again? Open a window, stand back.' (*Hangs out of window, gasping. Returns to desk.*)

'Oh, my God, those socks!' (*Covers eyes with hand, puts on sunglasses.*)

'Now who saw *Maxim Gorky* last night? That's the programme you tune into between Mickey Mouse and Long John Silver.'

By this form of humour the teacher retains control and reinforces status. It is a kind of humorous, rather than aggressive, domination technique, but the aggression lurks in the background.

Sometimes, however, a teacher directs laughter upon himself, frequently belittling his formal role. These divergences from the mainstream expected behaviour place him in a wider context and invalidate the narrowness of the immediate scene. Impersonation is a favourite vehicle:

Example 1

The teacher is talking about raising hands when the pupils wish to reply:

'In Germany – and don't do this here, please, other teachers might not like it – the pupils go (*here he snaps his fingers together*) . . . and at the back they even do this' (*does it with both hands, jumps up and down and shouts* 'Sir! Sir!')

Example 2

A pupil comes into the room and requests the 'German helmet and gas mask'. Teacher goes into cupboard and comes out wearing them: 'Mein Gott in Himmel: Ve haf ways of making you talk!', and gives a five-minute impersonation of Hitler.

Many aspects of modern 'progressive' teaching embrace the entertainment principle. The use of film, television, radio and records, and devising the projects, fieldwork and so on, have control as a major aim. Interestingly, most general courses, particularly ROSLA' depend almost entirely on film and television. Teachers also devise their own little tactics. Many of these, for example, took the form of quizzes of one sort or another. One teacher punctuated a formal question-and-answer technique with 'hangman' games when no one knew an answer. Class involvement and hence control was always greater during the games.

Another form of fraternization is indulgence. This is consciously to allow the pupils a far greater measure of liberty than is customary for teachers. In negotiating, the teacher goes to the extreme of his bargaining counters. His norm of behaviour is displaced entirely towards the pupil culture. Here is an extract from my note of the beginning of one such session:

> (I sat in a corner at the back, as usual, next to Mark Godfrey. He was peashooting away.)
>
> *Mark*: Great teacher this is!
>
> *PW*: I don't know, is he?
>
> *Mark*: Yeah, he fixes things up.
>
> *Steve*: It's a muck about.
>
> *Mark*: No, it's not that, 'e's great. (*He aims off another pea, scores a hit on Peter Matthews, who prepares to retaliate.*)
>
> *Paul* (loudly): Cor, Steve! You done a fart in English, you done one now! (*Paul gets up and moves over to teacher; suddenly there are more shouts from this corner, and a mass exodus.*)
>
> *Mark*: Bloody 'ell, Dunsley, you've dropped one again! (*He holds his coat collar up. Paul comes back, groans, and goes away again.*) On the other side of the room a group of girls are very noisy. Michelle is whooping and squealing — they have a letter. Janet appeals to teacher loudly, but humorously: 'Tell her off, sir, she's getting on my nerves!' Teacher (*attending to an individual*) ignores her.

The lesson continued in this vein for the whole period. Yet it was not the anarchy it appeared to be. The teacher did much individual and small group tuition. None of the disorder was directed against him, nor did it involve less yield of work than was normal for his form, whom I accompanied to all their lessons. Another indulgent technique is the indiscriminate backing of 'winners'. Sometimes pupils do become interested. Teachers capitalize on this interest. No doubt this frequently has pedagogical value, but equally it is often done unrelated to the lesson as planned, and justified only *post hoc*.

In co-educational schools flirting is a widely used technique, especially by male teachers with female pupils. Since sex is one of the most prominent interests of the more rebellious girl pupils, it can be a great aid in securing their goodwill and co-operation. As we saw in chapter 3, many of these pupils see school in purely 'social' terms, as compared with instrumental or vocational, and their idea of 'social' differs a great deal from the school's 'social training' or 'education for citizenship', so topical with ROSLA. It is much concerned with the basic elements of interaction, and is rooted in their own culture. Some teachers spend their careers fighting this, others capitalize on it, while perhaps denying it:

> *Teacher*: Don't flash your eyes at me, Susan. It might work with your dad, but it won't work with me! (*However, his expression and tone indicate that it is working.*)
> *Susan* (faking embarrassment): Oh! Oh!
> *Teacher* (mimicking): Oh! Oh! (*He carries on up the row, flashing* his *eyes at the girls, who smile and giggle in mock confusion.*)

The sex element is strong in games. I noticed during a mixed game of volleyball that occasionally, when serving or receiving, an individual would be the centre of attraction, but that one's failings in this arena are laughed at and experienced in a different way from lessons, when they might have felt embarrassment. In the role of 'female' as opposed to pupil, all seemed to recognize that it was quite acceptable, even perhaps desirable, to be incompetent at games. The girls responded with such feminine wiles as ogling, putting out the tongue, pretending to hide confusion and so on. Thus their participation in the game was sublimated, and they found salvation in the sexual front. This technique was more used by 'incidental' games teachers. Full-time games staff were much more dominative and aroused far more resentment, especially among teenage girls. This was because they were permitted only the role of 'sportswoman', and their failure at games was of prime importance.

Here is an extract from my observation notes of an incidental games male teacher and a group of teenage girls round the trampoline:

> *Teacher*: Who wants a double bounce? (*Pet puts her hand up.*) Right oh, give us a push up. (*Two girls help push teacher up by the backside.*) Hey, watch it! (*good humouredly*) (Teacher and Pet have a double bounce, teacher working Pet to state of collapse and confusion. As he gets off, he pulls another girl on, and she collapses, bouncing and laughing, in the middle of the trampoline.)

5 Absence or removal

'Teaching would be all right if it wasn't for the pupils'. (Teacher folklore)

One certain way of ensuring survival is to absent oneself from the scene of potential conflict. Some teachers achieve this by upward mobility at one end, or by never starting at the other.[31]

However, few achieve such absolute absence. Most have to make do with partial absence, some official, some unofficial. Because it is the most efficacious and the most relative (i.e. one usually gains only at the expense of others) of survival techniques, it is the cause of intense

159

and sometimes bitter struggles. This is why the timetable is of such critical importance. 'Survival' features prominently in its construction. 'Weak' teachers have to be protected, 'good' ones rewarded. 'Weak' ones can be given fewer lessons, none of the hard classes and the most favourable rooms (a good example of how incompetence might be rewarded in our educational system). Whence then come the rewards? Fortunately for the hierarchy there are some 'in-between' teachers consisting of a faceless group of those who have not yet 'arrived' at the school, a 'disloyal' group consisting of those who are leaving or applying for other jobs, and a 'rebellious' group who for some reason have got in bad favour with the hierarchy. These take up the slack of 'bad' forms, poor rooms and overloaded timetables.

Manipulation of the timetable protects the weak, rewards the good and penalizes the unknown and unworthy. The same applies to time-table adjustments that have to be made in the day-to-day running of the school. One of the 'rewards' is free periods. The importance of survival as an organizing principle in the teacher's day is evidenced by the neuroticism attending this topic. Losing free periods can be quite trau-matic, for survival becomes that bit harder; it can be very much harder if, in exchange for an idyllic 'free', one is confronted by somebody else's extreme survival problem — a 'bad' form in 'bad' circumstances.

Failing the legitimate acquisition of 'free periods', one can absent oneself in other ways. Unloading the worst troublemakers onto others is a common device, and is legitimated in schools where certain teachers have been given financial and status compensation in return for a 'counselling' function. One can take days off school, though the folk-lore regards this as defeatist. It also saddles equally hard-pressed colleagues with extra responsibilities. Thus it is more customary to steal extra minutes at the beginning and end of 'breaks', use delaying or de-ferring tactics during lessons or work absences into one's teaching. Many new courses and styles of teaching that have come into vogue since the Newsom Report are characterized by a large amount of absence. Link courses, work-based courses, Community Service, field-work, individual and group projects, all aid teacher survival by virtue of separating the combatants for much of the time. Techniques such as pupils taking assemblies, running parts of lessons or initiating and con-trolling work on their own cleverly turns the opposition back on itself and neatly fits into fashionable educational philosophy, while the teacher sits on the sidelines.

If teachers choose to maximize their survival programme, they will follow a policy of non-volunteering, 'keeping out of the way', and 'keeping one's nose clean'. Some teachers have their 'secret places'. Some feel the need to go out — often to a local pub — during the mid-day break. Some are strictly 'nine-to-four' teachers, often for sur-vival reasons rather than lack of interest or sense of vocation. Teachers can be absent in spirit. They can 'be away' and have their 'removal activities' as well as the pupils.[32] Teachers occasionally daydream, fall asleep, look out of windows, fail to pay attention, defer or ignore problems, pass or waste time, pretend something is happening which is not and otherwise evade the head-on conflict with reality.

6 Ritual and routine

'You'll be all right once you get into the hang of things'

Bernstein has described the symbolic function of ritual as[33]

to relate the individual through ritualistic acts to a social order, to heighten respect for that order, to revivify that order within the individual and, in particular, to deepen acceptance of the procedures which are used to maintain continuity, order and boundary and which control ambivalence towards the social order.

In British state schools, rituals[34]

facilitate the transmission and internalization of the expressive order of the school, create consensus ... deepen respect for and impersonalize authority relations. They also serve to prevent questioning of the values the expressive order transmits.

Much ritual is to be located in the expressive order of the school. But there are ritualistic qualities about certain forms of teaching. Bernstein again has noted the social control element that lies behind much systematization of our teaching.[35]

Where knowledge is regulated by collection codes, social order arises out of the hierarchical nature of the authority relationships, out of the systematic ordering of the differentiated knowledge in time and space, out of an explicit, usually predictable, examining procedure.

Elsewhere he has observed:[36]

It would also not be entirely wrong to suggest that the incentive to change curricula arose out of the difficulties secondary schools were experiencing in the education of the non-élite children.

In turn, this suggests the possibility that survival strategies based on ritual and domination were becoming counter-productive, and needed to give way to more negotiative strategies.

In pluralistic, industrialized societies the value systems are various or ambiguous, and because of other societal developments which I spoke of earlier,[37] the social basis for the ritualization of the expressive order of the school will be considerably weakened and the rituals may come to have the character of social routines.

Perhaps the best example of this is morning assembly. Morning after morning the school where I did my research went through the formula of mustering, saying a prayer, singing a hymn, and listening to a peroration and exhortation from the headmaster. I described in chapter 5 the survival problem this created for the pupils, and how they coped with it. It is another example of a survival strategy that has outlived its usefulness and degenerated into yet another problem.

However, teachers would find it difficult to do without routine. Musgrove points up the problem:[38]

> The computer will take much of the routine out of teaching in schools, and will make possible far more learning which is not school-based. Although most people complain about the routine in their jobs, they would probably go mad without it. Without routine we are constantly dealing with unique, unprecedented, non-recurrent and non-standard events. This may be exhilarating; it is also exhausting. We can expect teachers to be in a state of constant exhaustion.

That prophecy for the future is for all too many teachers ancient history: routine, systematization, drill, have provided a safeguard. Black School provides a vivid example. Because of the boys' 'irrepressibility, rule-breaking and spontaneity' and the teacher's fatigue and fear of playground chaos spreading into the classroom, he insists rigidly on good behaviour and adopts a rigid style of teaching. Consequently, only rather mechanical skills can be taught:[39]

> Only certain rigid work and conduct standards can be conveyed by drilling. And these make or maintain dislike and therefore the need for drilling.

Teachers become addicted to routine and ritual. Once instituted, they are extremely difficult to get rid of. Rituals become associated with 'tradition' and 'ethos' and to change them means discontinuity and disjuncture. Routine is a narcotic, taken to soothe the nerves and mellow the situation. Once established, to do without it would involve the teacher in severe withdrawal symptoms.

Routine imposes a structure on school life which pupils and teachers almost automatically come to accept, and serves as a basis for establishing control. Registration, form periods, assemblies, timetables, lesson structures and so forth are the bones of the school day. Within this overall structure, individual teachers establish their own routines. We are all familiar with the archetypical teacher of fiction, middle-aged, soberly dressed, extremely mannered and eminently predictable in all his movements.

As Webb noted, this carries implications for what and how one teaches. Gump has shown that self-paced activities involve more difficult pupil management problems than in externally paced activities.[40] Westbury has portrayed recitations and textbook teaching as coping mechanisms.[41] Furlong has noticed, from the pupils' point of view, that 'work' and 'learning' is a desiccated, skeletal, structured and measurable form of knowledge.[42] To them, learning is 'measured accomplishment'. A recent report found that a large percentage of the writing done in school is done for the 'teacher-as-examiner', and not for the purposes which might do more to foster pupils' learning and development.[43] 'Teacher-as-examiner', it must be realized, is masking 'teacher-as-survivor'.

Many a teacher who has tried an experiment, and felt it has not been working and disorder threatening, has reverted in mid-stream to more formal techniques. The best example is the dictating of notes. This is an extremely useful device from the survival point of view for it gives pupils to believe they are being spared doing their own 'work', and thus secures their co-operation, involving quiet application, for considerable periods at a time. This is not to say that much activity associated with 'new' teaching techniques does not have a strong 'routine' component. Work cards, structured exercises, group activities, programmed learning, audio-visual techniques all provide for it, and perhaps their persistence is to be explained by it.

7 Occupational therapy

'It passes the time'

The principle of pupil therapy is bodily involvement accompanied frequently by dulling of the senses. The aim is to take the edge off boredom or fractiousness, and thus prevent incident arising. Pupils sometimes try to provide their own therapy such as playing cards, carving on desks, doodling on paper, reading comics. But though therapeutic, these activities are counter-official. Education must be seen to be going on. This is the purport of the 'busyness' that Sharp and Green talk of. The injunction to 'be busy' is legitimated by the philosophy of child-centred education.

Within the secondary schools of my knowledge I have encountered many therapeutic techniques. Drawing maps, pictures, patterns is good therapy. This is one of the reasons why art is a popular subject, particularly among bored and rebellious pupils. History, geography and science teachers make good use of the knowledge. 'Play' is also useful. The simple experimental kits provided for pupils' tinkering in science lessons allow for this, and for this reason the practical subjects —

woodwork, metalwork, cooking, needlework, etc. – have strong therapeutic value. De-inhibiting activities such as free, unstructured swimming are wonderful therapy, and can spread their beneficial effect over several classroom periods before and after.

Pupils often fill in time with 'jobs'. 'Have you any jobs, sir?' is a common refrain from bored, inactive pupils. So teachers request blackboards cleaned, drawers tidied, corners cleaned up, pencils sharpened, files ordered and so on. It can be the major 'official' activity of older pupils outside the mainstream of the school, especially in their final year when there is common acceptance of the failure of the special 'official' programme designed for them. The girls can make tea and wash up for the staff, the boys can repair gates or glasshouses, paint sheds and so on. They are usually glad to do these jobs, for therapy is a more lasting and satisfying antidote to boredom than 'mucking about'.

A teacher can engage in therapy unilaterally. Busying oneself can help, when all around is chaos and threatening. Marking books, setting up equipment, giving individual guidance can occupy one's mind and cut out the general scene. Sometimes a teacher's whole programme is little more than therapy, like a series of science lessons I observed. Here the teacher carefully constructed the equipment for his experiment, and went dutifully through the procedure from beginning to end, explaining as he went, and elaborating on the application to the modern world of what he was doing. It was a model lesson in many respects, but none of the pupils in these classes listened. Moreover, they obviously were not listening, but clearly divided into their own groups and devised their own entertainment, often quite noisily. The two elements, teacher and pupil, though in the same room, seemed totally oblivious of each other. The only time when they came together was in the last ten minutes of the two-hour period when they were dictated the results of the experiment, and they recorded them in their exercise books. This teacher neutralized the control problem by concentrating exclusively on the 'stimulus' aspect of teaching and totally ignoring 'response'.

Another form of therapy takes the form of 'spinning-out' exercises. One example that came my way involved non-examination, nonscientific subjects allocated half-day slots because of their parallel grouping with science subjects which were reckoned to need that kind of block provision. I observed some of these sessions, and always enormous time-wasting and time-passing was resorted to as a survival technique. It was taken up with arriving late, finishing early, chatting with the pupils before and after, preparation of lesson and materials for it (during it), interruptions (which seemed to be welcomed and capitalized upon), peripheral story-telling and general nonchalant pace.

8 Morale-boosting

'We have to believe' (deputy headmaster)

Just as socialization is an anticipatory strategy, morale-boosting is a retrospective one. For teachers need a survival strategy to 'account for' their other survival strategies. They mentally neutralize the survival problem, and they do it in two ways — by rhetoric and by laughter. I am speaking of rhetoric here as Green has done, i.e. 'it explains and constructs the necessity of the conjuncture within the disjuncture. It constructs the paradox in the teacher's actions and perspectives as itself a conjuncture.'[44]

Aiding this is another aspect of commitment, group cohesiveness. Kanter defines this not in terms of sociability and mutual attraction but rather in terms of the ability to withstand disruptive forces and threats from outside the group ('sticking together'). This sort of commitment involves primarily 'forming positive cathectic orientations; affective ties bind members to the community, and gratifications stem from involvement with all the members of the group. Solidarity is high, and infighting and jealousy low.'[45] Group cohesiveness among teachers is high, though it frequently pertains to sub-groups within a staff. Friction between these is only another feature of the internal cohesiveness of the groups.

The deeper the commitment, both in terms of continuance and group cohesiveness, the more extensive the rhetoric, and attachment to it. Sharp and Green give a good example in their discussion of 'busyness' as already noted. To the teacher 'there is a logical relationship between her notion of busyness, her educational philosophy and her actions'.[46] If the children are 'busy' and 'getting on with it on their own' or 'finding something to do', this is well within the spirit of child-centredness.

Well-established rhetorics attend many of the techniques discussed here in relation to secondary schools. I have touched on the legitimation of certain forms of absence and removal. Pupils running lessons, taking assemblies, going on projects are in line with progressive philosophy, as are certain aspects of therapy ('more involvement') and fraternization ('treating the pupils like people'). There is now a vast thesaurus of 'progressive' vocabulary and idioms, from which the teacher might draw to construct his own vocabulary of motives (free expression, integrated learning, activity-based learning, project work, free choice . . .).

All of the specific instances I have mentioned have a rhetoric closely attending them. Young teachers, for example, are best 'thrown in at the deep end', it is 'good experience', and better known sooner than later whether they are going to last. School uniform is championed in the interests of 'equality', preventing the poor being exposed by the sartorial elegance of the rich, of school 'ethos' and the qualities of pride and loyalty, and of 'utility', for identification purposes. Mortification procedures and dominating techniques are represented as socializing devices in the interest of the individual, whose naturally savage and un-couth character must be tamed and channelled along the 'right' paths to a civilized society. The latent survival function of the separated form of potential trouble-makers with their teacher is occluded by a rhetoric which asserts the peculiar characteristics of these pupils – personal, environmental, mental – which 'entitle' them to special preferential treatment; and the relationship they develop with the teacher con-cerned, which ensures the success of the survival manoeuvre, is pre-sented as evidence of the justification of the rhetoric. Thus the problem is collapsed back into the situation and contained within a solution that masquerades, very powerfully and convincingly, as education. Even the 'jobs' that they do as therapy are justified as 'education'. In one case, for example, the boys in 5th year had to decide 'how much paint was needed', 'who was going to do which job', 'how they were going to order the materials', 'how much they were going to cost', 'how long it was going to take' and so on. This was the view of the teacher in charge of the educational value of one particular job the boys did. In essence though this is not far removed from Mr Squeers's technique:[47]

> We go upon the practical mode of teaching Nickleby – the regular education system. C-l-e-a-n, clean, verb active, to make bright, to scour. W-i-n, win, d-e-r, winder, a casement. When the boy knows this out of book, he goes and does it.

The growth of the counselling function in schools has legitimated the 'removal' technique, as mentioned above. Moral crusades and deviance amplification in the service of Parkinson's Law have provided a vast amount of rhetoric to support the counsellor's position, function and raw material.

In the struggle for survival, detection and celebration of the enemy's weakness is an enormous morale-booster. Hence the teacher's insistent representations of pupils in psychological terms as 'thick', 'idle', and the prevailing 'norm of cynicism' to be found in staffrooms.[48] One of the two beliefs on which the ideology of Black School staff was based was that the boys were rather hateful.[49] From this, the individual teacher might draw renewed strength, after flagging perhaps, towards the end of a double period and allowing the pupils to gain the upper hand. The greatest danger is that teachers should doubt what they are doing. Usually the supportive voice of colleagues available at key points of the day provides sufficient reassurance of his beliefs and reinforce-ment of status. Thus pupils invariably come to be held fully accountable for failings. They are responsible and free agents. Thus, with regard to the segregation that occurred in the school as the result of the subject-choice process, I was told by some that 'they had the choice'. There was no acknowledgment by these teachers of factors such as pre-conditioning, group perspectives and channelling procedures which constrain and direct these choices (though, as noted in chapter 1, *some* were well aware of them). Most of such factors are so completely beyond the control of the school that knowledge of them could possibly undermine commitment and hence powers of accommodation. As I have elaborated it, commitment provides for its own defence. Teachers, therefore, would resist such knowledge.

For teachers to 'get on' in their careers, they must 'believe' in these ways; and the more they get on, the more they must believe. The firmer the commitment, the greater the accommodation. This applies particularly to belief. There are several other reasons for this. Sharp and Green point out that the deputy head in their school had to 'contend more directly with the general crisis in school-parent relations than the other staff. The ideology of domestic pathology has become more sharply articulated for her as a device for understanding and handling her situation.'[50]

Webb imputed *guilt* to the upper hierarchy in Black School, though not to the teacher, whose drill-sergeant role was too narrow for him to have enough freedom to be held accountable. The headmaster eases his guilt by busying himself in administration, or exaggerating the school's achievements.[51] Perhaps also, guilt helps the upper hierarchy to invent and sustain a higher level of rhetoric.

However, it need not necessarily be a product of guilt. It is the responsibility of the head and his deputies to facilitate the teaching task for his staff. The provision or reinforcement of a rationale to support their survival strategies is a service to them, while, of course, this own responsibility for the school in general, as opposed to the teachers' classroom problems, causes him to have survival problems of a different order. He is supposed to lead and guide. Policy is his business, and where there is no scope for educational policy, he should be an expert in accommodation policy.

Less committed teachers who have less of an accommodation problem often see through this rhetoric and boost their own morale by merciless teasing and baiting of the upper hierarchy during their absence. This is one of the main subjects of staffroom humour, a supremely important factor in teacher survival; so much so that I devote the whole of chapter 9 to it.

Conclusion

I have outlined a model for the analysis of teacher behaviour which attempts to link the self with the system. At a systems level I have spoken of institutional momentum and societal developments, which may or may not run counter to that momentum. At the individual level I have spoken of commitment, which is bound up with institutional momentum, and the nature of the clientele, the pupils, which is bound up with societal developments. I have introduced the notion of accommodation, which is a product of the confrontation of these two factors. Where the confrontation is intense the teacher will meet with a survival problem which he will relieve by use of survival strategies. These do not necessarily facilitate teaching. They often take the place of it, and even assume its guise. Success ensures the establishment of a strategy, but many outlive their usefulness and turn into problems themselves. New teachers are quickly initiated, and so the system perpetuates itself.[52] If there is a 'hidden curriculum', there is also a 'hidden pedagogy'.[53]

Of the strategies I have identified, socialization is anticipatory, rhetoric retrospective. Domination and ritual and routine might be associated more with traditional forms of teaching, negotiation and fraternization with more progressive forms of teaching. The overall heuristic framework yields a number of hypotheses. Here are some examples:

(1) The bigger the commitment, the wider the accommodation.

(2) The bigger the commitment, the wider the use of rhetoric.

(3) The bigger the commitment, the more favoured will be the institutionally supportive strategies (socialization, domination, negotiation).

(4) The less the commitment, the more favoured will be the institutionally disruptive techniques (absence and removal, fraternization).

(5) The more 'professional' the commitment, the more professional strategies will be favoured (socialization, rhetoric, negotiation, domination).

(6) The more 'survival centred' the commitment, the more those strategies involving separation of teacher and pupil, and time passing will be favoured (absence and removal, therapy).

(7) The more accommodation, the greater the survival strategic orientation, and the less the education. And the converse of this. (This applies at both individual and institution level.)

What are the implications for teaching? Westbury concluded that[54]

> proposals for change in classroom behaviours that do not address the issue of tasks and resources do not show how change in teaching real groups of students can be effected, [and that] the ideology of open education articulates goals which the conventional school cannot address.

This is no surprise to such as Illich and Holly, who see schools as places where modern society puts children because it has nothing else to offer them, and that teachers and schools are trapped in the logic of custodial institutions.[55] Teachers, rather, are trapped in the logic of survival. Consider the raising of the school leaving age. By the time it was implemented there were more powerful reasons for bringing it down. But teachers have had to accommodate, and that very process will ensure its continuance, especially when the most committed and the most powerful — the headteachers — are so strong on morale-boosting. This has nothing to do with custodialism.

So much of what counts as 'teaching', therefore, can be a fake commodity. This is certainly alienation of a sort, but not in the sense that Illich and Holly talk about, whereby[56]

education is defined for the pupils by the dominant forces in society, [and] education is removed from the essential being of the learner and objectified as an alien commodity which can be consumed or rejected [or whereby] schools make alienation preparatory to life.

This alienation is a result of pressure on the teacher, not a conspiracy on the part of capitalist society. This appears to be Musgrove's meaning when he says 'What is alarming is not that we have a high degree of alienation (we don't), but that so many people invest meaningless activity with meaning, trivial work with high significance.'[57] This pressure is the reason why there has been so little real change in our educational system, despite a massive drive by theorists since the war, and why, in the light of the economies to come, there is likely to be little in the future. For example, there is much latent objection among teachers to team teaching, open-plan schools, integrated teaching. This is because they threaten the privacy of the teacher in his classroom; in other words, they threaten to destroy the whole basis on which their survival strategies have been constructed and on which they depend for continuance. In exchange they offer doubtful benefits, but certainly a whole new range of survival problems of unknown order. While teachers are shackled and threatened by present situational constraints, notably the teacher-pupil ratio, the required working week, compulsory education until 16, they will be unable to break out of the protective cocoon they have spun themselves. For they will be forced to continue to think of survival first, and education second.

Chapter 8

The professionalism of school reports

The following question is immediately raised: If the teacher's lot were improved such as to return him from the 'survival' to the 'educational' side of the threshold, what exactly would he be doing? Would he, for example, be freer to concentrate on 'transmitting knowledge', 'developing skills and aptitudes', 'facilitating the growth of the child', or other activities that have, from time to time, been defined as 'education'?

There could be no doubt where this would land the teachers of Lowfield — firmly with the transmission procedures so typical of institutions dominated by certification processes. And these are surrounded with professional, as much as with educational, considerations. It is very difficult, if not impossible, to find a 'pure' state of education. For it is masked on the one hand by the demands of self-preservation, and on the other by the requirements of professionalism. In the systematized processual pigeon-holing that is so typical of the technocratic society, teachers hold a supremely important position. They are the dispensers of keys, the judges of the worthiness of the recipients and the detectors of doors whose locks match the keys. Over the years the demands of the industrial state, the responding rationalizing process in the education system, the self-protecting and self-advancing interests and growth of corporatism among a growing body of teachers, the expansion of the compulsory education system to the point where it has taken up nearly one-quarter of the entire life-expectancy of society, all have interacted and compounded the process by which teachers have staked out undisputed claims to monopoly over this particular area. It is their preserve, and they have acquired the special attributes of a profession. Not quite as special as doctors and lawyers, to be sure, but still they are recognized as the guardians of an important passageway in life, armed with mystical knowledge, skills and power. Few parents can coach their children for 'O' level.

It is an ironic anomaly that teachers should legally be held to be acting *in loco parentis*. This, of course, refers only to bodily welfare. The schooling, selection and placing of children remain firmly the preserve of teachers. But once again the huge gap between the personal, human, individual, particular world of the parent's child and the public, dehumanized, mass universal world of the teacher's pupil is unrecognized in practice, cloaked by the misty veils of professionalism. Though teachers are beset by all manner of real difficulties, as discussed in the previous chapter, they must not only hold the fort and appear to be teaching in the classroom as capably as ever, for their own peace of mind, but also advance the cause of the profession in the eyes of the rest of society. Relentless advance is in the nature of the institutions of the technocratic society.

Thus professionalism is a key element in the understanding of teacher activity, and I found this well illustrated at Lowfield in the case of school reports. As the process of subject choice epitomizes the process and structure of school in their relation to society, so reports reveal the nature and degree of teacher professionalism. Reports constitute the pronouncements of the experts, their assessment of the material measured against standard aims and their diagnoses of remedy or improvement. Like doctors' diagnoses, there is something irrefragably incontrovertible about them. Few are in a position to argue with them. But an analysis of the process and factors surrounding the reports, before and after their constitution, exposes their professional, rather than absolute, basis. Teachers are not 'surviving' in this activity, but in a sense they are putting on just as big an act. Again, I should state that I am not castigating teachers for bad faith or wilful deception. Indeed, as 'persons', they appear to recognize these ironies, as we shall see in the next chapter. But, as teachers, they are part of the cogs and wheels of the system. Reports give us a good blueprint of its workings.

School reports

Teachers' categorization systems have recently become a prominent subject for study.[1] It might be claimed that nowhere are they so clearly evident and so succinctly crystallized as in school reports. These are the documents periodically completed by teachers, usually at the end of a term, and sent to parents, ostensibly to report on 'progress' (see Figure 8.1). A commonsense view regards them as a kind of objective measure of performance. Grades, usually from 'A' to 'E' or 'F', increase the appearance of objectivity and the notion of an absolute standard, with comments offering a key to the relationship between the grade and the individual's perceived ability, aptitude and attitude. Of all these factors the last is usually regarded as the only variable and hence invites most comment, especially if at all deviant.

NAME: ADRIAN SHARPE

	Form 2C	Spring 1973	Form 2C	Summer 1973
	Grade	*Remarks*	*Grade*	*Remarks*
English	D	Every effort required	D	Must work harder
Mathematics	D	Great drop lately. Seems to lack will-power to improve	B C	Improved
Science	—		C	Good progress recently
Practical Woodwork	C	More effort	B	Very good
Metalwork	C	Fair	B	Good progress
French	C	Drop this term	C	Improved
History	B	Improved	C	Marginal
Geography	C	Only Just	C	Not enough effort
Art	A	Works well	A	Very good
Craft (pottery)	—		B	Works very well
Music	C	Enthusiastic	B	Works well
RI		Satisfactory		A much better attitude
Games		Works hard		Good

Form teacher: Needs to improve a great deal in his attitude towards work. Behaviour also.

Form teacher: Has improved slightly this term, but still room for more, especially English.

Headteacher:

Headteacher:

Figure 8.1 A typical report (signatures of teachers and other details such as number in form, absences, etc., omitted)

Reports, of course, are a step removed from the action. We might take it that a great deal of that is socially constructed.[2] That is to say that much teaching does not take the form of transmitting absolute, objective bundles of knowledge to children and measuring the success of that operation by some universally recognized standards, but rather is predicated upon principles of selection and socialization. This can be easily verified by reference to the reports of an entire year group at Lowfield. The reports of pupils in the 'D' stream as 'C' 'Satisfactory' or 'B' 'Good', for example, have implications greatly different from the same comments made on pupils in the 'A' stream. The two just are not comparable, yet they masquerade, particularly with the classificatory grade, as a universally standardized form of measurement. In fact they measure against different standards and are decided by different criteria.

> Parents have little idea about their kids' capabilities. There are several anomalies; for instance, a kid who gets Bs in a lower stream might be, probably is, weaker than one in a higher who gets a C. Parents are deceived. They don't know the grade is class specific. Then there's the case of a kid who starts off well, then deteriorates at the end of the 2nd and in the 3rd year, and comments get more critical as well. Quite often all that means is the teacher getting the wind up as option time approaches. (A Lowfield teacher)

Typically, reports contain two indications relating on the one hand to the acquisition of skills and on the other to what kind of social person the pupil is becoming. They involve a notion of 'the ideal' but there are different ideal pupils according to (a) school aims (cf. contest and sponsorship systems, grammar and secondary modern schools), (b) teacher ideology (cf. 'Black Paper traditionals' and 'libertarian').

Teacher typifications

Consider the two lists in Table 8.1 These are typical categories derived from study of comments on reports of two senior year groups at Lowfield. They bear out Hargreaves's conclusion that teachers rate pupils

TABLE 8.1. Report categories

Desirable	Undesirable
Concentration	Easily distracted, lacks concentration
Quiet	Chatterbox
Industrious (works well)	Lazy
Willing Co-operative	Unco-operative
Responsible, mature	Immature
Courteous	Bad-mannered
Cheerful	Sullen
Obedient	Disobedient

according to their conformity to their instructional and disciplinary expectations:[3]

> the teacher defines the situation in terms of his own roles and goals, especially as they relate to his instructional and disciplinary objectives,

and assigns to the pupils roles and goals that are congruent with his own. He selectively perceives and interprets pupil behaviour in the light of his definition of the situation. On the basis of further inter-action with the pupils and separated perceptions of them, he develops a conception of individual pupils (and classes) who are evaluated, categorized and labelled according to the degree to which they sup-port his definition of the situation. He then responds to pupils in the light of these evaluative labels.

In a later work, Hargreaves and his colleagues elaborate a more com-plex theory of teacher typing.[4] It is proposed that there are three stages — 'speculation', when the teacher first comes to know about or meet the pupil; 'elaboration', wherein the teacher tests out his first impressions, verifies or revises his opinions; and the third, 'stabilization', at which point the teacher 'has a relatively clear and stable conception of the identity of the pupils'. The theory is elaborated in the interest of analysing 'how teachers come to recognize each pupil as a complex individual who is utterly unique'.[5]

Now this appears to be at variance with the scheme suggested by Keddie. She distinguishes between 'educationist' and 'teacher' contexts. In the former their views are more influenced by theory and by ideals; the latter is their world of practical action. There may be a big disjunc-tion between the two. For example, Keddie holds that in the teacher context:[6]

> What a teacher 'knows' about pupils derives from the organizational device of banding or streaming which in turn derives from the domi-nant organizing category of what counts as ability. The 'normal' characteristics . . . of a pupil are those which are imputed to his band or stream as a whole. A pupil who is perceived as atypical is perceived in relation to the norm for the stream: 'She's bright for a B' (*teacher H*); or in relation to the norm for another group: 'They're as good as Bs' (*teacher J of three hardworking pupils in his C stream group*). This knowledge of what pupils are like is often at odds with the image of pupils the same teachers may hold as educationists since it derives from streaming whose validity the educationist denies.

In some ways, this is quite compatible with Hargreaves's formulation, inasmuch as 'the pupil's educational identity is established in terms of the expectations the teacher has of him.'[7] But with Keddie the expecta-tions rest upon stereotypes, and to understand how these are constructed we need to examine the relationship between the social distribution of power and the distribution of knowledge. There is no such implication in Hargreaves's work. In fact the impetus of his thought on the matter takes him further and further into the actual process of typification, which increasingly emphasizes the uniqueness of each individual, and elaborates the process.

There is nothing wrong with this, indeed it is a necessary task, except that ultimately one is running a grave risk of reductionism. That is to say that actions and typifications are likely to be explained in their own terms, when a more powerful explanation lies elsewhere. There might also be an overrepresentation of complexity. All social life is complex. The sociologist's task is to unravel it, and search for prominent themes and patterns. Phenomenological investigations into the innermost recesses of the mind, which can be quite inventive when stimulated, can blind him to these.

In a more recent paper, Hargreaves seeks to show that a great deal of work on typifications has been static and stylized based on either a 'characteristics' or an 'ideal-matching' model; and that what we need is a more dynamic model of typification, which takes note of its fluctuating, emerging, processual nature, and which acknowledges the importance of different contexts.[8] There is some truth in this. On the other hand it does pull away from what I consider the more urgent task, which is to identify the nature and common themes of typifications, and thence their sources and recipes for action. A great deal of the work which Hargreaves characterizes as static, I take to be involved in this task.

It follows that, theoretically, there is not necessarily a difference between these two areas. Hargreaves's theory of typing might hold for those who come to know a lot about some, Keddie's for those who know a little about most. The Hargreaves model puts the pupil first and involves a careful and complex compilation of evidence about that pupil, before 'stabilization' of views. Keddie's would put the knowledge first, i.e. the typifications or stereotypes, and follow a process of 'identification', i.e. relating cues from the pupil to those typifications. There might be very few of these, piecemeal and fortuitous, which might be regarded as 'reinforcement' rather than 'elaboration'. 'Stabilization' can thus occur on the basis of extremely speculative data, and with many pupils it might not occur at all.

Such a process of rather rapid identification with rather crude stereotypes is typical of institutional, functionary life. Sudnow describes such categorization in a county hospital emergency ward.[9] 'The successful daily management of "dying" and "dead" bodies seemed to require that patients have a relatively constant character as social types.'[10] As long as they were elderly, poor and morally proper, their 'dying' fell within the established routines of 'death care'. These routines are 'built up to afford mass treatments on an efficiency basis, to obtain "experience", avoid dirty work, and maximise the possibilities that the intern will manage to get some sleep'.[11] On occasions, however, the routine was disturbed, when, for example, a successful middle-class person was brought in, and special measures were instituted, and especially when children died, which can lead to loss of self-control. Morally reprehensible characters such as 'suicides' or 'drunks' also attracted a 'special frame of interpretation' around the way care was organized and altered the institutional routine in significant ways.

The parallels with teaching are quite striking. Teaching routines are developed for the very same reasons: 'to afford mass treatments on an efficiency basis', etc., and the daily management of hundreds of children requires them to have fairly 'constant characters as social types'. As long as they are normal, conforming, or non-disruptive, their typification is a straightforward and institutionalized matter. The mechanics of it are to do with picking up and identifying 'cues' from the pupil and relating them to the stereotypes. Occasionally, however, these teaching routines are disturbed by 'special cases', usually because they are of uncommon excellence or an uncommon nuisance; also teachers independently, for idiosyncratic reasons, might form special associations with certain pupils. These are relatively very few in number though they might take up a disproportionate amount of a teacher's time. It is for these atypical pupils that Hargreaves's dynamic model of typification would appear more appropriate, even perhaps for certain schools where the teacher-pupil ratio is low, or where other special circumstances prevail, such as exceptionally close integration with the general community, also for exceptional teachers, perhaps too for some primary schools where the custom is for one teacher to teach only one form. But in the majority especially among state secondary schools, the static, stereotypical model appears quite appropriate. This is borne out in this particular study.

It holds, too, in American schools. Lortie reports that 'the people work of teaching is carried on under special circumstances'. The teacher's attempts to shape children are[12]

> continually constrained by the fact of 'classness'. Teachers do not establish entirely distinct and separate working contracts with each student — they establish general rules for class conduct and find it necessary to discipline deviation from these rules . . . the claims of 'individualised instruction' must be seen in light of these fundamental constraints.

These ideal models, therefore, together with the instances and causes of deviations from them, are more appropriate subjects for study as bases of teacher action than idealist and paradigmatic investigations.[13]

An example of teacher typification

I had many talks with teachers about their pupils. Here is a typical example of one such talk. I was interested in a particular class at the time, and this teacher had been their form teacher the previous year, and thus, I reasoned, had grounds for knowing more about them than most. I asked him what he could tell me about them as individuals, assuming that what I read about them on their reports was very abbreviated and possibly not the whole truth anyway. Thus the discussion was set deliberately to open up the typification world of the teacher acting in his professional capacity. He had in front of him a form list, and this was his reply, as recorded on tape:

Tony Bowyer — very disappointing. I noticed a decline last year and I spoke to him about it, and he's a right lout, isn't he? Always shuffling around with his hands in his pockets, instead of being a nice young man, as he was, but he's far from . . . This boy, John Cosin, he's got more introverted as time's gone on. He hasn't much to offer, but . . . now this little chap, Falding, he's alive and quite a promising little lad. No comment about Floxton, he's a reasonable lad. Now this one I understand has some problems at home. I don't think he's malicious or anything, but his manners and courtesy are less than you'd expect. Nice chap, Hodges, and this boy [Keele] and this one [Lewis], and him [Lane]. I got on well with Moore, though he had a bit of trouble — a bit of petty theft, you know. This boy [Muswell] is very poor but a very nice little kid, but he's illiterate, of course, but he's helpful, he'd do anything for you. I got on with him very well, very, very well, different from some of these illiterates — behind-your-back merchants, aren't they? This boy [Royle] — an unusual boy, I got on very well with him, though some didn't . . . and . . . I like that boy [Rudd] . . . has some family troubles, I don't know what the family history is; they haven't the benefit of a father at the moment. Whether he's died, or whether they have matrimonial troubles, I don't know. Soanes is all right, no trouble. Now they [Stewart] have trouble — the father told me, and he's a very nice little lad, John, when you get to know him. He always has a lot to say — very proud of his mother, who I think has left the family. Nice little lad, Keith. These people are all right . . . Stephen Woodcock a very mature boy.

Now the girls, I don't know so much about. Sandra, she's a pleasant girl. This one [Dianne] is very pleasant, not much ability but pleasant. Shirley is very difficult to get through to, always reserved, doesn't say much, a bit sullen. Judy Kershaw, a *lovely* girl, this. This girl's [Angela Mancroft] a nice girl now she's broken away from Dianne. Rebecca's a nice girl, she gets asthma and is away a lot; she's in real trouble there. This girl's [Geraldine Pitt] a very nice girl, not much ability I'm afraid; and here again, Pat — nice girl, she's a trier, she got involved with a bit of shop-lifting, but I think she's sorted it out. A live wire this one [Kerry], always in trouble, on report, particularly with others, and I must say she's never worked very well, but she's a happy disposition.

I then pressed the teacher to elaborate on certain individuals in certain respects, but though qualifications and extensions were introduced, no

177

further categories of thought were revealed. Now I am not suggesting this represents his total knowledge of these pupils by any means, nor that he always thinks in these terms, nor that these thoughts necessarily form the basis of his action in the classroom. What it does point to, however, is his differential knowledge of pupils, the categories he chooses to think of them in, in the professional context, and his confessed ignorance of some.

Looking at his comments on the boys, there are two polarities offered: (1) 'Introverted', 'not much to offer', against 'alive' and 'quite promising', and (2) 'helpful', 'very nice kid', etc., against other illiterates who are 'behind-your-back merchants'. He talks about all of them in terms of their disposition to school primarily, and his relationship with them. Within this chosen arena of discourse he emphasizes his ideals which show a commitment to the traditional image. Of all the boys, Rudd came closest to it. He was the only one who, in interview, emphasized the ultimate object of gaining as many and as good examination passes as possible, in order to get a good job. But if you had some hope, this was the first criterion; you 'had something to offer'. If you had not, another quality is called on — 'likeability' or 'niceness'. Some are 'nice', 'reasonable', 'mature', 'helpful', as opposed to others who are teetering on the brink of subversion. He chooses to inject some comments about home background, but again these follow a stereotypical pattern along the criterion of broken home equals disturbed child.

With regard to the girls, he admitted he knew little about them, and his remarks were mainly limited to a vague, affective category of 'nice' or 'pleasant'. Again one girl, Judy Kershaw, aspired closer to the ideal than the others — 'a *lovely* girl, this' (his emphasis) but the others were mostly converging around the median of niceness, except for Shirley and Kerry who are offending the norm in some way, but Kerry at least has 'a happy disposition'.

It would be a mistake to make too much of this example, but it does illustrate the terms in which teachers discuss children in their (i.e. the teachers') own confidential arena as one professional to another. It highlights one or two of the 'cues' which teachers look for to 'identify' the pupil ('illiteracy', 'broken home', 'niceness'), and the categories that emerge ('struggler', 'disappointing', 'promising', 'good relationship'). It also suggests stability — some firm judgments are made, at least about the boys, and some predominant typifications that suggest consistency from one context to another ('a right lout, isn't he?', 'very nice', 'very difficult to get through to'), a very strong affective area, focusing on his 'feelings' for them; and a certain vagueness about some, especially the girls. This is with a group of children that he knows better than any other. In no sense is this intended as an evaluation of this teacher personally. It is common among his colleagues, and in other schools, and indeed other professional areas, as Sudnow has demonstrated in hospitals, and is a commentary rather on the functional relationship between teacher and pupil. It is contributing to what I have called the static, stereotypical mode of teacher-typifying which lies behind most teacher judgments of pupils when considering them in mass, which includes when writing reports. (Of course, when considering them as individuals, unassociated with their colleagues and dissociated from pupil status a more complex typification structure *might* be brought into play, but that does not concern us here. Opportunities, and time, for that are few.)

Reports as typifications once removed

Many teacher typifications are thus stereotypified. Reports are even more stylized. For a start, they are a stage removed from the action. They result from the teacher 'reflecting' on the pupils in their absence, not constructing views about them in actual interaction. Of course, he will have his actuarial records — such as mark book — with him, but the context of his thought and cue-identification is different. Different factors shape his consciousness in the staffroom, as opposed to classroom. There, the teacher's pull towards norms distinguished chiefly by professionalism is stronger, and so is the influence of ideal-types. Figure 8.2 illustrates some possible routes between interaction and reports.

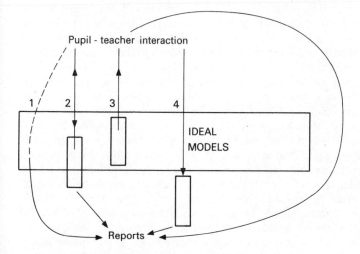

Figure 8.2 Routes between classroom interaction and reports

Note: Small rectangles represent teacher personal frameworks. Large rectangle represents ideal models.

Route 1 The teacher has 'taught' the pupil and has to write a report on him, but there is no data, no cues, and therefore nothing for him to process.

Route 2 These do involve teacher processing. The extent to which they are influenced by ideal models varies, of course, as does the direction of influence.

Route 3 Personal framework totally embodied in ideal models, and the typification begins there.

Route 4 Not at all influenced by ideal models. Personal and individual interpretation. Highly idiosyncratic in our system.

In classroom teaching, as we saw in chapter 5, teacher and class establish norms of procedure by negotiation.[14] This is a complex procedure which takes time. There is 'give and take' on both sides, as each feels out the other for maximization of their aims. The teacher might have to lower his standards to get any work out of his pupils at all. He might have to revise his notions of 'proper conduct' in the light of new cultural experience. The whole thrust of his teaching in this 'teacher' context might alter under those constraints, to, for example, survival, as I discussed in chapter 7. Reports do not reflect this classroom reality, but revert to the public official image of aims and standards. There is no concession to classroom negotiation.

In fact, reports implicitly deny it, building up a commentary on the pupil and a record of his achievement judged by absolute 'educationist' standards. Where the official aims and standards are capable of manipulation, as with non-examination forms, there is more room for manoeuvre. Here the pragmatic, survival element is nearer the surface at all times. Broad aims allow teachers greater personal definition, but even here 'ideal models' still very much hold in relation to social development, as I shall show later.

This demotion of the negotiative aspects and the supremacy of the educationist increases the chances of their inaccuracy. In making absolute judgments by formal criteria on standardized issues, reports are heavily weighted against individuals, not only in their 'individuality', but also in other areas. For example, it is well known that some pupils who show no ability at school do show considerable ability in other circumstances; and that some pupils who are 'badly behaved' at school might be very well behaved elsewhere.[15] Thus, in reporting on pupils' institutionally produced behaviour as if it were a decontextualized, genetic product, reports are adding to the accumulation of official information on individuals which goes towards providing them with an official identity. It might be highly stylized, and as a comment on inherent ability, qualities and dispositions, a misrepresentation of an individual's potential. The question is, how far does it, with all the other 'feedback', *become* the truth.[16]

Constraints operating on the construction of reports

Not only are reports a stage removed from the action, but they are cir-cumscribed by very severe constraints, which also effect their nature and content. Figure 8.3 illustrates the distribution of a typical teacher's time and energies on his pupils.

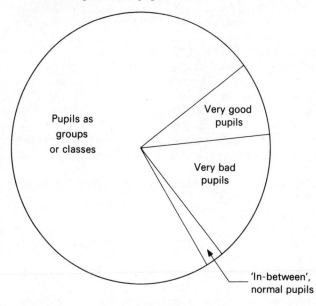

Figure 8.3 Distribution of teacher time

Most time is spent on pupils in groups or classes, with quite a lot going on very good or very bad pupils individually. Only a small propor-tion of time is spent individually on the 'in-between' pupils — yet these represent the vast majority, perhaps 95 per cent, of the total pupil popu-lation. As Lortie notes:[17]

> although there are dyadic contacts, a simple bit of arithmetic discloses that teachers can hardly spend more than a few minutes with each child in the course of a working day. Most of their teaching behaviour therefore must be addressed to groups of children.

Much of their efforts therefore go to establishing and maintaining work-ing rules for class activity; they 'groove' the students into regular patterns of joint action.[18]

The physical and temporal conditions are also very delimiting. At report time the teacher is faced with writing perhaps 300-400 reports on pupils, 75 per cent of whom he has limited knowledge of. He is given a very small space on the report sheet in which to write his comment, and a limited time, usually not more than two weeks. He is invariably extra fatigued while doing it; the task usually coming at the end of term, and he having to carry his usual workload while doing it. It is not surprising that there are a large number of 'neutral' comments such as 'fair', 'satisfactory', 'not bad', or the seemingly infinite number of combinations of them such as 'fairly satisfactory', 'quite good at times', and the one that intrigues me the most, 'very fair'. (Is this better, or worse, than 'fair'?)

It might be claimed that, after all, this is only a reflection of what has been and what is – most people *are* 'satisfactory' and even 'very fair'. This, however, in the light of the present argument, would be the wrong way of putting it. They would have to be regarded as 'satisfactory' or 'average' by that teacher's present standards and criteria. If he has a class that contains extreme groups which occupy most of his time, a neutral comment might simply indicate that the pupil concerned is not in one of those groups. 'Satisfactory', then, can have a number of very different meanings. Here are some of them:

(1) Is producing work and/or behaviour quite up to my, his, or the school's standard.
(2) Does not impinge on my consciousness.
(3) Is neither very good nor very bad.
(4) Is in the middle of the boat with regard to his particular group (as opposed to more universal criteria).
(5) The comment is intended to be as meaningless as possible, for any one of a number of reasons, e.g. lack of time, energy, knowledge or hope.
(6) Projects image of a 'succeeding' or 'coping' teacher, i.e. deliberately intended to reflect on teacher rather than a pupil.
(7) A palliative to troublesome parents or pupils.

A range of meanings could be inferred for any stylized comment. Take the 'not good enough', 'could do better' line. This could mean, among other things:

(1) Is not up to standard.
(2) Impinges adversely on the teacher's consciousness.
(3) Is verging towards the 'bad' end of the spectrum.
(4) Is good enough, but the pupil needs to think he is not, possibly as a motivation device.
(5) His work reaches the required standard, but behaviour does not match the ideal model. The reference to hidden reservations of ability is a kind of bait to lure them into conformity.

In addition to pressures arising basically from inadequate resources, there are others of a socio-political nature. One teacher whose opinion I sought on the usefulness of reports as message conveyors said, 'It would be all right if you could say what you thought, like, "Your little Ronnie wants a damn good kick up the backside."' In similar vein a parent made the observation that they were 'good if not doctored' and 'that you had to be prepared to read between the lines'. A teacher-parent, who once came to see me on a parents' evening about his son, greeted me with, 'Now come on, cut the cackle, I know what it's all about, tell me how Trevor *really is* getting on.' In their different ways these comments indicate some kind of filter or smokescreen through which teacher views are intentionally passed. What is its nature, and why is it there?

TABLE 8.2

Report given	Possible preferred report by teacher	Possible parental interpretation
Quite fair	Plain and undistinguished	Good
Needs to work hard ⎫ Finds the subject ⎬ difficult ⎭	Unintelligent and/or lacks other necessary personal qualities	The subject is difficult
Easily distracted ⎫ Lacks concentration ⎭	Prefers the pointless un-productive, dislocating mucking about with peers, to listening to my pearls of wisdom	Is misled by others in class
Well-mannered	Is no trouble (often academically weak)	Good

First, in Table 8.2, some examples of 'cackle' and its possible misinterpretation. Why do teachers not say what they feel on reports? Why do they qualify their statements? It might be supposed that it is a normal feature of human intercourse to pull one's punches and not tell people to their faces what you think of them or their children. We might with profit analyse reports through exchange theory or game theory. For the moment, however, let us note that reports are not written only for parents. They are also written for the headmaster, and through him for his employers, the LEA, the governing body, and the parental body as a whole. The headmaster, and/or his deputies, screens all reports and usually countersigns them. Sometimes he adds a comment, though not often, for if a teacher has hundreds of reports to do, the comments might run into thousands. He supervises standards, even sometimes specifying type of pen and ink to be used, and correcting for spelling and style. Above all, however, he ensures conformity to the classic ideals, and that nobody oversteps the mark.

Reports are also written for one's colleagues. They are passed around for completion, and comments are open for all to see. This can have both a restraining and channelling effect. One is unlikely to exceed the bounds of professional discretion as often tempted to do; then, as comments accumulate on reports, there is the danger that one might be influenced by what is already recorded, especially if the pupil concerned is, for this particular teacher, one of the 'faceless mass in the middle'. This process is similar to the one that goes on in staffroom discussions of pupils and the affixing of labels.

Functions of reports

If report comments are so inaccurate, or variable as descriptions, other functions are suggested.

Professionalism

This can be seen at work in various ways. It might be thought that parents receive reports as a right, and that they are given as a 'service'. However, the tone and organization of reports, and the way in which they are administered, make it clear that the balance of power is in the other direction. Teachers choose the content, define what counts as skills and social behaviour and arbitrate on standards. That is the basis of their professional expertise, and parents do not have access to it. At Lowfield they were often reminded of their powerlessness and 'ignorance' more pointedly, by for example the headmaster correcting parents' spelling mistakes on notes they had submitted to him on parents' evenings. Most parents, therefore, are not in a position to contest or even doubt teacher comments on reports. In this sense, reports have a strong political function, helping to sustain the impression of the subordinate role of parents and the professional image of the 'expert' pontificating without possibility of error; adding to the air of mystery about the content and expertise of teaching and 'the way school works'; integrating the staff in the common endeavour while separating out parents individually, yet seeking to enlist them in the reinforcement of their own power.

Reports occupy an important strategic position at the juncture of public and private spheres. Reports are similar in position and effect to institutionalized psychology (with which they are sometimes infused):[19]

> In the private sphere, it appears as one of the agencies supplying a population of anxious consumers with a variety of services for the construction, maintenance and repair of identities. In the public sphere, it lends itself with equal success to the different economic and political bureaucracies of social control.

By reaching into the private sphere, and appealing to factors which parents hold most dear — their children's life-chances — reports help lever parents into support of teachers' professional image in the public arena. Thus, like psychologism again, reports furnish 'the scientific legitimation of both inter- and intra-personal manipulation'.[20]

Thus within the general bureaucratic framework of school, reports, though ostensibly for parents' and pupils' benefit, help to insulate and protect teachers and indeed reinforce their power, and help to cultivate the impression of detachment and omniscience, such as is attributed to the professions.

Again there are interesting parallels with the medical profession. Friedson has observed how doctors protect themselves as a profession (against the emotional and intellectual demands of clients) by the use of 'avoidance techniques' (avoiding scenes and confrontations), and by control over access to information. They also protect their own self-image. 'Many institutionalised practices have developed to protect professionals . . . from unpleasant scenes . . . but also to cushion involvement with their own identity feelings.'[21] Thus they develop ways of resisting notions of professional failure that might arise, for instance, in cases of terminal cancer. 5 L are the 'terminal cancer' patients of school. The best practical treatment is to make them as 'comfortable' as possible until they leave. But while this goes on, the professional image and the individual's self-identity must be maintained. There is no public, and very little private, suggestion of the possibility that the teachers might have 'failed' 5L, or even that 5L and their kind present problems which they cannot, and ought not to be expected to, solve. The pole position of absolute standards and teacher infallibility is immutable, and the pupils are measured, unilaterally, against this.

Professionalism is another reason why punches are pulled in reports. Doctors do not tell patients that their case is 'hopeless' and their treatment 'useless', for that is an admission of professional failure. Similarly, teachers might use such terms among themselves in the privacy of the staffroom, but not in the public arena, of which reports are a part. There the general tone is one of hopeful urgency, and the content consists of shorthand diagnosis of the pupil's mental and behavioural health and prescriptions for success. That is what is expected from professionals, not admissions of perplexity, bewilderment, failure, weakness, frustration or resignation, which often is the actual case, as with Lortie's teachers:[22]

A seemingly simple question of problems of evaluating progress unleashed a torrent of feeling and frustration; one finds self-blame, a sense of inadequacy, the bitter taste of failure, anger at the students, despair, and other dark emotions. The freedom to assess one's own work is no occasion for joy; the conscience remains unsatisfied as ambiguity, uncertainty, and little apparent change impede the flow of reassurance. Teaching demands, it seems, the capacity to work for protracted periods without sure knowledge that one is having any positive effect on students. Some find it difficult to maintain their self-esteem.

Clearly, it would not do to convey this impression to parents.

Assessment and distribution

Winter has suggested that reports might not be intended to help the pupil, but as assessment, to help to fix the pupil's position in the division of labour.[23] Thus he thinks they are addressed primarily not to parents, but to the educational bureaucracy, providing information on how far the pupil is likely to be successful, and how much trouble he is likely to cause. They help fix his 'market value' both in the eyes of parents and of the educational bureaucrats.

Garfinkel's analysis of clinic folders supports this argument.[24] The items in the folders are 'tokens', he says, 'gathered together to permit a clinic member to formulate a relationship between patient and clinic as a normal course of clinic affairs'. That is to say they are serving the uses of contract rather than description — for whatever purposes their compilers want to put them to.

At Lowfield, this bureaucratic element was clearly evident, though I have no evidence to show if and how reports were used, as documents, in the assessment mechanism, or if they were related to private and confidential files. They seemed to be completed and regarded with immediate intent.

Advertising ideal models and recruiting parents

Teachers clearly assume the right to make decisions about what kind of person to aim to produce and also assume that this is generally acknowledged. Reports reflect the school's twin aims of providing skills and social training. An indication of the extent of the latter is given by a content analysis of six girls' school reports from 5L, selected at random (see Table 8.3). Having studied all the 4th- and 5th-year reports, I decided that these were the main items occurring:
(a) Character and personality
(b) Ability
(c) Behaviour and attitude
(d) Standard and rate of work.

Table 8.3 clearly shows the predominance of behaviour/attitude comments in all six cases. There are relatively few judgments on innate characteristics of personality or ability (these items occur more frequently on 'good' reports — as 'good' points and hence matters of congratulation and reward). There are more comments on standards of work, but except for one case, still many fewer than behaviour/attitude. There is not a higher proportion of bad points. I suggest that is indicative of the greater weight attached to this function — training for social relations (as compared with the other main function-skills), associated

TABLE 8.3 How comments were distributed among the six girls

Pupil		1st year	2nd year	3rd year	4th year	Totals
1	a	0	0	0	1	1
	b	4	8	9	0	21
	c	11	22	13	18	64
	d	1	2	5	10	18
2	a	0	3	0	0	3
	b	1	2	3	6	12
	c	14	12	12	13	51
	d	16	21	21	12	70
3	a	0	2	0	0	2
	b	8	7	0	4	19
	c	19	21	20	11	71
	d	7	5	13	6	31
4	a	2	2	3	0	7
	b	6	3	3	2	14
	c	15	22	15	11	63
	d	4	10	13	12	39
5	a	0	0	2	2	4
	b	3	3	2	2	10
	c	21	21	14	13	69
	d	10	11	10	9	40
6	a	0	2	2	0	4
	b	10	10	8	3	31
	c	17	22	18	17	74
	d	5	3	6	8	22
All	a					21
	b					107
	c					392
	d					220

with this non-examination form, especially in the context of their known inclinations to deviance. I had no time to make a similar analysis of top-form pupils, but I would hypothesize that their behaviour/attitude is less of an issue. It can be taken for granted that pupils are readily assimilating all the cues relating to their future dispositions in society, leaving teachers freer to concentrate on the provision of skills. We would expect, therefore, comments in the (d) category to increase and (c) to decrease. Since teachers are more disposed to being congratulatory than condemnatory (as a motivational principle), we would also expect a higher proportion of comments in the (a) and (b) categories. Pupils are congratulated for obedience, willingness, good manners, industry, application, consistency, neatness, good sense, and 'maturity' is reckoned by these criteria. An idea of the nature of these models is given by the following examples:

> 'A much better report. It would appear that Dianne has taken some of last term's comments to heart. A much more mature attitude this term, with obvious results. I really feel she must be congratulated, as she has come a long way. Please keep these standards up.' (Form teacher's comment on 4th-year girl)

The most vivid examples I came across were those relating to the 'ladylike' image required of girl pupils.

> 'Apart from French and music, Sara's report is below standard for a 3rd-year 2nd-stream pupil. Her slovenly ways, moodiness and inelegant speech are reflected in her work.'

> 'She is a cheerful girl who is rather boisterous, at times too much so. We must in this final year try to turn her into a quieter young lady.'

> 'Tends to make her presence heard forcibly and often uses rather strong language. I feel that if she can be made to see that this is not the behaviour we expect from young ladies, it will be to her advantage.'

The example above (on Sara) is rather unusual in its forthrightness. I came across very few of these and took them to be indications of despair. This suggests another function of reports – as an avenue for release of tension, even perhaps 'revenge'. Usually, however, comments are always nicely controlled, as in the other two examples. Too strong a statement can lead to opposition and resentment on the part of the parent, who might then support the pupil in counter-institutional activities. Better to work for their co-operation. To this end they are recruited into the motivational game. One of the things that impresses when reading through hundreds of reports is the atmosphere of urgency that they create. 'Time is running out . . .', 'there is an enormous wastage of potential and opportunities', 'there will be serious consequences', 'it will be for the individual's benefit', 'her life's career depends on it . . .' These are usually coupled with phrases of personal loss and regret.

Seeking further elaboration of the ideal models I did more content analysis on the reports of the non-examination forms in 4th- and 5th-years (4L and 5L). This study revealed the following list of 'blame' categories that teachers impute for pupils' failure to conform. As Berger and Kellner have shown, the pervasiveness of psychological models encourages these attributes being seen as inherent characteristics of individuals, whereas they are really products of social interaction.[25] I give some actual examples with each:

Peer group

This puts the blame for failure to reach required standards of work and behaviour on the activities of others, and the weakness of the individual in not resisting the temptation to join them. Implicit is the recognition of the individual's particular potential to reach the grade if he can only sever the connection. We must, therefore, rally to shore up the weakness.

On reports, this will feature as 'got into a bad crowd', 'is easily distracted', 'too busy mucking about with her mates'. Other examples:

'She must avoid inclusion in the pranks of her friends and thus inviting trouble.'

'Must make more effort and spend less time fooling around with her friends.'

Peer groups need not be nonconformist to be a nuisance:

'Shows little desire to get down to hard work, but relies on help from those around her.'

Immaturity (or 'irresponsibility', or 'lack of sense')

Like many of these blame categories, this is simply a euphemism for nonconformity. It contributes to a model of progressive socialization into the school's norms. One's maturity is then judged according to position along this scale. Thus *can* be retrogressive.

'Thelma must really take a much more mature attitude to her work. Time is running out for her. Next year is absolutely crucial to her.' [This also conveys the typical sense of urgency in some reports.]

'Susan's attitude to work is not sufficiently serious. Until she learns to concentrate and adopt a more responsible attitude to homework her progress will be very slow.'

'Kerry has been immature this term.'

'Would do well to mend her ways and get down to some sensible thinking and work for her own well-being.'

'Jean is becoming increasingly immature by comparison with the rest of the form.'

'Very immature. Has not yet shown ability or desire to work for his own benefit.'

Laziness

This is very common. Again it is often imputed as an inherent quality, but it is a similar laziness to that imputed to the thousands of unemployed by the 1834 Poor Law Commissioners. They were unemployed because they were 'lazy and didn't want to find work' — the economic system and provision of jobs were faultless.

Pupils therefore are 'lazy' in relation to the goals and means specified by the school. Thus 'laziness' is also a euphemism for nonconformity.

'Thoroughly lazy. Must learn to behave properly and let others get on with their work.'

'William is definitely lazy.'

'Far too fond of hiding away from anything approaching real mental effort.'

'This girl is basically lazy.'

'Has no idea of what work means.'

'He does not enjoy work and has constantly to be pushed to achieve anything. Too nonchalant.'

'Thoroughly lazy. Obtaining homework from her is like getting blood from a stone.'

'A very dilatory child.'

'Idle and pestilential.'

'She must learn that chance is no substitute for work.'

Lack of ability

These comments either suggest a 'total' deficiency, i.e. the pupil is lacking an essential mental component necessary for adequate performance; or they compartmentalize, i.e. draw a distinction between 'academic' or 'scholarly' mentality, and 'native wit'. Thus we often get the 'merry yokel' picture:

'Despite limited capability, John tries cheerfully.'

'An extremely low standard, not due to any lack of effort, simply to a lack of ability at the subject.'

'He has made an effort this year but his innate ability is very low.'

'Carol has found the work beyond her capabilities.'

'Work hampered by slow thinking and nervousness.'

'Quiet pupil who would do well to get down to some real reading and writing so as to improve his pretty low capabilities.'

Lack of other personal qualities

'Dianne needs more confidence in herself and a determination to improve.'

'She is rather a timid pupil.'

'Incapable of concentrating on any subject for very long. Must realize there is a need for greater effort to improve even when the interest is lacking.'

'Needs more drive about her.'

'Still capable but lacks drive.'

'She cannot be trusted to work without constant watch.'

'She does not work at all willingly and is not prepared to concentrate sufficiently.'

'Greater care and application needed. Dreadfully untidy at times.'

'Far too ready to accept low standards of work.'

'Must learn to control her giggling fits.'

'Complete lack of initiative and effort.'

'Slap-dash attitude with little pride.'

Thus one can come unstuck if one lacks confidence, courage, concentration, effort, drive, trustworthiness, care, application, ambition, control, initiative, pride. By the same token, possession of deplorable attributes can lead to problems.

Possession of deplorable attributes

'An annoying silliness has crept into her whole attitude.'

'So often a thorough nuisance because of her persistent chattering.'

'A little too quiet in the class.'

'Far too inclined to be ill-disciplined, noisy and rude, and in class she is simply being lazy. Next term she must pull herself together and work, before it is too late.'

'Her slovenly ways, moodiness and inelegant speech are reflected in her work.'

'Susan will be much pleasanter when she ceases to show off and when she realizes that she has an awful lot to learn. She'd do well to start before it's too late.'

'Lazy and impertinent.'

'Amiable but plodding.'

'Far too emotional. More mature approach needed.'

It will not pay off, then, to cultivate silliness, chattering, quietness, loudness, rudeness, strong language, moodiness, exhibitionism, impertinence, slowness, emotion. Although these are all cultural products, they are often presented as individual attributes. The question is, how far is the perpetual reinforcement of this kind of definition self-fulfilling, so that they become individual attributes?

The technicalities and mysteries of the subject

These are used in conjunction with some of the above, and occasionally the desperate efforts of teacher. This is operating, of course, in the interests of professionalism.

'The language of maths is incomprehensible to this pupil in spite of a hard slogging year to explain.'

'He finds the work difficult.'

In such ways are the ideal models exposed and highlighted, the pupils' weaknesses in relation to them pinpointed, parents wooed for their potential to motivate their children, and the cause of the profession secured and advanced.

Reports as cultural products

I want to show here (a) the inaccuracy of some comments and implications made about pupil ability and the misleading timbre of some comments on attitude and work, and (b) where some aspects of behaviour are more or less correctly described, that they are an institutional product rather than an inherent quality of the individual.

(a) In a staffroom discussion I asked some teachers how they defined the 'ability' in pupils they so often talked about. It revolves around three factors – (1) powers of expression and extensive vocabulary; (2) powers of analysis and discrimination, and ability to grasp ideas; (3) flair and imagination.

Labov has illustrated vividly how apparently unable and inarticulate children can undergo a metamorphosis in a different context.[26] As one 5L boy told me, 'Why worry around school, we just slouch around. Of course, we wouldn't if we were anywhere important.' In this instance the 'metamorphosis' might be present within the same context, but either simply pass unrecognized, or be lacking some other unstated or unrecognized quality. In the following interview extracts I suggest that all the above properties are clearly evident, yet they come from a pupil of low school achievement and low 'ability'. There are other admired qualities evident too – the ability to take the role of the other, tolerance, patience, humour, intellectual curiosity – 'maturity':

PW: The teachers might say they planned interesting lessons for you. Did you ever think that, at the beginning of the year, for instance?

Shirley: Well, when we started at the beginning of the year, I thought well, here we go again, we've got the same old lessons and same routine, but I can see from their point of view it's a hard job for them to find good lessons for us to do, that they think we'll enjoy, I mean I can understand they got to have a lot of patience to sort it out and take us on (*laughs*).

PW: Don't you have any interesting lessons?

Shirley: Yeah, we have some, there's two, there's social studies, that's with Mr Town, and that's like dealing with the outside world. And there's environmental studies with Mr Harvey, and there we're surveying the old-time villages of Bourne and Turkersville and the surrounding area. That's good that is, 'cos we use those old paper documents which are the school's and we get the information off of them.

PW: If you could make your own timetable, what would you put in it?

Shirley: Well, I'd put social studies first, I'd have all morning at that if I could, and careers, 'cos we can learn more about different jobs and how to get 'em and what passes you need for them. I'd put those two first. Then I'd probably put English and maths . . . because some of us need 'em for jobs that we're doing, but I don't really need it because I haven't got no passes, I don't need any . . .

PW (in a discussion about games): Do you try to get out of it if you can?

Shirley: Well, sometimes I feel I don't want to do it, that's not very often now, 'cos I've got used to getting into it, but some weeks I think 'Games! Ugh! What a rotten thought.' I try an' forget me kit, something like that, always end up taking it. But if I do do it when I don't want, I always sit there and mope about (*laughs*).

PW: Can you get out of doing it?

Shirley: Well, if you wanna get out of it you've either got to 'ave a note from your parents or you either got to 'ave something 'appened to you at school that they know about, or keep moaning at 'em until they tell you to go away.

PW: Any other dislikes?

Shirley: Oh no, the timetable's not all that bad considering what you 'ave to do. I know we've *got* to do it and there's nothing that we can do about it to say we can't really. Only way we can get out of it is by 'aving the day off or something. If you 'ave it off like that you probably get found out and then you're for it . . .

(Talking about teachers in general)

PW: What makes them more acceptable to you?

Shirley: I suppose it's the different ways in which they go about their subject, you know. One teacher you can bring in fun with the lesson, at other times you can just sit there and be bored stiff and get fed up and start moaning and complaining, and mucking around, but . . . it's like last year we 'ad music, this year we don't 'ave it 'cos we was always complaining, all we ever done was sit there and listen to records. I mean that was boring for us, 'e never used to let us sing . . . Mr James, he's very understandin', I get on all right with him, because last October I was away two weeks when my father died, an' you know when I went back to school he says if ever I 'ad problems or my Mum 'ad any problems, come and see 'im and he'd sit and listen to you, all afternoon he'd sit and listen . . . Some of the teachers have had more experience in teaching to children than what the others have, an' they know sort of the general routine, 'ow to talk to the children, and 'ow to get on with 'em more than the others do . . . Some can talk to you quite harshly, you know, an' be all nasty and bitter to you, yet you can turn round to another teacher an' he'll be ever so nice to you, much better, you know.

Not all her teachers were blind to Shirley's qualities. A content analysis of her reports during her five years at the school revealed the main distributions set out in Table 8.4. In some ways, however, this is

TABLE 8.4

Type of comment	Number
Good ability	11
Poor behaviour/attitude	31
Good behaviour/attitude	30
Good work	27
Variable work	37

misleading, for Shirley, like the vast majority of her colleagues in 5L, had been consigned to the bottom stream in the school on entry, and had stayed there, coming through eventually to the non-examination form. The criteria for ability and work differ in that route from the mainstream examination route, and can largely be collapsed into 'conformity'. This is borne out by the distribution of comments over the years, those for poor behaviour and variable work steadily increasing as

Shirley progressed through the school, especially from the end of the 3rd year onwards – the point at which the two routes formally separated. However, what the above interview shows is that, at the peak of her nonconformity, Shirley is displaying several eminently desirable qualities in the school's own terms, very readily and naturally, while being represented by some teachers as 'slovenly', using 'inelegant speech' which is 'reflected' in her work, 'loud', 'unladylike' and 'below standard'. One tactic is to recognize the ability but accord it a lower status. The headmaster told me: 'It's a sort of intelligence, a native wit and cunning, an ability to look after oneself in life, what I call "life-preservation wit".' Thus the intelligence is demoted to accord with the pupils' structural position in school, and in society.[27] The press of such attitudes and reactions and the determinism of the streaming fix her school identity, part of which is 'non-examination', that is, incapable of passing any examination. It becomes possible then to speak of her as 'good' for a non-examination pupil. But the interview shows she is good by any standards. Indeed her powers of application, expression and analysis – the key elements of general pupil ability in the teachers' view – and, one might add, depth of insight and understanding, were the equal of any pupil in the school.

(b) Reports, where they accurately describe behaviour, make no concessions to the heavy contextualizing of that behaviour, nor to the interaction that produced it. Behaviour and attitudes are reported as naturally emergent, in a manner appropriate to social Darwinism, as if the child is visited with original sin and is not responding to treatment. In fact much of this behaviour is a *reaction* – a reaction to the teacher, or some other institutional element. To understand it better we need to know, therefore, what it is a reaction to, and we must go to the pupils for this. The following comments illustrate their differential reaction to different teachers in terms used of them in their reports.

Example 1

Erica: You know she talks to us like real people.

Joy: Yeah, like *her* children.

Yvonne: As if we're grown up, she doesn't treat us like kids any more.

Erica: She makes you feel more older, more mature when she starts talking, don't she?

Joy: You can talk to her about anything.

Yvonne: I think she enjoys our lessons as well.

Example 2

> *David*: Some teachers, like Mr Jones, treat you like little children. Gives you work, makes you copy off the board.
> *Kate*: Yeah, then he gives you the answers!
> *David*: He treats you like you were a little primary school kid.
> *PW*: How do you prefer to be treated?
> *David*: Them what treat you like an individual. If I'm treated like an individual. I always work a bit better in those lessons. They always treat you as little kids.

Example 3

> *Jackie*: It's all right for juniors to 'ave uniform, but when you get to our age, I mean, I've got a Saturday job, an' you know, one week you're at school, the next week you're at work, you know, treatin' you like little children.
> *Fiona*: I reckon if they treat you like children we'll act like children — we'll muck about, an' if they treat us like grown-ups we'll act like grown-ups. It all depends on how they treat us.

Example 4

> *Amanda*: He's all right, 'cos you know where you stand with him, 'cos if he's in a bad mood, you know you've got to behave, but if he's in a good mood, he won't do anything, you can go up to him and tell him jokes.
> *Jane*: And speak back to him.
> *Penny*: Do anything with that bloke!

Example 5

> *Deborah*: He's all right, I suppose. If you have any problems 'e'll sit there an' listen to you. Sometimes he'll turn right nasty. He can be nice one day, and nasty the next, all depends how he feels.

Example 6

(In a discussion on a boy who was expelled from school.)
> *Valerie*: He swore at Mr Barney.
> *PW*: That's a good start!

Valerie: He didn't care, he just came out with any language he wanted to. He talked to all the teachers how he wanted.
Judith: But with Mr Town he'd be as right as rain. Yeah, funny that was, he seemed to like Mr Town.

These examples, in illustrating that typifications and reports are a product of interaction, remind us of some important facts attending that interaction. First, that teachers are human. They are not amorphous, bloodless, robot-like, people-processing professionals, *as they appear* on reports and other public and official documents, ceremonials and displays. They are subject to moods, whims, disabilities, misjudgments and temper. These essentially private characteristics invade the public sphere when they affect teacher-pupil interaction and judgments made on the basis of it. This is one area where teachers differ profoundly from other professionals such as doctors or lawyers. The nature of the work of the latter allows them more easily to separate the public and private arenas. Second, for the most part, teachers deal with pupils in groups. In any individual interaction the pupil is allocated a group persona, which might be far removed from any individual's view of him or herself. Hence David's plea in example 2 to be treated as an individual. But teachers who have time and flair for this, as in example 1, are very rare. Contrarily enough, however, the language of reports is highly personalized. Some of the comments, if made of a fellow adult, would be distinctly libellous. Third, it is quite clear that pupils differ between contexts, between teacher and teacher, lesson to lesson and school and home. These three basic contradictions in the teacher-pupil relationship are under-/or misrepresented in reports.

The models of behaviour encouraged by the school are assumed to have universal validity and regard. Any deviation or mismatch is regarded as deviant, and not as an alternative. However as the following interview extract makes clear, there are very strong, rich, complete and admired alternative models available, and these are deeply embedded in children's background culture. Since it is the one in which they have been reared and the one in which they will spend their lives (happily, for it has developed in reaction to the nature, conditions and environment of their work), they naturally see attempts to change it as attacks from the enemy.

(In a discussion on reports, and references therein to 'ladylike behaviour'.)

Yvonne: I don't think they're . . . Well, it seems stupid to me . . . We're women . . . I don't care what anyone says.
PW: What do you think they mean by 'ladylike'?
Yvonne: Someone that goes around stinking of perfume, 'aving 'er 'air up, an' wearin' little earrings.
Dianne: Rather like Miss Sparkes. (*Deputy head*)

Yvonne: Yeah, spittin' image of Miss Sparkes.

Dianne: That's what she's trying to get us to be like you know, trying to get us to be like her. But that's one thing I could never do, because ever since I've been five I've been climbing trees, climbing on top of garages at the back 'ere — you can climb up trees and swing over on the back of the garages. I don't think I could ever adjust to the way Miss Sparkes . . . Oh no!

Yvonne: We play football, don't we?

Dianne: Oh yeah, we like our game of footy in the dinner hour. Knocked old Jordan's hat off 'cos 'e took my matches away, so I said, 'Right, I'll have your hat.'

PW: Presumably Miss Sparkes wouldn't think that very ladylike?

Dianne: No, she wouldn't (*laughs*)

Yvonne: I hate anyone that's snobbish. There's this girl, she was ever so big-'eaded and one day she said to me, 'I don't know why you don't come to school in something decent for once', 'cos I used to go around in this little tank-top and little skirt, trousers sometimes, an' she used to come in 'er skirt an' little 'andbag . . . She always used to obey teacher. She was their pet — used to make me sick.

PW: Do they get on to you for the way you talk, at all?

Yvonne: Oh yeah, everyone moans at us for that.

Dianne: Not only swearing, but the way we talk. You know if we go up and say 'Oh yeah, all right, we'll do it' — they'll say, Oh no, you don't say it like that', then they say it the right way, and you have to repeat it. But it doesn't make any difference, it's the way you've been brought up and the way you've spoken. You can't adjust really to the way everybody else is.

PW: What about swearing, do they get on to you for that?

Yvonne: On and off, say, if we say it by accident, then they say, 'What did you say?' You 'ave to say it back, and we say we're sorry.

PW: Do you think it's wrong to swear?

Dianne: Some of the words, yeah. Some are worse than others. When I'm in a raging temper, I just come out with anything. I can't 'elp it, I'm like what me dad was. 'E would . . . it weren't all that strong, but 'e'd come out with most things over and over again, and that's like me. It was Tuesday, wasn't it, I 'ad a go at Kate Maxwell, I was raging at her. I went bombing around the gym. Oh, you should 'ave 'eard me!

This conversation is interesting for several reasons. First, Yvonne and Dianne's conception of the model in the image of the senior mistress, and their moral judgment on it — equally as reprehensible to them as their model is to the senior mistress. This is clearly a culture clash and not a question of socialization into a common citizenship, or adolescent waywardness on the path to maturity.[28] Another interesting feature is how accurately this is diagnosed by Dianne, who seems to show more sociological awareness than the senior mistress. These girls, in fact, display a great deal of sophistication and social etiquette in this conversation. Though perfectly frank about their speech, behaviour and so on, they clearly have standards conducive to good social order (hatred of snobs, 'some' swear words are wrong, etc.), and are able to discourse freely with me on a kind of 'middle ground'. For example, not once during three two-hour discussions with these girls did they use a 'swear word'. Where maturity, flexibility, adaptability, courtesy are concerned, they are very strong. Yet Dianne and Yvonne were two of those continually castigated for immaturity, rudeness, loudness and behaviour unbecoming to their sex.

Once more it seems that these qualities, professionally reported as observed characteristics of these girls, are, in fact, the product of two alien cultures impacting together, or the 'defence' of one against the threatened inroads of the other. They are not qualities inherent in the girls' biological or psychological make-up, or integral to their background culture, but institutionally produced in the attempt to 'reform' them.

Another example of a teacher imputing his own values on to pupils came when I was discussing a 4th-form miscreant, Tim Bewley, with Harry Timpson.

'You can never win an argument with Tim Bewley. He'll never back down, whereas Stephen Jones will. Steve will think, "Oh, I'm not going to win this one, it'll suit me better, make an easier passage if I give way." Tim Bewley will never give way. He's also gutless, have you noticed? He'll make a great show, make a lot of noise and splutter, but he's as weak as dishwater inside. A cricket-ball came to him yesterday along the ground and he got out of the way, whereas little Kevin Harris, a little lad with glasses, a third of his size, was breaking his neck to stop it. I slippered him the other day – one of the women had complained about him – and he argued, saying, "I wasn't the only one!" I countered that with, "I know you weren't the only one!" He was aghast at that, he expected a different retort. I didn't give him the old story about this hurting me more than it hurts you. I said, "Come on, it's a fair cop!" – that's what I expected of him, having been caught, an acknowledgment of it – "Take your punishment then it's over, I'm not going to carry on about it." But he went on, protesting away, he wasn't going to have it. No, he's a right coward, Tim Bewley.'

An alternative explanation is that the compliant boys mentioned more readily accept the cultural norms of the teacher, or possibly are better or more willing colonizers. Whereas Tim Bewley, something of an intransigent, remains more faithful to his background culture, which regards all authority and establishment men with suspicion, and demands a constantly vigilant and aggressive attitude towards them, with a touch of 'never surrender'. To admit the validity of Harry Timpson's 'fair cop' would have required him to turn his back on the criteria of survival and respect within his own culture. His persistence, then, was an act of courage and loyalty, not cowardice. As the likelihood of such polar opposite explanations of aspects of teacher-pupil relationships increases, so does the credibility of 'conflict' and 'dominance' interpretations of school.

The enormous power the teachers have over the pupils enables them to define what counts as proper standards of work and behaviour; and to exercise completely different standards in their own dealings with pupils as they choose:

> *Julie*: I can remember once when I went to take my maths book up to her, she marked it and I sat down, and she said, 'Come and collect your book, girl.' An' she just threw it at me, straight across the room [others: 'Yeah, she's always doing that'] an' tells you to go and pick it up. And if you go and ask her a question and you say 'Please, Miss', she'll say, 'It doesn't please me, so shut up and sit down.' She told me off once and I wet myself, I was so frightened – that was in the 1st years – I was so scared. She still gives me the jumps every time I see her.

Clearly, various standards of 'courtesy' are operating. Again 'conformity' seems to be the teacher's aim, and group conflict, complete with contempt, hostility, fear and hatred, the basic factor.

The following comments help to contextualize the categories of 'lazy' and 'unco-operative':

(In a discussion with some 'non-examination' pupils about teachers and lessons.)

> *Kathleen*: It's because when we were in the 2nd year, we were put in the lowest form, and from then on they didn't want to know.
> *Christine*: It's made us more lazy, in't it?
> *Kathleen*: I mean it in't doin' us no good, is it? We might as well 'av carried on with ordinary lessons.
> *Christine*: They never give us anything interesting to do.
> *Leslie*: My little brother could do what we're doing.

(In a discussion on attitude to work.)

> *Brian*: Not only that, we're not just as brainy, but we don't want to work like. If someone puts something on the blackboard and says we'll finish that tomorrow, we just rub it off, and when they come back, it's gone, so we don't do no work. An' all the form say, 'Go on, rub it off', none of 'em say, 'No, I wanna do it' – so – we're lazy.

Some elements of reports are meaningless, as stated above when discussing constraints operating on teachers.

(In a discussion about reports.)

> *Philip*: Well, some of them are stupid. Some can be fair. Some teachers — you don't 'ave 'em — and just put a silly remark in, an' I never 'ave 'er — really made me look a fool to me mum.
> *Gary*: I think they're stupid. Some comments teachers put down just don't make sense, you know, they just put down work I haven't done, or just sort of says 'doesn't try' or something like that.
> *Philip*: They're only concerned about those 5th-years who are going to take exams, you know.
> *Gary*: That's all they're concerned about.
> *Philip*: They just give us work to pass our time away really.

One of the functions of reports mentioned was to describe a pupil's market value. Some are in no doubt about this and claim it does have an effect on them:

(In a discussion on a lesson given by the headmaster.)

> *Kevin*: I sort of pretended I was listening to him. The trouble is we have to have him for our reference, to get jobs with, he's our headmaster.
> *Jane*: Yeah, that's right.
> *Kevin*: I'm being fairly well behaved at this school. I've got to be good in some ways just to get a good report. At my last school I would have got a terrible report. I wouldn't have got a job in a prison.

So, quite calculatedly, Kevin is deferential towards the headmaster because he knows he holds the passport to a good job. The headmaster in turn, equally as calculatedly, uses the threat of bad reports and references to secure good order in his school.

Of course, not all teachers have conflictual or insidious motives, conscious or unconscious, nor are all perceived as having them. Some pupils do perceive criteria which they accept as having universal validity.

> *PW*: Do you think teachers try to change people?
> *Ken*: Do you mean the way they behave? Yeah, most teachers do. They try to make you look smart, bring you up as hard-working as they can. What they're really trying to do is make you accept the fact that when you leave school you've got to work.

In summary, pupils' own speech reveals very clearly exactly those criteria of ability and attitude, of maturity, courtesy, responsibility and humour that some teachers accuse them of lacking. This again points to the inaccuracy of reports as description. They confound the teacher's human and professional reactions, his typification of the pupil by group and by individual, and they collapse several contexts into one. Much deviant behaviour is not the aberrant response of wayward pupils to an educative process, but the defensive counter-thrusts of a complete, fully-integrated and self-sufficient culture under attack from an alien culture. There may be strands common to both cultures which equip them to discourse on a middle ground, and most teachers are concerned to cultivate those; but in some cases, teacher behaviour seems simply an instinctive hostile reaction to the norms and values of an alien group. In those cases it seems more appropriate to speak of 'war' than 'education'.

If the analysis were to end here it would have been better to have forgotten about reports and to have based the discussion in the broader context of teacher-pupil interaction in the classroom. But reports are written for parents, and they have an impact on the schooling process. We have discussed their purposes and their inadequacies. We must now consider their reception. How do parents 'fill in' the sense of reports?

The reception of reports

The passage of compulsory school legislation in England[29]

> finally signalised the triumph of public over private influences as formative in social life and individual development; in particular, it tardily recognised the obsolescence of the educative family, its inadequacy in modern society in child care and training.

Not only has the family lost its educative function, technocracy has deprived the lay person of his power of judgment in the public sphere.[30]

> No longer can each person make his or her own contribution to the constant renewal of society. Recourse to better knowledge produced by science not only voids personal decisions of the power to contribute to an ongoing historical and social process, it also destroys the rules of evidence by which experience is traditionally shared. The knowledge-consumer depends on getting packaged programs funneled into him.

Both these developments are well signalled in this study. Indeed reports are 'packaged programmes' compiled by the 'scientific-professional'. However, they relate to an area where it is difficult, if not impossible, for people to achieve intellectual and emotional distance. 'To the parents, the child is a special prized person; to the teacher, he is one member of the category "student".'[31] Again, reports invade a private area with a public message through a public mechanism. Unsurprisingly, therefore, they can lead to conflict and distress. The different frameworks through which reports pass might be summarized as in Table 8.5. This is not to forget the adulteration of the teacher's framework by more 'private' factors. For the purposes of analysing parental response, the above framework holds. We have seen these clearly illustrated in the matter of subject choice. Naturally, when reading a report, a parent reads it as a report on his child, not on a group of children. Because of his ignorance of the internal mechanics of the system, he will accept the cues to objective criteria that are given. He will, for example, interpret 'satisfactory' as meaning that his child is meeting those criteria comfortably, though not brilliantly. The other nuances connected with the term, as discussed earlier, will not occur to him.

TABLE 8.5

Teacher	Parent
Universalistic	Particularistic
Institutional	Family
Professional	Amateur
Impersonal	Personal

Behind these teacher-parent frameworks are class-cultural frameworks, again as discussed in chapter 2. These permit some parents to effect the bridge between public and private more easily than others; while some parents experience the same kind of cultural assault on themselves as do their children.

'Teachers can be very sarcastic and big-headed, you know. At the parents' evening, Mr Henry made me feel quite small. "You know she gossips a lot, Mrs Overberry." Mr Fountain made me feel right guilty, as if it was all my fault she was no good at maths. Mr Taylor also made me feel small, running on about her behaviour, how she never listens and so on. My God, I felt I was back at school myself. I went to try and find something out, and came away with my tail right between my legs.' (Wife of foreman)

'No, we didn't go to the last parents' evening. When we go, we get such rotten comments, "Does not listen", "Does not pay attention", and so on, it has a depressing effect on both pupils and parents. A little encouragement would work wonders.' (Estate agent)

The latter comment from a solidly middle-class representative shows that teachers do not discriminate consciously between classes. Middle-class deviants get similar treatment — the lines are not as neatly drawn as all that. The following comments show what a mystical experience reports are for some parents:

'We don't know how good he is; I mean, teachers have more idea of his ability.' (Council worker)

'I don't really feel competent to advise Stephen because of my own lack of education. I can't appreciate fully what's at stake. I was going to take his exam report to a second teacher outside school to get an independent verdict.' (Fireman)

'We have a good hard look at them [reports]. Sometimes it's really disheartening. You can't argue with what they say, because we don't see him at school. We've accepted them – sometimes they've told us things we've virtually known, like "lack of concentration". His teachers are the people who are in the know. We sometimes look at his books and shrink in horror at the red marks on them. But they're the ones who know his potential.' (Police officer)

'You have to accept what they say, it's the only thing you can do. I go through her books and so on, but I've no way of knowing if all the heavily corrected bits are "hard" and the best bits "easy". We've no idea of the standard.' (Factory manager)

'This is my biggest grouse, really. They bring you an appointment card, and I fixed up to see those teachers he'd said he was bad at. They all told me how good he was. Then the report comes out and tells you all different.' (Toolmaker)

The conflicts, hurt feelings and sense of helplessness and outrage that can result are vividly illustrated in some of the comments above, though usually teacher diplomacy, like the doctor's 'bedside manner', wins the day. This, however, is difficult to put over in a sterile 'report'. It is always done better in a face-to-face meeting because in that situation one can say more, ask questions, explore possibilities, in short, contextualize, modify and seek the nature of any judgments that are being made. Besides, the balance of power is somewhat altered when parents enter the premises. Here is their opportunity to create an atmosphere of teacher accountability, break through the professional barrier and force consideration of their charges on an individual basis.

'Yes, I found the parents' evening very helpful. David had had a rotten report. The last one was the worst one he got. He got 'E' for maths, and was 127th out of 132. He got fed up with the homework early on. Well, I thought, is he going to do anything or not, so I went up to the school, saw most of his teachers, and they were very reassuring on the whole, very helpful.' (Petrol pump attendant)

The parent has to pad out his interpretation by whatever means are available to him.

'Reports are very stylized. They say the same things over and over again, and don't tell you very much really. The children are our main source of information, and that, of course, is filtered. They only tell us what they want to tell us. I feel very cut off from the situation, really.' (Wife of lorry driver)

Some claim more insight and broader knowledge base:

'Teachers can tell you what your child is capable of, but they don't know much about the outside world, so we try to match the two. As far as reports go, they can be very useful as long as they're dead true and not softened. You've got to be prepared to read between the lines a little. Then you weigh this up with what you get from your own child as well. For example, Jones apparently always gives everybody 'Cs', so you know if your child gets a C+ she's doing very well, and if she gets C− she's pretty poor. They give you some idea on how your child is progressing, providing they're not doctored.'

(Works manager, whose wife is a school secretary)

This last would appear to be the ideal parent in a sense, putting it all together, being on top of the situation and in command of the information. But he was the only *one* I met in sixty interviews. In short, of those parents expressing positive and unprompted feelings about reports, ten were left nonplussed by their apparent contradictions and often suspected inaccuracies; a further twelve were at a loss as to how to 'fill in' reports to arrive at a meaningful understanding and ended up frustrated and angry; four others remarked on the differential power element between teachers and parents; four more said that the reports on their children coincided with their own views and thus experienced no problems in 'filling in', since the information was already present in their own knowledge; and only one, as above, combined his knowledge of child, school and 'outside' worlds to contextualize the report. These last five are solidly middle-class parents; the others overwhelmingly working-

TABLE 8.6

Mediatory frameworks (main elements)	Kind of understanding	Response
Knowledge of system, and teacher frameworks	Diagnosis in complete contest	Satisfaction
Acceptance of system, but little knowledge	Decontextualized diagnosis	Bewilderment frustration
Rejection of system	None	None
Personal knowledge of child	Child-loaded	*Either* Confusion and/or contestation *Or* Satisfaction

class (except for four, which includes the estate agent mentioned above). Again, I would not wish to make too much of these distributions, or class connections — they are suggested, nothing more. The main point I wish to establish is the actual categories of response. These are summed up in Table 8.6.

Conclusion

Reports are not a sterile description of individuals. The views on which they are based are derived from a static stereotypical model of typification which has been decontextualized to form 'master typifications' wherein the educationist context and ideal models are supreme, and classroom negotiation discounted. The constraints that teachers work under, both concerning resources and of a socio-political nature, further circumscribe reports. Their functions are seen as professionalism, assessment and distribution, advertising the ideal models, and the recruitment of parents as motivators. As to their content, reports are cultural products. Pupils represented as lacking ability, discourteous, troublesome and lazy possess the desired characteristics as personal attributes, well evidenced in different contexts. Difficulty arises from the clash of alternative models embedded in alien cultures. The apparent simplicity of reports' comments is belied by the fact that it is a product of the messy interface where teacher-as-professional meets teacher-as-person, where child-as-pupil meets child-as-child, and where public institution meets private life. Few parents are equipped to unravel these intricacies and contextualize reports. This operates in the service of professionalism, though hardly in the interests of recruiting parents as motivators.

All this demonstrates what is by now a familiar axiom, that whatever we do, whatever judgments we make, whatever knowledge we come by, is firmly anchored in society. Reports are not a purely cognitive affair, giving omniscient judgment on objective states by absolute criteria. Nor are they entirely, or even predominantly in many cases, the result of the application of the current state of professional expertise and knowledge. They are particularly interesting sociologically because first, like subject choice, reports involve all three major parties in the educative process in interaction; and second, they invest a weak link in the system. Teachers have to commit themselves to public statements which reflect back on pupil-teacher interaction, refer to ideal models, and are addressed to third parties. They employ glosses which both disguise and contain heavily implicit references to how they perceive the relationship between those three parties, and to the functions of schooling.

We hear much these days of 'parental choice', 'community schools' (wherein parents have an integral place), the teacher acting *in loco parentis* (in acknowledgment, seemingly, of the parents' ultimate responsibility). In fact, parents have little choice, part or responsibility in their children's education. As this study shows, they are an adjunct to the system, of potential use as motivators in directions pointed to by the staff, for destinations perceived by them and in a manner defined by them. Even in America, where teachers are held to have less power, parents are seen by them in a similar light. Lortie's teachers thought 'good parents' 'should not intervene' and 'should support the teacher's efforts'; and they reserved the right to 'define occasions which justify parental involvement'.[32] One might also note the classic role of PTAs — as fund-raising bodies, and in no sense collaborators. This, of course, is in line with the development of the industrial society, the segregation of areas of activity and the division of labour. As Sockett attests, 'the most cursory review of legislation in the last 100 years may be regarded as a gradual erosion of the rights of the parents.'[33] And as he notes, 'it is a paradoxical feature of the system that the older it gets, the more generations go through it and become "educated", the less the parents have any right to decide what goes on.'[34] If, in some instances, parents seem to have been more in the formal operation of the school, frequently this can be interpreted as a move by the teachers to seek their aid in control. Musgrove and Taylor sought to show that teachers have become too powerful and unresponsive and inefficient.[35] They see the introduction of school 'counsellors', as a powerful indoctrination device which can operate against the influence of parents as the most sinister among the school's recent attempts to invade the private area. Clearly, the tone of the reports examined here show that the teachers concerned readily assume that they have the right to pontificate on such matters, even to the degree of making some *parents* personally experience the effects of their comments. Thus some parents, at least, far from being collaborators with teachers in the joint project of educating their children, are themselves objects of scrutiny for appraisal and comment.

Musgrove and Taylor recommended that parents should be treated as the teachers' clients, introducing a contractual relationship. However, this would appear unrealistic. It ignores or underestimates, for a start, the consequences of that teacher power, amply demonstrated here, in the case of reports, as professionalism. With each round of reports and parents' evenings, the conditions of the teacher-parent relationship are further consolidated. But it is also out of gear with the prevailing model of society, which is an accumulation of trends and experiences and cannot be overturned by a simple act of will. The features of this society have been well described, for example by Illich, Marcuse and Roszak.[36]

In the technocracy, nothing is any longer small or simple or readily apparent to the non-technical man. Instead, the scale and intricacy of all human activities — political, economic, cultural — transcends the competence of the amateurish citizen and inexorably demands the attention of specially trained experts. Further, around this central core of experts who deal with large-scale public necessities, there grows up a circle of subsidiary experts who, battening on the general social prestige of technical skill in the technocracy, assume authoritative influence over even the most seemingly personal aspects of life . . . In the technocracy, everything aspires to become purely technical, the subject of professional attention. The technocracy is therefore the regime of experts — or of those who can employ experts.[37]

Everybody to his trade, therefore, and to other trades, a recognition of their expertise and one's own ignorance.[38]

Within such a society, the citizen, confronted by bewildering bigness and complexity, finds it necessary to defer on all matters to those who know better. Indeed, it would be a violation of reason to do otherwise, since it is universally agreed that the prime goal of the society is to keep the productive apparatus turning over efficiently.

School reports are an expression of the technocracy. They illustrate how technocratic man has superseded private man. We have seen how, in certain areas, the bartering and bargaining, the affective ties, the individual interest and compassion push through the institutional crust of ritual and routine and find expression — for example in classroom interaction, in the staffroom and in parent-pupil relationships. But there is a tension between this, and the mass public technocratic order which operates by a different mechanism, in accordance with different norms. The two do not sit happily together, as we have seen; from the teacher's point of view in his compilation of reports — in the constraints and restriction, in a certain amount of hypocrisy, in the decontextualization; from the pupil's, in the inadmissibility of his own culture if it does not fit, his experience of the ensuing conflict, and his knowledge, firmly realized or merely sensed, of the underlying truth; and from the parents', in their bewilderment, confusion, ignorance and, sometimes, shame. Yet, if Winter is correct (see p. 186), school reports, and other accounts like them, form the basis of the pupil's social identity or 'market value'. This would appear to be an excellent recipe for further devaluation of the public sector of school and work, and increased elevation of an individual's private world, where he can more truly be 'himself'.

I have discussed the mechanics of teacher typifications. They are largely a function of the constraints teachers work under, the 'mass' nature of their raw material and the need for routine. This facilitates, perhaps necessitates, the emergence of ideal models and the relation of individuals to them. But what governs the content of these ideal models? Where do they come from? They might be seen as part of the traditional role of compulsory schooling as an agency of social and political discipline, and of training the workforce for the technological society. The factory-owners of the nineteenth century needed workers 'whose attendance was regular, who were punctual, and who could work for long periods at a consistent speed; and these were precisely the qualities which, through long habit, the domestic workers lacked.'[39] With the introduction of compulsory schooling in 1870, the first task was seen to be one of 'civilizing the masses'. Soon the school took over from the church as the prime agency for direct moral instruction, 'a good example of the way in which schools were coming to be accepted as the automatic surrogate for any social institution which was functioning inadequately.'[40]

These functions have stayed with the school, though now the emphasis is not so much on civilizing or controlling a barbaric populace as 'liberating' them to increase chances of personal advancement. Thus the principles that have served the successful over the years — those contained in the 'Protestant Ethic' — have come to be universally applied. Downes has summarized these into nine basic criteria:[41]

> the possession of ambition; the recognition of individual responsibility; the cultivation and possession of skills; worldly asceticism; rationality; the accentuation of manners, courtesy and personality; the control of physical and verbal aggression; the pursuit of 'wholesome' recreation; and the respect for property.

All of these can be seen at work in the reports' comments reviewed earlier. The irony of the situation is that the best intentions of teachers are confounded by the strategies and cultures developed by the less privileged over the years as a response to the conditions in which they work and live, and to their position in the power structure. These cultures have become self-sufficient in their own right, resistant both to adversity and to attempts to 'improve' them, which might be simply disguised attempts at subversion. They carry over into school, and operate there in the same way.[42] Reports on such pupils are part of the 'noise' given off by the clash between the two.

Chapter 9

The meaning of staffroom humour

Sociological analyses of schools invariably leave an impression of grim institutionalization, and analyses of teachers, one of either sinister conspirators in the service of the dominant groups in society or of judgmental dopes, innocently but naively unaware of what they are doing. Neither of these is the view I have formed of teachers, at least in as simple a form as that; and that particular image of the school, as we have seen, is one-sided.[1] As described in chapters 2 and 7, a large amount of rhetoric pervades the teaching game. Many ingenious explanations are devised to provide accounts that square with the professional ethic and naturally enough, when interviewed on this plane by researchers, teachers answer in those terms with entire conviction. However, it is a curious fact in a society characterized by sharply differentiated functionary roles that we can 'split' ourselves into components, each one self-sufficient and insulated from the others. So that we can, if we wish, stand outside ourselves and comment on the actions of another 'self'.[2] I take the line that much personal investment in the advanced industrial society is made in the private, as opposed to the public, sphere, a point I shall return to in chapter 10. For the moment it is clear that, for the reasons I have advanced in the two previous chapters, certain elements of the 'private' self are not to be found in the teaching process at Lowfield. But they are there in school, and performing an important function.

At Lowfield, I found them in the staffroom. There I discovered a great deal of awareness of the restrictions, ruses, shortcomings and subterfuges that make up teacher activity. This awareness posed a problem, namely how to resolve the great conflict and discrepancy between the appearance on the one hand, and the reality on the other. We have seen how the rhetoric solves a problem of dysfunction on the plane of professionalism. But where the dysfunction arises as a result of the invasion of the professional by the personal plane, rhetoric is clearly highly inappropriate. The panacea in this instance is laughter. Thus we have, by my analysis, the greatest paradox of all, namely that what appears to be the most trivial and peripheral activity of the school could be interpreted as the most serious and central. For it is through laughter that teachers neutralize the alienating effects of institutionalization; that they synchronize the public and private spheres.

In this chapter I examine the phenomenon of staffroom humour. First I look at the significance of its location – the staffroom – and its incidence. Then, to give some perspective to the examples that follow, I give a summary of sociological accounts of laughter and humour. The examples are arranged according to the main contexts that have been developed in these accounts. It will be seen that these are insufficient within the framework of my analysis to do justice to the essential properties of staffroom laughter. My alternative explanation sees staffroom humour against a broader backcloth. The key role played by laughter is further supported by the conflicts that arise when its emergence is obstructed. I conclude the chapter, therefore, with a consideration of laughter-inhibitors.

The staffroom – the laughter arena

It is important to grasp the physical and temporal properties of staff laughter. Here I refer to several staffrooms of my acquaintance, which all seem of a type, though I make no other claims to wider generalizations. In these schools, the main arena is the staffroom, the teachers' collective private area. Its privacy is well respected by headteachers and pupils alike. Pupils are often debarred from knocking on the door, or even approaching its vicinity, by 'out-of-bounds' corridors. Headteachers usually knock before entering, limit their visits to urgent matters of business, and conduct themselves discreetly while there. Its boundaries are usually clearly demarcated. One I know, regarded as ideal by its inmates, was a cellar in an outbuilding, protected from the rest of the school by ancient stone walls and two car-parks. It was the 'men's' staffroom, and the strength of its boundaries was well indicated by the women's confessed trepidation at entering it. 'Solidarity' was here expressed in distance, construction, site, and reinforced by others' recognition of it. The 'properties' of the staffroom often lend it a distinctive character – perhaps old battered armchairs which the teachers who 'belong' to them defend with great vigour, resisting charitable urges from the headteacher to buy 'brand new ones'; or stained tea mugs, which carry the evidence of many a happy break – both symbols of individuality; and frequently too, signs of vast disorder – masses of papers, books, journals strewn around flat areas – which contrasts strongly with the system and order outside. Above all the staffroom is characterized by a euphoric atmosphere, given off by the reactions of the people in it, whether they be smoking, doing crosswords, playing bridge, conversing or just relaxing.

This is indeed a haven in stormy seas, and recourse must be had to it at regular intervals. The 'collective' periods are again well indicated. The initial gathering at the beginning of the day is a leisurely and tension-free gathering, after which teachers register their forms, then go to assembly. This is followed by a short, transient but often highly significant episode in the staffroom, before lessons begin in earnest. There is then a mid-morning break of some twenty minutes, a lengthy dinner-hour and a mid-afternoon break. Some often stay behind after school for an 'un-winding session'. In between these times the staffroom is populated by one or two teachers enjoying 'free periods', but as these are used in preparatory work, or in marking, they are not our concern – the staff-room is being used on these occasions as a 'quiet area' in the service of the official work of the institution.

I want to say a little more now about functions of laughter as revealed in the literature, which I touched on in chapter 5. All of these can be seen at work in staffroom humour, but also, as I hope to show, there is something more.

Functions of laughter

Generally speaking, sociological work on humour and laughter has hung round two models, one featuring conflict, the other control. Conflict humour occurs in inter-group situations where one group expresses aggression or hostility towards another group through the medium of sarcasm, ridicule, irony, satire, invective, caricature, parody, burlesque and so on.[3] The value of humour as a device is that, not only is it a socially acceptable form of expressing aggression (of 'being malicious with dignity'), and hence of great interest sociologically since it reveals strains not evident elsewhere, but also peculiarly efficacious as a weapon in boosting one's own morale and undermining the enemy's, even if this is assumed rather than a reality.[4]

In the hierarchical and status-ridden structure of a school, interpersonal conflict is endemic. It is frequently dispersed in humour. 'Status' is functional in this respect – it provides scapegoats, but protects its holders. Much of the pupil laughter featuring in chapter 5 could be represented in conflict terms, especially 'subversive laughter'.

The 'control' functions of humour are to 'express approval or disapproval of social form and action, express common group sentiments, develop and perpetuate stereotypes, relieve awkward or tense situations and express collective *sub rosa* approbation of action not explicitly approved.'[5] The 'control' function more properly operates through the sanctions of a group to enforce conformity to norms established by the group. Thus deviations from the norm might be punished by ridicule, or the norms themselves expressed through humour as part of the socializing of a new recruit. The particular 'collective' and 'sharing' quality of humour and laughter reinforces group solidarity and supports rhetorics like 'being one of the boys' and 'fitting in to the staffroom'. One feature of this fitting in is conformity with the informal traditions of the group which enable it to survive as a group, and one prominent aspect of this is often the 'joking relationship'. 'From the individual's point of view, a successful joke is a means of winning the social approval of the group, but in the very process of his seeking such approval the bonds of the group may be strengthened.'[6] Again, the reciprocal cementing function of humour is evident. At Lowfield, the deviations most frequently punished were (1) stepping out of line professionally, especially attempts at exceeding the authority of one's status, (2) stepping out of line as a person, especially boasting, toadying or 'shopping', and (3) professional incompetence, especially unawareness of the 'hidden pedagogy', even more so where this was associated with incongruity of status, i.e. high status *and* high level of incompetence. These embody the norms and values of the professional community, and those generally operative in middle-class society. Stephenson's analysis of jokes in anthologies of wit showed an adherence to a set of values regarded as the 'traditional American creed'. This 'minimizes the importance of economic differences, stresses the notion and value of equality, ridicules the concept of any basic conflicts, asserts the soundness of the American system, and emphasizes the virtues of charity, initiative and ambition.'[7] An interesting study in English staffrooms would be to consider the extent to which these are 'mocked' in the hidden pedagogy of survival, for example volunteering for extra work, losing one's 'sense of mission', 'jollying' the pupils along.

Another aspect of the 'order' function derives from the anthropological work of Radcliffe-Brown.[8] Humour has a function of maintaining a satisfactory relationship between persons and parties who, as a result of their positions, social ties and competition for favours and advancement, might be expected to feel some hostility toward each other, but who nonetheless have to carry on working together for the institution, and hence their place in it, to survive. Not only then might humour enhance solidarity, it can also evaporate conflict, jealousies, envy, even hatred.

There are many variations of the conflict-order models which do not fit tidily into either. One variant is what we might call an 'order' function whereby a subjected group, through humour, comes to accept the situation. Coser has shown how 'jocular griping' performs integrative functions for the social structure of the hospital ward, and how it helps to shape the behaviour of patients according to the expectations of doctors and nurses. Thus the patients themselves, through laughter, help to enforce the norms of the hospital community.[9] Like the pupils who transform the reality of the school in order to make it tolerable, these patients change the definition of the situation to make it acceptable as it is. Other variants are 'humour as compensation' and 'humour as release' themes. The first is well expressed by Myrdal:[10]

> When people are up against great inconsistencies in their creed and behavior which they cannot, or do not want to, account for rationally, humor is a way out. It gives a symbolic excuse for imperfections, a point to what would otherwise be ambiguous. It gives also a compensation to the sufferer. The 'understanding laugh' is an intuitive absolution between sinners and sometimes also between the sinner and his victim. The main 'function' of the joke is thus to create a collective surreptitious approbation for something which cannot be approved explicitly because of moral inhibitions.

It is a short jump from this to the defence of professional failure and inadequacy through humour among teachers. And it adds some complexity to the straight 'conflict' line. Take, for example, the great amount of 'ribbing' of pupils that goes on among teachers in staffrooms. Nearly always, such pupils are academic or behavioural failures. They present problems, academic and disciplinary, and might well be perceived as an opposing hostile group. Humour can then boost morale, metaphorically shoot down the enemy and also ascribe to them the implicit reasons for the strife.

Theories of laughter as 'release' stem from Freud. One variant is provided by Hayworth, who suggested that laughter was originally a 'vocal signal to other members of the group that they might relax with safety'. He emphasizes its 'natural' qualities, and 'if laughing is not instinctive it is at least a conditioned response acquired early in life.'[11] One might even go in search of tension, for the sake of the subsequent relaxation. Laughter here is a kind of language, and 'by communicating the mood of gladness becomes of survival value in the social group'.[12] But more than this, according to Hayworth, it is a signal that the supposed danger is passed.

Coser also refers to the safety-producing functions of laughter. Her hospital patients were subject to a high degree of insecurity and generalized anxiety, deriving from their physical condition, and the type of authority relation to which they were submitted.[13] But their joking and laughter allowed them to cope. As Freud put it, 'Its meaning is "Look here! This is all this seemingly dangerous world amounts to. Child's play, the very thing to jest about."'[14] Joking can liberate, and lead to solidarity. The jocular gripe is peculiarly fit as a mechanism of adaptation to the hospital for it helps patients to regain their identity through collective triumph over their weakness, and at the same time to release their grudges in 'substitute complaints'.[15]

To summarize: humour has been interpreted in terms of (1) conflict, as a weapon with which to strike at an enemy; or (2) control, as a device to establish norms; or (3) order, in the furtherance of social bonds, solidarity, intimacy, and accounting for failure and inadequacies; or (4) release, from tension and anxiety. I have felt this brief account necessary because, while all might well be present in staffroom humour, as we shall see shortly from examples I came across in my research, I felt that none of them, either singly or collectively, captured the essence of that particular kind of humour. First, as a reaction agent, there is insufficient emphasis on the structures and forms of organization this humour is reacting against: second, there is hardly any acknowledgment of laughter as a creative, growth experience. The two are related, since the first stimulates the second. It is its counterbalancing force.

Georg Simmel, for one, saw that many forms of human interaction contained far more than could be reduced to their mechanical functions or the sum of their various roles. It is essentially joyful and pleasurable.[16]

A superficial rationalism always looks for this richness among concrete contents only. Since it does not find it there, it dispenses with sociability as a shallow foolishness. Yet it cannot be without significance that in many, perhaps in all European languages 'society' simply designates a sociable gathering. Certainly, the political, economic the purposive society of whatever description is a society. But only the 'sociable society' is a society without qualifying adjectives. It is this, precisely because it represents the pure form that is raised above all contents such as characterise those more concrete societies. It gives us an abstract image in which all contents are dissolved in the mere play of form.

Interaction, therefore, can be intrinsically satisfying, over and above the instrumental gains that might be got from it and indulged in for its sheer delight. It can involve fondness and affection, even when expressing conflict, and the former might in fact predominate. To reduce it to instrumental functions adulterates it. Because it does not lend itself easily to sociological analysis, it tends to get ignored, which is rather unfortunate for institutions like schools many of which have a high incidence of such interaction. And it takes place mainly in 'off-periods' and in private areas, whether it be a staffroom or playground. Perhaps that is why there are so few reports on these areas – they are 'off-periods' also for researchers.

Staffroom laughter

All of the previously mentioned functions of laughter are evidenced from time to time in the staffroom, together with the other, 'creative' element. To try to separate them out would be to abuse the essence of the humour. My impression was that some of the staff were as much on the lookout for laughs as the kids. 'You have to make a laugh of it', Harry Timpson told me after one uproarious session. Often it might have its origins in conflict, control, order or some frustration, but equally as often it would seem to lose that initial referent to which it was a reaction, and become a growth experience in itself. The main social referent then would be the immediate company, the function, the delight and pleasure of sociation.[17]

Conflict-initiated humour frequently involves the attacking through laughter of attempted subversions of status by senior personnel combining excessive bureaucratic features, which themselves call for neutralization. It is not surprising, therefore, that much staffroom humour takes the form of mocking, embarrassment, or compromise of senior personnel, often by 'subversive ironies'. In essence, this is no different from the pupils' 'subversive laughter' as discussed in chapter 5. The teachers' oppressors, of course, are the headmaster and his deputies. Senior teachers and deputy heads are marginal men, neither headteachers nor ordinary staff. They can fall either way. In this case the male deputy head identified strongly with the staff, and was never a laughter object. The headmaster and his deputy headmistress at Lowfield, however, who had separate offices, were both 'subversively derided'. In giving examples of this, I should make clear that in no way am I assessing characters or competence, but trying to show how roles and situations bear on teachers and how they accommodate them. Often these accommodations, like those of the pupils, paint rather cruel portraits. Hardly a break went by without laughter being raised in some form or other over 'Cheetah' and 'Flossie', and, as with the pupils, their physical and psychological compositions were exploited to maximize the benefit. For example, these remarks followed an assembly where the headmaster had talked about war experiences. Typically, the comments grow in outrageousness until the realm of pure comedy perpetrated by a real comedian is reached:

'Did he ever really fly an aeroplane?'

'He wouldn't half have needed some cushions to sit on!'

'They wouldn't have been able to see him.'

'I reckon the Germans must have thought we'd got a new secret weapon – the pilotless plane.' (*laughs*)

'Do you remember when he told the kids once that he'd bombed Brussels, and that kid asked, "But, sir, weren't they on our side?"' (*laughter*)

'Get out boy! Don't be insolent!'

'He must have had a time taking parties to Germany.'

'"I bombed over this area, you know." "Oh, jah, indeed, I was head

216

of ze Flak, how do you do?"' (*Pretends to shake hands, Cheetah's hand gets crunched.*)

'What about the experience of Tony Hancock's fighter ace. Do you remember how he put out a fire in his single-engined plane by dropping his bombs in the sea and flying back through the spray?' (*much laughter*)

This shows the caricature (and often unkind) aspect of conflict humour. But there is a more general principle involved than the expression of aggression through humour, and the undermining of the moral position of the enemy in the context of the school and their relative positions and statuses within it. That is the celebration of a common principle among people in general which calls for equalizing and levelling.[18]

The humor in such situations is seen in the attempt to be something one is not or in trying to assume characteristics which one cannot have by virtue of his previous experience. These jokes thus function to express the value of being one's self, average, and 'just like anybody else' ...

Ceremonies and rituals frequently seemed designed for the greater glory of the role structure. Barney seemed rather status conscious. The more he tried to build up the image of headmaster, so the staff, particularly the 'wits', pulled it apart afterwards. Thus his fire drills were passed off and acted out as Nürnberg rallies, complete with the caretaker's wife being sent to the gas chamber for not clearing up the school yard properly. (Of course, when somebody told Barney that he could take his gas-mask off, he replied he hadn't got one on!) And his hymn practice assemblies were similarly acted out as if at the palace of varieties, or a Frankie Vaughan attempting, vainly, to conduct the Wembley multitude. Here is an extract from my notes of one such assembly:

'Lester introduces the hymns, and talks about how the chaps on the football trains used to sing in four-part harmony. Then he announces the first hymn, "Alleluia, sing to Jesus". Both Barney and Lester open their mouths wide and sing very loud indeed. The band also play very loud, but there is not much coming from the body of the hall. Barney comes round from behind the table to the front of the stage to inspire. Lester, who had been conducting the band, turned to face the assembly, emphasizing once more the last lines of the verse.
  Hark! the songs of peaceful Sion
  Thunder like a mighty flood;
  Jesus out of ev'ry nation,
  Hath redeemed us by his blood.
Barney stops the band with an imperious wave of the arm. "The band

is playing! Me and Mr Lester are singing, with about twenty others in the hall, now come on, heads up, books up, fill your lungs with air and sing!" After another verse, with no perceivable increase in volume, Barney suddenly shouts, "Girls only!" ("Oh Christ!" says the girl next to me.) There is a pathetic noise, like a behind-the-hand mumble, for Barney and Lester, of course, are no longer singing. "Now come on!" urges Barney. "This is a damn good tune, some good words . . ." and he intones roundly the words of the next verse:

Alleluia, Alleluia
Glory be to God on high;
To the Father, and the Saviour,
Who has gained the victory . . .

". . . now come on, sing up, sing up!" After this first hymn, Barney says, "It's coming. It takes a lot out of you, doesn't it? It takes more out of you than a game of rugby, but if you want enjoyment you've got to pay for it. The more you put into it, the more you get out of it. Thank you, Mr Lester." Lester introduces the next hymn. He runs on about background, capabilities, etc., philosophical stuff. The hymn is softer, more dulcet, "Take My Life". The band plays the introduction, then Barney interrupts. "Now come on, heads up, books up, let's hear it!" After one verse, it was, "Girls! 'Take my voice'." But they were still unable to find theirs. After that verse it was "Without the band, this time!", which yielded the most miserable noise of the morning, like one or two creaky doors opening and shutting. One girl later told me she actually started to sing, but they all stared at her so she stopped. "Boys! 'Take My Silver, take my gold!'" Oh, what a groaning!'

The headmaster and music master achieved little in terms of their intentions during this hymn practice, despite formidable exertions. Teachers on the stage said they could see whole wedges of silent faces. And so, for the pupils, it was merely an extension of the usual bore. But it was an extremely important component of the teachers' day, a brilliant start, in fact. I could see faces twitching as they sat at the back on the stage. And as soon as they reached the staffroom, Harry Timpson went into his master of ceremonies routine.

'For this verse, I give you your own, your very own, Flossie Sparkes!'
'This time we'll have the boys, the girls, the band, but chiefly — yourselves!'
'Is there any truth in the rumour that he's practising for Wembley next year?'
'It's sing-a-long with Cheetah time, folks.'
'He gets just about as much response.'
'When the band stops you can hear a pin drop, can't you?'

The staff went off happy to their lessons, and when they returned at break they immediately recaptured some of the early morning mirth, '. . . but chiefly yourselves!'

Mirth is compounded when the opposition falls out amongst itself, such as, for example, when Barney rounded on Flossie. Once she had altered arrangements for an assembly, because, it was rumoured, she didn't want to take it herself. At a subsequent staff meeting, Barney kept saying, 'Who changed it?' 'Yes, but who changed it?' Timpson said she tried to wriggle out of it, but only landed herself further in it. 'It *was* the first Monday, and the first Monday of the half term.' The staff were hugely amused to see them bickering. 'He can't stand her, can he? I was knocking round the office one day, and he came storming out, "Where the flaming hell is it?" he roared — and she had it, whatever it was.' They amused themselves during staff meetings by taking bets on what she would do first, this — rubbing her arms crosswise, or this — smoothing or straightening her clothing.

The point about Flossie is that, whatever her abilities, which were not necessarily in question, she provided tension release, as did Barney, which helped them through the day. This does not mean, of course, that it was an adequate substitute for resources, but it was a considerable consolation. During my time there, the amusement she caused vastly outweighed the exasperation. I was reminded of another senior mistress I once knew. Gertrude Harmer had become a legend in one school I taught in. New facts about her supposed incompetence were always coming to mind in the restorative staffroom chats that took place after the ceremony of the school dinner. And her howlers were always delivered with the panache of an eccentric, elderly spinster.

'Paul Entwhistle has been fudging in my drawers again. Next time I'll put a mousetrap in it.'

'Now, somebody's been trampling my flowers. You must understand that the playing areas of the field are public. But these gardens are mine. They are my private parts, and the only person allowed in there is the gardener.'

A favourite lesson of hers was 'where to put the apostrophe'. The example she always chose to use was 'cats balls', covering the blackboard with all manner of permutations. The pupils had great fun with the board rubber after she had left the room!

The social role Flossie, Gertrude and, to some degree, Barney are playing here is that of 'fool', rather than senior personnel in the hierarchy, making threatening onslaughts onto others' statuses.[19]

The fool is distinguished from the normal group member by a deviation in person or conduct which is regarded as ludicrous and improper. He is usually defined as a person lacking in judgment, who behaves absurdly or stupidly.

The fool deviates from the normal in three main ways.[20] The deviation is:

> an extreme exaggeration or deficiency; it is an evidence of weakness or irresponsibility, and it is an offense against propriety rather than against mores. With regard to the first of these . . . the role of the fool involves a striking exhibition of some incongruity or shortcoming. With respect to the second, the role of the fool inherently involves failure, weakness or comic frustration. Because of his ineffectuality, the fool is regarded as incompetent and irresponsible. Despite his shortcomings, therefore, he is distinguished from the villain by the fact that his pranks involve no evil intent or are too stupid to be taken seriously. The fool is thus tolerated and is regarded with amusement rather than being punished.

These incidents also quite clearly promote solidarity. With a large school staff there is always some regular turnover, and the input of new personnel unacquainted with these backroom legends and traditions offers an excuse for their regular recall. The spontaneous laughter of the initiates is shared by those familiar with the tales, even if they have rehearsed it a hundred times. The humour in the material is constant. The laughter is sparked off, and then spread, contagiously, and then frequently compounded by other tales.

> 'Do you remember the time the head announced in assembly about the kids coming over from the hills? "When you get to the gym, you must go straight on, you must not fork off to the dining-room."'

The mental image of those kids 'forking off' to the dining-room was another 'banker' among the staff's humour sessions. There would be input from others' experiences elsewhere, contributions heightening the individual's identification with the group. Laughter is an enormous aid to solidarity, and in the harshness of the conditions in which teachers work it is important that they have this support. Group solidarity is often aided by demarcation from other groups, hence the persistence of such themes as 'senior personnel' or 'the women's staffroom' (if indeed they are separate), or 'the kids', or other departments (such as 'the PE department'). The more ludicrous or ridiculous these can be made to appear the better — hence the added spice in the examples above that were public announcements to very large audiences. But it would be quite wrong to present this as entirely a kind of vindictive delight in the failures and embarrassments of superiors. There might be some of that, more especially when less amusing consequences of incompetence are actually being experienced. Then there might be an overriding tone of ridicule.

But on occasions, especially in recollection, and in legends, the ridicule and ill-feeling has evaporated, and the overriding tone is one of fondness. These howlers, errors and misjudgments are accepted as a contribution to sociation, and the endearing qualities of human failure, and that is how they are celebrated. The ecstasy of the humour lies not so much in the content by itself, as in the extreme incongruity, in relation to it, of the people perpetrating it. These are senior personnel – headteachers, their deputies – who, as previously noted, are more committed to the institutionalized structure and have performed more accommodations. In their responsibility for, and dedication to, the overall running of the school, they have a preoccupation with administration and policy, with rules and timetables, with 'appearances' (e.g. the public image of the school) and the 'forms' (i.e. the way in which things are done) of a completely different degree and order from the rest of the staff. That such institutionalized people can, on occasions, act in such outrageously 'foolish' fashion is an implicitly shared delight, where all concerned are allies, and the common foe, the institutional framework of the school. 'There's nowt so queer as folk', one member of staff was always declaiming. The comedian or fool who sets off a chain of humour is a person of special worth, since he promotes 'a bit of the transcendence designed to make sport of those situations, events and taboos that lie heaviest upon us if seen only from an earnest and serious perspective'.[21]

There is a lot of this in the sniping at rituals, as in assemblies, hymn practices, fire-drills, as discussed above. There might be elements of personal animosity and restoration of professional status, but there is also ridicule of the ritual as an enterprise in itself, as some kind of uncomfortable transmutation of life. It needs this humorous treatment to expose its pretentiousness. Laughter can be a great leveller. One example of this was the school's Sports Day, one of the great annual rituals of the school year. This called for considerable organization on the part of the games staff and complete co-operation from the rest, who were required to act as starters, stewards, convenors, recorders, announcers, calligraphers, policemen and cheer-leaders. It was not to everybody's taste. Indeed, to many it was an added burden, completely incidental to their main function as teachers. There were problems of motivation and order – since for many pupils it was simply a bit of a giggle – of a change of role and arena and of interdepartmental rivalry. This latter was particularly acute among some members of staff who resented the PE department's assumption of plenipotentiary powers on these occasions especially as they were using those powers to subject them to unpleasant experiences.

The gloom that had settled over the staffroom during the dinner-hour break in anticipation of the sports afternoon was suddenly dispelled when it was noticed that it had begun to rain, very, very slightly. The 'wits' went quickly to work:

'Can I have a runner – I mean a swimmer – please?' (*Using pretend binoculars, through the window.*) 'Are you ready? On your marks!'

'Calling Mr Lewis, glug, glug, glug . . .'

'Can we have all runners at the deep end?'

'That boy with the outboard engine is disqualified!'

'The shot is sinking!'

'With a boy underneath!'

'Ten to one on the one in the diver's helmet.'

'Don't forget to go straight to the decompression chamber when you've finished the race.'

'I've just seen Julie Marne. She said it was only a little shower. "We're certainly going to get a little wet this afternoon, but I don't think it'll be too bad," she said.'

'So saying, she dived into the playground and struck out manfully for the gym.'

'Ted, can you get your band to strike up "A Life on the Ocean Wave", and a few sea shanties, just to drop her a hint? Or "Fierce Raged the Tempest o'er the Deep"?'

'We'll all change into bathing costumes, goggles and flippers and come and join in.'

'I hear they're going to issue us with shooting-sticks and polythene bags this year.'

'Cor, look at it, it's making dents in Sandra's car roof!'

'Where's Fuller, for heaven's sake!'

'He was last seen tacking up the causeway . . .'

'. . . dropping anchor over the girls' changing room.'

The joking intensified with the rain, and eventually Julie Marne came in and announced to universal applause and merriment that the sports had been cancelled. The feelings that lay behind this humour were articulated to me by Ted Lester. He was quite happy to miss 'sports afternoon'. He was envious of the PE department — it was one of the 'sacred cows'.

'The kids don't want to watch, they don't want to run, you're forever chasing them up for being in school, writing in the toilets, smoking and so on. It's a hell of a job to get them to compete, or to watch, worse than trying to teach them — at least you know where you are with your own room and your own subject. Then they have their hierarchy of jobs. If you're a starter for the 400 metres that's a cushy number. But if you're race co-ordinator, that's a hell of a job. You've got to get them all together. They're in these four pens, and they're always going missing. Jack Fuller allocates jobs all off his own bat, without the courtesy of asking.'

In short, sports afternoon challenged the day-to-day survival mechanisms which were the ordinary teacher's safeguard, and disturbed the status equilibrium of the staff by elevating the PE department to a position of high authority. These two factors deprived the great amount of organizational detail that was necessary of its credibility, thus laying it open for ridicule. In the example above, certain features of it are seized on with alacrity and lampooned in the overall expression of opposition to the activity. It is a good example of the use of humour to disguise enmity, anger and frustration, but again, with evidence of the 'growth' element, which appears, is indulged in and enjoyed on its own account.

This levelling or neutralizing is often marked by a return to basics. Male staffroom chat and laughter often has a certain earthiness, especially among younger or less professionalized members. And there is nothing more basic than sex. Flirtation is common in mixed staffrooms – thus it would appear important to have some attractive people, as well as some incompetent ones, on the staff.

'You should have been here yesterday! She had a bruise which she was showing around. No, first of all she comes in and says, "Cor! I've got a big one!" Then they got over in that corner to examine it, and all the women gathered round, saying, "Cor! What a whopper! What a beauty! What do you put on it? It mustn't half hurt when you ride your horse! How did you get one as big as that, there?" Some people got a private viewing, but I didn't get one . . .'

Humour can often be seen running along the edges of the institutional framework. The line of quivering lips on the stage during hymn practice assemblies, the asides during fire-drills, the ruses to alleviate the boredom of doing reports (such as trying to fill a whole line with 'satisfactory', or drawing pictures and running a book on what it is, with such comments as 'Fair' and 'Good') all indicate the fine balance between role and person, paradigm and practice, programme and survival. One hilarious lunch-hour was spent in filling in forms (than which there is no more bureaucratic feature) for a colleague doing a project for a diploma:

'What have you put for "occupation"?'

'Teaboy to a steeplejack, What have you put?'

'Deep sea diver, unreturned.'

'Irish peat-cutter's mate.'

Another institutional symbol frequently ridiculed is school uniform. Though as teachers they might support the principle in all seriousness, they can still make light of it. Thus after one stern announcement from Barney that there would be an 'inspection' in the morning, there was much hilarity in the staffroom, focusing mainly on the colour of the girls' knickers – again the return to basics.

'The green knicker brigade will be out in force again tomorrow.'

'The girls will be going round all their aunts and cousins to borrow a pair of green ones.'

'It will make a change for Trudy Wilson to have any on at all.'

'Cheetah will be there inspecting, going up and down the rows . . .'

'. . . with little mirrors on the end of his boots . . .'

'. . . and his long cane, with a torch tied on the end.'

'My girls are dead worried. I told them they'd have to take everything off on Monday, and I hoped none of them were tatooed, and I think they believed me.'

'That wouldn't worry *my* lot. They'd be only too willing to oblige.'

'My girls have just about got one set of regulation kit between them. Whenever any of them wants to go out and has to go and report to Flossie, they have a quick whip round for the right tie, socks, shoes . . .'

'There'll be some quick-change acts along the line with your girls on Monday, then!'

'Jimmy Sloan's green sleeve will come in useful, won't it?' [The nearest any part of Jimmy's ragged clothing came to the uniform colour was a huge green ink stain on one grey jacket-sleeve.]

Chorus: 'Greensleeves is my delight . . .'

At times, someone will, deliberately I suspect, aim to create a mirthful atmosphere, again through the well-known technique of incongruities, offering him or herself as the butt of the joke. Thus one whole mid-day break was once taken up with Frank Boundley's defence of queueing as a restful experience.

'You're in the queue, you can't do nothing about it, so you might as well relax and shut off. Everybody else is hustling and bustling about. There's too much dashing about in this world, not enough pausing to think . . . queues stop you dashing around, make you stop and think. You know you won't do it unless you're forced to do it, and queues are the only thing I know about that make you do it . . . Oh yes, if I go to the bank, or Sainsbury's, and see a number of queues, I'll always join the largest one, or if I'm on the road and get in a jam or come up behind one of them MIT lorries, I'll think, "Good, we're in for a nice, relaxed drive now." I'll never try to overtake; why should I deprive myself of what I enjoy most?'

Frank sustained this line of talk for the whole of the lunch-hour, while the staffroom 'wits' spun variations on it:

'Oh dear, I've punctured my basket, I'll have to sit down till the floor manager repairs it.'

'What do you do, Frank, if when you come to go out, there aren't any queues? Keep going round till there are some?'

'Sometimes I will actually go looking for queues, if I'm feeling in need of relaxation. If I see a big one I'll get in it, whatever they're queueing up for.'

'Now, sir, when is your baby due?'

'When did you have your last period?'

'Is this the tooth that's hurting?'

'This is the last job we're offering you; you've refused six already.'

'Men's toilets are round the other side, sir.'

Thus a pleasant dinner-hour was passed and people went off smiling to their lessons. The humour was developed out of nothing in particular; in other words it could not be represented as a reaction or response to threatening people or situations, or as dissipating conflict or as tension release. It was a creative act in itself. This gives it a broader setting. 'Humour as an example of the creative act in its full range of potential, or humour as play, is a sensitive means of coping, an adaptive vehicle for making life's compromises, and is, therefore, a *growth experience*.'[22] This fondness and affection which marks the human bond is often forgotten amid the overriding conflict that prevails in many schools.

'There's nowt so queer as folk.' One wonders whether the eccentricities are being celebrated in honour of the individual or ridiculed from the profession's view. Thus in one school stone-deaf Caldicott might have been an 'old bugger', an expert in survival at others' expense, but at times one was forced to admire his animal cunning, and his deafness led to some amusing consequences. At one staff meeting, from which he was thought to be absent, he was savagely attacked from all sides. When they came to leave the room at the end of the meeting, to everybody's surprise and consternation he was found in the wing armchair, near the door. To this day nobody knows if his hearing aid was switched on or off. That chair has been christened 'the Siege Perilous' and has become another laughter symbol, the key to an experience that will cure a few pains and forge a few bonds.

Fondness for the pupils as individuals is evident in the following teacher's remarks on some of her pupils:

'John Hurley, he's a charmer; he always says "Cheers, Miss!" if I ask him to do something. I think he fancies his chances with me, always telling me risqué jokes, and I'll laugh, others are quite embarrassed. Paul Hopkins is very expansive. If I'm trying to find something out, he comes in saying, "You'll never find out, Miss, you'll never find out!" I say, "Do you mind, *I*'m conducting this!" "Oh, sorry I spoke, sorry I spoke!"'

The sense of individuality coming over from these comments contrasts strongly with the stereotyped comments of the teacher in chapter 7 operating in the professional plane. It also contrasts strongly with laughter arising from conflict, or from professional failure. This is certainly very common. As with the writing of reports, laughter helps sustain a view of self as expert, and infallible. Shared experiences of failure are accounted for in terms of the object, and often ridiculed. Thus one teacher read out to the class a 'hoot' of an essay somebody had written during an examination. Killing himself with laughter as he read it (it was a preposterous tale about the Last Supper), he left the class in no doubt about the idiocy of the author. A similar motive might be held to lay behind the recounting of howlers.

'Queen Elizabeth was known as the virgin queen. She had a unique way of getting what she wanted.'

'The ancient Britons had rough mating on the floor.'

'The French executed people in a pubic place.'

Again these have an earthy ring and the laughter raised is serving a variety of functions. The professional motive appears uppermost, though glee at the enormous incongruity revealed by the slightest human error is a universal phenomenon. Teachers, too, can make 'howlers', such as the one who wrote on a girl's report, 'I do not like to see her bottom.' There is nothing as tedious, or professional, as writing reports. Such slips provide personal relief for all concerned, including the perpetrator.

Some psychological elements

I have mentioned tension release agents or 'fools' as laughter-producers. The other main suppliers of humour are the staffroom 'wits'. These might be individual humorists in their own right, or, like Phil Harvey, born raconteurs and/or impressionists. His version of the 'Hindenburg-Ludendorf' duo (as he called Barney and Miss Sparkes) never failed to amuse. It would be inaccurate, however, to suggest that the staff were always all equally amused. Jim Martell confided in me once that 'sometimes he thought they went too far'. For him, at times they overstepped the bounds of respect that he felt for his superiors – it was the merciless baiting of Barney and Flossie that disturbed him most. Teachers in a staffroom are not the unity they sometimes appear to be by the character given them by the most talkative and the biggest laughter-raisers. They differ in the staff hierarchy, in their attachment to role, in their degree of commitment, in their accommodation capacity, in their ability to laugh and in their perceived need for it. There is often a 'fifth column' element in the staffroom, or at least one agent who will identify more with the hierarchy than with the staff in general. Their perceptions of what is humorous, or what calls for humour, differ and they have ways of accounting for the laughter of others that reflect deficiency not in the institution, nor in the upper hierarchy, but in the laughter-makers themselves. This puts a different slant on some staffroom humour, and suggests strong psychological elements.

A hint of these comes from a consideration of the most consistent staffroom laughter-makers in one school of my experience. Three teachers were mainly concerned.

According to another teacher, what united this group was not their laughter but their own insecurity. The laughter, in large part, was a product of that — a search for esteem, status and power, in their own eyes and in those of their colleagues. Since laughter works well in dyadic and tryadic relationships, they found strength in this union, feeding off each other, creating humorous sessions, taking gratification from their individual input and gaining strength from the overall development. One in particular promoted as much conflict as humour among the staff. He had been very aggressive, and personal, about a paper I had presented to the staff.

'He would,' said another teacher. 'We've all had difficulty there, don't worry, that was inevitable. He would have taken it personally, he argues with anything, all the staff have difficulty with him. He's a pain in the neck at times. He wouldn't see the point of it, he'd put peculiar twists on anything he could find.'

This teacher thought the alliance a very brittle one, and far from a corporate union in the name of humanity, sheer personal indulgence. 'They'll only listen to one another for as long as they want to, then they'll switch off.' Two of them, Eric and Steve, might seem a pair, but Eric was relatively new, didn't know Steve like the rest of them did, and when he did, he would 'chuck him up'. In the meantime Eric had his problems, notably an 'insatiable and intolerable desire to have the last word in any decisions that were made'. The way to deal with Eric was to allow him a great deal of voice, and let him think a large part of any decision was his. He seemed to need this reward for his ego and self-esteem, and could not brook opposition and argument. The ploy then was not to argue with Eric, but to engineer him into your position, so that he could himself articulate it. Only then would he attach any status to it.

This is by no means intended as a definitive assessment of these teachers' characters, merely to point to the possible importance of psychological elements in the creation of laughter. Humour has many forms and functions, and it is something of a paradox that some of its extreme expressions are but one step from extreme despair. For while humour and laughter can be a rescue agent, it can also be a despoiler. To reduce everything to a joke is to tread continually in a no-man's-land, a limbo with no roots in the 'real' world, a comic mirror image of how things are. The distortion becomes the reality, and ultimately turns in on itself in anomic confusion. In this respect laughter is like a beneficent but powerful drug, highly efficacious if used in the appropriate doses, but dangerous and inhibiting if these are exceeded.

Laughter inhibitors

Occasionally, however, certain combinations of factors produce incidents for which laughter is no antidote. These are the real disturbers of the peace and it is important to identify them. I have noticed the following factors obstructing laughter:

(1) The psychological and physiological state of the teacher

There seems to be a higher incidence of staffroom 'explosions' towards the end of a term, during or just after examinations, or at other times of high tension. With some, all social poise is lost and customary civilities, such as passing the time of day, forgone. Others might invert the process and actually invade the staffroom with their distress. The staffroom has been swamped by the tide of their misery and offers no relief; and, like drowning men, they threaten to pull the others down with them. At such times staffrooms are 'unhappy' places, and staff sectionalize, some going to the local pub, or to department rooms, store-cupboards, the games field, or even home.

(2) Injustice

Some things just are not funny and cannot be made so. Bureaucracies operate on the assumption of equal work and responsibilities according to status, and equal distribution of resources. If you get less work and more resources than average, that might be cause for self-congratulation — but if you get more work and less resources, that is without doubt the very worst thing that can happen to you in state secondary schools. Hence the trauma of the 'free period' ritual every morning. The teacher who can smile at the loss of a 'free' is very rare indeed. He is more likely to have others smiling at him, in relief that it is not they.

(3) The undermining of status, or threats to professional equilibrium or personal insults

Of course, some pupils threaten teacher status continually but not, usually, irretrievably. Sometimes, however, they go too far. Also it is up to each teacher to negotiate his own position not only *vis-à-vis* the pupils, but also his colleagues and the headmaster. Laughter presupposes this kind of equilibrium. It assumes that though there may be frustrations, difficulties and altercations, on balance the flow of activities is on the credit side, and that, to some extent, one is achieveing one's personal aim, however negotiated that might be. Otherwise, sour feeling is likely to predominate, unrelievable by humour.

All these factors are evident in the following examples which all promoted 'heavy' conflict (as opposed to 'negotiable' conflict):

Example A

One particular instance that occurred during my stay concerned Jerry Horne and Harry Timpson, major laughter-makers as a rule. They discovered one day, from pupils as I gathered, that there would be no spectators at the swimming gala. Disappointment at not gaining some extra 'frees' was compounded by the empathetic feeling of injustice they felt on behalf of the kids and their resentment at the high-handedness of the PE department in making decisions they felt should be more appropriately made by the headmaster. Significantly this lunchtime debate was totally lacking in humour, and highly charged with inter-staff animosity. It came to light that, because of problems of discipline, Jack Fuller had decided that the staff-school hockey match was better played in the lunch-hour. Again the autocracy of the decision, the loss of valuable free time and the denial of the gain of free time doing a pleasurable activity — a great aid to survival — led to disappointment, frustration and anger, and totally precluded laughter. The very next day, Jerry Horne learnt, again from the kids, that some House cricket matches were to be played during two periods when there was to be a staff meeting. Five teachers had been 'excused' the staff meeting to supervise the rest of the school, but these cricket matches would consume three of them, leaving two — Jerry, since he knew nothing about cricket, and a student — to 'control' the five hundred other pupils, who would in all probability be rather boisterous at the break in routine. Jerry felt particularly aggrieved, since the other form teachers concerned had volunteered their absence from the staff meeting, cutting the ground from under his feet. When the headmaster asked him, he felt he had little option but to agree. Now there was this further injustice.

> 'Jack Fuller says he's been to higher authority, but I know the old man — Jack would mumble something to him and Barney would mumble "Yes, all right" back without realizing what was going on. It's Fuller's direct responsibility . . . It's all right for him . . . "I'm all right, Jack" . . . He'll get his cricket in, get his umpires, and be nice and comfortable in the staff meeting. What about us poor sods trying to cope with that mob out there?'

As noted, laughter is frequently both a symptom and a reinforcer of solidarity. Threats to, and rifts in, solidarity promote the obverse, conflict and anger.

Example B

Another outstanding example was the shattering of David Sylvester's 'inner peace'. Here was a man of great conviction who lived the message that he put about, that peace lay within the individual, not in all these frenzied activities that took place outside. This extract from my notes of an assembly talk given by him one morning gives some idea of the history of arriving at that conviction. It is much condensed.

'The story of his life was basically one of anti-establishmentarianism throughout school and college. He had all the feelings and trappings, supported the right groups. He championed the "Rolling Stones" against the establishment's "Beatles", grew his hair long, wore zany clothes. He went crazy when Pete Townsend smashed his guitar on the microphones, ecstatic when Jimi Hendrix performed. As he went up the school he changed, from supporting the "Stones" to Hendrix, for example. None of them quite suited exactly. Later, at college, he met many people who claimed to have found the ultimate solution, but none of them suited him. Then he went to America and he came across a group who made a lot of sense to him, called the "drop-ins". One guy there particularly drew his attention. He stood apart from the others, a gentle, quiet, guy. He plucked up courage one day and went up to him and said, "This is it, man, this is where it's all at!" He said gently, "That may be so, but it's what goes on in here (i.e. in the mind) that matters, this has to be at peace with itself." And that guy really put him in his place. He realized that all his previous attachments had been based on hate. What he sought was peace . . . The talk was illustrated by appropriate tracks. Yes, he had always aligned himself to movements that promised revolution in some form or another — until he found peace with the "drop-ins". And he hoped he still carried a bit of it around with him. It was not too late for them — yet. After the talk, Clem Marne sang a song to his own guitar accompaniment of a dream he had had about no more war . . .'

This is interesting in several respects, but here let us note the firmness of the conviction and the length and highly-charged nature of the journey getting to it. David's 'peace' withstood all manner of buffetings, but Barney, the headmaster, managed to undermine it, and in a comparatively short space of time. They had had several altercations along the lines of Barney's traditionalism versus David's libertarianism, all successfully resisted by David, until the day Barney visited one of David's lessons.

Again I quote from my field notes the story as told me shortly afterwards by a far from peaceful David.

'David was showing a film to a 5th form on housing. All had gone pretty well in the project they were doing. Barney came in and stood at the opposite end of the room, hesitated then came in far enough, so a number stood up, whereupon he waved them down. David wished he'd make up his mind what he wanted. "Anyway I went over to him and thought I'd better say something, so I started to tell him what the film was about, putting it in context. Half-way through — he clearly hadn't been listening — he suddenly bellowed to Mervyn Waters to get his feet down — and strode across the room to him, thus obscuring the film and concentrating all attention on him and Mervyn Waters. There was some altercation with Mervyn, remonstrating as is his wont, then Barney finally stormed back across the room, his image all over the screen, and out, having taken over and ruined the entire lesson. I'd resisted getting steamed up over him till then — but it went then — I seethed! (He gestures.) The ignorance of it!"'

In fact Barney's intervention in this way might not have been all that ignorant — on the contrary. Up to that point, David had resisted all Barney's attempts to 'cut him down to size'. Humour had been a useful weapon in his defence, joining in the general lampooning of the headmaster. But it was of no avail to him now. We might interpret what happened like this: Barney, continuously on the look-out for 'constitutional' ways of putting down David, found one in this film lesson in the form of Mervyn Waters's lounging posture, which epitomized for him the dangers in David's radical style of teaching. Using this symbol, Barney conveyed a loud and clear message to David, nicely dramatized by the circumstances: (a) that this form of teaching was unwelcome, and (b) that he was the headmaster, and would, if necessary, use his superior authority. David's distress was an indication that he had got the message. He now had to decide whether to allow himself to be socialized into the Lowfield way of doing things, or whether to continue to go his own way and develop unbearable conflict. In fact, the commitment to his ideals allowed for no compromise, and it was the latter course that he took, ultimately to resign his post after a stay of little over a year. The point, for our present discussion, is that this conflict, bared of all its camouflaging gloss, allowed for no mediation by humour, or by any other device. It was too open, too revealed, too frank, too oppositional, and the opposing parties' commitments to their respective positions too complete, to allow any room for reconstruction or manoeuvre. From this point on David saw nothing funny whatever in Barney no matter what high pitches of merriment on that account were struck in the staffroom. For him, the issue was much too real, much too earnest to allow for its transcendence.

Example C

A typical laughter-resistent item occurred in the last week of the Christmas term. During a 'reading competition' two 4th-year boys — Clanton and Willcock — hid under the stage and refused to come out. They made noises through the grill, such as 'Yoo-hoo, Miss Travis!', thus effectively spoiling proceedings without actually stopping them. However, the headmaster was on the stage behind the curtains (unbeknown to the boys, in the staff's opinion) but was unable to detect their presence conclusively. One teacher thought this was what irked him — they were getting the better of him. He had the piano moved over the trapdoor to block their escape. Then, coming down the steps from the stage he forgot the organ and banged his head, much to the glee of the children in the hall. There was a welter of suppressed giggles hurriedly stopped as he glowered at them. He then 'had a go' at Miss Travis and Mr Whitlock, who were supervising the reading competition, in front of the assembled children.

Paternalism will become inverted if its own armaments are turned against it, and will reply with vindictive assault. In this case the headmaster had been well and truly 'shown up' and Clanton and Willcock had scored a great triumph. Barney had contributed to his own discomfiture by banging his head, which compounded the irresolution and failure to detect. The balance of respect had to be restored. For Clanton and Willcock it was the worst punishment he could administer — suspension. But he had been shown up before the senior school, so they too must be made to pay. They were assembled in the hall and given a general dressing-down. Things were going to be different from then on. They were 'denigrated as human beings', according to one account. School uniform was going to be rigorously inspected and boys were to have hair cut above collars. David Sylvester, now continually smarting from his losing battle with the head, and whose own hair was shoulder length, came into the staffroom afterwards and declared, 'That's it, I'm leaving, I'm off, can't stay in this school any longer.' Even Jack Fuller, with what he called his 'armchair traditional views', disliked it intensely. The staff said it was his 'tone' and 'irrationality', especially the fact that 'the huge majority of kids in there were completely innocent of any wrongdoing'. Moreover, he associated his staff with this 'new totalitarian, oppressive policy'. Sylvester resented this. He wasn't 'going to bloody do it'. A group of 4th-year boys told me later that the head's influence was mediated through his teachers. 'It's like the SS, you know, with him as Hitler.' One said, 'It's bad enough as it is — he says you're here to be educated, but I can't learn in a forced situation. I have to be relaxed. Now we're not going to be allowed to do a damn thing. I'll be glad when he leaves.'

It would appear that the only beneficiaries of this incident, and the only ones entitled to 'laugh', were Clanton and Willcock. Everyone else — headmaster, staff and pupils — were outraged. Thus a situation which might have been interpreted as a bit of innocent mucking about was transformed into a criminal and rebellious assault on the headmaster's status, the restoration of which had to be made up by sacrifices from the rest of the school. No 'fun' could be made out of this incident by anybody — except perhaps the two perpetrators. It was too wilful, irrational, vicious, unjust, arbitrary. It overstepped the limits of accommodation. And it shows the extraordinary and quite unreasonable power of the headmaster within the school to reign, as he chose, by whim. 'The most original thing Clanton's ever done,' commented Sylvester. 'And he gets suspended for it!' There were, of course, no mass hair-cuts, nor uniform reformations — the display of rage and power had been sufficient.

This incident combines all three of the conflict-producing contingencies mentioned above — exhaustion at the end of a term, injustice and a disturbance of the finely balanced equilibrium in the school, which takes weeks and weeks of subtle and complex negotiation to attain. Both staff and pupils were deprived of the right of appeal to secondary adjustments. Laughter was no antidote. It is not difficult to see that it would not take many such incidents to reduce the whole school to strain and misery, making survival for all intensely difficult.

Example D

Another instructive incident arose during the school examinations. Because of different 'sets' in maths, and because each set had different teachers for different aspects of the subject, the circumstances arose where nine different examination papers were needed within the same rooms. Some did not appear. Allan Groves, for example, had only seven, though he searched diligently for the other two, even asked some of the maths staff for them. There was general chaos. Many had finished their 'bits' of papers by break, others had not even started. The maths department were outraged that their examination had been 'sabotaged'. The staff who had been supervising were equally outraged at the incompetence of the maths department's arrangements. Insults were hurled about, and physical assault threatened:

'He was bloody rude to me . . .' 'If he says that to me I'll stick him one on . . .!' 'Ridiculous! Forty minutes for a 1¼-hour paper! . . .' 'I'm not marking 2Ws, I'm *not* marking them, and that's that! . . .' 'It's the kids I think about, done all that revision, one little lad came to me this morning, crying he was . . .

Allan Groves astutely observed that because so many people were involved in the difficulty, the maths department should have known it was not the supervisory teachers' fault as individuals, but the system's. By causing so much disturbance they were covering their own tracks, or trying to. Disguising professional failure is one of the functions of staff laughter, but sometimes it is inappropriate; for example, when the failure is peculiar to one group on the staff and not others, when it adversely affects the others, and when its consequences are going to be evident and incriminating. Bigger guns are then brought to bear, and heavier smokescreens laid.

Interdepartmental rivalry frequently hovers on the borders separating humour from malice, in ridicule for example. But it is a thin divide, and the scales are often tipped by minor, even trivial, factors. If there is humour, it disguises the real grievance within, and helps one to conduct one's business.

Some other examples

Some relationships are unamenable to resuce by laughter. While some might joke about 5L, Jim Martell was unable to see anything funny in them at all.

> 'They're terrible, particularly the girls, they're revolting, they really are − filthy, vile, despicable. *(I asked him in what way.)* In their minds . . . I don't catch what they say, thank God, I just hear the guffaws − you wonder how much is directed at you. There's Carol Landers and Sandra Turner − great big lump − really coarse, horrible she is, disgusting. The boys aren't so bad, just won't work − idle and lazy. Yet on their own they're different. Sharman, for example, that very tall boy, an idle waster in class, yet as an individual . . . I had a talk with him the other day − his background, family, what he's going to do − and for the first time I felt I was getting through to him. They're all OK as individuals, I suppose, but in a group! If there were a 5th-form dinner this year, I wouldn't go. It will be the first one I've missed for over twenty years, but I shan't go. Yet there was no group we did more for, as a staff, by way of preparation, countless hours spent, hundreds of meetings among staff making sure we didn't overlap on subject-matter.'

Even here one sees redemption in the individual, but as a group, for Jim, 5L were beyond the pale. The feeling, it must be said, was mutual. They staggered on, from lesson to lesson, under clouds of bad feeling and perpetually on the brink of breakdown. Some individual relationships were of this kind; for instance, those between Ted Lester and Phil Harman. Quite regularly, each would tell me how much he hated the other. Senior and long-serving teachers both, they had not spoken to each other for eight years. 'Loathsome, pompous individual!' said

Harman. 'I'll never understand', said Lester, 'why someone who hates kids so much could stand teaching so long. He's a funny feller, you know!' Therein lies the irony. There was no fun. Their gorges rose at the mere thought of each other, so much so that Harman had removed himself from the staffroom and lived a hermit's life in his formroom, in a separate building

Thus the psychological and physiological state of the teacher, perceived injustices, the undermining of status, threats to professional equilibrium, interdepartmental and interpersonal rivalry or hatred, and the obstruction of routes to secondary adjustments, all work as blockages to laughter, either dispelling its efficacy or pre-empting its use. But these all imply breakdown or non-survival. They represent cracks in the system. Invariably they are repaired by humour, or at least humour is a sign of its repair. Laughter is the coping mechanism *par excellence*. Lack of it might suggest non-survival. Its presence is a sure indication of managing.

Conclusion

The obstruction of humour in institutional life is a serious matter. It heralds the breakdown of order. The presence of laughter is a sure sign of coping. This is why headteachers like a 'happy school' and a 'happy classroom'. In the ordinary course of events, humour and laughter operate to resolve conflict, maintain control, preserve order or release tension. But staffroom humour has another, more transcendent, quality. In this chapter I have taken a view of humour which sees it as extra- and supra-institutional and which locates it within a conception of man struggling to get on terms with the social forms and structures that assail him.[23]

> Humor alone, that magnificent discovery of those who are cut short in their calling to highest endeavor, those who falling short of tragedy are yet as rich in gifts as in affliction. Humor alone (perhaps the most inborn and brilliant achievement of the human spirit) attains to the impossible and brings every aspect of human existence within the rays of its prism. To live in the world as though it were not the world, to respect the law and yet stand above it, to renounce as though it were no renunciation, all the favorite, commonly formulated propositions of an exalted, worldly wisdom, only humor has the power to make those paradoxes obvious . . . it is a third kingdom wherein the spirit becomes tough and elastic, a way of reconcilement, of extolling the saint and the profligate in one breath, and making the two poles meet . . . You should not take things too seriously . . . the immortals will tell you that . . . seriousness is an accident of time, it puts too high a value on time. Eternity is a mere moment, just long enough for a joke.

Much staffroom laughter might be put into this context — a reassertion of the basic rights of man, a ritual to remind one of a wider faith, using as content those aspects of the situation which appear to subvert the principles on which it rests. By this interpretation the 'conflict' or 'control' evident in the humour is a lesser factor, even a misleading one. It is to assign humour a place within the institutional structure, wherein it plays its part among the checks and balances — but no more. It thus misses the most outstanding quality of all belonging to laughter and humour — its ability to transcend the immediate situation and appeal to a broader scale of criteria. By this token, it is a supremely important part of school life, allowing the restoration of a perspective more in line with preferred identities.

Chapter 10

Summary and conclusion

In this study I have described particular aspects of life in a particular school interspersed with considerations of the influence on those aspects of institutional and external factors. In this final chapter I want to draw these themes together and also point to the implications for educational practice. The overall connecting theme has been posited as one of *division*. Some divisions are promoted by factors external to the school, such as social class and the technological nature of society;[1] others by institutional elements. Teacher, pupil and parent perspectives both reflect and promote those divisions, while teacher and pupil strategies and adaptations are the expression of them, consolidating and promoting in turn. I will argue that divisions arise from different sources, that some are less deeply-rooted than others, that influence is injected into the dividing at various levels, and that these levels are not necessarily inextricably linked with each other. On the one hand, there is the press of powerful forces in society, but on the other, a range of choices for the individual teacher. In the interstices of the prevailing system, as evidenced at Lowfield, lie the opportunities for change.

Perspectives

These refer to the frameworks through which people make sense of the world. They are the essential starting-point for a study of school life, for it is through these that pupils and teachers construct their realities.[2] There are both group and personal perspectives, those that are held in common with others, and those that are differentiated within the self.

Some key elements in two prominent pupil group perspectives identified at Lowfield were suggested in chapter 2 in relation to subject choice. Those associated with a working-class background appeared to be contributing to a diffident, social, counter-cultural model, others to

237

a utilitarian, ability, interest model. There was evidence, too, that some pupils employed different perspectives in and out of school. To some, the school was an alien and hostile environment prompting defensive and cushioning adaptations. Outside, within their own culture, they expressed themselves within a context they understood, often ironically exhibiting the qualities some teachers struggled to impose upon them at school.

The reflection of similar criteria in parents' perspectives was also discerned. There were pointers as to how they differ among themselves on roughly social-class lines, corresponding to pupil perspectives and how they differ as a body from teachers in viewing the pupil. With regard to the former, middle-class parents show more complex reasoning by 'school' criteria in advising their children and are more persuaded by 'school' factors; working-class parents are less instrumentally oriented, appear to have some suspicions of school and teachers, are more persuaded by social and personal factors. With regard to the latter, parents show particularistic, familial, amateur and personal criteria, as opposed to the teacher's universalistic, institutional, professional and impersonal ones. It should be repeated that these indications derive from small numbers within one case study whose major focus was elsewhere. But they are worthy, I would maintain, of further research, and suggestive of other possibilities. Since behaviour and action are a product of mediation through these frameworks, then it is of major importance to identify their range, nature and properties. This study is a small beginning in that respect.

Access to pupil and parent perspectives was by informal interview (see Appendix 1). For teachers I had my own knowledge as a participant, as well as using interview and observation. I have characterized teacher perspectives as having three major orientations: survival, professional and personal. As survivor, problems of control have become paramount. It is not simply a question of 'more or less teaching' depending on resources. The teaching has become transmuted into a different activity. The transmission of knowledge or awakening and developing of skills associated with 'educating' is relegated to a minor role. The teacher gives priority to factors such as promoting greater ease and quiet, and less personal strain, while fulfilling the letter of his obligations. This was the major disposition toward the classroom at Lowfield. Toward the outside world, however, the teachers presented a 'professional' front. Here they are guided by considerations of solidarity, 'expertise', 'self-protection', separateness. Thus the perspective changes according to context, and depending on what it is directed towards. The third teacher perspective I identified at Lowfield was the 'personal' one, most clearly evident in the staffroom at times when it served as a private area or 'back region'.[3] Here the teacher might be released from the exigencies of role, either as survivor or as professional, and might view school activities through a 'private' framework. This enables him to identify and to evaluate his other perspectives. One of the major staffroom activities at Lowfield — laughter — was seen as an important mechanism easing the transition from survival or professional contexts into private, personal ones.

These by no means complete the range of teacher perspectives. I have not, for instance, considered the teacher as pedagogue, or careerist or bureaucrat, which possibly prevail in less beleaguered situations. My aim has been not to foreclose on the range of teacher and pupil categories, but to explore more features of the many-sided nature of their own views and activities.

Distinguishing between various perspectives promises to aid our understanding of many crisis points and issues that arise in school — the showing-up of pupils, moments of 'heavy conflict' in school, teacher schizophrenia, parental frustration and bewilderment over reports, or how parents should advise their children over choices and decisions they form at school. Often these crises and issues emerge from interfaces between, for example, teacher as professional against teacher as person, or child as pupil versus child as child, or public institution versus private life. 'Battles' such as those between the 5L girls and the senior mistress over 'ladylike' behaviour are better understood as clashes of cultural perspective than as socialization attempts against intransigence. A focus on perspectives also enables us to get behind apparently consensual feelings such as 'happiness at school' or 'liking for teacher', as shown in chapters 4 and 5. Vastly different criteria are being employed.

Strategies and adaptations

A large part of the book has been concerned with the actions resulting from how teachers and pupils have interpreted reality through their various perspectives; in other words how they have adapted to school and its various demands, what aims they have had and how they have gone about securing their ends. This is not a straightforward task, since many of these accommodations are hidden behind some form of rhetoric, or other disguise. Another task has been, therefore, to identify those disguises. This was the case, for example, with teacher survival. In chapter 7 I described the various survival techniques that I witnessed at Lowfield, together with their associated rhetorics.

How teachers' strategic action works out in a particular organizational area was illustrated in chapter 2 in relation to subject choice. Here the notion of freedom of choice, the same as embodied in child-centred and progressive teaching, was portrayed as having far outrun the realities. Teachers bridged the gap between idea and reality by some ingenious argument and actions. Most areas of the teacher's job have a strategic element. School reports provided another example, operating to a considerable extent in the services of professionalism. This involves techniques which cut them off from parents and emphasize the boundaries of the school, but at the same time seek to enlist the aid of parents in promoting the ideal models the teachers have defined. At the extreme we have seen that some parents at times have felt themselves castigated as a result of their errant child's behaviour — such is held to be their responsibility in producing malleable material. Some parents are lucky enough to possess some negotiating power through 'knowledge of the system', but most appear to be at the teachers' mercy on questions of their children's education.

Questions that arise requiring further research are: In these survival strategies, what degree of transmission of knowledge is there, and how intended is it? How do survival strategies differ from some 'progressive' forms of teaching and conception of the curriculum? Other areas of teacher activity that might repay examination are teachers' initial allocations of pupils to forms, and their use of initial 'socializing' tactics in these different groups; individual teachers' ongoing techniques in 'cooling-out' and 'warming-up' pupils and methods concerned with placement in jobs. Other questions are: What other elements of their task are strategic, and to what degree? How do teachers differ among themselves with regard to strategic activity; between, for example, age groups, or 'departments', or 'cliques'? And how do these compare with strategic action in institutional life elsewhere? More research is needed into all aspects of parents' interpretations of school and the factors bearing upon them. The headteacher is an especially important figure. Much teacher pressure is mediated through him. The investigation of other interactional chains bearing on the headmaster would therefore be of interest. They would reveal the mechanisms by which society makes its influence felt on the school through the interpretations and constructions of personnel. Such linkages might be, for example, the headteacher's relationships with the Education Committee, the Board of Governors, and his/her personal relationships with the Chief Education Officer, the Chairman of the Board of Governors and influential parents. Lowfield, as a secondary modern about to become a comprehensive school, was the subject of a large number of meetings during this period. One wonders how the headmaster interpreted these proceedings and internalized others' expectations, and if they squared with others' interpretations. They certainly had major repercussions for Lowfield.

I have pointed to the importance of the staffroom and its activity for any conception of the teacher's task. I was particularly impressed at Lowfield with the use and importance of laughter as a device or strategy, and I have suggested various ways in which it might be viewed. Primarily, I see it as a device in sustaining equilibrium among perspectives. Further studies on the nature of laughter would be rewarding.

Particularly, we might ask if we have become so fond of drawing political implications, detecting functions, correlations and hidden agendas and so forth, that we have overlooked one of the most important elements in our schools, namely their sociability. There was ample evidence of this on both sides of the fence even in Lowfield, a comparatively disadvantaged school in our system as a whole. In other words, there was a certain amount of unstrategic action and laughter, and this may hold the key to the resolution of problems thrown up in the areas traditionally studied by sociologists.

As for pupils, I have suggested a typology of adaptations which, I argue, captures much of the activity that is important both to them and to the school. The strategic nature of the techniques within, for example, ingratiation, colonization or intransigence, is clear. The typology enables us to distinguish different motives and principles behind sometimes similar products. The analyses in chapters 4 and 5 present two sides of what is essentially the same picture. The first gives the pupils' views of official processes and organization, the second incorporates observations of their activity. It describes what seemed to me to be the chief expressions of colonization and intransigence, namely 'mucking about' and 'subversive laughter'. This latter clearly shows the importance and strategic nature of laughter, either as a boost for their own morale, a cure for boredom or a weapon against the enemy. What is often branded as meaningless behaviour, and which indeed is actually known as 'messing about', is often quite orderly and rational in the pupils' terms. We must then try to identify the rules governing the behaviour, and the pupil categories upon which they are based.

My analysis here was focused largely on the lower non-examination streams of the upper school where colonization was rife, tinctured at times with a touch of compliance on one side and of intransigence on the other. There are, of course, other kinds of pupils, notably those more conformist, and other areas of the pupils' activity, especially out of school, worthy of examination. Indeed it is urgently necessary if we are to accord pupil activity its rightful status. Thus 'having a laugh', 'being bored', 'being shown up', 'being picked on', 'mucking about' become matters of some importance. One category that I have not systematically explored here is 'work', which certainly figured prominently in pupil accounts.[4] Interviews with and observations of conformist pupils would probably reveal other categories.

The negotiation of rules

Among other concepts emphasized in this study are contexts, rules and negotiation. To study teacher and pupil strategies separately is to run the risk of minimizing the actual interaction between them. But neither teachers nor pupils fall into these types of activity and set up camp in them. Rather, school life is a continuous process of *negotiation* and bargaining. This is particularly evident with regard to *rules*. Both teachers and pupils are very rule conscious. But there are two kinds of rules. There are the formal rules of the institution, and there are the informal rules, often implicit only, of the classroom and everyday interaction. The latter constitute the reality for the inmates. Such rules are not immediately obvious, and knowledge of them is a matter of entering the negotiation. In chapter 5 I spoke of pupil rules and various types of teacher negotiation. Often those rules were far removed from both letter and spirit of the formal rules. As Waller said, 'what rules secure is not conformity but a different type of non-conformity.'[5] The negotiation of rules makes a fascinating study – it is what 'becoming a teacher' is all about. More especially the study of 'negotiation gone wrong' or 'bargains exceeded' are illustrative of the real boundaries of tolerance. We have seen instances at Lowfield of pupils transgressing group-negotiated rules with teachers (the blazer-ripping incident in chapter 5), of an individual teacher transgressing traditional, though still implicit, classroom rules in dealing with pupils (the young teacher in chapter 5 who tried to exert her authority with 5th-form girls) and of a teacher who offended against some heavily implicit rules binding on all teachers in our society and was successfully 'negotiated' out of the school by the headmaster (chapter 9). The importance of *contexts* is already apparent from the discussion on perspectives. Here again they are of relevance in the cross-referencing of life in the school. For rules negotiated in one context may be inappropriate in another; for example, between different teachers. Action that constitutes high fulfilment of the spirit of the rules in one place might be the most shocking transgression of them in another. The adventure of the two boys under the stage, described in chapter 9, was the height of originality to the liberationist teacher David Sylvester, but the basest insolence to the headmaster.

Institutional factors

I am referring here to those aspects of the school that are considered necessary for its efficient running as an organization, which over the years often become a matter of routine and ritual. Some obvious examples are the temporal divisions of the school day; routines associated with establishing necessary conditions of work, such as registration, distribution of teachers and pupils; rules and regulations concerning behaviour, dress, work, play; organization of the curriculum, and teacher methods and behaviour. Institutional properties are created, altered or added to by people, of course, but under certain conditions they can exercise an influence of their own on action, which seems quite independent of human agency. One of those sets of conditions is induced by increase in size, such as had gradually happened at Lowfield in the years immediately preceding this study. There have been many references throughout this study to the press of institutional factors in their own right on school processes and outcomes.

I have noted the parallels between Lowfield and Cicourel and Kitsuse's Lakeshore. Rosenbaum also, in his research in an American high school, thought that[6]

> much of what goes on in this school suggests that it is responsive first to the professional and bureaucratic imperatives of itself as an institution, second to those of the large society, and only then to the needs and desires of the family and its students.

At Lowfield, the actual bureaucratic organization of the school into streamed classes in the lower school, and 'examination' and 'non-examination' in the upper, also helped to create the problem. It is a factor in the vicious circle which helps to strengthen the circle. The group perspectives identified in chapter 2 may originate outside the school, but they are certainly reinforced by school organizations. As Hargreaves and Lacey showed (see chapter 3), this promotes consolidation reactions. In turn these bring retribution if they are inappropriate, rewards if appropriate; cultural defences and identification are reinforced and contribute toward the imperviousness of the background culture. Nothing illustrates this better than the re-routing of misguided choices, driving the boundaries of advantage further in. If such routes were not there, or their boundaries more flexible, the chain of circumstances would be at least weakened.

Such processes become legitimated over time. They become self justificatory. The procedures, routines, both at a general and individual level, become taken for granted and individuals adjust to them. Official areas are designated to teachers with special responsibility who then 'grow' into such areas. In a very real sense, processes such as that of subject choice, which have been worked through for a number of years and refined by many open and clandestine manoeuvres to achieve a high degree of workability, create their own impetus and make their own demands.

The institution also contributes towards pupil adaptations. I located these within pupil cultures, which the school helps to foster. It also imposes itself in a more subtle way, as was demonstrated in chapter 4. At Lowfield the degree of dislike of certain institutional factors was remarkable, indicating that control of those processes had been lost, and they were felt to be exerting an influence of their own. This was as true for the teachers as for the non-examination form and, interestingly, even more true for the examination form. For these, I suggested that the mainstream school was more of a reality, hence more pressing. Apart from instrumental aims, however, there was a more general feeling, widely held among pupils and staff, that the school was no longer a 'friendly place'. As it had grown in size and changed in character, rules and routines increasingly took over the running of the school, and fuller expression of human nature was reserved for playground and staffroom.

Even so, teachers differ in their accommodation to the institution, and pupils clearly distinguished between those predominantly display-ing the symptoms of what I have summarized as teacher-bureaucrats and those of teacher-persons. The former are more bound by institutional forms and processes and more geared to the formal definition of the teacher role. They are more likely to show a higher degree of rule con-sciousness, exert their authority, and foster formal and depersonalized relationships. They are categorized by pupils in this study as 'too strict', 'full of moans', 'won't laugh', 'treat you like kids'. Teacher-persons capitalize on humour and togetherness. They are 'more natural', 'more like a friend than a teacher', 'have a laugh with you', 'talk to you like real people'. They are still in control of the institution, using it for their ends.[7] Teacher-bureaucrats, however, are governed by it. The teachers at Lowfield did differ in these respects, but not in such hard and fast form. It is perhaps better to view the degree of attachment to formal role as a dimension along which teachers can be differentiated as a body, but also along which a single teacher can oscillate according to certain factors – the day of the week, the particular class he is teaching, his overall work-load, his age.

The difference, frequently referred to in pupil descriptions, is neatly summarized in the following comments from some 5th-form girls:

Amanda: Mr Groves, you see him as a person. We see him outside, and he's always the same.
Debbie: They take everything as it comes.
Liza: Mr Martell, as soon as he walks into the class, he's a different person.
Christine: I think the only time I ever saw him as a human was when his wife had a baby, and they announced it from the stage, and you could see he had a great beaming smile all over his face – and that was about the first time you'd seen him human.
Amanda: He came up to the lesson and said his wife had just had a baby, and he was a completely different person, totally changed.

The teachers themselves are not unaware of these changes. Thus the majority agreed with the pupils that the teachers frequently used their power unreasonably, but, as one said, it was 'largely a consequence of the difficult position they had been put into'. At Lowfield all felt there had been a general shift towards formality, but some teachers still sur-vived as 'persons' in the pupils' eyes. Here also the importance of humour was noted. The more institutional pressures exert themselves, the more of a life-saver laughter becomes. If a teacher provides it, it is welcomed — not as a frivolity, be it noted, for the pupils also wanted to work, but as a life-line to a shared definition of humanity. It was the straight-laced authoritarian who rankled, and who, ironically enough, invariably drew forth bouts of subversive laughter, but ultimately heavy conflict.

It may sound a commonplace to say that much pupil and teacher behaviour is 'institutionally produced'. However, it is frequently taken as symptomatic of one's basic personality. This study shows the mistake of the latter view. Some teachers are veritable Jekylls and Hydes between staffroom and classroom. In some cases certain aspects of the teacher role have become reified in the same way as some organizational processes. That is to say that through growing pressures on the job owing to mounting external demands and inadequate resources (including inability to cope) some teachers opt for routine and ritualistic features. They identify more with the formal features of the role. After all, the lines of institutions and their associated roles are drawn for efficiency. Problems arise when the institution and the roles take over.[8]

The pupils resolve the problem by 'mucking about' and 'having a laugh'. The first is largely a product of boredom induced by the dead, ossified hand of drab, institutionalized teaching or institutional processes (such as assembly or Speech Days). In chapter 5 I gave examples which leave no doubt of the crashing boredom experienced by some pupils because of 'repeating lessons', 'doing useless, meaningless work' or 'blackboard and blackboards of writing'. The antidote is vandalism, 'silly' behaviour, teacher-baiting, sabotage and so on. I would argue that there are more 'human' properties about these activities than there are about those to which they are a reaction. The same is true of 'subversive laughter'. Several forms of this, for example subversive ironies or confrontational laughter, can be seen as attempts to neutralize alien properties, to cut down to size, to strip away the trappings of authority inappropriately used, to repel unwarranted inroads on their own private resources. Others, like symbolic rebellion, are often directly aimed at institutional symbols such as school property or school uniform.

I pointed out how pupil behaviour can be misconceived if the wrong context is attributed to it. In chapter 4 I described three pupil contexts within which their behaviour might be viewed — subject, teacher and institution. Opposed to the latter is what we might term a 'natural' context (i.e. that perceived as the predominant reality), for most pupils, apparently, an out-of-school one. The pupils themselves have provided ample testimony as to how their attitude and behaviour differ among them.[9]

'Why worry around school, we just slouch around. Of course, we wouldn't if we were anywhere important.' (chapter 8)

'Of course, we don't act silly out of school.' (chapter 5)

This is not, in other words, a matter of psychological traits of laziness or immaturity working themselves out, nor, on these occasions, a matter of resistance to socialization into another culture. Basically at Lowfield it was often institutional resistance, compounded by teacher misinterpretation and culture clash. Or pupils having made their peace with the school and established some pupil core norms, teachers would fail to recognize the adaptation and seek to establish official rules, thus producing conflict. Or contexts would get confused, as in the blazer-ripping incident (chapter 5), pupils on that occasion jumping the gun that freed them from school. Both teachers and pupils make adaptations to school. Sometimes they harmonize, sometimes they conflict, and sometimes they do not address each other through similar adaptations.

Some teachers find common cause with the pupils and 'aid colonization'. I came across many instances of 'tacit conspiracies' usually directed at school rules of one sort or another (such as the 'smoking game'). This is a form of teacher adaptation to the institutional problem at the opposite pole to sinking oneself fully into the teacher role, which requires exact prosecution of the rules.

But this reaction of the pupils is almost exactly mirrored by the teachers in their staffroom laughter, and I have suggested that it has a similar origin. Some certainly can be interpreted in traditional 'conflict' or 'control' terms, but a large proportion of it equally can be interpreted in a way akin to the 'subversive laughter' of pupils. In their case it is directed toward institutional elements. Since these are usually designed and perpetrated by the upper hierarchy, and that often constitutes their whole job, much of this humour is directed against the headteacher and his deputies. Doubtless it intermingles with 'conflict' motives, but the institutional element is clearly discernible. Unfortunate personal characteristics are often the weapons, not the objects, of attack, and are seized on with alacrity to help to pile ridicule on this or that aspect of a new rule, a certain ritual (like hymn practice) or ceremonial (like Speech Day or Sports Day). Deliberate sabotage is perpetrated at times when bureaucracy exceeds the limits, as in form-filling, and 'games' spice the tedium of such activities as writing reports. I described how, at times, this form of humour might be discerned running along the edges of the institutional framework — for example, in a row of barely disguised smiling faces at the back of the stage during assembly. And how the most celebrated instances of mirth are provided by the sudden and utterly complete demolition of high institutional form and ceremony, as when the headmaster in full, formal, robed official majesty, in the school's most sacred and formalized ritual, before the whole of the school mustered in serried, supervised and hierarchical ranks, told them solemnly not to 'fork off' to the dining-room on their way to the hall. This one simple *double entendre* is sufficient to bring the whole of the massive institutional edifice tumbling down.

However, sometimes teachers separate out in the schizophrenic way described. Thus, as teachers within the teacher role, they might champion the cause of school uniform, while in the staffroom as persons, they might ridicule it. School is full of such anomalies, traceable to these basic divisions. Perhaps the most remarkable one is the love-hate relationship with pupils, both clearly discernible within the staffroom. I would claim that, although in the same place, the contexts are different. Pupil-baiting and recrimination occur in a 'teacher' context and arises from both pupils' and teachers' inability to fulfil the formal requisites laid down by the institution. The wider the gulf, the stronger the tones, until they can become very abusive indeed, as was shown with the study of school reports. When this is relaxed, however, fondness and affection are readily apparent, often, interestingly enough, for the biggest miscreants. Again, this is reciprocated by the pupils – often the biggest villains expressed their 'genuine' fondness for the teachers while still trying to make their lives hell. However, one of the central elements of the institution – its 'massness' – militates against 'personal' relationships between teachers and pupils. The fact that teachers have to deal with various large groups of pupils draws them away from individuals and towards 'group thinking', towards static typifications and rigid ideal models to which individuals are then related. Nor would it be difficult to lay at this particular door other consequences of high concern at Lowfield. How far are pupil 'showing-up' and degradation rituals a function of the formal organization of school or class, carried out when a pupil transgresses the formal code or contests the prevailing ideal model? Do they exist to the same degree in less formal, more personalized contexts? And how far are the blockages to relief, the 'laughter-inhibitors' identified in chapter 8, also a product of purely institutional factors? In this way, the institution threatens to swallow its own placebo and the inmates with it. Thus are the principles of education subverted by the institution.

Identity

The comments above remind us of another conflict point frequently arising: that between the 'mass' approach of the teacher and the individuality of the pupil. Whether by 'childish' treatment, misinterpretation of context, 'showing-up', 'picking-on', contravening pupil rules, failure to recognize adaptations or trying to socialize, what the teacher is doing is assailing the pupil's desired presentation of self, attacking his very identity. Herein lies the greatest humiliation for pupils, and the reason why so many are perpetually on the defensive. Pupils are engaged in a continual battle for who they are and who they are to become, while the forces of institutionalization work to deprive them of their individuality and into a mould that accords with teachers' ideal models. We have seen, at Lowfield, 'mortification techniques' typical of institutional life as described by Goffman; degradation rituals, 'socialization' into the mores of the school and away from both the background culture and the individual self. Repeatedly with regard to their everyday interrelations with teachers, pupils have distinguished between personal and bureaucratic treatment of them.

But the institution impinges on all. Teachers, too, bound by commitment, oppressed by growing demands and dwindling resources, guided now by professionalism, now by humanitarian interest in their charges, and subject to the same bureaucratic forces, also are concerned with establishing and maintaining identities within the school. Whether parrying a perceived insubordinate pupil threat by showing-up, or deflecting some high-handed action of the headmaster by ridicule, seeking the aid of parents to support their own constructions, or fending off perceived attacks on them, using institutional devices for their own ends, as in survival, or seeking to neutralize them when they impinge too harshly on the sensitivities, teachers are engaged primarily in promoting and protecting their self-images, the sorts of persons *they* are.

Lowfield appears to verge towards the ideal-typical bureaucratic structure 'which approaches the complete elimination of personalized relationships and non-rational considerations'.[10] As Berger and his colleagues say, 'the more frequently the individual comes into contact with bureaucracy the more frequently he is forced into structures of meaning beyond those of his private life', and 'encountering bureaucracy is an experience of being ongoingly surrounded by strangers'.[11] Is this what was behind the complaint of the boy and the teachers in chapter 4 that the 'friendliness of the school had gone'? Clearly it is heavily weighted against progressive ideologies which emphasize individualism. Kanter, for example, has suggested how many of the central characteristics of bureaucracy are reproduced in nursery school, for example, its stress on security and rationality, and its reduction of personal accountability. Even in nursery school, 'the organization child was oriented to organizational reality, his play was highly routinized, he had little personal responsibility, and he had developed adaptive techniques for the maintenance of ascendancy.'[12] Moreover, there is something artificial and highly inappropriate about bureaucratic structures in people-processing institutions. Berger and his colleagues view playing a role as *'ipso facto,* to engage in hypocrisy. The real self (that spontaneous un-"repressed", to-be-intuited entity) is presumed to lie beneath or beyond all roles, which are masks, camouflage, obstacles to the discovery of the real self.'[13] Thus tradition can no longer vouchsafe a reasonably watertight world within the institution with its own insulated conceptions of respect, honour and identity.[14]

The disintegration of this world as a result of the forces of modernity has not only made honour an increasingly meaningless notion, but has served as the occasion for a redefinition of identity and its intrinsic dignity apart from and often *against* the institutional roles through which the individual expressed himself in society . . . Institutions cease to be the 'home' of the self; instead they become oppressive realities that distort and estrange the self.

Modern society's solution to this problem, according to Berger *et al.*, is the creation of the 'private' sphere, and the division of the individual's involvement between 'private' and 'public' spheres.[15] We saw this illustrated in chapters 2 and 8 with teachers' negotiations with parents, and in chapters 2 and 5, which showed the dichotomization of pupils' lives. Lowfield, for me, strongly suggested that the most severe forms of division for teachers, pupils and parents arose from the institutional framework of the school and its bureaucratic forms of control.[16]

External factors

Some indications have been given of possible connections between school processes and the world outside. The institution impinges on all, both staff and pupils, but it impinges on some more than others – pupils more than teachers, and some pupils more than others. Teachers try to inculcate their models into pupils, and to create the necessary conditions bring institutional forces to bear. In both respects some pupils – those primarily of middle-class background – respond more readily than others, for they are already equipped with the relevant frameworks. In this sense some pupils are doubly disadvantaged. Becker wrote:[17]

Professionals depend on their environing society to provide them with clients who meet the standards of their image of the ideal client. Social class cultures, among other factors, may operate to produce many clients who, in one way or another, fail to meet these specifications and therefore aggravate one or another of the basic problems of the worker-client relation . . .

Becker himself demonstrated how social class differences contributed to three major problem areas for his Chicago teachers – teaching, discipline and moral acceptability. In this country Bernstein has demonstrated the importance of social class identity in the area of language, and Ford, Box and Young have examined class cultural differences in the areas of justice, friendship and privacy.[18] Willis has remarked on the similarities between school counter-cultures and shop-floor culture.[19] Similar differences along similar lines to these studies were evident at Lowfield. Pupil and parent perspectives appear to differ along these lines, and at times there seems to exist a state of what I described as 'cultural warfare', complete with strategies, cold wars, skirmishing and set-piece battles. I have remarked on possible relationships between social class and distribution of pupil adaptations and careers among them (chapter 3), pupil views of curriculum, teacher and institution (chapter 4) and certain features of pupil lifestyles (chapters 5 and 6).

There can be little doubt that these connections exist. It is equally clear that the divisions fostered by social class differences are aggravated by school processes and organization. However, the question of whether this is inevitable, and if so, why, is a moot one. Social control theorists such as Sharp and Green, and Bowles and Gintis, seek to show how schools 'reproduce' the society they serve. How, for example, they are organized like factories, with their hierarchies and division of labour, and how they legitimate inequality by claiming to route pupils in accordance with ability, but in reality with social class factors.[20] The meritocratic, egalitarian, 'fair' mask that the school puts on its processes, such as those of subject choice, is explained as intentional illusion or a means of ideological control.[21] However, there often may be no question of 'intentionality' here on the part of teachers, rather that, whatever those intentions and sometimes in spite of them, powerful, wider forces constrain teachers to act in certain ways. Whatever the appearance, the substance is always the same, the reproduction of the way things are with the same forms of division and difference, dominance and disadvantage. In this rather inexorable system, school plays a key role. Its 'covering' devices, by which it pretends to be doing something else, are particularly important. Through these, it is held, an impact is made on consciousness. People come to 'believe' in the 'rightness' of the system and the appropriateness of their own place in it.

Now it may be thought that the analysis in chapter 2 largely supports this argument and illustrates how the mechanism of connecting linkages works. The school is divided into two broad channels that are reflected in individual groups by those chosen for examinations and those not. Parents used to gaining from the selective, sponsored system make their influence felt upon the school through the headmaster. The teachers then seek to achieve those groupings which will yield optimum results, which benefits some, penalizes others. But the penalties are legitimated through a number of 'fair procedures', including the inculcation of the notion that that is the natural way of the world. The idea that much of school life, and possibly the most important part of it, is concerned with social relations and takes the form of one culture seeking to destroy another might also appear to be supported by the argument in chapter 8.

Such findings do lend some substance to the social reproduction argument. However, there are problems about accepting it in its entirety. In the first place there is the astonishing failure of the legitimating tactics to 'legitimize'. The pupils of 4C and 5C and their parents, if persuaded into the 'right' choices, were mainly under no illusions as to how the system worked, neither for that matter were the other pupils and parents, *and* a large proportion of the staff. Their political consciousnesses were stimulated rather than appeased or seduced. Not only were they not taken in by the rhetoric, many pupils were not even convinced that they had fallen down on the school's criteria. The reflections of the 5th-form girls in chapter 5 and 4th-years in chapter 4 show the range of views on this.

Then, if the prevailing system is composed of different groupings, each with their supporting cultures, one might argue that schools would better serve that system by helping to sustain those cultures. Of course, this is, in effect, what they do — the counter-culture thrives in schools, Lowfield included, as never before. As Richard Johnson notes, 'schools reproduce *forms of resistance too*', not 'the perfect worker in complete ideological subjection'.[22] But this is the *opposite* of what is intended. The lower classes then, destined to be the workers of the future, provide for their own social relationships, largely against the intentions and will of the teachers. One could still say that this is one instance of powerful system-wide forces steam-rollering over the good intent of individuals — it works out in the end as system-supportive, regardless.

However, while Lowfield might add some support to the social reproduction argument, it also exposes weaknesses in it. One important feature overlooked or relegated, is that of individual choice. But we have seen that at Lowfield at least, if in some respects 'choice' was rather an euphemism, in others a considerable range of choice existed. Teacher style, for example, was a matter of much variation. They are not all constrained, either by the institution or by society, to act in roughly the same way. The blueprint of the ideal teacher given by the pupils in chapter 4 was based on their real experiences; and arguably he or she is judged by qualities that cut across social class divisions. Qualities of warmth, friendship, understanding, ability to explain and so on, as discussed in chapter 4, which these 4th-year pupils valued above all things, owe nothing to social class, but everything to remaining human against institutional pressures, and to teacher skill and ability. This contrasts with the class-bound culture clash between teacher and pupils recounted in chapter 8. The class element is certainly there, but it is not all pervasive, and it differs from teacher to teacher. Inasmuch as its effects are mediated through people, some teachers are more powerful mediators than others. Thus it may be said to exert a pressure on basic school organization, but may have little or no consequences at all for what takes place between teacher and pupil. It often does of course, but that, at least, is a matter of choice for the teacher. In other words, a selective society might exert a strong influence over the basic organization of the school, and the distribution of pupils within it, and institutionalization might force the teacher into constructing ideal models, but he does not necessarily have to be governed by criteria valued by the so-called dominant culture. In fact, one suspects there are large phalanxes of teachers in the state system opposed to such criteria, who find common cause with all pupils, along the lines articulated by pupils in chapter 4. And this helps to sustain counter-cultures. These are not legitimating tactics. There is a transparency about subject-choice strategies and about survival rhetorics that teachers themselves see through, especially when in the 'personal' context. There is no such transparency about the kind of 'warm' teacher-pupil relationship discussed above.

Even where teachers are more or less forced into certain lines of action, as in grouping children and arranging classes, there is doubt about the cause and the mechanisms involved. The exposition in chapters 2 and 7 brings out the situational exigencies that immediately bear on teachers and press them into certain lines of action. I would argue that this helps to provide a better explanation for certain aspects of teacher action, embodied in 'socialization' and 'domination' techniques, than theories of social control which often ignore the situation, or speculate about it. It is sometimes argued that these operàte at a different level of abstraction. If this is so, other theories are devisable which better accord with the situational facts. I outlined such a theory at the beginning of chapter 7, which, through the concept of commitment, links the self with the system. It has certain functionalist elements, but works through interaction with people.

Institutions, once established, generate a certain momentum and inter-dependence. This is well illustrated in the case of 'school', whose place in the industrial society has become virtually unassailable. However, it is important to realize that this necessity and interdependence comes about, not through some mystical property of the institution which renders it 'functional' for society, but through the consciousness of its members. As Berger and Luckmann put it:[23]

> *De facto,* then, institutions *are* integrated. But their integration is not a functional imperative for the social processes that produce them; it is rather brought about in a derivative fashion. Individuals perform discrete institutionalized actions within the content of their biography and this biography is a reflected-upon whole in which the discrete actions are thought of, not as isolated events, but as related parts in a subjectively meaningful universe whose meanings are not specific to the individual, but socially articulated and shared. Only by way of this detour of socially shared universes of meaning do we arrive at the need for institutional integration.

Individuals also contribute to the institution's functions and further legitimacy in accordance with their own personal investment in the institution. A very important part of oneself is left for extra-institutional reflection. And the degree of one's own institutionalization might be measured by the degree of one's commitment. Thus institutionalized consciousness comes about, not necessarily through a process of sociali-zation in which one learns about the inevitability of certain parts of the world, but through one's own personal dependence on it. Institu-tional order and integration then might be seen as a product of the sum of the dependencies of the people who contribute to it. Thus preserva-tion of the self is linked with preservation of the system, and the self, if reconstituted accordingly, divided into various components. This 'com-ponentiality' is a feature of life in the modern industrial state, as is the separation of work from private life, the dominant position of the 'expert', and anonymous social relations of which I shall say more shortly.[24] School reflects the pluralistic nature of modern life, now representing a mechanistic functionality, now a warm humanity; hours of tedium, moments of joy; pain and humiliation, gladness and laughter; conflict and opposition, togetherness and sociability; with certain linkages with society which promote a reproduction of the way things are, but with large interstices around them that are potential areas of choice, and seedbeds of change.

This book has been a case study of the implications for educational processes of an institution in the technocratic/bureaucratic society. It has included descriptions and analysis of 'getting the worst of it' (chap-ter 6 and parts of chapters 5 and 9); 'making the best of it' (chapters 2 and 7); 'fulfilling the obligations of it' (chapters 4 and 8); and, perhaps, 'transcending it' (chapters 5 and 9). Within this framework there is another, brought out in chapter 2, linking school process to the actual structure of the particular society in which we live. Such linkages, power-ful and pervasive (together with the cultural forms and social class dif-ferences with which they are associated), have led some to conclude that they are paramount. But behind these hangs a greater influence, common to all forms of modern advanced industrial societies, which embraces capitalist and communist, teacher and pupil, middle-class and working-class alike.

This influence derives from technological production and bureau-cracy. It promotes increasing rationalization and systematization of life, concentrating man's impact on society in his instrumental aspira-tions and functionary relationships. One consequence has been the separation of the public and private spheres of life, with much of man's personal investment in the latter.[25]

'Ultimate' significance is found by the typical individual in modern industrial societies primarily in the 'private' sphere — and thus in his 'private' biography. The traditional symbolic universes become irrelevant to the everyday experience of the typical individual and lose their character as a (superordinated) reality. The primary school institutions, on the other hand, turn into realities whose sense is alien to the individual. The transcendent social order ceases to be

253

subjectively significant both as a representation of an encompassing cosmic meaning and in its concrete institutional manifestations. With respect to matters that 'count', the individual is retrenched in the 'private sphere'.

This division is well in evidence at Lowfield between classroom and staffroom (or playing field), between teacher as functionary pedagogue and teacher as private person, between pupil as pupil and pupil as child. Other consequences resulting from the technologizing of society are equally well in evidence – the emphasis on expertise, the division of labour and the curriculum.

Teachers are the 'experts', the 'professionals', most of them with their own specialist preserve, which protects them not only against lay people, but also against colleagues. A headmaster of a secondary school might have overall responsibility for the school, but he would be quite unable to teach or master the range of specialisms involved. The curriculum has become divided and subdivided, the areas thus created tending first to ensure their own self-preservation, then gathering strength with a view possibly to some further fission. Thus have teachers become more and more 'expert' as their area of preserve becomes increasingly digested in this rationalizing process. Some of this is brought out in chapter 8 on reports. The overwhelming and exclusive pressure is on the certainty of the school's aims, the rightness of the content of the curriculum (if not always its form), the media of its relaying, its forms of assessment, the relationships between teacher and taught, the sanctity of the teacher as judge of the future by virtue of his knowledge of 'what is required in this particular world', and of a particular child. Only the teacher, by virtue of his expert knowledge of both, can solve the equation and 'properly' predict a child's future. But, as we saw in chapter 8, the knowledge of the child is invariably stereotypical. The teacher makes group assessments and attributes them to individuals, and he does this for a rationalistic framework of society. It is this kind of process perhaps that led Illich, for example, to conclude that 'the safeguards of individual freedom are all cancelled in the dealings of a teacher with his pupil'.[26] In the campaign for equality of opportunity (palpably unsuccessful to date) one must reconsider the question – opportunity for what?

However, my conclusion is not quite so pessimistic as Illich's. For the Lowfield study, while certainly showing these signs, also shows the strong existence in certain areas of individuality, ingenuity, inventiveness and *joie de vivre*. This results from the dual function of school, expressed in concern for the production of man both for the public and for the private arena of life. Here is Weber's classic distinction between the 'specialist' and the 'cultivated' type of man:[27]

Behind all the present discussions of the foundations of the educational system the struggle of the 'specialist type of man' against the older type of 'cultivated man' is hidden at some decisive point. This fight is determined by the irresistibly expanding bureaucratization of all public and private relations of authority and by the ever-increasing importance of expert and specialized knowledge.

At times they complement each other, at times they clash, for basically they are in tension with each other. We have seen how teachers resolve this at Lowfield with a variety of adaptations, ranging from, on the one hand, teacher-as-teacher in a well-demarcated and rationally oriented role, and on the other, teacher-as-person, free of the bureaucratic structures which both constrain and direct him, a 'whole' person in the sense that there is no split between 'public' and 'private', nor rational and other components in the prosecution of his job, and in command of, rather than subservient to, the teacher role. In this guise, teachers often display 'charismatic' qualities.

We could say that the dilemma is resolved in one of three basic ways. Either the teacher assumes one guise — teacher-person or teacher-bureaucrat — for the whole of his time in school, or he oscillates between the two. We might hypothesize that teacher-persons are largely to be found where the bureaucratic processes press least — in the 'easy' subjects like art, or with specialist non-examination-form teachers, while teacher-bureaucrats congregate at the policy-making end, among headteachers, deputies, other senior personnel and keen aspirants to these positions. The continual co-operation of teacher-bureaucrats into the positions of authority in schools and influential educational organizations might be another powerful reason for system-continuance.[28] The majority, however, seem to conform to the third type, the oscillator, the split personality, the teacher-schizophrenic who moves, often uncomfortably, between the two states.

The transition is not always sudden or clear cut. The teacher-role is often sustained by group pressure in the staffroom depending on circumstances and who is present. But at Lowfield its main function was as a disrobing room, a private area, where you could send up, without fear of redress, the artificial contours of the school, the paradoxes and inconsistencies of your own position in it, and the requirements made of you.

What this amounts to is a fractionalizing of activity in the school, mirrored in a fractionalizing of consciousness. But it has still that other division, within the teacher-role, made possible and tolerable because of the very fact that the teacher is professionally — not personally — committed. The latter involves total dedication, the former allows room for more schizoid manoeuvring. At one level the teacher does his professional job, and teaches. This is the most obvious level, so taken for granted that its share of teacher application compared to other fractions of his activity have not been examined. The second level, by contrast, at which a teacher operates is one of a 'hidden pedagogy' that is not concerned with teaching at all, but 'surviving'. Either one has become preoccupied with the systematic pursuit of appropriate means to have lost all sight of the ends, or one is caught up in a continuous struggle to master the most elementary means, such as controlling large groups of recalcitrant children, or inventing adequate resources. This in turn reinforces the teacher-person division, the teacher seeking more personal fulfilment in private areas and periods, and in his own free time, the more that, in his teacher capacity, he is forced to concentrate on survival. The further this three-fold division in teacher activity advances, the more institutionalized and mechanical it becomes. The reluctant schoolchild is joined by the reluctant teacher. The joy of relief in playground or staffroom laughter, and in other marginal areas and moments, is common to both pupils and teachers. Apart, in separate groups, they are whole persons. When they come together in the educative process, they break up into splinters.

The predominant theme running throughout the book is one of 'division' — division of the 'self' and of 'consciousness' on the part of both pupils and teachers, division of public and private spheres of life, between choice and direction, of laughter and conflict, pleasure and pain, as well as divisions between and within groups of pupils, teachers and parents owing to their different social locations, both in regard to the school and to the social structure. The manifestations of these divisions make the concept of the 'divided school' my overriding impression of Lowfield and they are of such an order that they threaten to increase, if anything, under comprehensivization.

Implications

A full discussion of the practical significance of this study falls outside the boundaries of this book, but I will end with a brief personal statement of the implications as I see them. I have argued that this study does not support 'hard, deterministic approaches'. There are inevitable connections with the prevailing social structure, and with the nature and distribution of occupations; and there are institutional and professional pressures. But their influence is uneven and sporadic, and leaves gaps in the system where a range of choices exists at a number of levels — governmental, local, professional, within the school, departmental, personal. Change is possible at all these levels, to some degree or other.

We need to be honest about, and give a little more thought to, our aims. If the school is primarily instrumental in the sense that its main efforts are directed toward certification, then a high degree of systematization and bureaucracy would appear desirable. Such precise ends require precise means. At the same time, however, some strong 'personal' compensation would be required in the form of high provision of 'off-moments' and 'private areas' to avoid dissatisfaction with the major process, and possibly reduced performance. Traffic between the two areas can be only one way. That is to say that one can personalize bureaucracies, but not bureaucratize personal areas. Thus, in a certification-centred school, personalized aims such as may be implied in 'education for leisure' or 'education for life' – i.e. training for the personal, private sphere, whatever one's occupation – are unlikely to be realized. The basis for such education is inappropriate. Indeed, where it is held to operate, it may only disguise a form of social control which facilitates the school's main activity.

But if schools have a genuine wider aim and 'education for life' is not simply rhetoric or an ideology, then we need to reconsider their organization and structure, and teachers their own identities. School cannot escape the society it serves. This was shown in chapter 2. Even without the critical external influence of extra parental pressure demanding even better examination results, the constraint would still operate, albeit, a little more diffused. Certification, rationalization or social class are all well entrenched. The question is, rather, do we recognize this? Are we masters of our own destinies? For understanding means control. Non-recognition means slavery, with faceless institutions and their factotums as our slavemasters. We have seen some of the convolutions teachers go through to make acceptable sense of a number of profound contradictions that attend their work. One of them is to assume a bureaucratic identity, to invest their person in the role, to elevate the criteria of the institution to prime position. Lots of things that happen in school 'make better sense' from that position. It eases accommodation. If this has to occur, then I would appeal for 'partial' or 'incidental' investment which did not call for total commitment of the self. Some elements of this would then be left free to enrich the interstices of the school day and the lives of all within it. Without this saving mechanism, the institutional consciousness will encroach ever more on the few personal areas remaining – putting the 'far side of the field' out of bounds, and rendering staffrooms places of business rather than sanctums of laughter.

This is assuming no change in the situation. The only change we can make in such a circumstance is within ourselves. But if we seek to change the situation then clear recommendations follow from this study. Chapters 7, 8 and 9 have shown how, at Lowfield, the teachers' energies and talents were expended in three main activities – surviving, being professionals and being persons. The preoccupation with 'survival' follows from pressures and low resources; the 'professional' concern is mainly with matters of certification, the school's instrumental aims; it is in the third area, the personal, I would argue, that the broad aims of 'education for life' are to be realized, if they are to be realized at all. But this area can gain only at the expense of the other two.

We need to save our teachers, relieving them of the preoccupation with survival; and they need to de-professionalize. To lessen survival concerns would entail increasing resources and/or lessening demands. This is not simply, or even essentially, a matter of injecting more money and more teachers into the system. It would appear more realistic to experiment with the system; the length of the school day, the forms of education the young are offered, especially at secondary level, so that, for example, groups were of more manageable size, and 'frees' readily available. But beyond this fairly obvious fact lies a less obvious one, and hence possibly more important. Part of the pressure on the teacher has arisen from increased interest in 'education' as an activity, and the attentions of an army of educational theorists, other educationists, curriculum innovators and teacher trainers. Many of these have operated at a different plane from the teacher struggling with the realities of the classroom, being concerned with 'pure' aspects of education untainted with details of application. Many of their urgings and recommendations, delivered with the force, authority and backing of real powers in the education system, cause problems for teachers, for they cannot be ignored. Again, perforce, they must be accommodated. But if financial restrictions cannot be helped, we as educationists should know better. Curriculum reformers, for example, need to take into account the primitive level at which many teachers are forced to operate, and possibly transform an irresolvable pressure into an aid. I would not wish to claim that this omission is always the case, nor deny the possibility and existence of much cohesion between reformers and practitioners. Lowfield, however, for me, demonstrated how easy it is to lose sight of the mediating mechanisms between idea and practice.

Deprofessionalizing teaching does not mean demoting teacher knowledge and skills. It means getting rid of all the spurious ways in which teachers, and others, promote a sense of their indispensability, infallibility and inevitability, and the many supporting mechanisms of this, such as separation from other groups, like parents; their own elaborate forms of hierarchy, and the bureaucratic framework of the school. Perhaps this is why the notion of 'community schools' seems to be becoming popular. It promises to cut across many of these boundaries which have been erected in defence of professionalism, though how entrenched these attitudes are remains to be seen. The abolition of the post of headteacher would be in the spirit of such a reform. The effect of such a range of reforms would be to dispel the enormous impulsion teachers have felt under in recent years to close ranks, and to undertake a new co-operative venture with parents and children in a common task. There would be a re-arrangement of responsibilities uncommon in the technocratic society. But if we are not to find it in our schools, where are we to find it?

It might be argued that such an enormous increase in 'personal investment' in school that must accrue with such life-saving injections and deprofessionalization is unrealistic in our society, and is not good preparation for the occupations that lie ahead of our pupils. But that itself is a technocratic view. The nature of much present-day work makes it all the more necessary that people are able to explore the possibilities of personal enrichment in their own leisure throughout their working lives. This is one of the great driving forces behind the notion of recurrent education. But it needs a firm basis, one that is established during the formative years of childhood, instead of the monotonous conformity to prevailing standards and conditions as described in chapter 2, which becomes the accepted practice by all.

Even without concerted or large-scale reform, there is much that teachers can do. In forging relationships with each other, and with their pupils of a less 'role-bound' nature, 'stepping outside' the institution, using it instead of allowing it to use them, mellowing the alienating features of bureaucracy, they can help counter-balance the worse effects. As the monasteries in the Dark Ages preserved culture, so schools in the technocratic age can preserve humanity. At Lowfield, as at so many of our state secondary schools, it was evident mainly in the margins, the 'interstitial areas' of school life. It needs to be more of a conscious and central policy, and less of an incidental and peripheral happening. It is the only way we can master our institutions before they master us.

This is not a utopian plea for complete 'freedom' for the individual, nor a metaphysical one for recovery of a human essence that has somehow got lost along the way. Rather, like Simmel, it is in the hope that[29]

the unforeseeable work of mankind will produce ever more numerous and varied forms with which the human personality will affirm itself and prove the worth of its existence. And if, in fortunate periods, these varied forms may order themselves harmoniously, even their possible contradiction and struggle will not merely disrupt that work, but rather will stimulate it to new demonstrations of strength and lead to new creations.

Appendix 1

The involved observer

In this appendix I give a little more detail about the methods behind the research on which this book is based. As space is limited, I concentrate on what I consider to be the prominent features and important issues of the methodology. These are: the nature of my 'participation' in the school; the collection of material through 'talk'; the generalizability of the findings; the generation of theory; and the collective and ongoing aspects of what might appear to be, on the face of it, a rather individualistic 'snapshot'.

Participant and involved observation

The appropriate research style for symbolic interactionism is participant observation. Problems, issues and kinds of interaction are not specified before the research begins. For example, it would not be assumed that teachers were 'teaching' and pupils 'learning' to some degree or other; those very terms become problematic — we need to find out what they mean to the people involved.[1] One difficulty, however, with members providing accounts is that it is not always easy to articulate reasons, or identify motives or intentions. This is where the sociologist stands to gain from *participation,* that is assuming a recognized role within the institution, or group, and contributing towards its function. In time the sociologist becomes a member and can proceed by reflection and analogy, analysing his own reactions and motives as and when they occur during the process of which he is a part. Hargreaves points to other advantages:[2]

> [It] permits an easy entrance into the social situation by reducing the resistance of the group members; decreases the extent to which the investigation disturbs the 'natural' situation; and permits the

investigator to experience and observe the group's norms, values, conflicts and pressures, which (over a long period) cannot be hidden from someone playing an in-group role.

The researcher tries to combine deep personal involvement and a measure of detachment. Without the latter he runs the risk of 'going native'; that is, identifying so strongly with members that he finds himself defending their values, rather than studying them. Sharing in life activities, after all, involves learning and using the language, rules and mode of behaviour, and role requisites, assuming the same dress and appearance, tasks and responsibilities and becoming subject to the same pressures and constraints. The diligent recording of 'field-notes' and a generally reflective attitude help to guard against being swamped by the experience. Reflection might lead to awareness of changes in the researcher himself.[3]

Special roles, then, designed to fit the researcher's purposes, are not created. However, the nature and degree of the participation might vary according to the aims of the research, the researcher and the culture concerned. In schools, for example, it seems to have been customary to take on a teaching load of half a timetable.[4] Some sub-cultural studies have required almost complete immersion.[5] Others adopt marginal positions.[6] My own, at Lowfield, was of this nature, and was of such a character that I preferred to think of myself as an *involved* rather than as a participating observer. I did not take on an accepted role in the institution, although I occasionally helped out with supervisions, took part in activities such as playing chess, umpiring cricket matches, accompanying pupils on Community Service to hospitals, town halls or old people's homes and, above all, shared in staffroom life with the teachers. The involvement was in the relationships entered into with staff and pupils, an identification with the educative process, and a willingness to go along with their perceptions of my role. These perceptions incorporated me into the framework of the school. For example, I was seen variously as, among others:

(1) A relief agency, or counsellor, by both pupils and some staff. Phil Harman told me, 'It helps me to get this off my chest', in one private discussion I had with him, and Angela Brown in 5L said, 'We like talking to you, it helps make us feel better about it.' On some days, when I was working all day in the staffroom, different individuals would come in in succeeding periods and confide to me their opinions of the school, the headmaster or a current topical issue. In this sense I persuaded myself that I was functional for the school. Not having any ties with the school, not being dependent on it for my livelihood, not having to teach or be taught or keep order, not having an official role (and hence no role conflict),[7] not having to take sides, I could lend a sympathetic ear to all, and not be regarded as 'belonging' to anybody, at least until

I had presented the first paper to the staff, by which time my stay at the school was more than half over.

(2) A secret agent. I would be surprised if some pupils did not suspect my motives and identify me with the teachers, or at least the cause that they represented. Certainly the headmaster saw me in that light and was interested only in whether I had discovered any fornication or drug-taking on school premises. He tried to persuade me to travel to school on the school bus, as I would 'act as a force for order' in that problem-bound vehicle. Had I done so, I would have experienced severe role conflict, since I would have been more interested in identifying the cultural patterns that pertained on the bus, rather than enforcing school rules which they contravened.[8]

(3) A factor to be used, or appealed to, in power struggles. This was a following-through of the counselling function. At times I felt people 'rehearsed' their case with me, sought out my 'bird's-eye' view of the situation (denied to them because of their total particular commitment to their sectionalized teaching responsibilities) and consulted my specialist knowledge, all to reinforce a position in a particular conflict that might have arisen.

(4) A substitute member of staff. Given that a fairly large staff will frequently have some absentees, and that the loss of 'free' time to fill in for them is so traumatic (see chapter 7), it was not surprising that pressure should be put on me to help out there. It was a matter of reciprocal obligations. I wanted to observe a form's lessons, which included one with the senior master. The following day he asked me to register a form and collect their dinner money, and fill in for an absent teacher for a double lesson with the 4th-year bottom stream maths. If there was a touch of *touché* about this I was able the following day to decline his invitation to do substitutions, on the excuse that I was too busy. My own survival strategy was acknowledged with, 'You're learning, boyo, you're learning!' To partake in the hidden pedagogy, further to the official administration of the school, I took to be a welcome sign of arrival at the strategic heart of the school.

(5) A fellow-human, who shared in the company of both teachers and pupils. I felt this to be the most important aspect of my involvement, as perhaps is clear from the analysis in chapters 5, 9 and 10. Whether reliving 'laughs' or sharing boredom with the pupils, partaking of staffroom merriment or exchanging grumbles, drinking in the pub with various groups of staff, chatting with pupils in playground, corridors and some in their own homes – in all these respects, I felt very much 'involved' in the scene, and in the action.

I was also 'involved' by previous experience. Having recently taught for over ten years in state secondary schools, I felt that participation in an official role was unnecessary.[9] With some understanding already of school life, the teacher's subjective experience, hidden agendas and in-group behaviour and strategies, I felt that I might be in a position to capitalize on the advantages of participant observation without having to suffer the difficulties. The difficulties arise mainly from becoming inundated with the responsibilities of the job, and over-involved emotionally in power struggles and survival strategies which can lead to physical, mental and nervous strain, 'going native' and deep problems of role conflict and ethics.[10] While I did not entirely avoid these problems, I did feel that they were lessened and made more negotiable.[11] My previous experience also facilitated access. Participation is often a bargaining counter in gaining entry, for where human resources are scarce, it is an aid to the institution. But as Harry Timpson told me on one occasion: 'The staff put great trust in your teaching experience. They don't see you as one of these boffins riding roughshod through the place and making a nonsense of it all. You know what it's about.' In fairness, I do not know how many staff contributed to this view, or how long it was maintained. The first paper I produced (on pupil views of school, see chapter 4) I circulated to the whole staff. It met with a mixed response, from very supportive to very critical, which reflected, as I discovered, staff personalities and/or ideologies. I accepted the practical fact that I could not present the same face to all the people all of the time, and that from then on I had stronger relations with some and weaker relations with others. It is another indication of becoming part of the scene, and how one's own interaction in it pulls one in certain directions.

Understanding through talk

Though the research style is termed 'participant observation' and there is, indeed, a great deal of 'observation' done, many studies based on it rely equally, if not more, on interviews, discussions, conversations: in short, some form of 'talk'.

I favoured forms of what I call naturalistic or behavioural talk, as opposed to reported talk, that is talk heard and noted by me in the ordinary course of events. However, how ordinary is ordinary? For a start I detected three levels of ordinariness associated with three levels of access. When I first went to the school I was shown carefully preselected scenes and witnessed 'educationist' performances. This was the public, outer face of the school in its Sunday clothes. The second level came with the relaxation of this strict control and shop-window performance and allowing me general freedom – the school divested of its clothes, as it were, but not until more time had elapsed had I built up enough trust and concord with the inmates for them to confide in me their innermost thoughts and feelings and thus reveal to me how the school operated in its very vitals. I was not aware of being given directly contradictory information, though it may have been limited and hence distorted, out of context. To guard against this I employed the usual precautions — distinguishing between subjective and objective data, invoking the criteria of plausibility and reliability of informants, but chiefly by triangulation and cross-checking of accounts.[12]

I was fortunate in finding some key informants. They helped to give perspective to the entire methodological front from the very beginning, for example to identify the nature of other people's talk and behaviour. One instance of this arises from the distinction between educationist and teacher talk.[13] It is not surprising that in some contexts there is a big difference between what teachers say they do and what they do. In a different context they might say things that accord more with that performance. The gap will be wider if one does not progress beyond the first two levels of access, and it might be difficult to spot if there were no informants. Similarly, key informants can alert us to alternative explanations of the talk and behaviour of others that we perhaps have no other means of knowing about, so that we can get a grip of the various rhetorics presented to us, and how consciously and seriously they are held. It helps here to have various kinds of informants. The more they constitute a cross-section of the population in question, the better. I was lucky in being able to forge close ties not only with the reformist left-wing art teacher and libertarian social studies man, but with the traditional-conservative head of games who had academic aspirations, and the traditional-liberal humanities teacher. On the important temporal dimension also, informants provide a sense of history, interpreting present events as part of a long, on-going process.[14]

My general practice was to use as many cross-validating methods and instruments as I could. For example, I wouldn't know what to make of the content of a personal talk with the headmaster, say, on the matter of subject choice, without the benefit of other vantage-points. Among these I would include his talk to the 3rd-year pupils and to their parents, their views on it, and the views of those he has taken into his confidence — other members of staff, preferably both for and against — sought, if possible, in various different situations which might include public house as well as staffroom and classroom. I never held any formal interviews. The nearest I approached was with the headmaster, a reflection possibly of the social distance between us. But even then I made no notes on the spot, had no formal schedule and simply tried to conduct a man-to-man discussion, leaving him to fill the scene that I set, as it were. I did as little talking as I could get away with, being intent, as Cicourel advises, on elaborating his meaning.[15] So with other members of staff. Teacher ideologies are revealed not by head-on confrontation but by naturalistic observation and discussion of other topics. For example, the teacher quoted at length in chapter 8 on reports, in talking about pupils revealed the bases of his own categorizations of them; the teacher talk in chapter 2 on subject choice had to be penetrated for underlying ideologies; and teachers' responses to the paper on pupil views reported at the end of chapter 4 were seen as comment on both the pupils' views, *and* on their own, individual, relationship to them.

At least we can identify more readily with teacher culture. The road to understanding is a longer one with pupils. Here I am using 'understanding' as Rosalie Wax does, not as some mysterious empathy but as a phenomena of shared meanings, when one feels part of the culture and can interpret words, gestures and so on, as they do.[16] We know some of the problems from, for example, Labov's work – explaining defensive, monosyllabic behaviour in terms of the asymmetrical interview situation.[17] The problem of putting them at their ease cannot be met by the normal forms of proclaiming anonymity, universality and impersonality, disclaiming teacher and associate identity and trying to get across to them in words that this was *their* platform.[18] I felt that I had to make it situationally their platform. This I tried to do by having conversations with them in friendship groups. I would go to a class at the beginning of a day, with the permission of the teacher concerned, of course, and arrange a timetable for the day, seeing groups of about four pupils in double-period slots. Pupils were invariably split up into groups when I entered. If they were large groups, I asked them to split themselves up. Pairs of pupils I asked to invite another pair along. This technique, I believe, had several advantages. The company of like-minded fellows helped to put them at their ease. The bond between them and the way it was allowed to surface shifted the power balance in the discussion in their direction. As long as my interventions were not too intrusive, it might facilitate the establishment of their norms, and I might become privy to their culture, albeit in rather a rigged way. Other advantages were that they acted as checks, balances and prompts to each other. Inaccuracies were corrected, incidents and reactions recalled and analysed. Many of the conversations became, I believe, part of their experience rather than a commentary on it, and this was particularly true of the 'laughter' discussions.

This leads me to consider what these discussions actually did, in a Garfinkelian sense.[19] First, they did provide me with information and I think the structure of the group facilitated this. Pupils volunteered information in the company of their friends – and often to them rather than to me in the context of ongoing exchanges with them – that I would not otherwise have been privy to. At other times they prompted each, other – 'Go on, tell him' – 'What about when you . . .?'

There is another side to the unstructured, naturalistic, group identification approach, of course. More forthright individuals can dominate discussions and there is a danger that the outcomes can be biased in favour of the most outspoken and aggressive individuals. If we couple with this the pupils' natural tendency in a conflict situation to regard an external interviewer as a kind of relief agency, we get an idea of the

kind of bias that can creep in. I felt that, on occasions, the actual incidence of the discussion made grievances. People can talk themselves and
others into a temper, or into laughter for that matter, and sometimes I
felt there was a thin divide between the two. This clearly has repercussions for their representations of past events. Such discussions should
be regarded as data rather than sources of information. Thus misrepre-
sentations, outrageous lies, melodrama, put-ons can all in fact be turned
to research advantage, as long as they are identified. Perhaps the best
examples again are in connection with laughter. Many of the discussions
held with me were 'laughs' in their own right; that is to say that 'laughs'
were generated in the discussion; possibly the particular configuration
of circumstances subscribing to it as reported by them had not led to
laughter previously. The discussion thus became part of their school life
rather than a pause in it.[20] Also the laughter is certainly the important
element. For added ribaldry, the facts will probably have suffered some
distortion, but that is a natural concomitant of laughter-making.

Surrendering the initiative can lead to results that are very time-
absorbing, tedious and discomforting. There is a great deal of repetition.
People occasionally wander off into peripheral monologues. I remember
one boy describing at great length his plans for becoming a jockey; a
couple of girls their experience with a gang of hell's angels in Luton;
several risqué discussions with both boys and girls about sex and fornication. This last is clearly very relevant to my interest in the pupils'
cultural experience with their environment. But it reminds me of another
of those ethical problems. In a sense, talk is legitimation. For me to talk
about some things with the pupils might have the effect of legitimating
them in their eyes. Even 'listening' can go half way towards this. Smoking, fornication, teacher-victimization, all figure prominently in the
pupil's school life, and thus we need to know about them. But it can be
uncomfortable at times, while operating under the auspices of, enjoying
the hospitality of and making friendships with those who make a career
of trying to eliminate these activities. The obvious solution is to take
sides, and I suppose if one is going to identify successfully with a culture,
it is imperative to do so. But one does it as researcher, not as political
agent, and this enables identification with any cultural form in the
school without the charge of hypocrisy. This leads me on to another
effect of these discussions, which touches on the 'mysterious empathy'
I spoke of earlier. Redfield described how the form in which he came to
understand the Mayan culture came to be phenomenologically constituted in his experience, and in some ways I went through a similar
process.[21] In the early days of my study I recorded my impressions of
the cultural experiences of the pupils. I noted down what the teachers
did, what the pupils did, and what they told me about it. As this was
during the first stage of access it had only limited value. Later, after
many discussions, when I had become what Janes calls a personalized

member and had developed a certain rapport with the pupils, I was keyed in to their experience via talk, and it was the talk which led to the empathy.[22] This might be already clear from the 'laughter' examples. Having listened, for example, to their accounts of how they occupied themselves during school assembly, it was easy to do some of the same things and share in the fun. Obviously one catches something in laughter that is not necessarily expressed in words. The same is true of other experiences, when the talk assumes an onomatopoeic quality. I am thinking here of what I discovered to be the main impact of the school on one group of pupils — boredom. The point I am making is that the way in which they expressed it cued me in to the actual experience of it. One of my one or two outstanding memories from the enormous mass of experiences at the school is that of pupils talking to me about boredom. They managed to convey, in a very few words largely, years of crushing ennui that had been ingrained into their bones. A great wealth of expression was got into 'boring', 'boredom', 'it's so bo-or-oring here'. The word, I realize now, is onomatopoeic. I could never view lessons in company with that group again without experiencing that boredom myself. They would occasionally glance my way in the back corner of the room with the pained expression on their faces, and I knew exactly what they meant. This then provided a platform for my understanding of the school life of one group of pupils. The group conversations also enabled me to distinguish fairly easily between groups, on the lines described in chapter 2, a division which was a basic feature of the model developed of pupil experience of the school.

In my use of talk, the criteria for selecting extracts in my accounts are basically four — validity, typicality, relevance and clarity. I have used extensive quotation — the subjects do a great deal of speaking for themselves. The themes are theirs, the categories are theirs ('having a laugh', 'being shown up', different kinds of 'choice', and see the teacher aphorisms below the sub-headings in chapter 7 on survival strategies). The sociologist acts first as a roving microphone, then as a book-keeper and filing clerk. By presenting a sample from his file he can give a tidy, descriptive account organized round certain features which will have a value in its own right. These member typifications are then subjected to social scientific analysis. They are two distinct processes and ideally should not be confused. The 'rhetoric of interaction' should not be coloured by the analysis and should be available for alternative analyses.[23]

Generalizability

How applicable might these findings be to other schools? There are two different approaches to ethnography. Some see it as exclusively idiographic, that is to say, descriptive of particular situations; these emphasize the holistic nature of ethnography and the distinctive nature of information discovered, which consequently is not covered by the assumptions of statistical assessment. It does not in itself, therefore, permit generalization, though it might serve as a basis. As we have seen earlier, the situation is fluid, emergent, consisting of multiple realities which are in constant negotiation. There are no 'truths' to be discovered, or 'proofs' to be made; rather the aim is greater understanding of the social action in the situation under study. One's descriptions might be full of details of content, meanings, style and pattern, features which are not easily quantifiable.

On the other hand there are those who prefer to see it as nomothetic, that is to say, generalizing, comparative, theoretical. There are a number of ways we can generalize through ethnography. We can, for example, take an area of special interest, say a curriculum innovation, and carry out intensive studies of it within several schools; then as the study reveals certain particular aspects of interest concerning the innovation, widen the sample of schools. Because the focus is narrower, the base of operations can be wider. Then we could accumulate case studies of particular features, aspects or areas, such as the classroom, the 'express stream', school assemblies. Or one can move from the study of small-scale items to a larger-scale in a logical and interlocking sequence, for example, from a school class to a year group or sub-culture, to a school, to a community. Occasionally, participant observations have been quantified, though more usually by 'quasi-statistics'.[24] For instance, observations may frequently be implicitly numerical without lending themselves to actual counting. One might observe that in one lesson most of the class pay attention for most of the time, while in another they do not, or one might discover by talking to people that a few, some or many of them hold certain views or have certain concerns. This all involves frequency and distribution.[25] My own view is that 'idiographic' and 'nomothetic' approaches are not mutually exclusive, and that we can have both rich and intensive description *and* generalizability. As far as schools are concerned, one can work from the other way round, that is to say, select a 'typical' school, class or group, using such indices as numbers, type of school, curriculum, area, neighbourhood, sex, age, social mix and so on. The more 'representative' the school, the greater the chances of the external validity of the results. There are many schools like Lowfield, with similar structural and cultural patterns and forms of interaction. It follows from my theoretical framework, as elaborated in chapters 1 and 10, that there must be some common features and some idiosyncratic ones. Generalizability is strengthened as the theory is strengthened, and this might be done in a number of ways – by more case studies of schools, by other forms of empirical evidence which bear on the theory, or parts of it, by improving the internal logic of the theory, or increasing the explanatory power of its parts, and not least, in the reader's head as he deploys his own knowledge and experience of such institutions.

The generation of theory

Some do consider the chief merit of ethnography to be 'good reporting, and that ethnographic facts clearly and accurately presented are likely to survive the theoretical frame of reference of the man who revealed them'.[26] Others might engage in purely descriptive work, but in clear recognition that it is in the service of the grander design. Wolcott, for example, is satisfied as an ethnographer if someone is willing to use one of his accounts 'in an attempt to create some larger scientific super-structure. That's what these bricks are for.'[27] Robinson pleads for more long-term case studies of schools which will 'help us generate theoretical statements having a wider applicability than the local classroom'.[28]

Too much pre-formulated theory at the start can prejudice the out-come of ethnography.[29]

> If the observer focuses his attention on specific hypotheses, or ques-tions, or categories, he will see meanings within the framework of these preconditioning factors, but he will miss other meanings . . . which could be more important to people in the context of a culture.

Others think that sociology has become theoretically and methodologi-cally hidebound, imprisoning the 'sociological imagination' and recom-mend dispensing with traditional methodological requirements and concentrating on the 'realities of society'.[30] This, it should be said, would be in the service of new insights which themselves might go towards the making of new theoretical structures, which would embrace more of the problems which interest us now. These theoretical structures could *then* guide research for as long as they were considered relevant.

Thus ethnographers often prefer to proceed by 'induction'. That is to say, rather than seeking evidence to support or refute hypotheses derived from *a priori* theory (the hypothetico-deductive method), they seek to induce concepts and theory from the data as it is revealed. This theory is 'discovered' and is 'grounded' in the situational facts.[31]

Glaser and Strauss distinguish between 'substantive' and 'formal' theory.[32]

> By substantive theory, we mean that developed for a substantive, or empirical area of sociological inquiry, such as patient care, race rela-tions, professional education, delinquency, or research organizations. By formal theory, we mean that developed for a formal, or concep-tual, area of sociological inquiry, such as stigma, deviant behaviour, formal organization, socialization, status congruency, authority and

power, reward systems, or social mobility. Both types of theory may be considered as 'middle-range'. That is they fall between the 'minor working hypotheses' of everyday life and the 'all-inclusive' grand theories.

In this book I have suggested, at times, some ways in which the gap between interactionists and structuralists might be bridged, that is the gap between the 'minor working hypotheses' of everyday life and 'grand theory'. Chapter 2 contains perhaps the most detailed example, but a briefer one, which will serve description here, is the discovery and study of the 'showing-up syndrome' discussed in chapter 6. Once one has negotiated access to the stage where, if not exactly privy to innermost councils, one is permitted to witness *normal* processes, data collection begins in earnest. All the techniques of fieldwork are brought into play (observing, interviewing, examining, reports, reflection, etc.), and the tapes, notes and records grow quickly and rather chaotically. If recorded faithfully, they will reflect the muddle and messiness of everyday life. Ultimately, however, I became aware of regularities in the pupils' conversations with me which provided certain 'themes'.

What governs their appearance is frequency of occurrence, strength in terms of cataclysmic effect on people, or strangeness in terms of paradoxes, inconsistencies and deviations from routine. In this case, all of these seemed to apply. One of their preoccupations was an aversion to being 'shown up' by teachers. Satisfied that this was acutely felt and common enough to warrant further investigation, I engaged in 'theoretical sampling'; that is, I purposely began to seek and accumulate material from all sources which bore on the phenomenon,[33]

(a) to examine the extent of the possibilities,
(b) to see how well the facts fitted,
(c) to examine their common properties, and
(d) to investigate its theoretical potential.

Inevitably for a while, a certain amount is tentative and there is a deliberate stretching of the limits, and experimentation (viz. in the 'mind', not in the situation). This first distillation of material and theme was, for me, an essential stage. During it, triangulation and all the rest of the participant observer's armament of techniques continue.

I constructed a typology, examined the internal structure of the process, considered its functions and results and who was involved. Much of this was at the level of substantive theory, but some formal theory came in in relation to functions and who was involved. This is because the functions are connected with general sociological concepts like power, socialization and status, and could therefore be related to other contexts. 'Who was involved' led to a consideration of other distinctive features they might have in common, and a tentative identification with one of the pedagogical paradigms outlined in the literature, and an elaboration of a 'paternalist' style of control. This is the point where personality meets system, and there are opportunities for a related analysis at the wider level.[34] Here, then, is a possible connection with 'grand theory', followed through from one feature of interaction clearly identified and analysed at ground level.

The stages of my research match Becker's three stages of field analysis — (a) the selection and definition of problems, concepts and indices, (b) the check on the frequency and distribution of phenomena and (c) the incorporation of individual findings into a model of the organization under study.[35] I would add a fourth stage — (d) a consideration of the relationship of this model and its component parts to external forms and structures. Of course, one does not 'prove' the connection with any grand theory — the theory might well have to be revised in the light of subsequent research and analysis. But this is perfectly natural in 'analytic induction', the strategy that 'directs the investigator to formulate generalizations that apply to *all* instances of the problem with which he is concerned'.[36] Denzin sees the strategy taking the following steps:[37]

(1) A rough definition of the phenomenon to be explained is formulated.

(2) A hypothetical explanation of that phenomenon is formulated.

(3) One case is studied in light of the hypothesis, with the object of determining whether or not the hypothesis fits the facts in that case.

(4) If the hypothesis does not fit the facts, either the hypothesis is reformulated or the phenomenon to be explained is redefined so that the case is excluded.

(5) Practical certainty may be attained after a small number of cases has been examined, but the discovery of negative cases disproves the explanation and requires a reformulation.

(6) This procedure of examining cases, redefining the phenomenon, and reformulating the hypotheses is continued until a universal relationship is established, each negative case calling for a redefinition, or a reformulation.

Clearly the link with 'grand theory' is impossible to 'ground' in the same sense. One tends to merely add to or subtract from its plausibility. This is not surprising since much grand theory is incapable of verification in the same way.

A danger in participant observation 'immersion' is 'macro-blindness'. Deep involvement in the scene can blind to external constraints, and the researcher might find himself explaining things in their own terms when more powerful forces operating on the action lie elsewhere. This is the other side of the coin from that wherein he takes existing theory and concepts as his guide and runs the risk of blinding himself to the more significant and interesting parts of the action. Sharp and Green claim they have demonstrated how structural factors are reproduced in interaction, and how interactions are socially structured by the wider context.[38] Interestingly, and as with several others, it was only when they 'had left the field that many of the crucial insights emerged and with them the crystallization of the overall approach to our accounting.'[39] Thus they were not engaged in 'grounded theorizing' as discussed above. They did not 'saturate' their categories, nor 'induce' their theoretical propositions. Hargreaves and his co-authors in *Deviance in Classrooms* keep more to the grounded theory rubric, but more easily so since the authors invoke no structural theory.[40]

A collective and ongoing enterprise

In some respects, participant observation is an intensely individualistic task and many field studies give an impression of 'hit and run', that is, gaining access to an institution, 'cracking' its secrets, and then escaping, before the ethical problems catch up, to write the definitive version in the sanctuary of one's own study. However, this kind of research, like any other, is a collective enterprise, and, equally, is an ongoing one.

For example, after the first distillation of material, the search for both internal validity and theoretical potential requires the participation of other people. Internal validity requires the aid of people in the institution, and of others in the profession elsewhere. Of course, there are the difficulties mentioned earlier. In the 'survival strategy' thesis, for example, in chapter 7, if teachers have constructed defence mechanisms which protect their exposure, they will hardly countenance an interpretation which threatens to undermine this reality. (Is this the source of the gulf which exists between teachers and educational researchers, rather than the latter's tendency to abstraction?) If teachers are still bound by commitment problems, their interpretation is sure to differ, being governed by those very same criteria which the theme may claim to expose. After all, they do have to continue teaching in the school. We would expect, therefore, not so much a confirmation of views of the paper as further illustrations of survival strategies in practice. However, there might be some teachers in the school who are not likely to see themselves so threatened: for instance (a) those who are not included personally in the examples, (b) those of low commitment, (c) those who contribute to certain ideologies (liberal reformists, deschoolers, liberationists) and (d) those with whom the researcher might have forged certain personal links which transcend the institutionalized role. These might hold views quite contrary to the researcher, but the personal bond is strong enough to stand the strain. They are a useful counterbalance to the liberationist ideologies.

To investigate the theoretical possibilities, he will show the paper to colleagues in the usual way, inviting their comments, and consult the literature, thus generating new thoughts and ideas, while locating his work within a trend or a genre and the discipline as a whole. The theoretical sampling of the first stage continues, hopefully aiding refinement of the categories. He will discard those that are thin ('unsaturated'), and he will rule out examples that are problematic. The explanation – the overall theoretical import – may be one-sided; it might not be intended as a *complete* explanation of all that goes on (i.e. all the phenomena) in that institution, nor even as a complete explanation of the phenomena it presents. I much prefer to view society, and man in his relationships, as complex, manifold, loosely-structured and quite often contradictory. To take a one-sided view is legitimate practice in sociology, and is accepted as contributing to a general scheme. But as a one-sided view, the other sides of the view might come to prevail in some respects as the research proceeds. For example, is a 'fraternizing' teacher aiming simply to pass the time more equitably, or seeking to facilitate the learning situation? Clearly he could be doing either, and often there must be a thin divide. This must be allowed for in the new model.

A second account of the phenomenon is thus produced which draws on the literature for both theoretical and empirical support and compares alternative theories. Yet this is by no means the final stage. What we have so far in the research process is (a) access, (b) immersion, (c) idea, (d) distillation, (e) consolidation. In a sense, this last, 'consolidation', might be seen as a beginning. In fact it *is* the beginning of survey research, which *assumes* all these other preliminaries. This in fact might be the style of future work, some kind of quantification, whether done statistically, or by an accumulation of case studies. How widespread is this amongst our profession as a whole, what proportion of teachers' work is to be interpreted in this way, and how are the distributions affected by other factors, career structures and so on?

Together with this kind of extension must go further theoretical refinement and underpinning. Its value as a model must be put to the test and this can be done only by more ethnographic work. The 'consolidation' phase might raise as many questions as it answers. For example, we need to explore in more detail the *nature* of commitment, how it varies in kind and degree among teachers, and according to what factors, and how it relates to institutional and social change. The whole needs broadening to the realms of formal sociology. This leads to a new level of abstraction, and more general applicability so that it can more easily be applied to all walks of life. Clearly, one suspects strongly that 'commitment', 'survival' and 'accommodation' are just as constraining and determining in hospitals, prisons, town halls, supermarkets, factories, universities. It is a feature of modern society, which in its development of technocracy and mass institutions has forced the human consciousness through all manner of convolutions. It is our task to trace those convolutions, and not to be seduced by them.

Appendix 2

The questionnaire to parents

Please complete the form as indicated. If you wish to add any comments; please do so in the spaces following the questions. Please ignore any questions you may find difficult to answer.

The name of your child in the 3rd year . . . .

His or her present class. . . . .

Your relationship to child (Mother/Father/Guardian). . . . .

Your occupation . . . .

1. Did your child ask your advice about what subjects should be chosen?

Yes/No

2. How important do you consider the following pieces of advice to pupils considering what subjects to take? (Place a tick in the box that applies for each statement)

	Very import.	Quite import.	Of some import.	Not very import.	Not at all import.
(a) Do those subjects you're best at					
(b) Do those subjects you're interested in					
(c) Do those subjects with the best teachers					
(d) Do those subjects you want to					
(e) Do those subjects likely to lead to a good job					
(f) Do those subjects your teachers advise					

3. Do you feel fully competent to advise your child on such a matter?

Yes/No

If not, please explain.

4. Did you attend either of the 3rd year parents' evenings at the school?
   Yes/No

5. Do you think the school offers a reasonable choice of subjects?
   Yes/No/Don't know
   If not, please explain why you think not.

6. Do you think the school gives enough information and advice to pupils and parents on the matter of subject choice?
   Yes/No/Don't know
   If no, can you say what it is that you would like to know more about?

7. Do you think that the school does as much as it reasonably can to see pupils get the subjects which they choose?
   Yes/No/Don't know
   If no, please explain.

8. How important do you think the following aims should be for the school? Please tick the relevant box.

	Very	Quite	Of some	Not very	Not at all	Don't know
To teach children about life						
To teach children so that they get as good qualifications as possible						
To teach good manners and courtesy						
To prepare children for a job						
To keep children occupied till they go out to work						
To teach children to be good citizens						
To teach children to think for themselves						

9. How suitable do you think your child is for the following subject groups? Please tick the relevant box in each case.

	Very suitable	Quite suitable	Not very suitable	Don't know
Practical subjects (e.g. Woodwork, Housecraft)				
Commercial subjects (Typing, Shorthand, etc)				
Science subjects (Physics, Chemistry, Biology, etc)				
Arts subjects (e.g. History, Geography, English lit.)				
Non-examination subjects (e.g. Environmental Studies) Social Studies				

275

10. How far do you feel each of the following has influenced your views of your child's suitability? Please tick the relevant box in each case.

	Very influential	Quite influential	A little	Not very influential
Past reports from school				
Your child's performance in exams				
Your own knowledge of the child				
Your knowledge of the rest of the family				
Teachers' recommendations				
The child's own view of him or herself				
Your knowledge of other children like him/her				

11. Have you any idea of what sort of work you hope your child will be going into when he/she leaves school?

Yes/No

If yes, please say what it is.

12. What sort of work do you *expect* your child to be doing when he/she leaves school?

Please add further comments you wish to make about 3rd year subject choice in the space below.

13. Please put a tick in the box if you would be willing for me to call round to discuss this matter briefly with you.

Note on sources

Some of the articles cited in the Notes have appeared subsequently in collected volumes and, for ease of reference, page numbers have been given from these volumes, with the titles abbreviated as follows:

CCC Class, Codes and Control, by B. Bernstein.

P of S The Process of Schooling, edited by M. Hammersley and P. Woods, Routledge & Kegan Paul, London, 1976.

S & S School and Society, edited by B.R. Cosin *et al.,* Routledge & Kegan Paul, London, 2nd ed., 1977.

Notes

Introduction

1 R.D.Laing *The Divided Self,* Penguin Books, 1970.
2 R. Sharp and A. Green, *Education and Social Control,* Routledge & Kegan Paul, London, 1976, p. 17.

Chapter 1   Theoretical approach

1 Best illustrated in the work of A.H. Halsey and J. Floud. See, for example, A.H. Halsey *et al.,* eds, *Education, Economy and Society,* Free Press, Chicago, 1961; and J.E. Floud *et al., Social Class and Education Opportunity,* Heinemann, London, 1956.
2 For illustrations of these, see R. and B. Gross, eds, *Radical School Reform,* Simon & Schuster, New York, 1969.
3 The most famous of these was, of course, Ivan Illich. See *Deschooling Society,* Harper & Row, New York, 1971 (Penguin Books, 1973). A useful summary of the movement is given in I. Lister, *Deschooling,* Cambridge University Press, 1974. For a consideration of their implication, see D.H. Hargreaves 'Deschoolers and New Romantics', in M. Flude and J. Ahier, eds, *Educability, Schools and Ideology,* Croom Helm, London, 1974.
4 See especially the work of Wolcott and Wax, in H.F. Wolcott, *A Kwakiutl Village and School,* Holt, Rinehart & Winston, New York, 1967; M.L. Wax, S. Diamond and F.O. Gearing, eds, *Anthropological Perspectives on Education,* Basic Books, New York, 1971; R.V. Dumont and M.L. Wax, 'Cherokee School Society and the Intercultural Classroom', *Human Organization,* 28 (3), Fall 1969, pp. 217-26 (*S & S,* pp. 70-8). Also important was interactionist work on other institutions, the most influential being E. Goffman, *Asylums,* Penguin Books, 1968.
5 L.H. Smith, and W. Geoffrey, *The Complexities of an Urban Classroom,* Holt, Rinehart & Winston, New York, 1968; P.W. Jackson,

278

Life in Classrooms, Holt, Rinehart & Winston, New York, 1968; D.H. Hargreaves, *Social Relations in a Secondary School*, Routledge & Kegan Paul, London, 1967; C. Lacey, *Hightown Grammar*, Manchester University Press, 1970. See also T. Partridge, *Life in a Secondary Modern School*, Penguin Books, 1968.

6 R.A. King, *Values and Involvement in a Grammar School*, Routledge & Kegan Paul, London, 1969; J. Ford, *Social Class and the Comprehensive School*, Routledge & Kegan Paul, London, 1970; E. Richardson, *Authority and Organization in the Secondary School*, Macmillan, London, 1975.

7 The most notable exponent being N.A. Flanders, *Analyzing Teacher Behavior*, Addison-Wesley, New York, 1970.

8 As recommended in D. Hamilton and S. Delamont, 'Classroom Research: a Cautionary Tale', *Research in Education*, no. 11, May 1974, pp. 1-15. For an account of this particular development, see S. Delamont, *Interaction in the Classroom*, Methuen, London, 1976; and for examples, see the collections, G. Chanan and S. Delamont, eds, *Frontiers of Classroom Research*, NFER, Slough, 1974, and M. Stubbs and S. Delamont, eds, *Explorations in Classroom Observation*, Wiley, Chichester, 1976.

9 M.F.D. Young, ed, *Knowledge and Control*, Collier-Macmillan, 1971; *School and Society*, Open University Press, Milton Keynes, 1971 (especially units 1-7).

10 D. Gorbutt, 'The New Sociology of Education', *Education for Teaching*, Autumn 1972, p. 6.

11 N. Keddie, 'Classroom Knowledge', in M.F.D. Young, ed., op. cit., p. 133.

12 J. Beck, 'Transition and Continuity: a Study of Educational Status Passage', unpublished M.A. thesis, University of London, 1972.

13 G. Vulliamy, 'School Music as a Case Study in the New Sociology of Education', in J. Shepherd *et al.*, eds, *Whose Music? A Sociology of Musical Languages*, Latimer New Dimensions, London, 1977.

14 E. Fuchs, 'How Teachers Learn to Help Children Fail', in N. Keddie, ed., *Tinker, Tailor . . . the Myth of Cultural Deprivation*, Penguin Books, 1973.

15 R. Nash, *Classrooms Observed*, Routledge & Kegan Paul, London, 1973.

16 G. Whitty, *School Knowledge and Social Control*, Open University Press, Milton Keynes, 1977 (units 14-15 of E202, 'Schooling and Society'), p. 16; for his extended critique of the new sociology, see G. Whitty, 'Sociology and the Problems of Radical Educational Change', in M. Flude and J. Ahier, eds, *Educability, Schools and Ideology*.

17 The Plowden Report was published in 1967, and presumably became of most use to schools in the 1970s. This illustrates the considerable 'lag' in practical action. Some intellectuals were committed to the development of which Plowden was a culmination; others with no such commitment condemned it almost before it appeared. See B. Bernstein and B. Davies, 'Some Sociological Comments on

Plowden', in R.S. Peters, ed., *Perspectives on Plowden*, Routledge & Kegan Paul, London, 1969.

18 It should be noted that charges of wilful 'teacher-bashing' can hardly be made to stick. The climate of political opinion, given failure to abolish or even modify selection by comprehensivation, forced attention on the nature of teaching, a shift encouraged by growing interest in progressive methods of teaching. That there should be a strong undercurrent of 'critique' is hardly surprising, and this in itself constituted a pressure on teachers, as I discuss later in chapter 7. But nobody was out to 'get' teachers.

19 D.H. Hargreaves, S.K. Hester and F.J. Mellor, *Deviance in Classrooms*, Routledge & Kegan Paul, London, 1976.

20 R. Sharp and A. Green, *Education and Social Control*, Routledge & Kegan Paul, 1976.

21 Ibid., p. 114.

22 Ibid., p. 35.

23 For an extended discussion of these two works, see M. Hammersley, *Teacher Perspectives*, Open University Press, Milton Keynes, 1977 (unit 9 of E202, 'Schooling and Society'). For a critique of Sharp and Green, see D.H. Hargreaves, 'Whatever Happened to Symbolic Interactionism', in L. Barton and R. Meighan, eds, *Issues Relating to the Classroom*, Nafferton Books, Driffield (forthcoming), and for an appreciation, see M. Apple, 'Power and School Knowledge', *Review of Education*, 3 (1), January–February 1977.

24 For illustrations of current approaches in the field, see P.E. Woods and M. Hammersley, eds, *School Experience*, Croom Helm, London, 1977; M. Hammersley and P.E. Woods, eds, *The Process of Schooling*, Routledge & Kegan Paul, London, 1976; G. Whitty and M.F.D. Young, *Explorations in the Politics of School Knowledge*, Nafferton Books, Driffield, 1976.

25 R. Morton-Williams and S. Finch, *Young School Leavers, Schools Council Enquiry* 1, HMSO, London, 1968; A. Smithers, G. Avis and D. Lobley, 'Conceptions of School Among Pupils Affected by the Raising of the School Leaving Age', *Educational Research*, June 1974.

26 R. Nash, 'Pupils' Expectations for their Teachers', *Research in Education*, November 1974.

27 W.G. Quine, 'Polarised Cultures in Comprehensive Schools', *Research in Education*, November 1974; S. Delamont, 'Academic Conformity Observed', unpublished Ph.D. thesis, Edinburgh, 1973; V. Furlong, 'Interaction Sets in the Classroom: Towards a Study of Pupil Knowledge', in M. Stubbs and S. Delamont, eds, *Explorations in Classroom Observation*, pp. 22–44 (*P of S*, pp. 160–70).

28 B. Torode, 'Interrupting Intersubjectivity', in Woods and Hammersley, eds, *School Experience*; R. Harré and E. Rosser, 'The Rules of Disorder', *Times Educational Supplement*, 25 July 1975. See also E. Rosser and R. Harré, 'The Meaning of "Trouble"', in Hammersley and Woods, eds, *The Process of Schooling*, pp. 171–7 and P. Marsh, E. Rosser and R. Harré, *The Rules of Disorder*, Routledge & Kegan Paul, London, 1978.

29 D.H. Hargreaves, *Social Relations in a Secondary School*; C. Lacey, *Hightown Grammar*. See also Quine, op. cit., and Furlong, op cit.
30 Quine, op. cit.
31 Morton-Williams and Finch, op. cit.; Smithers *et al.*, op. cit.; Nash, 'Pupils' Expectations for their Teachers'.
32 N. Keddie, 'Classroom Knowledge' in M.F.D. Young, ed., *Knowledge and Control*.
33 Nash, 'Pupils' Expectations for their Teachers'; Harré and Rosser, op. cit.
34 H.L. Foster, *Ribbin', Jivin' and Playin' the Dozens*, Ballinger, Cambridge, Mass., 1974. See also Nash, 'Pupils' Expectations for their Teachers', and Harré and Rosser, op. cit.
35 See H. Gannaway, 'Making Sense of School', in M. Stubbs and S. Delamont, eds, *Explorations in Classroom Observation*, for a more dynamic account of pupil perceptions of teachers. For a critique of studies of pupils' perceptions, see D.H. Hargreaves 'The Process of Typification in the Classroom: Models and Methods', *British Journal of Educational Psychology*, September 1977. I discuss this article in chapter 8.
36 See R. Woolfe and K. Giles, *Deprivation, Disadvantage and Compensation*, Open University Press, Milton Keynes, 1977 (units 25-6 of E202, 'Schooling and Society').
37 B. Bernstein, *Class, Codes and Control*, vol. 1, Routledge & Kegan Paul, London, 2nd ed., 1974.
38 An interesting attempt is made by Paul Willis. See his article, 'The Class Significance of School Counter-Culture', in Hammersley and Woods, eds, *The Process of Schooling*, pp. 188-99, and his book, *Learning to Labour: How Working-Class Kids get Working-Class Jobs*, Saxon House, Farnborough, 1977.
39 G.H. Mead, *Mind, Self and Society*, University of Chicago Press, 1934; H. Blumer, *Symbolic Interactionism*, Prentice-Hall, Englewood Cliffs, N.J., 1969; E. Goffman, *The Presentation of Self in Everyday Life*, Penguin Books, 1971; H.S. Becker, *Sociological Work*, Allen Lane, London, 1971
40 For a theory of the 'definition of the situation' see R.A. Stebbins, 'A Theory of the Definition of the Situation', *Canadian Review of Sociology and Anthropology*, no. 4, 1967, pp. 148-64.
41 This is based heavily on E. Goffman, *The Presentation of Self in Everyday Life*.
42 This parts company with some interactionists, e.g. H. Blumer, *Symbolic Interactionism*.
43 See, for example, S. Bowles and H. Gintis, *Schooling in Capitalist America*, Routledge & Kegan Paul, London, 1976.
44 See H.H.Gerth and C.W. Mills, eds, *From Max Weber*, Routledge & Kegan Paul, London, 1967, chapter 8, pp. 196-266; E, Goffman, *Asylums*, and *The Presentation of Self in Everyday Life*; P.L. and B. Berger and H. Kellner, *The Homeless Mind*, Penguin Books, 1973.
45 Gerth and Mills, op. cit., pp. 215-16.
46 F. Musgrove, *Youth and the Social Order*, Routledge & Kegan Paul, London, 1964.

47 In J. Wakeford, *The Cloistered Elite: a Sociological Analysis of the English Public Boarding School,* Macmillan. London, 1969.
48 *Ecstasy and Holiness,* Methuen, London, 1974, p. 166.
49 Ibid., p. 165.
50 The question of a 'real' or 'true' self, and 'public' and 'private' areas, is taken up in chapter 10. It should be said, however, that the theories that underwrite such models are rather speculative, and inasmuch as Lowfield appears to contribute towards their substance, it is a qualitative matter. That is to say that Lowfield illustrates how the mechanisms with such theories might work within one school, but other schools might manifest different features.
51 See R. Walker and I. Goodson, 'Humour in the classroom', in Woods and Hammersley, eds, *School Experience,* and R. Walker and C. Adelman, 'Strawberries', in M. Stubbs and S. Delamont, eds, *Explorations in Classroom Observation.*

Chapter 2   Patterns of choice

* A version of this chapter was first published under the title 'The Myth of Subject Choice', in *British Journal of Sociology,* June 1976.
1 This follows the methodology recommended by B.G. Glaser and A.L. Strauss in *The Discovery of Grounded Theory,* Weidenfeld & Nicolson, London, 1967.
2 H.S. Becker *et al., Boys in White,* University of Chicago Press, 1961, p. 34.
3 For useful summaries and recent reflections on this position, see Section V of J. Eggleston, ed., *Contemporary Research in the Sociology of Education,* Methuen, London, 1974.
4 These terms are used by D.N. Ashton in 'Careers and Commitment: the Movement from School to Work', in D. Field, ed., *Social Psychology for Sociologists,* Nelson, London, 1974.
5 B. Bernstein, 'A Socio-linguistic Approach to Socialization: with some Reference to Educability', in D. Hymes and J.J. Gumperz, eds, *Directions in Socio-linguistics,* Holt, Rinehart & Winston, New York, 1971 (*CCC,* vol. 1, 2nd ed., 1974, pp. 143-69).
6 Ibid., p. 152.
7 Op. cit., p. 174.
8 A.V. Cicourel and J.I. Kitsuse, *The Educational Decision-Makers,* Bobbs-Merrill, New York, 1963.
9 As, for example, in T. Parsons, 'General Theory in Sociology', in R.K. Merton *et al.,* eds, *Sociology Today,* Basic Books, New York, 1958; A.B. Hollinghead, *Elmtown's Youth,* Wiley, New York, 1949; J.S. Coleman, *The Adolescent Society,* Free Press, Chicago, 1961.
10 H.Becker, *Outsiders: Studies in the Sociology of Deviance,* Collier-Macmillan, 1963.
11 D.T. Dickson 'Bureaucracy and Morality: an Organizational Perspective on a Moral Crusade', *Social Problems,* 16, 1968, pp. 143-56.
12 Pupils were interviewed in friendship groups of two to four pupils

previously ascertained by sociometry and observation. I have no doubt that this aided free and frank discussion. It might be argued that they would influence each others' responses. But I believe this to have been a beneficial influence, in that our discussions frequently drew upon discussion they had had among themselves on the subject, and they assisted each other's recall.

13 D.H. Hargreaves, *Social Relations in a Secondary School,* Routledge & Kegan Paul, London, 1967.

14 C. Lacey, *Hightown Grammar,* Manchester University Press, 1970.

15 R.A. King, *Values and Involvement in a Grammar School,* Routledge & Kegan Paul, London, 1969.

16 See Bernstein, op. cit.

17 A.W.H. Pitt, 'A Review of the Reasons for Making a Choice of Subjects at the Secondary School level', *Educational Review,* 26 (1), November 1973.

18 M.T. Reid, B.R. Barrett and H.A. Rosenberg, *A Matter of Choice,* NFER, Slough, 1974.

19 L. Cohen 'Role Conflict in Headteachers', unpublished Ph.D. thesis, University of Keele, 1969.

20 It might equally be said that they show a connection with academic achievement, but, of course, I am assuming also a connection between *that* and social class. Also, as pointed out previously, I was able to establish from the interviews that the connection with social class predominated over connection with academic stream.

21 For the effects of streaming see B. Jackson, *Streaming: an Educational System in Miniature*, Routledge & Kegan Paul, London, 1964; Central Advisory Council for Education (England), *Children and their Primary Schools* (Plowden Report), HMSO, 1967; J.B. Lunn, *Streaming in the Primary School,* NFER, Slough, 1970.

22 For teachers' knowledge of pupils based on institutional channelling, see N. Keddie, 'Classroom Knowledge', in M.F.D. Young, ed., *Knowledge and Control,* Collier-Macmillan, London, 1971.

23 For an extended discussion along these lines, related to subject choice in a girls' secondary school, see Y. Beecham, 'The Making of Educational Failures', *Hard Cheese,* no. 2, May 1973.

24 It is important to note that the teachers did not feel this directly. Pressure was put on them by the headmaster, and from his words and actions they thought this the most likely, indeed the sole, explanation.

25 These comments were made during a lunchtime conversation involving six members of staff.

26 B. Bernstein, 'On the Classification and Framing of Educational Knowledge', in M.F.D. Young, ed., *Knowledge and Control,* Collier-Macmillan, London, 1971 (*CCC*, vol. 3, 2nd ed., 1977, pp. 85-115).

27 R.H. Turner, 'Sponsored and Contest Mobility and the School System', in E. Hopper, ed., *Readings in the Theory of Educational Systems,* Hutchinson, London, 1971.

28 To date, the field of subject choice has been largely the preserve of psychologists interested in correlations between personality factors

and subject choice. The most well-known one perhaps is Liam Hudson's famous distinction between divergent and convergent thinkers, and their predisposition for arts and science subjects respectively; see *Contrary Imaginations,* Methuen, London, 1966. In a recent review of the literature, five times as much space is taken up with personality factors as with 'other possible causes'; see A.W.H. Pitt, op. cit. The most recent, comprehensive work on subject choice takes for granted the general context of school and society, though much of the basic data supports the social structural model outlined in this chapter; see M.I. Reid *et al., A Matter of Choice.* The model is also supported by another sociological study currently in preparation; see S. Ball, 'Subject-Option Choice: Selection and the Management of Knowledge', unpublished paper, University of Sussex. In fact the parallels between this study and my own are quite remarkable. For instance, Ball concludes: 'In effect then the selection decision for 4th-year options and subsequent examination attainment at O level and CSE at the end of the 5th year, and later entry into the occupational hierarchy or higher or further education, are all critically influenced by the allocation to bands at the beginning of the first year. This is in its turn based upon educational identities created in the primary school. The separation into bands is linked closely to a stratification of knowledge and the differential access to high status knowledge with high negotiable value . . . given the relationship between banding and social class the basis of the differentiation of access is primarily that of socio-economic status even here in a Comprehensive school. This form of early selection and the subsequent "warming up" of the band 1, predominantly middle-class pupils, and "cooling out" of the bands 2 and 3, predominantly working-class pupils fit . . . an elitist sponsorship selection ideology' (p. 40).

If the basic model holds, then it applies to all processes of choice throughout the school. This is supported by studies of occupational choice (see especially D.N. Ashton and D. Field, *Young Workers,* Hutchinson, London, 1976; and K. Roberts, *From School to Work: a Study of the Youth Employment Service,* David & Charles, Newton Abbot, 1971; for a general summary of work in this area, see M. Speakman, *Occupational Choice and Placement,* Open University Press, Milton Keynes, 1976 (unit 5 of DE351, 'People and Work') and for studies of attitudes of senior pupils to higher education see '16 and 18-year-olds: Attitudes to Education', *DES Reports on Education,* no. 86, July 1976, and W.A. Reid, 'Choice and Selection: the Social Process of Transfer to Higher Education', *Journal of Social Policy,* 3 (4), 1974, pp. 327-40; though Reid, in the area of university applicants, prefers to relate social class with a number of other factors as possible determinants of choice, and suggests that 'it might be more worthwhile to look for differential success rates within, rather than between, the conventional social class groupings' (p. 338).

Chapter 3 Pupil adaptations

1 J. Wakeford, *The Cloistered Elite: a Sociological Analysis of the English Public Boarding School*, Macmillan, London, 1969; R. Merton, *Social Theory and Social Structure*, Free Press, Chicago, 1957; E. Goffman, *Asylums*, Penguin Books, 1968.
2 F. Harary, 'Merton Revisited: a New Classification for Deviant Behavior', *American Sociological Review*, 31 (5), 1966.
3 Merton, op. cit.
4 Goffman, op. cit., p. 67.
5 Wakeford, op. cit., p. 139.
6 For a good illustration of this, see R.V. Dumont and M.L. Wax, 'Cherokee School Society and the Intercultural Classroom', *Human Organization*, 28 (3), Fall 1969, pp. 217-26 (*S & S*, pp. 70-8).
7 D.H. Hargreaves, *Social Relations in a Secondary School*, Routledge & Kegan Paul, London, 1967, p. 36.
8 Hargreaves, op. cit.; C. Lacey, *Hightown Grammar*, Manchester University Press, 1970.
9 Op. cit., pp. 169-70.
10 Op. cit., p. 95.
11 Hargreaves, op. cit., p. 172.

Chapter 4 Pupils' views

* Some of the material in this chapter was originally published under the title 'Pupils' Views of School', *Educational Review*, 28 (2), February 1976.
1 E. Goffman, *Asylums*, Penguin Books, 1968.
2 Ibid.

Chapter 5 Having a laugh

* A short version of this chapter is published in M. Hammersley and P. Woods, eds, *The Process of Schooling*, Routledge & Kegan Paul, London, 1976.
1 *Previous work on laughter*. Sociological work on humour and laughter might be seen as leaning towards either of two models, conflict or control.[15] Among the latter, which focus on the way laughter mellows the abrasive qualities of institutions, joking relationships between teachers and pupils have been explored by Walker, Goodson and Adelman.[16] They show that joking is heavily situated; that is, it might not be appreciated by an outsider unfamiliar with the history and general context of the relationships under observation. This in itself suggests there might be more humour in schools than meets the eye. Using conversations with teachers as leads and as illustrations, Walker and his colleagues suggest various ways in which joking might facilitate the teachers' task; mainly it has to do with

establishing personal relationships with students, but jokes can also 'mark areas of vulnerability in the frame'.[17] However, as observers, they are mostly impressed by the way 'jokes short-circuit social situations in a way that allow them to become personal and unique. Joking is one way in which social structures are made human.' Fifty years ago D. Hayworth was advancing a theory that laughter was originally a vocal signal to other members of the group that they might relax with safety.[18] A similar point is made by Emerson with regard to hospitals, when she talks of joking being the negotiation of a private agreement to suspend a general guideline of the institutional setting, bargaining to make unofficial arrangements about taboo topics.[19] Other features of bureaucratization have been seen to be assailed by humour. Coser, for example, found that 'negative democratization' encourages a colleague-type of relationship between nurses and doctors rather than a service one – 'hence the banter and joking which help further to cancel out status differences and the relative frequency of interaction'.[20] Anthropologists have noted how, among primitive societies, joking seems to maintain equilibrium among persons and groups who, because of their relative positions and social ties, might otherwise feel antagonism toward each other and threaten the disruption of the society.[21] This function is claimed to have been identified in a London department store.[22] On the conflict side, Coser elsewhere suggests three main social functions of laughter among hospital inmates – the alleviation of boredom, elevation of status and the counteraction of ritual and routinization with expression of individuality.[23] Freud remarked that 'what is fine about humour is the ego's victorious assertion of its own invulnerability'.[24] Obrdlik made a similar point on a nation-wide scale in his study of 'gallows humour' which he claims arises in difficult and dangerous situations and which might be taken as an index of strength or morale on the part of oppressed peoples; it could have a disintegrating effect on those toward whom it is directed.[25] In these situations the humorist triumphs over his own weakness and gains added strength from a collective nature of the victory. It can strengthen boundaries and demarcate separate cultures. The relevance of such work to schools will immediately register with anyone familiar with them. I consider the literature on humour in more detail in chapter 7.

2 E. Goffman, *Behavior in Public Places,* Free Press, New York, 1963.

3 E. Goffman, *Encounters,* Penguin Books, 1972.

4 E. Goffman, *Asylums,* Penguin Books, 1968.

5 *Ribbin', Jivin', and Playin' the Dozens,* Ballinger, Cambridge, Mass., 1974.

6 Ibid., p. 179.

7 V. Furlong has discussed the changes in general behaviour within one class both among different teachers and according to the composition of the class: 'Anancy Goes to School: a Case Study of Pupils' Knowledge of their Teachers', in P.E. Woods and M. Hammersley, eds, *School Experience,* Croom Helm, London, 1977.

8 E. Bittner, 'The Police on Skid Row: a Study of Peace-Keeping', *American Sociological Review*, 32 (5), October 1967, pp. 699-715.

9 N.W. Braroe, 'Reciprocal Exploitation in an Indian-White Community', in H.A. Farberman and E. Goods, eds, *Social Reality*, Prentice-Hall, Englewood Cliffs, N.J., 1973.

10 'Friends, Enemies and the Polite Fiction', *American Sociological Review*, 18, 1953, pp. 654-62.

11 E. Goffman, *Asylums*.

12 A.J. Obrdlik, '"Gallows Humor": a Sociological Phenomenon', *American Journal of Sociology*, 47, 1942, pp. 709-16.

13 Ibid., p. 715.

14 Ibid., p. 716.

15 M.L. Barron, 'A Content Analysis of Intergroup Humor', *American Sociological Review*, 15, 1950, pp. 88-94; J.H. Burma, 'Humor as a Technique in Race Conflict', *American Sociological Review*, 11, 1946, pp. 710-15; R.M. Stephenson, 'Conflict and Control Functions of Humor', *American Journal of Sociology*, 56, 1951, pp. 569-74.

16 R. Walker, I. Goodson and C. Adelman, 'Teaching That's a Joke', paper presented at the Open University Conference on 'The Experience of Schooling', Cranfield, 1975.

17 B. Bernstein, 'On the Classification and Framing of Educational Knowledge', in M.F.D. Young, ed., *Knowledge and Control*, Collier-Macmillan, London, 1971 (*CCC*, vol. 3, 2nd ed., 1977, pp. 85-115).

18 'The Origin and Function of Laughter', *Psychological Review*, 36, 1928, pp. 367-84.

19 J. Emerson, 'Negotiating the Serious Impact of Humor', *Sociometry*, 32, 1969, pp. 169-81.

20 R.L. Coser, 'Authority and Decision-Making in a Hospital: a Comparative Analysis', *American Sociological Review*, 23, 1958, pp. 56-63.

21 A.R. Radcliffe-Brown, *Structure and Function in Primitive Society*, Cohen & West, London, 1952.

22 P. Bradney, 'The Joking Relationship in Industry', *Human Relations*, 10, 1957.

23 R.L. Coser, 'Some Social Functions of Laughter', *Human Relations*, 12, May 1959.

24 S. Freud, 'Humour', in *Collected Papers*, Hogarth Press, London, 1950, pp. 215-21.

25 A.J. Obrdlik, '"Gallows Humor": a Sociological Phenomenon'.

Chapter 6 Showing them up

* A version of this chapter first appeared under the title 'Showing Them Up in Secondary School', in G. Chanan and S. Delamont, eds. *Frontiers of Classroom Research*, NFER, Slough, 1974.

1 All those who work in institutions are inhibited by this constraint, but because the education of children is veiled in idealism, rarely is sufficient allowance made for the extent to which this acts as a bar or brake on a teacher's good intentions.

2 Bernstein *et al.* make a similar point in their discussion of 'consensual' and 'differentiating' rituals in schools, which function to 'maintain continuity, order, boundary and the control of dual loyalties and ambivalence'. But they are thinking mainly of formalized ceremonials. There is a kind of second-order ritual, apparently informal but in fact quite stylized, which functions to the same end, and which paradoxically includes some ritualized opposition. B. Bernstein, with H.L. Elvin and R.S. Peters, 'Ritual in Education', *Phil. Trans.* B, 251, 1966, p. 249 (*CCC,* vol. 3, 2nd ed., 1977, pp. 54-66).

3 G.M. Mead, *Mind, Self and Society,* University of Chicago Press, 1935. See also H. Blumer, 'Society as Symbolic Interaction', in A.M. Rose, ed., *Human Behavior and Social Processes,* Houghton Mifflin, Boston, and Routledge & Kegan Paul, London, 1962.

4 D.J. Bennett and J.D. Bennett, 'Making the Scene', in G. Stone and H. Farberman, eds, *Social Psychology through Symbolic Interaction,* Wiley, New York, 1970.

5 E. Gross and G.P. Stone make this point in 'Embarrassment and the Analysis of Role Requirements', *American Journal of Sociology,* 70, 1964, pp. 1-15.

6 R.L. Coser, 'Some Social Functions of Laughter', *Human Relations,* 12, May 1959.

7 E. Goffman, 'On Face-Work', *Psychiatry,* 18, August 1955.

8 Goffman makes this point in his *Interaction Ritual,* Anchor Books, New York, 1967, pp. 101-2 (also Penguin Books), 'To appear flustered, in our society at least, is considered evidence of weakness, inferiority, low status, moral guilt, defeat and other unenviable attributes.'

9 Gross and Stone, op. cit.

10 Mead, op. cit., p. 255.

11 For example, L. Stenhouse, 'Discipline and the Dynamics of the Classroom', in L. Stenhouse, ed., *Discipline in Schools,* Pergamon, London, 1967.

12 Though it is regarded as outside the boundaries of professional ethics, teachers often show each other up. It is interesting to speculate which of these functions operate in situations where, for example, a headteacher shows up one of his staff in front of colleagues and/or pupils.

13 This is a good example of one of the vicious spirals that teachers and pupils can get caught up in. Among the senior pupils I spoke to, the biggest plea was for a status more appropriate to their age. One teacher told me 'they want to be treated as adults, but they don't *act* like adults, they behave like children.' A senior girl told me 'they treat us like little kids, so we act like little kids'. The self-fulfilling prophecy is well known (see R. Rosenthal and L. Jacobson, *Pygmalion in the Classroom,* Holt, Rinehart & Winston, New York, 1968). But who starts it?

14 D.H. Hargreaves, *Interpersonal Relations and Education,* Routledge & Kegan Paul, London, 1972.

15 Ibid., p. 246.

16 A. Schutz, *The Phenomenology of the Social World*, trans. G. Walsh and F. Lehnert, Northwestern University Press, 1967.

17 The teacher's dilemma is illustrated by this anecdote taken from Kounin. When teaching a course he noticed a student reading a newspaper that he was holding completely unfolded in front of himself. 'Contrary to what I advocated in the course, I angrily reprimanded him without diagnosis or understanding (I failed to administer psychological tests, to invite him for a counseling session, to interview his parents, or to study his community).' Thus he took into account only the student's intentions. J.S. Kounin, *Discipline and Group Management in Classrooms*, Holt, Rinehart & Winston, New York, 1970, p. 1.

18 This is an example of the pay-off that can come from talking to people in friendship groups. Often I felt I was favoured with privileged access to information which I certainly would not have got from individuals or randomly selected groups.

19 H. Garfinkel, 'Conditions of Successful Degradation Ceremonies', *American Journal of Sociology*, 61, 1956, pp. 420–4.

20 E.M. Lemert, *Human Deviance, Social Problems and Social Control*, Prentice-Hall, Englewood Cliffs, N.J., 1967, p. 42.

21 C. Lacey, *Hightown Grammar*, Manchester University Press, 1970, p. 178.

22 D.H. Hargreaves, *Social Relations in a Secondary School*, Routledge & Kegan Paul, London, 1967, p. 105.

23 Lacey, op. cit. Also see Eileen Moody, 'Right in Front of Everybody', *New Society*, 26 December 1968.

24 *Interpersonal Relations and Education*, p. 246.

25 F. Redl, *When We Deal with Children*, Free Press, New York, 1966.

26 Kounin, op. cit.

27 A.M. Rose, 'A Social-Psychological Theory of Neuroses', in A.M. Rose, ed., *Human Behavior and Social Processes*, p. 541. Charles H. Cooley's concept of the 'looking-glass' self holds that part of the self is reflection, possibly distorted, of other people's reactions to the person in question. *Human Nature and the Social Order*, Schocken Books, New York, 1964.

28 See, for example, G. Esland, 'Teaching and Learning as the Organization of Knowledge', in M.F.D. Young, ed., *Knowledge and Control*, Collier-Macmillan, London, 1971; D. Barnes and D. Shemilt, 'Transmission and Interpretation', *Educational Review*, **26** (3), June 1974; M. Parlett and D. Hamilton, *Evaluation as Programme*, Centre for Research in the Educational Sciences, University of Edinburgh, Occasional Paper 9, 1972; I. Lister, 'The Whole Curriculum and the Hidden Curriculum', in I. Lister, ed., *Deschooling*, Cambridge University Press, 1974, pp. 92–3.

29 M. Hammersley, *The Teacher's Perspective*, Open University Press, Milton Keynes (unit 9 of E202, 'Schooling and Society'), 1977, p. 38.

30 As opposed to 'socially constructed knowledge', as described by P. Berger and T. Luckmann, in *The Social Construction of Reality*,

Penguin Books, 1971. For changes in child-rearing techniques during the first four years of life, see J. and E. Newson, *Four Years Old in an Urban Community*, Allen & Unwin, London, 1968.

31 P.E. Woods, 'The Generation Game', *Youth in Society*, December 1974.

32 M. Abrams, 'How and Why We Spend Our Money', *Twentieth Century*, autumn 1963.

33 Though I am using 'culture' in a wider sense here, the 'cultural deprivation' thesis is part of the syndrome connected with traditional paternalism. Most children's experiences and ways of life are seen as inadequate and of limited value and are frequently deprecated. This often provides substance for the showing-up, as in the example on p. 130. See N. Keddie, *Tinker, Tailor ... The Myth of Cultural Deprivation*, Penguin Books, 1973.

34 E. Goffman, *Asylums*, Penguin Books 1968, p. 24.

35 Ibid., p. 35.

36 D. Holly, *Beyond Curriculum*, Hart-Davis, MacGibbon, London, 1973, p. 49.

Chapter 7 The hidden pedagogy of survival

1 R.M. Kanter, 'Commitment and Social Organization', in D. Field, ed., *Social Psychology for Sociologists*, Nelson, London, 1974, p. 126.

2 Ibid., p. 132.

3 H. Becker, 'Notes on the Concept of Commitment', *American Journal of Sociology*, 66, July 1960, pp. 32-40.

4 I. Lister, 'Drifting into More and More Trouble', *The Times Educational Supplement*, 1 November 1974.

5 F. Musgrove, 'Education of Teachers for a Changing Role', in J.D. Turner and J. Rushton, eds, *The Teacher in a Changing Society*, Manchester University Press, 1974, p. 46.

6 J. Webb, 'The Sociology of a School', *British Journal of Sociology*, 13 (3), 1962, pp. 264-72.

7 F. Musgrove, *Ecstasy and Holiness*, Methuen, London, 1974, p. 165.

8 W. Waller, *The Sociology of Teaching*, Wiley, New York, 1932, p. 198.

9 P.H. Hirst, 'What is Teaching?', *Journal of Curriculum Studies*, 3 (1), May 1971, pp. 9-10.

10 H. Judge, *School is not yet Dead*, Longmans, London, 1976, p. 21.

11 P.W. Jackson, *Life in Classrooms*, Holt, Rinehart & Winston, New York, 1968.

12 I. Deutscher, 'Evil Companions and Naughty Behavior: Some Thoughts and Evidence Bearing on a Folk Hypothesis', duplicated, Case Western Reserve University, 1969, pp. 28-9.

13 H.S. Becker, 'Personal Change in Adult Life', *Sociometry*, 27 (1), March 1964, pp. 40-53 (*S & S*, p. 59).

14 C. Jenks, 'A Question of Control: a Case-Study of Interaction in a

Junior School', unpublished M.Sc.(Econ.) thesis, London University Institute of Education, 1971, p. 28.

15 M. Denscombe, 'The Social Organization of Teaching: a Study of Teaching as a Practical Activity in Two London Comprehensive Schools', unpublished Ph.D. thesis, University of Leicester, 1977, p. 252.

16 Ibid., p. 253.

17 Ibid., p. 385.

18 R. Sharp and A. Green, *Education and Social Control,* Routledge & Kegan Paul, 1976, p. 121.

19 I. Westbury, 'Conventional Classrooms, "Open" Classrooms and the Technology of Teaching', *Journal of Curriculum Studies,* 5 (2), November 1973, p. 100.

20 A similar model of coping is expounded by A. Hargreaves, 'Progressivism and Pupil Autonomy', *Sociological Review,* 25 (3), August 1977, p. 593. Hargreaves suggests that 'the response of teachers to structural pressures is a creative one. In this sense, progressive educational practice embodies a set of coping strategies which have been created in the sense of the forging of *new* roles which have the capacity to resolve the conflictual demands contained within liberal-progressive ideology'.

21 P. Freire, *Pedagogy of the Oppressed,* Penguin Books, 1972.

22 H.S. Becker, 'The Career of the Chicago Public Schoolteacher', *American Journal of Sociology,* 57, March 1952, pp. 470–7 (*P of S,* p. 77).

23 E. Goffman, *The Presentation of Self in Everyday Life,* Penguin Books, 1971.

24 J. Webb, 'The Sociology of a School', p. 269.

25 See V. Furlong, 'Anancy Goes to School: a Case Study of Pupils' Knowledge of their Teachers', in P.E. Woods and M. Hammersley, eds, *School Experience,* Croom Helm, London, 1977.

26 B. Bernstein, 'On the Classification and Framing of Educational Knowledge', in M.F.D. Young, ed., *Knowledge and Control,* Collier-Macmillan, London, 1971 (*CCC,* vol. 3, 2nd ed., 1977, p. 99).

27 Waller, op cit., p. 207.

28 Ibid.

29 J. Welton, 'Comprehensive Education and the Egalitarian Dream', unpublished, paper, University of Bristol, 1973, part II, p. 9.

30 Denscombe, op. cit., p. 253.

31 Lister, op. cit.

32 Goffman, *Asylums,* Penguin Books, 1968, p. 67.

33 B. Bernstein, with H.L. Elvin and R.S. Peters, 'Ritual in Education', *Phil. Trans.* B, 251, 1966 (*CCC,* vol. 3, 2nd ed., 1977, p. 54).

34 Ibid., p. 65.

35 B. Bernstein, 'On the Classification and Framing of Educational Knowledge', p. 106.

36 B. Bernstein, 'The Sociology of Education: a Brief Account', in *Eighteen Plus: the Final Selection,* Open University Press, Milton Keynes, 1972, p. 103 (*CCC,* vol. 3, 2nd ed., 1977, p. 164).

37 B. Bernstein, 'Ritual in Education', p. 60.
38 F. Musgrove, 'Education of Teachers', p. 45.
39 Webb, op. cit., p. 265.
40 P. Gump, 'What's Happening in the Elementary School Classroom', in I. Westbury and A.A. Bellack, *Research into Classroom Processes,* Teachers College Press, New York, 1971, pp. 155–65.
41 Westbury, op. cit.
42 V. Furlong, 'Anancy Goes to School'.
43 J. Britton *et al.*, 'The Development of Writing Abilities, 11–18', *Schools Council Research,* Macmillan, London, 1975.
44 A. Green, 'Structural Features of the Classroom', in P.E. Woods and M. Hammersley, eds, *School Experience,* Croom Helm, London, 1977.
45 Kanter, op. cit., p. 128.
46 Sharp and Green, op. cit., p. 121.
47 C. Dickens, *Nicholas Nickleby,* Nelson, London, 1839.
48 D.H. Hargreaves, *Interpersonal Relations and Education,* Routledge & Kegan Paul, London, 1972.
49 Webb, op. cit.
50 Sharp and Green, op. cit., p. 121.
51 Webb, op. cit.
52 That the primary mode of adaptation is one of compliance to role demands is well attested in the literature. See, for example, B. Morris, 'Reflections on Role Analysis', *British Journal of Sociology,* 22 (4), 1972, pp. 395–409; and L.B. Hendry, 'Survival in a Marginal Role: the Professional Identity of the Physical Education Teacher', *British Journal of Sociology,* 26 (4), December 1973.
53 The term is used by Deuscombe, op. cit.
54 Westbury, op. cit., p. 18.
55 I. Illich, *Deschooling Society*, Penguin Books, 1973.
56 D. Holly, *Beyond Curriculum,* Hart-Davis, MacGibbon, London, 1973, p. 59.
57 F. Musgrove, *Ecstasy and Holiness,* p. 179.

Chapter 8 *The professionalism of school reports*

1 N. Keddie, 'Classroom Knowledge', in M.F.D. Young, ed., *Knowledge and Control,* Collier-Macmillan, London, 1971; D.H. Hargreaves, 'The Process of Typification in the Classroom: Models and Methods', *British Journal of Educational Psychology,* September 1977; R. Nash, *Classrooms Observed,* Routledge & Kegan Paul, London, 1973, and *Teacher Expectations and Pupil Learning,* Routledge & Kegan Paul, 1976.
2 Young, op. cit.
3 D.H. Hargreaves, *Interpersonal Relations and Education,* Routledge & Kegan Paul, London, 1972, p. 161.
4 D.H. Hargreaves, S.K. Hester and F.J. Mellor, *Deviance in Classrooms,* Routledge & Kegan Paul, 1976.

5 Ibid., pp. 145, 143.
6 Keddie, op. cit., p. 139.
7 Ibid., p. 154.
8 D.H. Hargreaves, 'The Process of Typification in the Classroom'.
9 D. Sudnow, 'Dead on Arrival', in I. Horowitz and M.S. Strong, eds, *Sociological Realities: a Guide to the Study of Society*, Harper & Row, New York, 1971, pp. 225-32.
10 Ibid., p. 231.
11 Ibid.
12 D.C. Lortie, *Schoolteacher*, University of Chicago Press, 1975, pp. 137-8.
13 Hammersley argues that: 'while paradigms are grounded in conceptions of how the world is, these conceptions relate to the essentials or ultimate features of the world not to the particular situation faced. Given the social location of the actor the action possibilities open to him are limited and these may well exclude some or all of the paradigmatic prescriptions to which he is committed. The pragmatic component of teacher perspectives is concerned with what is or is not possible in given circumstances, and with strategies and techniques for achieving goals.' In M. Hammersley, *Teacher Perspectives*, Open University Press, Milton Keynes, 1977 (unit 9 of E202, 'Schooling and Society'), p. 38.
14 See also C. Werthman, 'Delinquents in Schools: a Test for the Legitimacy of Authority', *Berkeley Journal of Sociology*, 8 (1), 1963, pp. 39-60 (*S & S*, pp. 34-43); D. Reynolds, 'When Pupils and Teachers Refuse a Truce', in G. Mungham and G. Pearson, eds, *Working-Class Youth Culture*, Routledge & Kegan Paul, London, 1976.
15 W. Labov, 'The Logic of Non-Standard English', in P. Gigliolo, ed., *Language and Social Content*, Penguin Books, 1972.
16 For a critical account of labelling theory, see chapter 1 of Hargreaves, Hester and Mellor, op. cit. For the 'self-fulfilling prophecy', see R. Rosenthal and L. Jacobson, *Pygmalion in the Classroom*, Holt, Rinehart & Winston, New York, 1968.
17 Op. cit., p. 152.
18 L.M. Smith and W. Geoffrey, *The Complexities of an Urban Classroom*, Holt, Rinehart & Winston, New York, 1968.
19 P. Berger, 'Towards a Sociological Understanding of Psychoanalysis', *Social Research*, spring 1965.
20 Ibid.
21 E. Friedson, *Medical Men and their Work*, Aldine, Chicago, 1972.
22 Op. cit., p. 144.
23 R. Winter, 'Keeping Files: Aspects of Bureaucracy and Education', in G. Whitty and M.F.D. Young, eds, *Explorations in the Politics of School Knowledge*, Nafferton Books, Driffield, 1976.
24 H. Garfinkel, 'Good Organizational Reasons for Bad Clinic Records', in R. Turner, ed., *Ethnomethodology*, Penguin Books, 1974, p. 123.
25 P.L. Berger and H. Kellner, 'Marriage and the Construction of Reality', *Diogenes*, 46(1), 1964, pp. 1-23.
26 Labov, op. cit.

27 The social construction of intelligence is discussed in P.G. Squibb, 'The Concept of Intelligence: a Sociological Perspective', *Sociological Review*, February 1973, pp. 57-75.

28 That adult–child interaction is not socialization but cultural assimilation is strongly held by R. Mackay, 'Conceptions of Children and Models of Socialization', in H.P. Dreitzel, ed., *Recent Sociology, no. 5, Childhood and Socialization*, Macmillan, New York, 1973.

29 F. Musgrove, 'The Decline of the Educative Family', *Universities Quarterly*, 14, 1960, p. 377.

30 I. Illich, *Tools for Conviviality*, Calder & Boyars, London, 1973.

31 W. Waller, *The Sociology of Teaching*, Wiley, New York, 1961, p. 61.

32 Lortie, op. cit., p. 190.

33 H. Sockett, 'Parents' Rights', in O. Bridges and P. Scrimshaw, eds, *Values and Authority in Schools*, Hodder & Stoughton, London, 1975.

34 Ibid.

35 F. Musgrove and P.H. Taylor, *Society and the Teacher's Role*, Routledge & Kegan Paul, London, 1969.

36 I. Illich, *Deschooling Society*, Penguin Books, 1973; and *Celebration of Awareness*, Calder & Boyars, New York, 1971; H. Marcuse, *Eros and Civilization*, Beacon Press, Boston, 1955, and *One-Dimensional Man*, Routledge & Kegan Paul, London, 1964; T. Roszak, *The Making of a Counter Culture*, Faber, London, 1968.

37 Roszak, op. cit., pp. 6-7.

38 Ibid.

39 D. Wardle, *The Rise of the Schooled Society*, Routledge & Kegan Paul, London, 1974, p. 93.

40 Ibid., p. 99.

41 D. Downes, *The Delinquent Solution*, Routledge & Kegan Paul, London, 1966, p. 35.

42 See P. Willis, 'The Class Significance of School Counter-Culture', in M. Hammersley and P.E. Woods, eds, *The Process of Schooling*, Routledge & Kegan Paul, London, 1976.

Chapter 9   The meaning of staffroom humour

1 See R. Walker and C. Adelman, 'Strawberries', in M. Stubbs and S. Delamont, eds, *Explorations in Classroom Observation*, Wiley, London, 1976 and R. Walker and I. Goodson, 'Humour in the Classroom', in P.E. Woods and M. Hammersley, eds, *School Experience*, Croom Helm, London, 1977.

2 E. Goffman, *The Presentation of Self in Everyday Life*, Penguin Books, 1971.

3 R.M. Stephenson, 'Conflict and Control Functions of Humor', *American Journal of Sociology*, 56, 1951, pp. 569-74; R. Middleton and J. Moland, 'Humor in Negro and White Subcultures: a Study of Jokes Among University Students', *American Sociological Review*, 24, 1959, pp. 61-9.

4 A.J. Obrdlik, '"Gallows Humor": a Sociological Phenomenon', *American Journal of Sociology*, 47, 1942, p. 570.

5 Stephenson, op. cit., p. 570.

6 Middleton and Moland, op. cit., p. 69.

7 Stephenson, op. cit., p. 574.

8 P. Bradney, 'The Joking Relationship in Industry', *Human Relations*, 10, 1957.

9 R.L. Coser, 'Some Social Functions of Laughter', *Human Relations*, 12, 1959.

10 G. Myrdal, *An American Dilemma*, Harper, New York, 1944, pp. 38-9.

11 D. Hayworth, 'The Origin and Function of Laughter', *Psychological Review*, 36, 1928, pp. 367-84.

12 G.T.W. Patrick, *The Psychology of Relaxation*, 1916, p. 126, quoted in Hayworth, op. cit., p. 383.

13 Coser, op. cit., p. 173.

14 S. Freud, 'Humour', in *Collected Papers*, Hogarth Press, London, 1950, p. 220.

15 Coser, op. cit., p. 177.

16 G. Simmel, *The Sociology of Georg Simmel*, trans. and introduction by K.H. Wolff, Free Press, New York, 1964, pp. 122-3.

17 On the influence of different compositions of groups see V. Furlong, 'Interaction Sets in the Classroom', in Stubbs and Delamont, op. cit.

18 Stephenson, op. cit., p. 572.

19 O.E. Klapp, 'The Fool as a Social Type', *American Journal of Sociology*, 55, 1949, pp. 157-62.

20 Ibid., p. 158.

21 H.R. Pollio, and J.W. Edgerley, 'Comedians and Comic Style', in T. Chapman and H. Foot, eds, *Humour and Laughter*, Wiley, London, 1976, p. 240.

22 W.E. Fry and M. Allen, 'Humour as a Creative Experience: the Development of a Hollywood Humourist', in Chapman and Foot, op. cit., p. 252.

23 H. Hesse, *Steppenwolf*, Henry Holt, New York, 1929; quoted in Fry and Allen, op. cit.

Chapter 10 Summary and conclusion

1 Roszak refers to the technocracy as 'that social form in which an industrial society reaches the peak of its organizational integration'. Its prominent features include rationality, as evidenced in extensive systematization, division of labour, the creation of standards, production norms and the like. It encourages a belief in technological solutions to all problems in all spheres of life, and the existence of the right means to achieve them. Consequently all talents and energies are devoted to finding and refining them. We are in the era of the 'expert' and of faith in the expert. The technologizing of the world has brought many benefits and represents man's most ambitious

attempts yet to master nature. Its 'technique', as Ellul calls it, is the 'translation into action of man's concern to master things by means of reason, to account for what is subconscious, make quantitative what is qualitative, make clear and precise the outlines of nature, take hold of chaos and put order into it.' Therein lies both its strength and its weakness. For 'technique' by Ellul's definition, tends to encourage artificiality and automation and exclude spontaneity, drive, enterprise, personal choice and creativity. These have no place in well-oiled systems serviced by functionaries, who do better to concentrate on punctuality and precision and other forms of self-discipline.

See T. Roszak, *The Making of a Counter Culture: Reflections on the Technocratic Society and Youth Opposition,* Faber & Faber, London, 1970, p. 5; J. Ellul, *The Technological Society,* Cape, London, 1965, p. 43. For other commentaries on the 'technocracy', or the social and psychological effects of industrial and technological development, see H. Marcuse, *One-Dimensional Man,* Routledge & Kegan Paul, London, 1964; H. Arendt, *The Human Condition,* University of Chicago Press, 1958; V. Ferkiss, *Technological Man,* Heinemann, London, 1969; E. Fromm, *The Revolution of Hope: Towards a Humanized Technology,* Harper & Row, New York, 1968; E. Fromm, *The Sane Society,* Routledge & Kegan Paul, London, 1956; J. Habermas, *Toward a Rational Society,* Heinemann, London, 1971; E. Mayo, *The Human Problems of an Industrial Civilization,* Harvard University Press, 1933; M. Mead, ed., *Cultural Patterns and Technical Change,* Merton Books, New York, 1955; W.H. Whyte, *The Organization Man,* Cape, London, 1957; L. Mumford, *Technics and Civilization,* Routledge, London, 1934. For a brief account of the effects of 'industrialization' and 'rationalization' on personality, see chapter 9 of B. Berger, *Societies in Change,* Basic Books, 1970. The classic accounts are by E. Fromm, *The Fear of Freedom,* Routledge & Kegan Paul, London, 1942, and W.H. Whyte, *The Organization Man.* For another account of rationalization processes on schools, see A.E. Wise, 'Why Educational Policies Often Fail: the Hyperrationalization Hypothesis', *Journal of Curriculum Studies,* 9 (1), 1977, pp. 43-57.

2 See M. Hammersley, *Teacher Perspectives,* Open University Press, Milton Keynes, 1977 (units 9 and 10 of E202, 'Schooling and Society'); S. Delamont, *Interaction in the Classroom,* Methuen, London, 1976. For 'sub-universes of meaning' and 'institutional segmentation', see P. Berger and T. Luckmann, *The Social Construction of Reality,* Penguin Books, 1967; and for an empirical application, see S. Chibnall and P. Saunders, 'Worlds Apart – Notes on the Social Reality of Corruption', *British Journal of Sociology,* 28 (2), June 1977.

3 E. Goffman, *The Presentation of Self in Everyday Life,* Penguin Books, 1971.

4 See P.E. Woods, 'Relating to Work', *Educational Review,* June 1978, and 'Negotiating the Demands of Schoolwork', *Journal of Curriculum Studies* (forthcoming).

5 W. Waller, *The Sociology of Teaching*, Wiley, New York, 1932, p. 193.
6 J.E. Rosenbaum, *Making Inequality: the Hidden Curriculum of High School Tracking*, Wiley, New York, 1976.
7 Though Paul Willis argues that teacher style is likely to have little effect on disaffected working-class kids. This might be true with extreme intransigent or rebellious groups, but clearly, at Lowfield, teacher style was important for all groups. See *Learning to Labour*, Saxon House, Farnborough, 1977, pp. 188-9.
8 P.L. Berger, *The Social Reality of Religion*, Penguin Books, 1973; P.L. Berger and T. Luckmann, *The Social Construction of Reality*.
9 On multiple realities, paramount realities and sub-universe, see A. Schutz, *The Phenomenology of the Social World*, Springer, Vienna, 1960; and *Collected Papers*, vols 1 and 2, Nijhoff, The Hague, 1971.
10 R. Merton, *Social Theory and Social Structure*, Free Press, Chicago, 1957.
11 P.L. and B. Berger and H. Kellner, *The Homeless Mind*, Penguin Books, 1973, p. 60.
12 R.M. Kanter, 'The Organization Child: Experience Management in a Nursery School', *Sociology of Education*, 45 (2), 1972, pp.186-212 (*S & C*, p. 172).
13 Berger *et al.*, *The Homeless Mind*, p. 190.
14 Ibid., p. 86.
15 For other theoretical formulations of a shift of 'self', see D. Bell, *The Cultural Contradictions of Capitalism*, Heinemann, London, 1976. Bell speaks of a disjunction of 'realms', between a 'social structure that is organized fundamentally in terms of roles and specialization, and a culture which is concerned with the enhancement and fulfilment of the self and "the whole person"' (p. 14). Also see R.H. Turner, 'The Real Self: from Institution to Impulse', *American Journal of Sociology*, 81 (5), March 1976. Turner proposes that the self is variously located in the institution on the one hand, and in 'impulse' on the other, and that there has been a shift from the former to the latter during this century. Under the institution locus, the self is achieved, created, through planning and control; under the impulse locus, the true self is something to be discovered through the lowering of inhibitions. Perhaps the best illustration of the latter quest for self is the youth movements of the 1960s. I have considered youth cultures along these lines in P. Woods, *Youth, Generations and Social Class*, Open University Press, Milton Keynes, 1977 (units 27-8 of E202, 'Schooling and Society'). For other discussions on the 'self' in 'technocratic society' see S. Cohen and L. Taylor, *Escape Attempts: the Theory and Practice of Resistance to Everyday Life*, Penguin Books, 1978; and L. Taylor, *Man's Experience of the World*, Open University Press, Milton Keynes, 1976 (block 9 of D305, 'Social Psychology').
16 For a recent report of institutional impact on staff and students in American comprehensive schools, see P.A. Cusick, W. Martin and S. Polonsky, 'Organizational Structure and Student Behavior in

Secondary School', *Journal of Curriculum Studies,* 8 (1), 1976, pp. 3-14. See also H. Gracey, *Curriculum or Craftsmanship: Elementary School Teachers in a Bureaucratic System,* University of Chicago Press, 1972; and K. Marjoribanks, 'Bureaucratic Orientations, Autonomy and the Professional Attitudes of Teachers', *Journal of Educational Administration,* 15 (1), May 1977.

17 H.S. Becker, 'Social-Class Variations in the Teacher-Pupil Relationship', *Journal of Educational Sociology,* 25 (4), 1952, pp. 451-65 (*S & S,* p. 113).

18 B. Bernstein, *Class, Codes and Control,* Routledge & Kegan Paul, London, vol. 1, 2nd ed., 1974; vol. 2, 1973; J. Ford, D. Young and S. Box, 'Functional Autonomy, Role Distance and Social Class', *British Journal of Sociology,* 18 (4), 1967, pp. 370-81.

19 *Learning to Labour.*

20 R. Sharp and A. Green, *Education and Social Control,* Routledge & Kegan Paul, London, 1976; S. Bowles and H. Gintis, *Schooling in Capitalist America,* Routledge & Kegan Paul, London, 1976.

21 See, for example, P. Bourdieu, 'Cultural Reproduction and Social Reproduction', in R. Brown, ed., *Knowledge, Education and Cultural Change,* Tavistock, London, 1973; L. Althusser, 'Ideology and Ideological State Apparatuses', in B.R. Cosin, ed., *Education: Structure and Society,* Penguin Books, 1972.

22 'Notes on the Schooling of the English Working Class 1780–1850', in R. Dale *et al.,* eds, *Schooling and Capitalism,* p. 52.

23 P. Berger and T. Luckmann, *The Social Construction of Reality,* p. 82.

24 P.L. Berger, B. Berger and H. Kellner, *The Homeless Mind.*

25 T. Luckmann, *The Invisible Religion,* Macmillan, New York, 1967, p. 109. On the segmentation of the institutional order and the 'private school' sphere, see also T. Luckmann, 'On the Rationality of Institutions in Modern Life', *Journal of European Sociology,* 16, 1975, pp. 3-15. Luckmann states, 'The personal identity of the individual is relatively independent of institutional constraints. Such constraints are no longer effectively transmitted by the family during primary socialization and it appears that the educational systems are following this trend (p. 13). Thus, the typical modern personality mediates rather less successfully between the elementary structures of the human condition and the quasi-autonomous and quasi-objective laws of the great institutional domains' (p. 14). On child-rearing practices and their effect on consciousness, see P. Woods, *Youth, Generations and Social Class.* On the 'marginality' of the 'typical modern personality' in relation to education, see F. Musgrove, 'Marginality, Education and the Reconstruction of Reality', *Journal of Curriculum Studies,* 8 (2), 1976, pp. 101-9.

26 *Deschooling Society,* Penguin Books, 1973, p. 37.

27 H.H. Gerth and C.W. Mills, eds, *Max Weber's Essays in Sociology,* Oxford University Press, 1946, p. 243.

28 Teacher-bureaucrats come out with a bad press in this book, largely because of the antipathy of the bulk of the pupils. However, there

can be no absolute evaluation. Rather, teacher-bureaucrats locate their 'selves' within the achieved domain of institutional structures, while teacher-persons and the majority of the pupils locate their 'selves' within the uninhibited sphere of 'impulse' (see Turner, 'The Real Self'). This is another source of teacher-pupil clash arguably independent of social class. See A. Brittan, *The Privatised World*, Routledge & Kegan Paul, London, 1977, pp. 152-3.

29 G. Simmel, *On Individuality and Social Forms*, ed. D.N. Levine, University of Chicago Press, 1971, p. 226.

Appendix 1

1 As S.T. Bruyn observed: 'If the researcher is aware of the hazards and the rules of the method of participant observation, then he should be able accurately to find the cultural meanings contained in any group he studies — some meanings of which may lie at the root of man's existence in society'; *The Human Perspective in Sociology: the Methodology of Participant Observation*, Prentice-Hall, Englewood Cliffs, N.J., 1966, p. 21. H. Wolcott also observed that 'the ethnographer's compelling interest is his continuing enquiry into human social life and . . . the ways that human beings confront their humanness'; 'Criteria for an Ethnographic Approach to Research in Schools', *Human Organization*, 34 (2), 1975, p. 125.

2 *Social Relations in a Secondary School*, Routledge & Kegan Paul, London, 1967, p. 193.

3 R. Redfield urged his anthropologist colleagues not to hide behind a 'mask of neutrality'; *The Primitive World and its Transformations*, Cornell University Press, 1953, p. 156; P. Robinson, 'An Ethnography of Classrooms', in J. Eggleston, ed., *Contemporary Research in the Sociology of Education*, Methuen, London, 1974, p. 251.

4 This was the case with C. Lacey, *Hightown Grammar*, Manchester University Press, 1970 and Hargreaves, op. cit.

5 For example, L. Yablonsky: 'At a certain point in the research I decided it was of vital importance for me to *personally experience* some core hippie behaviour patterns in order to truly tune-in to what was happening. When the opportunity emerged in the flow of my trip, I decided it was crucial to my research to enter into several acts that conflicted with the primary life-style values of a generally law-abiding middle-class professor'; *The Hippie Trip*, Western Publishing, New York, 1968, p. xiii.

6 Such as H.J. Parker, in his study of a group of deviant boys in Liverpool: 'My position in relation to theft was well established. I would receive "knock off" and "say nothing". If necessary I would "keep dixy" but I would not actually get my hands dirty. This stance was regarded as normal and surprised nobody; it coincided with the view of most adults in the neighbourhood'; *View from the Boys*, David & Charles, Newton Abbot, 1974, p. 219.

7 D.H. Hargreaves, for example, describes how, as soon as he began

classroom observation, the teachers' perception of his role changed, and hence their behaviour, in Hargreaves, op. cit., pp. 195-6. This mars the 'naturalness' of the scene, but the ethical predicament for the researcher comes from his felt role conflict. Is he as researcher free to use information to which he has been given privileged access as a teacher? Some think not, favouring complete openness in information use and collection (as, for example, R. Frankenberg, 'Participant Observers', *New Society,* no. 23, 7 March 1963). Others think this is impractical, since much valuable information is frequently revealed in 'asides'. Hargreaves feels that 'the moral question is one of the uses made of the material so obtained', op. cit., p. 199. This seems to me to be correct, but I would add, 'and the extent to which it impinges on the individuals concerned'.

8 P. Willis experienced a similar problem. See *Learning to Labour,* Saxon House, Farnborough, 1977.

9 This was decided after half a term's exploratory work in the school, when the terms of association were agreed.

10 See, for example, A. Lambart, 'The Sociology of an Unstreamed Urban Grammar School for Girls', unpublished MA thesis, University of Manchester, 1970.

11 On ethics, see chapter 13 of N.K. Denzin, *The Research Act in Sociology: a Theoretical Approach,* Butterworth, London, 1970.

12 One of the best collections of articles on techniques of observation is still G.J. McCall and J.L. Simmons, eds, *Issues in Participant Observation: a Text and Reader,* Addison-Wesley, New York, 1969.

13 N. Keddie, 'Classroom Knowledge', in M.F.D. Young, ed., *Knowledge and Control,* Collier-Macmillan, London, 1971. See also I. Deutscher, *What we Say – What we Do: Sentiments and Acts,* Scott, Foresman, Glenview, Ill., 1973.

14 The classic informant is 'Doc' in W.F. Whyte's study: 'That's right. You tell me what you want to see, and we'll arrange it. When you want some information, I'll ask for it, and you listen. When you want to find out their philosophy of life, I'll start an argument and get it for you. Not a scrap you know, but just tell me what you want, and I'll get it for you'; *Street Corner Society,* University of Chicago Press, 1955, p. 292.

15 A.V. Cicourel, *Method and Measurement in Sociology,* Free Press, New York, 1964.

16 R.H. Wax, *Doing Fieldwork,* University of Chicago Press, 1971.

17 W. Labov, 'The Logic of Non-Standard English', in P. Gigliolo, ed., *Language and Social Content,* Penguin Books, 1972.

18 See McCall and Simmons, eds, op. cit.

19 H. Garfinkel, *Studies in Ethnomethodology,* Prentice-Hall, Englewood Cliffs, N.J., 1967.

20 And thus, by nature, more of an 'unobtrusive measure' than one requiring subjects to 'react' to a stimulus, as in a more formal interview, structured or unstructured. See E.J. Webb *et al., Unobtrusive Measures: Nonreactive Research in the Social Sciences,* Rand McNally, Chicago, 1966.

21 R. Redfield, *Peasant Society and Culture,* University of Chicago Press, 1967.
22 R. Janes, 'A Note on Phases of the Community Role of the Participant Observer', *American Sociological Review,* 26, 1961.
23 D. Ball, 'Sarcasm as Sociation: the Rhetoric of Interaction', *Canadian Review of Sociology and Anthropology,* 2 (3), 1965.
24 H. Becker, *Sociological Work,* Aldine, Chicago, 1970.
25 For examples and more discussion see D. Hamilton *et al.,* eds, 'Whatever Happened to Daniel Stufflebeam', unpublished manuscript.
26 P. Kutsche, 'Review of Tijerina and the Courthouse Raid, La Raza and Chicano', *American Anthropologist,* 73, 1971, pp. 957-8.
27 Wolcott, op. cit., p. 124.
28 Robinson, op. cit., p. 263.
29 Bruyn, op. cit., pp. 265-6.
30 C.W. Mills, *The Sociological Imagination,* Oxford University Press, New York, 1959, Penguin Books, 1970; D.L. Phillips, *Abandoning Method,* Jossey-Bass, San Francisco, 1973.
31 B.G. Glaser, and A.L. Strauss, *The Discovery of Grounded Theory,* Weidenfeld & Nicolson, London, 1967.
32 Ibid., pp. 32-3.
33 Ibid., p. 44.
34 For some possibilities connected with a similar representation of a pedagogical paradigm to that discussed in chapter 6, see G.M. Esland, 'Teaching and Learning as the Organization of Knowledge', in M.F.D. Young, *Knowledge and Control,* Collier-Macmillan, London, 1971.
35 H. Becker, 'Problems of Inference and Proof in Participant Observation', *American Sociological Review,* 23, 1958, pp. 652-60.
36 Denzin, op. cit., p. 194.
37 Ibid., p. 195.
38 *Education and Social Control,* Routledge & Kegan Paul, London, 1975, pp. 218-19.
39 Ibid., p. 233.
40 Routledge & Kegan Paul, London, 1976.

Index

Authors

Abrams, M., 290
Adelman, C., 282, 284, 287, 294
Ahier, J., 278, 279
Allen, M., 295
Althusser, L., 298
Apple, M., 280
Arendt, H., 296
Ashton, D.N., 27, 282, 284
Avis, G., 280

Ball, D , 301
Ball, S., 284
Barnes, D., 289
Barrett, B.R., 283
Barron, M.L., 287
Barton, L., 280
Beck, J., 11, 279
Becker, H., 15, 26, 28, 56, 144,
    150, 249, 271, 281, 282, 290,
    291, 298, 301
Beecham, Y., 283
Bell, D., 297
Bennett, D.T., 288
Bennett, J.D., 288
Berger, B., 296, 297, 298
Berger, P.L., 18, 188, 248, 249,
    252, 281, 289, 293, 296,
    297, 298
Berlak, A., 292
Berlak, H., 292
Bernstein, B., 15, 26, 154, 161,
    249, 279, 281, 282, 283,

287, 288, 291, 292, 298
Bittner, E., 113, 287
Blumer, H., 15, 281, 288
Bourdieu, P., 298
Bowles, S., 250, 281, 298
Box, S., 249, 298
Bradney, P., 287, 295
Braroe, N.W., 113, 287
Bridges, D., 294
Brittan, A., 299
Britton, T., 292
Brown, R., 298
Bruyn, S.T., 299, 301
Burma, J.H., 287
Burns, T., 115

Chanan, G., 287
Chapman, T., 295
Chibnall, S., 296
Cicourel, A.V., 27, 28, 51, 55,
    56, 243, 282, 300
Cohen, L., 283
Cohen, S., 297
Coleman, J.S., 282
Cooley, C., 135, 289
Coser, R.L., 213, 214, 286, 287,
    288, 295
Cosin, B.R., 298
Cusick, P.A., 297

Dale, I.R., 298
Davies, B., 279

303

Subjects

307